AUTHORITY, PARTICIPATION AND CULTURAL CHANGE IN CHINA

ESSAYS BY A EUROPEAN STUDY GROUP

Other publications in the series are:

Party Leadership and Revolutionary Power in China (1970) *edited by John Wilson Lewis*

Employment and Economic Growth in Urban China, 1949–1957 (1971) *by Christopher Howe*

Democracy and Organisation in the Chinese Industrial Enterprise, 1948–53 *by William Brugger*

A Bibliography of Chinese Newspapers and Periodicals in European Libraries

AUTHORITY PARTICIPATION AND CULTURAL CHANGE IN CHINA

ESSAYS BY A EUROPEAN STUDY GROUP

Edited and with an introduction by
STUART R. SCHRAM

With contributions by

MARIANNE BASTID   JOHN GARDNER
JACK GRAY   CHRISTOPHER HOWE
WILT IDEMA   JON SIGURDSON
ANDREW J. WATSON

CAMBRIDGE UNIVERSITY PRESS

CAMBRIDGE
LONDON NEW YORK NEW ROCHELLE
MELBOURNE SYDNEY

CAMBRIDGE UNIVERSITY PRESS
Cambridge, New York, Melbourne, Madrid, Cape Town, Singapore,
São Paulo, Delhi, Dubai, Tokyo, Mexico City

Cambridge University Press
The Edinburgh Building, Cambridge CB2 8RU, UK

Published in the United States of America by Cambridge University Press, New York

www.cambridge.org
Information on this title: www.cambridge.org/9780521098205

First published 1973
Reprinted 1975, 1977, 1980
Re-issued 2010

A catalogue record for this publication is available from the British Library

Library of Congress Catalogue Card Number: 73-80482

ISBN 978-0-521-20296-1 Hardback
ISBN 978-0-521-09820-5 Paperback

CONTENTS

PREFACE

The activities which culminated in the production of this volume took place during the last two years of my tenure as Head of the Contemporary China Institute; editorial work has gone forward subsequently with the encouragement and support of the present Head of the Institute, Christopher Howe. At a preliminary meeting in London in April 1971, attended by approximately twenty scholars from France, Germany, Holland and the United Kingdom, plans were drawn up for the organization of a European Study Group on China after the Cultural Revolution. Preliminary drafts of papers on various aspects of China today were discussed at meetings of this 'core group' of authors and discussants held in Hamburg in February 1972, and in Leiden in May. Revised versions were then presented at a week-long conference at Urchfont Manor, near Devizes, in Wiltshire, England, in September 1972, with the participation of an additional ten specialists from countries in Europe and North America. At this final gathering, a total of nine countries were represented.

Not all of the members of the Study Group wrote papers, and not all of the papers which were produced could be revised for inclusion in this book. All those who attended the sessions did, nevertheless, contribute substantially to the success of the enterprise, not only by enriching the discussions at the time, but by putting forward ideas which have helped the authors represented here to revise and improve their articles. The debts thus incurred are so numerous and varied that it would be invidious to single out any of them here. One name must, however, be mentioned: that of Erik von Groeling. Dr von Groeling's paper, 'The Impact of Power Politics on Party Building: the CCP 1969–72', gave rise to lively and fruitful discussions at Urchfont. In the light of these, he had drawn up, late in 1972, plans for extensive revision and updating, which he unfortunately did not live to carry out. He died in hospital on 10 January 1973, at the age of 32. All of us who attended the meetings in which he participated will remember him for his keen and lively intelligence, and for his friendly and modest demeanour.

As this project draws to a conclusion, our thanks must go first of all to the Stiftung Volkswagenwerk, which provided the totality of the funds for travel, subsistence and entertainment incurred in the course of the four meetings of the Study Group. This sum was part of a larger grant to the School of Oriental and African Studies, in behalf of the Contemporary China Institute, for the development of contacts and cooperation on a European basis among students of contemporary China. There is no doubt that it has effectively served this end.

I also wish to express my own personal appreciation to Averill Norton, Viola Shaw, and Janet Wilson, secretaries to the Institute, for working long and hard to produce transcripts of the Urchfont discussions, and to type and re-type manuscripts. I am grateful to David Wilson for the assistance of his deft and vigorous editorial hand in preparing the final manuscript of the volume, and to Christopher Howe and Denis Twitchett, who read the draft at an earlier stage. My own contribution was unfortunately not completed in time to be discussed at Urchfont. Thus, while I must thank all the participants for the stimulus I derived from the proceedings, none of them are in any way responsible for failing to point out the short-comings of the introductory essay.

STUART R. SCHRAM

NOTE TO THE 1975 REPRINT

These essays are being reissued substantially in the form in which they were first sent to the printer in the spring of 1973. Some typographical errors have been corrected, and a few small substantive changes have been made in order to place events in a truer perspective, but no information has been incorporated regarding developments of the past two years. Thus the book retains its character as an attempt to describe and analyse certain aspects of Chinese society at the moment when they first began to take shape after the Cultural Revolution. In the opinion of the authors, much of this description remains valid and relevant, but the reader must be warned that the significance of one key symbol has changed: early in 1973, Lin Piao was re-classified as a rightist instead of a leftist. His name, which occurs frequently in these pages, should therefore be understood to evoke ultra-leftism, as it did in 1972, and not Confucian reaction.

S.R.S.

INTRODUCTION
THE CULTURAL REVOLUTION IN
HISTORICAL PERSPECTIVE

Stuart R. Schram

This volume, like the study group out of which it grew, seeks answers to the question: 'What has happened to China as a result of the Cultural Revolution?' Such an enterprise must, of course, take the current situation as one of its essential points of reference. The essays which follow accordingly look at aspects of Chinese reality as they appeared at the end of 1972. Since our object is not to present a tableau of China today, but to grasp the dynamics of change, there has been no attempt at encyclopaedic coverage. We have concentrated rather on a series of problems intimately related to the central theme of leadership and participation in the Chinese pattern of economic development and social change.

The flow of events can be charted only by comparing conditions in the most recent past with those before and during the upheaval of 1966-9. All the chapters in this book have thus, to some extent, an historical dimension. One of them, the contribution by Jack Gray, traces the emergence of two opposing approaches to development from the 1940s to the 1960s. Limitations of space have, however, made it impossible in most instances to pursue the antecedents of current policies back to 1949 and beyond. Moreover, a revolution is more than the sum of its parts. The changes which are visible in particular domains of Chinese society take on their full significance only in the context of the Chinese revolution as a whole.

By 'Chinese revolution' I mean in the first instance the struggle carried out by Mao Tse-tung and his comrades during the past half century, first to achieve power, and then to transform their country. But I am also referring, more broadly, to the many-faceted process of change initiated in the mid-nineteenth century under the Western

I

impact. This Chinese revolution grew out of the attempt, begun under the empire and continued by all those who have striven to rule China since 1911, to strengthen the nation in order to resist the political and economic penetration and domination of the foreigners. It rapidly became apparent, however, save to the most obstinate conservatives, that such a national revolution necessarily implied a cultural revolution as well. For the incursions of the West could be ended only by borrowing ideas and techniques from the West, and thus by calling into question certain aspects at least of the Chinese tradition. The republicans who emerged in the first decade of the twentieth century held that modernization, which for the most part they equated with Westernization, was impossible without political revolution; and the overthrow of the imperial system in 1911, though at first it did not appear to have initiated any very deep changes, did in effect deal a blow to Confucian values which ultimately hastened their demise. Meanwhile, a majority of the generation which came to the fore with the May 4th Movement of 1919 drew the more sweeping conclusion that the changes in attitudes and customs necessary to China's resurgence could be carried forward only in conjunction with a fundamental reordering of the economic and political system – in other words, through a social revolution inspired by Marxism or some other radical ideology.

Thus, both in fact and in the eyes of those who have participated in it, the Chinese revolution of the twentieth century has been made up of many strands: national revolution, cultural revolution, political revolution, economic revolution, social revolution. By baptizing 'Cultural Revolution' the movement which he launched in 1966, thus refurbishing a term current during the May 4th era, and which he himself had used extensively in Yenan days,[1] Mao Tse-tung chose to emphasize rather the unity and continuity of the Chinese revolution as a whole, despite the sharp differences between its successive phases. By so doing, he did not, of course, mean to reduce reality to its cultural dimension (though the cultural struggle in the narrow sense was much in the foreground in the early stages of the movement), but rather to suggest that we should take cultural change as

[1] See, in particular, 'On New Democracy', *Selected Works of Mao Tse-tung* (Peking, Foreign Languages Press, 1961–5), vol. II, pp. 369–82. (Hereafter *Selected Works*, followed by the volume number.)

the guiding thread for interpreting the process as a whole. Such an approach is in harmony with the traditional Chinese way of looking at things, with its overwhelming emphasis on patterns of thought (especially on moral and political philosophy) as that which both defines and gives meaning to a society. It is also in keeping with the Leninist and Stalinist interpretation of Marxism, which affirms the decisive importance of ideology in social change. It is therefore not surprising that it should be adopted by Mao, who is the heir to both these outlooks.

These recent developments are, in any case, part of the ongoing effort of the Chinese people to come to terms with the modern world without sacrificing their own identity. For Mao, both aspects of this process are equally important. The Chinese must master science and technology, and develop their economy, but they must do so by carrying out a revolution of a new and distinctive type, adapted to their circumstances and traditions. In a sense, it is hardly legitimate to separate these two strands, for a firm grasp of the organic linkage between social change and cultural change is one of the hallmarks of Mao Tse-tung's approach to revolution, and of the Chinese experience in general. Nevertheless, it will perhaps serve to clarify the issues if we look first at the cultural dimension of the problem, before turning to such matters as development strategies and levels of decision-making.

I. MAO TSE-TUNG AND CHANG CHIH-TUNG:
METAMORPHOSES OF THE 'T'I-YUNG' RATIONALIZATION

It may appear paradoxical to begin a discussion of the Cultural Revolution with a reference to the so-called *t'i-yung* formula – the classical, pre-revolutionary expression of the view that China should borrow only techniques from the West, while preserving the substance of her own tradition. Did not the advent of Marxism-Leninism in China radically change the terms of the debate regarding this problem, opening the door to a new synthesis? Such was the view expounded by Mao Tse-tung himself in 1949, on the eve of the foundation of the Chinese People's Republic. Recalling that successive generations of reformers and revolutionaries, from the Taipings to Sun Yat-sen, had 'looked to the West for truth before

3

the Communist Party of China was born', Mao noted that in his youth, he too had studied the 'new learning' from the West. And he continued:

For quite a long time, those who had acquired the new learning felt confident that it would save China...Only modernization could save China, only learning from foreign countries could modernize China. Among the foreign countries, only the Western capitalist countries were then progressive, as they had successfully built modern bourgeois states. The Japanese had been successful in learning from the West, and the Chinese also wished to learn from the Japanese. The Chinese in those days regarded Russia as backward, and few wanted to learn from her. That was how the Chinese tried to learn from foreign countries in the period from the 1840's to the beginning of the 20th century.

These 'dreams' about learning from the West were shattered, Mao indicated, not only by imperialist aggression, but by the ineffectiveness of Western solutions in the Chinese context. On the one hand, the 'teachers' of the European capitalist countries were 'always committing aggression against their pupil'. On the other hand, though the Chinese 'learned a great deal from the West', they 'could not make it work and were never able to realize their ideals'. The revolution of 1911 'ended in failure', and conditions in the country continually got worse. At this juncture:

Under the leadership of Lenin and Stalin, the revolutionary energy of the great proletariat and labouring people of Russia...suddenly erupted like a volcano, and the Chinese and all mankind began to see the Russians in a new light. Then, and only then, did the Chinese enter an entirely new era in their thinking and their life. They found Marxism–Leninism, the universally applicable truth, and the face of China began to change.

...The October Revolution helped progressives in China, as throughout the world, to adopt the proletarian world outlook as the instrument for studying a nation's destiny and considering anew their own problems. Follow the path of the Russians – that was their conclusion.[1]

It is obvious that, in Mao's view, the Chinese had entered 'an entirely new era' because they had found, in Marxism–Leninism, an instrument for working out their destiny which was free of both the defects which marred the 'new learning' borrowed from the Euro-

[1] Mao Tse-tung, 'On the People's Democratic Dictatorship', in *Selected Works*, IV, p. 413.

4

pean bourgeois democracies. Russia was no longer imperialist; and this new doctrine, unlike Western liberalism, *did* work in Chinese conditions. Thus the alternative was no longer nationalism *or* Westernization. China would pursue simultaneously the objectives of modernization and national resurgence, through new, revolutionary methods. The fact that the theory underlying this revolution was ultimately of Western origin was immaterial, since it enabled China to affirm her independence in the face of the West.

With due allowance for differences in vocabulary, Mao's views just quoted have been widely shared during the past two decades by social scientists and other political observers, who have seen in Leninism a doctrine which teaches revolutionaries in the non-European countries how to assimilate Western values and techniques, but to turn these against the domination of the West. Thus, when the confrontation between Communists and Kuomintang, between revolution and neo-traditionalism ended in 1949, it was generally assumed that China had finally chosen the path of 'wholesale Westernization', though this Westernization would take the Soviet rather than the American or European form. But what if the Russians were not content to allow the Chinese to follow the path blazed by the October Revolution in their own way, but undertook to guide them, and in the process control them? What if Russian methods proved *not* to work in China – at least without drastic modification? And what if the Chinese ultimately found it wounding to their national pride to follow the Russian example even if it did work, and therefore resolved to strike out on their own? Would not the controversies of the late nineteenth and early twentieth centuries then re-emerge in a new form, and would it not be discovered that all the crucial problems had in reality not yet been resolved?

This is, of course, exactly what did happen. In the event, wholesale Westernization in Marxist terms, like wholesale Westernization along lines inspired by John Dewey, was to prove a passing phase in China, lasting scarcely a decade. Two quotations from Mao Tse-tung, relating specifically to Chang Chih-tung's *t'i-yung* formula, nicely summarize the change. In the summer of 1956, after rejecting 'complete Westernization' as 'impracticable' and not acceptable to 'the common people of China', Mao stressed the need to learn from foreign countries, especially in the domain of theory:

Some people advocate 'Chinese learning as the substance, Western learning for practical application.' Is this idea right or wrong? It is wrong. The word 'learning' in fact refers to fundamental theory. Fundamental theory should be the same in China as in foreign countries... Marxism is a fundamental theory which was produced in the West. How then can we make a distinction between what is Chinese and what is Western in this respect?[1]

To be sure, he added that the universally applicable 'general truth' of Marxism must be combined with the concrete practice of revolution in each country and he even declared that the purpose of studying foreign things lay in the impetus it would give to the development of Chinese things. Still, half a dozen years after coming to power, he saw the universal essence of Marxism as somehow transcending its adaptation to the conditions and culture of each nation. In 1965 he put it exactly the other way round:

At the end of the Ch'ing Dynasty, some people advocated 'Chinese learning for the substance, Western learning for practical application.' The substance was like our General Line, which cannot be changed. We cannot adopt Western learning as the substance, nor can we use the substance of the democratic republic. We cannot use the 'Natural Rights of Man', or the 'Theory of Evolution'. We can only use Western technology.[2]

This text should not, of course, be taken to mean that Mao had turned his back on Leninism and relapsed into the conservative nationalism of the late nineteenth century. For him, the salvation of China continued to reside not in the preservation of an immutable 'national essence', but in revolution. He was increasingly persuaded, however, that the revolution must find its primary source and inspiration in China herself. Certain lessons which he had learned from Lenin (and Stalin) he would endeavour to retain, and he continued to call himself a Marxist–Leninist. In the last analysis, however, only iconoclasm from *within* the Chinese tradition, in a form immediately

---

[1] 'Talk to Music Workers' (24 August 1956), as translated in *Mao Tse-tung Unrehearsed: Talks and Letters 1956–1971*, translations by John Chinnery and Tieyun. Edited, and with an introduction by Stuart R. Schram (Harmondsworth, Penguin, 1974, and New York, Pantheon, 1975), Text 2. (The American edition of this book is entitled *Chairman Mao Talks to the People*.)

[2] 'Speech at Hangchow' (21 December 1965), *Mao Tse-tung Unrehearsed*, Text 13.

accessible to the Chinese people, would make it possible to dissolve and transcend the Confucian heritage.

In pursuing this intuition, Mao would find himself grappling, within the intellectual and political universe of Marxism, with problems not unlike those which dogged the conservative modernizers such as Chang Chih-tung at the end of the last century. By postulating that Leninism, in order to play its proper role in China, must be transmuted to such an extent that it lost its foreign essence – and thereby perhaps its identity – Mao was proposing, in effect, to use the Leninist heritage primarily as a storehouse of techniques. But could one borrow *political* techniques from the West – any more than one could borrow techniques for making cannons – without smuggling in Western (or Soviet) values as well?

Mao, clearly, believes that this is possible. Indeed, the Cultural Revolution could be defined as one vast attempt to achieve this result – to overcome the evils inherited from the past, but to do so in original and specifically Chinese terms. This ambition is not, of course, of recent origin. Like many others of the May 4th generation, Mao has long been persuaded that the Chinese people can and must play a distinctive role in world history. Meditating, in 1919, on the contrast between China's past greatness and her present humiliation, he attributed to the Chinese people special and unique qualities, residing not only in their past achievements, but in their capacity for renewal:

Our Chinese people possesses great inherent capacities!...I venture to make a singular assertion: one day, the reform of the Chinese people will be more profound than that of any other people, and the society of the Chinese people will be more radiant than that of any other people...We must all exert outselves! We must all advance with the utmost strength. Our golden age, our age of glory and splendour, lies before us![1]

This strand in Mao's thought can be traced straight through from that day to this. Discussing, in 1962, the history of the Chinese People's Republic up to that time, which he divided into the first eight years, when the Chinese had for the most part followed the Soviet example, and the period since the Great Leap For-

[1] Mao Tse-tung, 'The Great Union of the Popular Masses', translated in *The China Quarterly*, 49 (January–March, 1972), 87.

ward of 1958, when they had sought to strike out on their own, he declared:

in the first few years. . .the situation was such that, since we had no experience in economic construction, we had no alternative but to copy the Soviet Union. In the field of heavy industry especially, we copied almost everything from the Soviet Union, and we had very little creativity of our own. At that time it was absolutely necessary to act thus, but at the same time it was also a weakness – a lack of creativity and a lack of ability to stand on our own feet. Naturally this could not be our long-term strategy. From 1958 we decided to make self-reliance our major policy and striving for foreign aid a secondary aim.[1]

In other words, Mao saw 'wholesale Westernization' in Leninist or Soviet terms as a temporary crutch, which had enabled the Chinese to move forward during a limited period, but could not, in the long run, provide a substitute for walking on their own two feet. Irrespective of whether or not in fact the Great Leap Forward marked a rupture with the Soviet model, the political implications of such a stand on Mao's part are evident. Moreover, despite Soviet attempts to explain recent developments in China solely by Mao's 'nationalist fanaticism', a distaste for foreign tutelage is not the prerogative or invention of one man. The point has often been made that the Chinese communist movement did not take the form of guerrilla warfare in the countryside because Mao willed it so; it is rather because he was capable of conducting such a struggle that he rose to supreme leadership. Similarly, with reference to the issue raised here, it is not Mao alone who has turned the Chinese revolution away from primary reliance on Soviet guidance; he has remained at the helm because the vast majority of the Chinese people share his attachment to national dignity.

These attitudes, both on Mao's part and on that of his compatriots, do not simply grow out of the legendary Chinese 'ethnocentrism' – though the influence of centuries of splendid cultural isolation cannot be ignored. They are also the product of more recent historical experience. There is, first of all, the impact of a century of semi-colonial humiliation at the hands of the West – the carving out of spheres of influence, the unequal economic relations, the smug

---

[1] Speech of January 1962 to an enlarged central work conference known as the '7,000-Cadres Conference', in *Mao Tse-tung Unrehearsed*, Text 8.

missionaries, the insolent foreigners of the treaty ports. The bitter-
ness engendered by these memories is deep, but it is less important,
in explaining the genesis of the Cultural Revolution, than the fruits
of half a century of unequal relations between 'fraternal parties'
within what used to be called the 'World Communist Movement'.
Moreover, the problem of the 'Sinification of Marxism', and of the
search for an original pattern of revolution in China, is inextricably
linked to the struggle for power, in the 1930s and 1940s, between
Mao Tse-tung and the Moscow-oriented faction in the Chinese
Communist Party.

Stalin had rapidly come to accept the tactics of guerrilla warfare in
the countryside which Mao Tse-tung and Chu Te were developing
in the Chingkangshan, in the years 1928–9, as the most important, or
in any case the most effective, form of struggle in China for the time
being. He continued to regard these activities, however, as in the last
analysis a holding operation until the urban working class could
recover from the bloody repression of 1927 and once more play an
active role in the revolutionary struggle. As the time scale lengthened,
and the eagerly-awaited 'high tide' of revolutionary activity failed to
materialize, Mao's 'holding operation' in the countryside assumed
greater and greater importance in the eyes of the Comintern, which
devoted extensive passages in its directives to the problems of
enlarging the Red Army and the base areas it controlled, setting up
Soviets, carrying out agrarian reform, and so on. Nevertheless,
'working-class hegemony' remained for Moscow not merely an
article of faith, but a basic operational principle, and a decisive
advance in the Chinese revolution was regarded by the Comintern as
inconceivable without the participation of at least some of the 'large
proletarian centres'. A whole series of directives of the period
1928–31 made this crystal clear.[1]

Li Li-san, who dominated the leadership of the Chinese Communist Party in the years 1928–30, laid even heavier emphasis than
Stalin on the importance of the cities and of the working class. On
doctrinal grounds, and also, no doubt, because he looked on Mao as a

---

[1] See the extracts in H. Carrère d'Encausse and S. Schram, *Marxism and Asia*
(London, Allen Lane the Penguin Press, 1969), pp. 242–7; also the letter of 7 June
1929, in Jane Degras (ed.), *The Communist International 1919–1943. Documents*, vol. III
(London, Oxford University Press, 1965), pp. 31–6.

rival, he adopted at first a sceptical and even contemptuous attitude toward the activities of the Red Army in the countryside. Early in 1930, he suddenly reversed his tactical position and began elaborating plans for a great revolutionary offensive combining attacks by the Red Army on key cities with a general strike by the workers culminating in an armed uprising. Until recently, the predominant view among Western scholars has been that Li was encouraged to make this move by the Comintern, which had sent to the Chinese Communist Party, in December 1929, a letter hailing the emergence of a 'revolutionary upsurge' in China and calling simultaneously for the development of the guerrilla movement in the countryside and for general strikes in the cities.[1]

Those who saw the Li Li-san line as made in Moscow have commonly assumed that Mao Tse-tung opposed from the outset Li's plan to hurl the Red Army against the cities because it not only jeopardized the basis of his own power, but threatened to destroy the instrument on which the future development of China's rural revolution depended.[2] An alternative interpretation first put forward a decade ago stands the earlier view completely on its head, making it appear not only that Li Li-san really *was* a leftist heretic (as both Moscow and the official Chinese historiography had long claimed), but that Mao was Moscow's man.[3] The fullest and most recent statement of this position relies extensively on Russian sources, but while it was in the process of publication, the Soviets themselves had begun to draw from their archives still another view,

[1] The full text of this crucial message, as originally published in *Pravda* on 29 December 1929, is reprinted in *Strategiya i Taktika Kominterna v Natsional'no-Kolonial'noi Revoliutsii, na primere Kitaya* (*Strategy and Tactics of the Comintern in the National-Colonial Revolution, on the Basis of the Chinese Example*) (ed. Pavel Mif), (Moscow, Izdanie Instituta MKh i MP, 1934), pp. 252–8. A partial English translation appears in Degras, *op. cit.* pp. 84–9. The view that the Li Li-san line was basically similar to that of the Comintern, and that Li was only discovered to be a heretic after it had failed, was first put forward by Harold Isaacs in 1938; it was espoused in the 1950s by writers of widely differing outlooks. (For a list, see Tso-liang Hsiao, *Power Relations within the Chinese Communist Movement, 1930–1934* (Seattle, University of Washington Press, 1961), pp. 23–4.)

[2] John E. Rue, who has advanced the novel view that the Li Li-san line was the result of a 'trap' laid for Li by the Comintern representative Pavel Mif (*Mao Tse-tung in Opposition* (Stanford, Stanford University Press, 1966), p. 189), likewise holds that Mao was opposed from beginning to end to the attacks on the cities. (*Ibid.* pp. 213–18.)

[3] This view was first stated by Tso-liang Hsiao, in his book *Power Relations*.

according to which Mao Tse-tung supported and shared in Li Li-san's leftist errors in 1930.[1]

It is obviously not possible, in the context of this introduction, to clarify fully the extremely complicated questions of historical fact involved in this dispute. It is, however, vital to our discussion of Mao's role as spokesman for Chinese national sentiment, and of the roots of his quarrel with Moscow, to define briefly his position in the face of the head-on clash which developed in the summer and autumn of 1930 between Li Li-san and the Comintern.

In a word, the conclusion which appears to emerge from an examination of the available materials is that Li Li-san had indeed deviated further from Comintern policy than has hitherto been generally recognized, but that Mao, far from being Moscow's man, stood in some ways very close to Li. There were, of course, important ideological differences between the two men – quite apart from the personal rivalry between them. Mao's heart was in the countryside, Li's in the cities. Nevertheless, from the moment that Li Li-san put forward the idea of joint action by the Red Army and the workers' movement to achieve a great revolutionary victory, two areas of convergence were immediately evident: their impatient and optimistic temper, and their commitment to China.

[1] Richard C. Thornton, *The Comintern and the Chinese Communists, 1928–1931* (Seattle, University of Washington Press, 1969). In a footnote on p. 224, Mr Thornton takes note of this recent Soviet position, and rejects it. Among the innumerable accounts of these matters recently published in the Soviet Union, perhaps the most serious and fully documented is that of A. M. Grigor'ev, 'Komintern i Revoliutsionnoe Dvizhenie v Kitae pod Lozungom Sovetov (1928–1930)' (The Comintern and the Revolutionary Movement in China under the Slogan of the Soviets, 1928–1930), in *Komintern i Vostok* (*The Comintern and the East*) (Moscow, Nauka, 1969, pp. 313–49). The political motivations of these recent Soviet historical writings are all too obvious, and become even more so when, after denouncing Mao for his complicity with Li Li-san, these authors proceed to claim that he learned from the Comintern all the lessons he subsequently applied in the course of his road to power, including the idea of encircling the cities from the countryside. Thus Moscow claims the credit for the successes of the Chinese revolution, and dissociates itself from the errors. Nevertheless, despite their bias, these writings present important evidence which challenges both of the contrasting Western interpretations. The same is true of the semi-official history published in Taipei. See Warren Kuo, *Analytical History of the Chinese Communist Party*, Book Two (Taipei, Institute of International relations, 1968), chapter XIV. While agreeing with recent Soviet writings that Mao in 1930 shared Li Li-san's leftist extremism, Mr Kuo naturally cannot admit that there were any divergences between either of the two men and Moscow. In his view, the 'fanatical' line of 1930 was inspired by the Comintern, and applied by both Mao and Li.

With reference to the first point, it is worth pointing out to begin with that Mao had concluded, as early as August 1927, that the Chinese revolution had already entered the socialist stage.[1] He abjured this 'leftist' error after receiving, in early 1929, the resolutions of the Sixth Congress of the Chinese Communist Party, which declared that the revolution was still in its bourgeois-democratic phase,[2] but he continued to believe that the revolution could and should advance rapidly. Thus, in April 1929, he criticized the 'pessimistic spirit' of Li Li-san and the Central Committee, and put forward a plan for the conquest of the whole of Kiangsi province, including major centres such as Nanchang, within one year. In January 1930, in a letter to Lin Piao, he reiterated the view that such an offensive was feasible.[3] The limited geographic scope of Mao's strategic thinking did not, in fact, mark it off sharply from Li Li-san's country-wide approach, once the two of them had agreed that the time had come to take the offensive. For Li saw a preliminary victory in one or several provinces as the first step to a nationwide revolutionary conflagration, while Mao, for his part, conceded that his goal of taking Kiangsi would be 'unthinkable' unless a nationwide revolutionary high tide were imminent, and believed that victory in one province would in turn hasten the coming of the tide.[4] Moscow, which had encouraged the Chinese Communists to

[1] For extracts from a letter summarizing his views at this time, see my article 'On the Nature of Mao Tse-tung's "Deviation" in 1927', *The China Quarterly* 18 (April–June, 1964), 58–9.

[2] Mao's 'Leftist' deviation of 1927 had been explicitly denounced by at least two speakers at the Sixth Congress, held in Moscow in June and July 1928. See the quotations from the stenographic report in Grigor'ev, 'Komintern i Revoliutsionnoe Dvizhenie v Kitae', p. 320, and N. I. Kapchenko, *Pekin: Politika, Chuzhdaya Sotsializmu (Peking: a Policy Alien to Socialism)* (Moscow, 'Mezhdunarodnye Otnosheniya', 1967), pp. 55–6. For his part, Li Li-san had declared at the congress that Mao's 'socialism' was the expression of 'petty-bourgeois illusions'. (Cited in Thornton, *The Comintern and the Chinese Communists*, pp. 40–1.)

[3] For the full contemporary text of this letter, see Bill Jenner's translation in *New Left Review* 65 (1971), 59–68.

[4] The classic expression of the 'Li Li-san line' is the resolution of 11 June 1930, translated in Brandt, Schwartz, and Fairbank, *A Documentary History of Chinese Communism* (Cambridge, Mass., Harvard University Press, 1950), pp. 184–200. Mao's view, stated in his letter to Lin Piao, about the links between the local and the national struggle, was put ever more forcefully in the course of the summer and autumn. See Grigor'ev, 'Komintern i Revoliutsionnoe Dvizhenie v Kitae', pp. 331–3, for references from Chinese and Japanese sources.

believe that a 'revolutionary upsurge' was at hand by its letter of December 1929, was alarmed by Li Li-san's impetuosity in ordering an offensive before sufficient preliminary work had been done either in the cities or in strengthening the Red Army, and explicitly refused to sanction the plan for an attack on Wuhan, Changsha, etc., and for coordinated uprisings in those cities.[1] Stalin's anxiety regarding the risks involved in such a policy must have been greatly heightened by Li Li-san's explicit aim of provoking Japanese and other imperialist intervention in Northeastern China, and thereby drawing the Soviet Union into a 'world revolutionary war'.[2] There are, of course, important differences between this 'Sinocentric' vision of world revolution and the ideas, which Mao was subsequently to develop, of a self-reliant Chinese revolution serving as the model for revolution in other Asian countries, but Li Li-san's conception of China as the powder keg, rather than the path-breaker, can be explained to a considerable extent by the apocalyptic outlook which Mao shared with him at the time. In any case, his statements to the effect that his basic loyalty was to China rather than to Moscow, his faith that revolution would break out in China before it did in Europe, and his conviction that foreigners could not understand China, were all strictly parallel to the attitudes adopted by Mao Tse-tung then and later.

Mao Tse-tung, it now appears, continued to support the Li Li-san line on this and other points at least until mid-October. A resolution, adopted under his guidance on 7 October, noted the existence of 'a revolutionary situation in the whole world, in the whole country, in all provinces', and concluded: 'In the course of this revolutionary "high tide" (*kao-ch'ao*)...soviet power must undoubtedly burst upon the scene in the whole country and in the whole world.'[3]

[1] Grigor'ev, 'Komintern i Revoliutsionnoe Dvizhenie v Kitae', pp. 333–7, provides many precise details, taken from the Comintern archives, regarding the efforts of Moscow and of the Far Eastern Bureau of the International to restrain Li Li-san, beginning in June 1930. There is every reason to believe that these are authentic.

[2] For a brief summary of some of Li's statements about China's role in the world revolution in the summer of 1930, see S. Schram, *Mao Tse-tung* (Harmondsworth, Penguin Books, 1967), pp. 148–9. Li's 'plot' to involve the Soviet Union in a war in support of the Chinese revolution naturally excites great indignation on the part of the Soviet authors; see, for example, Grigor'ev, 'Komintern i Revoliutsionnoe Dvizhenie v Kitae', pp. 330–1).

[3] Ch'ü Ch'iu-pai, article in *Shih Hua* (*True Words*) (Shanghai), 2 (9 December 1930), 3–4.

13

Subsequently, the attempt to hold even a minor centre such as Chi-an in Kiangsi having demonstrably failed, Mao's chiliastic excitement subsided, at least for the time being, and he began to think once again in terms of the gradual development of the revolution in the countryside.

I have dwelt at some length on the episode of the Li Li-san line because it is the first instance of an open clash between Moscow and a leadership of the Chinese Communist Party determined to put China first. Moreover, not only has Mao's attitude at this time often been incorrectly understood, but a very large proportion of those who were subsequently to play important roles in the Party shared some degree of responsibility for Li's policies, either because they had supported them, or because (as in the case of Chou En-lai and Ch'ü Ch'iu-pai) they had not opposed them energetically.

The members of the Moscow-trained 'Returned Student' faction, headed by Wang Ming (Ch'en Shao-yü), Ch'in Pang-hsien, Chang Wen-t'ien and others, had been present in China since March 1930, but they succeeded in taking control of the Party only when their mentor, Pavel Mif, arrived from Moscow at the end of the year backed by a mandate from the Comintern to put an end once and for all to the Li Li-san line. Thus, this affair was marked not only by lengthy and acrimonious ideological differences, but by the first direct organizational confrontation between the Comintern and the majority of its Chinese section. The Russians had 'spent a lot of money' sending the 'Returned Students' back to China, and therefore felt that these young men had a *prima facie* right to leadership over the Chinese Communist Party.[1] At the Fourth Plenum of the Central Committee, in January 1931, presided over and tightly controlled by Mif, this right was at last formally recognized.[2]

Having assumed control and got rid of Li Li-san, the new leadership undertook to set the Party's house in order in all respects, and to stamp out heresies of every kind wherever they might be found. In this situation, Mao's 'military deviation', and his rural orientation, strengthened and confirmed by the lessons he had learned from

[1] Schram, *Mao Tse-tung*, p. 150.
[2] Thornton, *The Comintern and the Chinese Communists*, pp. 203–16, gives a full and accurate summary of the proceedings. As he points out (p. 208, note), Western specialists (myself included) have erred in the past in stating that Mif had accompanied his protégés back to China in the spring of 1930.

the failures of 1930, once more became vital issues. The 'Returned Students' would never, as Li Li-san had done for a time, underestimate the importance of the Red Army. They were, however (as Stalin continued to be[1]) sharply critical of Mao's inadequate attention to the working-class movement in the cities, and of his failure to recruit an adequate number of workers into all the leading organs of the Party and of the Army. These anxieties on their part were undoubtedly compounded by personal jealousies on both sides. As a result, the 'Returned Student' leadership proceeded systematically to limit Mao's power. This struggle has been often chronicled, and the details are of little importance here. It is generally agreed that by 1932 Mao's influence over both Party and Army had been sharply curtailed, and that by the middle of 1934 little was left to him but his ceremonial functions as Chairman of the Chinese Soviet Republic.

Despite this background of conflict, when Mao achieved in January 1935 at the Tsunyi Conference a *de facto* position as supreme leader of the Party, the change was endorsed in Moscow. For nearly three decades, until the beginning of open Sino-Soviet polemics in the 1960s, these past differences were glossed over on both sides, but it is clear they continued to rankle.

On the Soviet side, the Comintern veteran Otto Kuusinen declared, in his speech of February 1964, that the neglect of the workers' movement by the leadership of the Chinese Communist Party was 'not something new', and added: 'In its time, it provoked justified criticism by the Communist International. I am far from thinking that all the decisions of the Comintern, including those on the Chinese question, have always been faultless. But on this important question of principle the Comintern was a hundred per cent correct.'[2] Kuusinen was here referring, of course, precisely to those directives cited above.

Mao also remembered these events, but he judged them differently. 'Speaking generally', he said in 1962,

it is we Chinese who have achieved understanding of the objective world of China, not the comrades concerned with Chinese questions in the Communist International. These comrades in the Communist Inter-

---

[1] For a concise statement of the Comintern's overall strategy for China, see the resolution of 26 August 1931, translated in Degras, *The Communist International*, vol. III, pp. 169–76.　　　　　[2] *Marxism and Asia*, p. 333.

national simply did not understand, or we could say they utterly failed to understand, Chinese society, the Chinese nation, or the Chinese revolution. For a long time even we did not have a clear understanding of the objective world of China, let alone the foreign comrades![1]

In the 1930s, Mao Tse-tung could not, of course, treat the authority and wisdom of Stalin and the Comintern so lightly. Nevertheless, he deliberately based his claims to leadership not on Soviet connections, but on knowledge of his own country. In October 1938, speaking to the Sixth Plenum of the Central Committee of the Chinese Communist Party, he denied not only the relevance, but the very existence, of what he called 'abstract Marxism', and demanded instead the adaptation of Marxism to Chinese conditions:

The history of our great people over several millennia exhibits national peculiarities and many precious qualities...Today's China is an outgrowth of historic China. We are Marxist historicists; we must not mutilate history. From Confucius to Sun Yat-sen we must sum it up critically, and we must constitute ourselves the heirs of all that is precious in this past. Conversely, the assimilation of this heritage itself turns out to be a kind of methodology that is of great help in the guidance of the revolutionary movement. A communist is a Marxist internationalist, but Marxism must take on a national form before it can be applied. There is no such thing as abstract Marxism, but only concrete Marxism. What we call concrete Marxism is Marxism that has taken on a national form, that is, Marxism applied to the concrete struggle in the concrete conditions prevailing in China, and not Marxism abstractly used...Consequently, the Sinification of Marxism – that is to say, making certain that in all of its manifestations it is imbued with Chinese peculiarities, using it according to these peculiarities – becomes a problem that must be understood and solved by the whole Party without delay.[2]

Mao did not claim in 1938 that he himself had carried out this enterprise of Sinification, but it must have been evident at the time to his listeners that he was bent on undermining the credentials of those whose knowledge of revolution had been acquired sitting in offices in Moscow, rather than fighting in the Chinese countryside. This was made crystal clear when Mao went on, in the speech just quoted, to call for 'an end to writing eight-legged essays on foreign

[1] *Mao Tse-tung Unrehearsed*, Text 8.
[2] S. Schram, *The Political Thought of Mao Tse-tung* (Harmondsworth, Penguin Books, and New York, Praeger, 1969), pp. 172–3.

16

models', and the replacement of such 'dogmatism' by 'a new and vital Chinese style and manner, pleasing to the eye and to the ear of the Chinese common people', adding that the separation of 'internationalist content from national form' was 'the way of those who understand nothing of internationalism'. The 'foreign dogmatism' thus rejected was, of course, Soviet ideology mechanically copied by the Moscow-trained intellectuals in the Chinese Communist Party. The so-called 'International Faction' in the leadership, made up of such intellectuals, had, Mao suggested, less grasp of true internationalism than those, such as himself, who approached questions of international solidarity from a firm stance in national reality.

Mao's speech of October 1938 thus announced, in effect, the terms of the final show-down between himself and the 'Returned Student' faction which was to work itself out over the next five years, culminating in the 'Rectification Campaign' of 1942–3. Wang Ming had returned to China in 1937 with a directive from Stalin regarding the leadership of the Chinese Communist Party which would, he anticipated, give him the opportunity to replace Mao as the principal figure in the Party, but which in fact proved to be his own undoing. On the one hand, Stalin declared that Mao Tse-tung had many defects; he did not understand Marxism, and he lacked a broad world view, relying too much on his own narrow experience. Nevertheless, since he had now become the leader of the Chinese Communist Party, those cadres with experience acquired in the Soviet Union should help him to overcome these weaknesses, and to play his role better. Secondly, Stalin suspected Chang Wen-t'ien, another Moscow-trained intellectual, who had succeeded Ch'in Pang-hsien as Secretary General at Tsunyi, of Trotskyist tendencies, and therefore regarded him as unsuitable for this post. The first of these points worked, in the last analysis, to consolidate Mao's authority. The second, which Wang Ming had hoped would permit him to take over the Secretary Generalship, gave rise to internal conflicts within the 'Returned Student' faction enabling Mao to play them off against one another, and ultimately to eliminate them all from the centres of power.[1]

[1] This is spelled out most explicitly by Warren Kuo, *Analytical History*, vol. III, pp. 328–30 (pp. 248–9 of the Chinese edition), but the broad outlines are confirmed by many other sources.

The significance of these circumstances in Mao's eyes was obviously that once more, as in January 1931, those who looked to Moscow for ideological guidance proved to regard the Soviet Union as the ultimate source of authority as well. To put it another way, they regarded Stalin as the supreme leader of the Chinese revolution; Mao, despite many statements hailing Stalin as the leader of the world revolution, was persuaded that the Chinese revolution could only be led by a Chinese.

Mao himself alluded to this aspect of the problem when, in the spring of 1941, his campaign for the adaptation of Marxism to Chinese conditions – and, in the last analysis, for the adoption of his own thought as the standard of orthodoxy – really got under way. In the preface which he wrote then to the re-publication in book form of a collection of *Rural Surveys* dating from the Kiangsi period, he reaffirmed the slogan he had coined in 1930: 'No investigation, no right to speak.'[1] Those who ridiculed this view as 'narrow empiricism' he stigmatized as 'imperial envoys', who rushed here and there the moment they alighted from their carriages spouting opinions about a reality of which they knew nothing.[2] A decade or so earlier, the directives of the International had been referred to, within the Chinese Communist Party, as 'imperial decrees' (*ti-ming*).[3] It is hard not to read Mao's statement of 1941 as a veiled but clear assertion that henceforth such 'imperial decrees' had no force in China. He had, in fact, said explicitly to Edgar Snow in 1936: 'We are certainly not fighting for an emancipated China in order to turn the country over to Moscow!'[4]

In his talk entitled 'Reform our Study', delivered in May 1941, shortly after he had written the preface to the volume just quoted, Mao Tse-tung started from the wholly orthodox axiom (supported

[1] For the first known statement of this idea, see Mao's 'Oppose Bookism', in *Selected Readings from the Works of Mao Tse-tung* (Peking, Foreign Languages Press, 1967), pp. 33–41. (Hereafter *Selected Readings*.)

[2] *Selected Works*, III, p. 13.

[3] See the translations from *Chung-yang t'ung-hsin* in C. Martin Wilbur, 'The Ashes of Defeat', *The China Quarterly* 18 (April–June, 1964), 35, 51. (Professor Wilbur interprets 'imperial decree' to mean the orders of the central organs of the Chinese Communist Party; I see it rather as a reference to the authority of Moscow.)

[4] Extracts from this interview (which was published in the *Shanghai Evening Post and Mercury* in February 1937, and may or may not have come to Stalin's attention at the time) can be found in *The Political Thought of Mao Tse-tung*, pp. 418–20.

by copious references to the authority of Marx, Engels, Lenin, and Stalin) that the 'universal truth of Marxism–Leninism must be combined with the concrete practice of the Chinese revolution'. He went on, however, to elaborate on the idea, thrown out in his report of October 1938, that the study of Chinese history would not only provide raw material for the analysis of Chinese reality, but constituted in itself a 'methodology' useful for guiding the revolution. Too many comrades, he said:

are not ashamed, but proud, when they understand very little or nothing about their own history. They really understand very little about the especially important history of the Chinese Communist Party or Chinese history for the hundred years since the Opium War...Many are ignorant of anything which is their own, yet hold on to Greek and foreign tales (they are nothing more than tales) which are pathetically abstracted and presented from a pile of old foreign papers. For the past few decades, many returned students have been making this mistake. They return from Europe, America or Japan, and all they know how to do is to recite a stock of undigested foreign phrases. They function as phonographs but forget their own responsibility to create something new.

It was obvious that the 'Europe' from which these students had returned included the Soviet Union. Apart from their ignorance of Chinese reality, Mao attacked them once again for dogmatism. 'Seventeen and eighteen-year-old babies', he declared, 'are taught to nibble on *Das Kapital* and *Anti-Dühring*...Their inclination is to regard what they have learned from their teachers as never-changing dogma.'[1] Evidently Mao felt that they were quite as incapable of understanding these books as the average Chinese elementary-school student was of understanding the Confucian *Analects* when they were first presented to him, and could therefore only learn them by rote.

When the *cheng-feng* or 'Rectification' campaign was formally launched in February 1942, Mao Tse-tung once again developed these two accusations of dogmatism and ignorance of Chinese

---

[1] These quotations are from Boyd Compton's translation of the contemporary version in *Mao's China* (Seattle, University of Washington Press, 1952), pp. 62–3. Is it an accident that Wang Ming and Ch'in Pang-hsien were seventeen or eighteen when they first went to Moscow?

realities. He added to them an increasingly strong emphasis on the futility of 'book learning' as such:

A man studies from grade school to university, graduates, and is then considered learned. Yet, in the first place, he cannot till the land; second, he has no trade; third, he cannot fight; fourth, he cannot manage a job – in none of these fields is he experienced nor does he have the least practical knowledge. What he possesses is merely book knowledge. Would it be possible to regard such a man as a complete intellectual? It would be very difficult; at most I would consider him a half-intellectual, because his knowledge is still incomplete... I advise those of you who have only book knowledge and as yet no contact with reality, and those who have had little practical experience, to recognize their own shortcomings and become a bit more humble...

On hearing this, some people will lose their tempers and say, 'According to your interpretation, Marx was also a half-intellectual.' I would answer that it's quite true that, in the first place, Marx could not slaughter a pig, and second, he could not till a field. But he did participate in the revolutionary movement and also carried out research on commodity production... He did personal research on nature, history, and proletarian revolution, and created the corresponding theories of dialectical materialism, historical materialism, and proletarian revolution. Thus Marx is to be regarded as a complete intellectual.[1]

Despite the concluding sentences hailing Marx's theoretical achievements, Mao's initial response to his own question, 'It's quite true that Marx could not till a field', opens the door to the view that first-hand experience of *rural* reality (especially of China's rural reality) is an indispensable attribute of a fully qualified revolutionary thinker. It thus prefigures Liu Shao-ch'i's 1945 statement that Mao had been 'boldly creative' in the theoretical field, 'discarding certain specific Marxist principles and conclusions that were obsolete and ill-adapted to concrete conditions in China'.[2]

Though the Cultural Revolution of 1966–9 is, in the true sense of the word, unique, the Rectification Campaign of 1942–3 offers interesting and suggestive parallels with these recent events. Like the Cultural Revolution, *cheng-feng* was both a struggle for power and a conflict about basic principles. Though the Rectification Campaign

---

[1] *The Political Thought of Mao Tse-tung*, pp. 176–7.
[2] From his report at the Seventh Party Congress of April 1945, translated in *Marxism and Asia*, p. 261.

was not a blood bath, as has been suggested by some recent Soviet accounts, neither was it, any more than the Cultural Revolution, simply a matter of education and persuasion.[1] The aim was no doubt, in most cases, to 'cure the sickness to save the patient', as demanded by Mao in his speech of 1 February 1942. None the less, this campaign took place more or less simultaneously with one to ferret out enemy espionage agents, and in this context, there resulted not only intense psychological pressure, but the use of torture to extract confessions, as K'ang Sheng recognized in a report of 1944.[2] Though the movement as a whole did not lead to the decimation of the Party membership in the manner of Stalin, and in this sense was not a 'purge', it aimed not merely to rectify the Party's style of work, but to break the power of the 'International Faction'.

Mao's long and complex struggle against the 'dogmatists' in the Chinese Communist Party was not brought to a successful conclusion until the autumn of 1943, a year and a half after the Rectification Campaign had been formally launched, and five years after Mao, in his report to the Sixth Plenum, had put forward the slogan

[1] The form and consequences of the power struggle at this time constitute yet another obscure and controversial question in the history of the Chinese Communist movement. The positions taken range all the way from that of Mark Selden, who concludes that rectification was 'not a purge', and did not lead to the imprisonment or exclusion from the Party (still less the execution) of even a single cadre (see Mark Selden, *The Yenan Way in Revolutionary China* (Cambridge, Mass., Harvard University Press, 1971), pp. 188 n., 196–7) to that of the Soviets, who have spoken of it in recent years as a bloody purge involving the liquidation of as many as a hundred thousand or more 'veteran revolutionaries' and other innocent people (Moscow radio, in Chinese, 26 April and 5 May 1970, quoted in Kuo, *Analytical History*, pp. 427–8). This latter picture of events is patently absurd. Indeed, the Soviets themselves have ventured to put forward such extravagant figures for the number of victims only in propaganda broadcasts; in print, they have been infinitely more prudent. Thus, one of the most scurrilous attacks on Mao Tse-tung published in the Soviet Union in recent years says merely: '. . . during the second and third stages of this campaign (or rather this mass purge), there came into being in the Party and in the Liberated Areas as a whole a climate of psychological terror, as well as conditions permitting the elimination (extending even to physical liquidation) of persons who did not agree with Mao Tse-tung and his coterie'. The victims of the campaign are naturally identified as the 'bearers of Marxist–Leninist ideas, the international communists' (O. Vladimirov and V. Ryazantsev, *Stranitsy Politicheskoy Biografii Mao Tse-duna (Pages from the Political Biography of Mao Tse-tung)* (Moscow, Politizdat, 1969, p. 42). For a balanced evaluation of the degree of violence associated with the campaign, see Compton, *Mao's China*, pp. xxv–xxvi.

[2] Quoted in Kuo, *Analytical History*, pp. 412–13 (Chinese edition, pp. 274–80).

of the Sinification of Marxism. The publication in the Yenan press, in July 1943, of an article by Liu Shao-ch'i hailing Mao Tse-tung as a true Bolshevik, and denouncing the adherents of the 'international line' as Mensheviks in disguise, may be taken as marking the symbolic ending of the campaign.[1]

As in the case of the Cultural Revolution, Mao's aim in launching the struggle which took place in Yenan in the 1940s was not merely to consolidate his own position, but to secure the implementation of those policies which he believed best adapted to Chinese realities. Mao's own slogan of the 'Sinification of Marxism', which I have been using as the shorthand expression of his line at this time, is a suggestive symbol, but an incomplete and ambiguous one, which requires spelling out. It was not for Mao an end in itself, though he undoubtedly regarded it as a good thing, because it displayed both his own creativity and that of the Chinese people. Despite his reference to Marxist theory in 1956 as 'substance', he regarded it in fact as a tool for practical use, and said so plainly in his speech launching the Rectification Campaign:

The arrow of Marxism–Leninism must be used to hit the target of Chinese revolution. If it were otherwise, why would we want to study Marxism–Leninism?...Our comrades must understand that we do not study Marxism–Leninism because it is pleasing to the eye, or because it has some mystical value, like the doctrines of the Taoist priests who ascend Mao Shan to learn how to subdue devils and evil spirits. Marxism–Leninism has no beauty, nor has it any mystical value. It is only extremely useful.[2]

Clearly Marxism–Leninism could serve to 'hit the target of the Chinese Revolution' only if it were understood and grasped by the Chinese people. In Mao's view, it could be understood only if it were adapted to the experience and patterns of thought of the Chinese. Therefore it must be Sinified, as he believed he had done. A central aim of the Rectification Campaign was to ensure that this interpretation of Marxism should be assimilated as widely as possible by Party members, and by the population at large. The membership

[1] For a brief summary of the steps leading to Liu's endorsement of Mao's ideological claims, see my article, 'Mao Tse-tung and Liu Shao-ch'i, 1939–1969', *Asian Survey* XII (4) (April 1972), 278–80. The text of Liu's article of July 1943 is translated in Compton, *Mao's China*, pp. 255–68. (See especially pp. 261–5).
[2] Compton, *Mao's China*, p. 21.

of the Party had increased at least ten-fold between 1937 and 1942, and many of those who had been thus drawn into the Party lacked even an elementary knowledge of Marxist ideas in general, and of Leninist organizational principles in particular. To give them such knowledge was vital if they were to be welded into an effective instrument of leadership.

To Sinify the outward form of Marxism was relatively easy, but insufficient. A Marxism 'Sinified' in vocabulary and logic, but marked, as regarded substance, by the wrong aspects of the national environment, might have been useless, or even harmful. The question was not merely an abstract and hypothetical one, for it so happened that the worst vice of traditional Chinese society overlapped to a very large extent with the greatest weakness of Leninism: an exaggerated respect for those with 'learning' (the Confucian term) or 'consciousness' (the Leninist term), and a tendency to elevate them too far above the common run of human beings. In the end, Mao came to call into question not only the traditional form of elitism, but elitism in its Leninist guise of the mystique of the Party, and to reject not only the Confucian prejudice regarding the superiority of mental over manual workers, but the Marxist prejudice regarding the superiority of the worker over the peasant.

On the eve of the conquest of power, Mao Tse-tung himself was acutely conscious of the limitations of his own experience. Despite an apprenticeship of two decades in administrative and economic work, both in the Kiangsi Soviet Republic and in the Yenan base area, he was aware that governing the entire country would pose problems of an entirely different order, and in 1949 he could imagine no other way of solving these than to follow the Soviet example. As we have already seen, he still felt, in 1962, that this decision had been the only possible one at the time. In his essay of June 1949, 'On the People's Democratic Dictatorship', he formulated the problem as follows:

Twenty-eight years of our Party are a long period, in which we have accomplished only one thing – we have won basic victory in the revolutionary war. This calls for celebration, because it is the people's victory...But we still have much work to do; to use the analogy of a journey, our past work is only the first step in a long march of ten thousand *li*...The serious task of economic construction lies before us.

We shall soon put aside some of the things we know well and be compelled to do things we don't know well. This means difficulties...

We must overcome difficulties, we must learn what we do not know. We must learn how to do economic work, from all who know how, no matter who they are. We must esteem them as teachers, learning from them respectfully and conscientiously...The Communist Party of the Soviet Union is our best teacher, and we must learn from it...[1]

In setting about this task of modernization and economic development, Mao deliberately reversed the relationship which had taken shape in the course of the struggle for power between the cities and the countryside. After the disaster of 1927, the Chinese Communist Party had been reformed as a political and military force in the countryside, intimately linked to the peasants and enjoying their support, and it was this Party which assumed power in 1949. But although Mao admired the peasants for their revolutionary qualities, the economic and social transformation of China to which he was committed involved raising the technical level of the rural areas and changing the peasants' traditional patterns of thought and behaviour. 'The serious problem', he declared in his essay already quoted on People's Democratic Dictatorship, 'is the education of the peasantry.'

The primary agents in the education of the peasants, and in leading them toward agricultural collectivization and a new life, were to be the Party cadres. 'It is only through the cadres that we can educate and guide the masses', Mao had declared in 1942 at the Yenan Forum on art and literature.[2] And though in 1949 very many Party members were of peasant origin, a systematic effort was made during the years immediately after the victory of the revolution to draw into the Party more urban workers, in order to make of it a proletarian party as the term had always been understood in the Soviet Union. It was, in part, looking forward to such developments, that Mao stated categorically in March, 1949:

From 1927 to the present the centre of gravity of our work has been in the villages - gathering strength in the villages, using the villages in order to surround the cities and then taking the cities. The period for this method of work has now ended. The period of 'from the city to the village', and of the city leading the village has now begun.[3]

[1] *Selected Works*, IV, pp. 422-3.   [2] *Ibid.* III, p. 83.   [3] *Ibid.* IV, p. 363.

What Mao was saying here was, in essence, 'Hitherto we have been doing it the unorthodox way, because that was how we had to do it in order to win power, but henceforth we will do it in the orthodox, Marxist way, relying for leadership on the cities and on the urban proletariat.' When, however, policies along these lines had actually been in operation for a few years, Mao became aware that they held dangers flowing not only from traditional Chinese patterns of behaviour, but from the logic of Marxism itself.

In the China of the 1950s, the cities were regarded both as centres of administrative authority, as in traditional China, and as centres of enlightenment, as in the Marxist distillation of the European experience. Peasants, in the Marxist view, were endlessly 'dark' (Lenin's favourite term for them) and ignorant, incapable of organizing themselves and solving their own problems. They must therefore receive from the cities not only the leadership which could be provided only by the party of the industrial proletariat, but the modern knowledge which was generated only in the urban environment. Mao had explicitly endorsed this view in 1949, but he had increasingly grave misgivings as he observed how this Marxist conception of the relations between town and countryside served to reinforce the ingrained tendency of educated Chinese – to which even he, by his own admission, had succumbed in his youth[1] – to look down on those engaged in manual labour.

Mao's conviction that the countryside, though it must assimilate modern knowledge, is not inferior to the city, is intimately linked to his belief that the Chinese need not regard themselves as inferior to the foreigners. Here lies the nub of his rebellion, not only against Soviet domination, but against the whole Europe-centred logic of Marxism. For Marx, the only salvation for the backward and stagnant societies of Asia lay in what he called 'Europeanization'.[2] Similar premises have informed the thinking of the Russian Communists about the Orient, from Lenin to the present day. This does not mean, of course, that Marx and Lenin were racists – their view that Europeans must show Asians 'how it is done' was based partly

[1] See his remarks on this theme in his talk to the Yenan Forum on Art and Literature, in *The Political Thought of Mao Tse-tung*, p. 362.

[2] For a discussion of Marx's ideas regarding Asian society, and some of the essential texts, see *Marxism and Asia*, pp. 7–16 and 115–33. The reference to 'Europeanization' occurs on p. 116.

on the fact that only Europe (and its extension in North America) possessed a working class which could lead the revolution, and partly on the conviction that only European culture could supply the Promethean thrust that would enable non-European countries to develop their economies and thereby acquire a proletariat of their own. Hence the conclusion that the world revolution must be led from Europe – which has meant, since 1917, from Moscow. Unfortunately, it is only a step from this interim practical conclusion to a belief in the ingrained inferiority of Asia to Europe – a step which Mao, at least, is persuaded that Lenin's successors have already taken. Needless to say, he does not accept either the premise about the inferiority of Asian culture, or the practical conclusions which flow from it.

Though fully aware of China's present backwardness, Mao is resolved that the Chinese people shall overcome this condition primarily by their own strength, and in their own way. 'Ours is an ardent nation, now swept by a burning tide', he declared in 1958, justifying the policies of rapid and self-reliant economic development then being initiated in the course of the Great Leap Forward. 'There is a good metaphor for this: our nation is like an atom... When this atom's nucleus is smashed, the thermal energy released will have really tremendous power. We shall be able to do things which we could not do before... We shall produce forty million tons of steel annually...'[1]

Although, as the reference to forty million tons of steel makes clear, Mao is vitally concerned with increasing production, he is resolved not only to raise China's economic level, but to do so in a way which will manifest the independence and creativity of the Chinese people. In 1964, he referred once again to the need to 'smash conventions' rather than 'crawling step by step behind others', and concluded: 'Why is it that what the Western bourgeoisie could achieve, the Eastern proletariat cannot achieve also? The great Chinese revolutionary, our precursor Mr. Sun Yat-sen, said at the beginning of the century that in China there would come a great leap forward. This prediction of his will certainly be realized within a few decades.'[2]

To achieve a great leap forward in economic development and

[1] *Mao Tse-tung Unrehearsed*, Text 3.
[2] *Ibid.* Text 12.

national power, and thereby to restore China's place in the world, has indeed been the goal of all Chinese revolutionaries and reformers since 1900 and before. In this respect, the Cultural Revolution can well be seen as the continuation and culmination of trends which began a century ago. But Mao's 'Sinified Marxism' is not marked only by the chiliastic hopes which, as we have seen, he has entertained since the days of the Li Li-san line. The Chinese revolution, under his leadership, has also been characterized by prudence, realism, and a patient effort to devise a pattern of modernization and economic development adapted to the concrete circumstances obtaining in China. A fundamental aspect of the reality he seeks to shape is the mentality of the citizens and their attitude toward the policies put forward by the Party. Mao has always placed a concern with changing man at the very core of his conception of revolution. An emphasis on the ethical dimension of social and political questions is, of course, altogether in harmony with the Chinese tradition, but the methods by which the Chinese Communists pursue this goal are radically new. Let us now turn to a consideration of these 'mass line' methods for mobilizing and educating the people of China, as they have taken shape over the past three decades.

II. DEMOCRACY AND CENTRALISM IN THE CHINESE REVOLUTION, 1942–1965

A revolution requires leadership, but it also requires the effective participation of the whole population. This much is obvious, but it is not so obvious how these two imperatives can be successfully combined. An excess of leadership may discourage participation at the grass roots; undue reliance on initiative from below may lead to confusion and paralysis.

Both of the traditions within which Mao Tse-tung and his comrades stand have always been far more concerned about the second of these dangers than about the first. The hostility of the imperial bureaucracy, not only to spontaneously formed social or political organizations, but to any kind of economic activity which might possibly escape from official control, is well known.[1] As for

[1] See, for example, Etienne Balazs, *Chinese Civilization and Bureaucracy* (New Haven, Yale University Press, 1964), especially pp. 34–54.

Lenin, 'spontaneous' was perhaps the nastiest epithet in his entire lexicon. The workers, in his view, were capable only of what he called 'trade union consciousness', that is, of perceiving their own immediate material interests. If they were to be made to fight for broader political goals, revolutionary consciousness would have to be instilled into them from without, by intellectuals of bourgeois origin, who would educate the workers and enlighten them as to their own real will. These intellectuals would constitute the leading core around which the 'party of the proletariat' would be organized. To proceed in the opposite way – i.e. for the intellectuals to seek to learn from the workers what the workers actually wanted, rather than to tell them what they ought to want – would, in Lenin's view, lead only to the 'crushing of consciousness by spontaneity', which he regarded as the worst sort of catastrophe.

Thus, for Lenin, the whole revolutionary movement was something highly stratified and hierarchical. At the top were the leaders, who must be men of exceptional talent, such, he said, as are born by the dozens, and not by the hundreds;[1] then came the far more numerous group of intellectuals, who were capable, under the guidance of the leaders, of inculcating proletarian consciousness into the workers and setting up the Party; and only then, some distance behind, came the actual workers, whose role it was to supply the rank and file of the 'proletarian party'. As for the peasants, their role was, as already suggested, still more lowly. The workers, in Lenin's view, though incapable if left to themselves of engendering proletarian consciousness, could play within society as a whole a role which might be described as that of non-commissioned officers. In other words, they could serve as the human agents who transmitted the ideas and orders coming down from the leadership to the still more inchoate masses of the rural population. The roots of this attitude, of course, go back to Marx, whose early diatribes against 'rural idiocy' are well known, and who later in his life spoke of the 'town working men' as the 'natural trustees' of the 'rural producers.'[2]

This fundamentally elitist cast of Lenin's approach to politics

[1] Lenin, 'What is to be Done?' in *Selected Works* (Moscow, Progress Publishers, 1967), vol. I, p. 197.
[2] K. Marx, 'The Civil War in France', in Marx and Engels, *Selected Works* (Moscow, Progress Publishers, 1968), p. 289.

was to be sure tempered in some degree by a realistic awareness of the need to secure the support of the masses for the policies of the leadership. Democracy in the sense of participation in decision-making was, however, restricted in his scheme of things essentially to the Party. The nature and limits of such give-and-take between the upper and lower levels of the Party were summed up in the concept of 'democratic centralism'. Lenin defined this term to mean freedom of discussion, but absolute acceptance of decisions once adopted; consultation with the rank and file, but absolute obedience of lower organs to higher organs.

These principles have, of course, long been in honour in the Chinese Communist Party. In his speech of 1 February 1942, Mao Tse-tung reasserted the validity of the concept, stressing as heavily as ever Lenin had done the importance of discipline and leadership. Some comrades, he said,

do not understand the Party's system of democratic centralism; they do not know that the Communist Party not only needs democracy, but needs centralization even more. They forget the system of democratic centralism, in which the minority is subordinate to the majority, the lower level to the higher level, the part to the whole, and the entire membership to the Central Committee.[1]

The impression, which might be conveyed by this quotation, that the Chinese Communists are even more elitist than Lenin, is corrected if one views Mao's interpretation of 'democratic central-ism' in conjunction with his exposition, in a directive of 1 June 1943, of the concept of the 'mass line'. In this classic text, Mao declared:

all correct leadership is necessarily from the masses, to the masses. This means: take the ideas of the masses (scattered and unsystematic ideas) and concentrate them (through study turn them into concentrated and systematic ideas), then go to the masses and propagate and explain these ideas until the masses embrace them as their own, hold fast to them and translate them into action, and test the correctness of these ideas in such action. Then once again concentrate ideas from the masses and once again take them to the masses so that the ideas are persevered in and carried through. And so on, over and over again in an endless spiral, with

[1] *Selected Works*, III, p. 43.

the ideas becoming more correct, more vital and richer each time. Such is the Marxist–Leninist theory of knowledge, or methodology.[1]

Thus the formulation of the problem of leadership in organizational terms, in the concept of democratic centralism, was completed and placed in perspective by the concept of the mass line, which interpreted the problem in terms of epistemology. The term 'democratic centralism' was still reserved, however, as in Soviet usage, to relations within the Party. In his speech of 1957 on contradictions among the people, Mao extended the application of this principle to the relations between the leaders and the led throughout society as a whole.[2] He then proceeded, in his 7,000-cadres speech of January 1962, to draw the two strands together in a broader definition of the concept of democratic centralism itself. After asserting once again that centralism and democracy must be combined 'both within the Party and outside' and stressing that centralism was even more indispensable than democracy, Mao went on to say:

Without democracy there cannot be any correct centralism because people's ideas differ, and if their understanding of things lacks unity then centralism cannot be established. What is centralism? First of all it is a centralization of correct ideas, on the basis of which unity of understanding, policy, planning, command and action are achieved. This is called centralized unification. If people still do not understand problems, if they have ideas but have not expressed them, or are angry but have still not vented their anger, how can centralized unification be established? If there is no democracy we cannot possibly summarise experience correctly. If there is no democracy, if ideas are not coming from the masses, it is impossible to establish a good line, good general and specific policies and methods. Our leading organs merely play the role of a processing plant in the establishment of a good line and good general and specific policies and methods. Everyone knows that if a factory has no raw material, it cannot do any processing... Without democracy, you have no understanding of what is happening down below; the general situation will be unclear; you will be unable to collect sufficient opinions from all sides; there can be no communication between top and bottom; top level organs of leadership will depend on one-sided and incorrect material to decide issues, and thus you will find it difficult to avoid being subjectivist;

[1] *The Political Thought of Mao Tse-tung*, pp. 316–17.
[2] *Selected Readings*, pp. 350–87, especially pp. 354–5.

it will be impossible to achieve unity of understanding and unity of action, and impossible to achieve true centralism.[1]

Here the term 'democratic centralism' is made to cover both the fundamental dilemma of leadership as such, namely that of combining effective 'centralised unification' with active support and initiative from below, and the problems of the upward and downward flow of ideas evoked by the slogan of the 'mass line'. Though priority is given in principle to centralism, it is the democratic aspect which really comes alive. The way in which Mao Tse-tung has thus retained, and at the same time transmuted, a key Leninist concept, provides a concise illustration of his basically utilitarian approach to the Leninist heritage. On the other hand, the Leninist conception of the Party – despite the many attempts to employ it in widely differing political contexts, including that of the Kuomintang – is not a tool which can be turned to any arbitrarily-defined purpose. Not only does it carry a built-in elitist bias, but it is specifically designed to impose the hegemony of the working class over the peasantry, and of the cities over the countryside.

Despite the illusions entertained by some in the early stages of the Cultural Revolution, Mao has never wholly rejected either of these fundamental traits of Leninism. He has, however, persistently sought to diminish the gap between the Party and the masses, and between the workers and the peasants. There are sound reasons, rooted in Chinese conditions, which not only justify this revision of Leninism on practical grounds, but link together its two facets. The workers, in Lenin's view (as in that of Marx), have acquired in the factories not only a sense of organization, but the technical knowledge which will enable them, after the victory of the revolution, to carry forward the enterprise of extending the mastery of man over nature initiated by the bourgeoisie. Since they were assumed to be already trained, it was possible for Lenin to regard them as potential units in a centrally-commanded army of production. The Chinese peasants, on the other hand, commonly had, prior to the revolution, no familiarity whatsoever even with those very simple forms of technology directly relevant to their own lives. It was therefore, as Mao said, necessary to 'educate' them, in the dual sense of changing their attitudes and providing them with modern knowledge. Education,

---

[1] *Mao Tse-tung Unrehearsed*, Text 8.

however, is a process which requires the active participation of the person to be educated, and such participation can more easily be obtained if the distance between the leaders and the led is not felt to be too great. Thus, the attenuation of the Leninist sense of hierarchy in the theory and practice of the Chinese revolution can be seen as a direct and logical result of the adaptation of Leninism to the conditions of a largely peasant country.

These modifications in the practice of revolution first began to assume coherent shape during the early 1940s in Yenan, simultaneously with Mao Tse-tung's efforts to define the ideological basis of the Chinese revolution.[1] The policies involved covered an exceedingly wide range, from land reclamation to culture. In the domain of administration, the main thrust was indicated by the movement for 'Crack Troops and Simple Administration'[2] launched at the end of 1941. Despite the reference to the army in the first half of the slogan, the emphasis was rather on the cuts in the bureaucratic apparatus called for by the second two characters.[3] This movement was accompanied by changes in administrative methods of continuing relevance. The system of vertical rule, in which authority at the basic level was exercised by the representatives of the relevant department, was replaced by that of dual rule, in which the responsible political officer (at this time still called the District Magistrate) played a greater role. Secondly and perhaps even more important, the practice of 'sending down' cadres and intellectuals to work in the countryside (then referred to as *hsia-hsiang*, or going down to the villages, rather than *hsia-fang*, as in the 1950s) was introduced.[4]

In the economic sphere,[5] the very moderate land policies followed since 1937, in the context of the second united front with the

[1] The best and clearest account of the 'mass line' policies is that of Mark Selden (*The Yenan Way*, chapter 6, pp. 208–76; see also the earlier and slightly different version in A. Doak Barnett (ed.), *Chinese Communist Politics in Action* (Seattle, University of Washington Press, 1969), pp. 99–151).

[2] As pointed out below by Marianne Bastid, this slogan (*ching-ping chien-cheng*) was actually derived from the *Shih chi* of Ssu-ma Ch'ien.

[3] The outcome in this respect was at best ambiguous; as Mark Selden points out, by early 1943, the number of government cadres had actually increased slightly, rather than diminishing by 20 per cent as planned, though some simplification of the administrative structure was achieved in the course of 1943 (*The Yenan Way*, pp. 212–16).

[4] Selden, *The Yenan Way*, pp. 216–28.

[5] On economic policies in the Border Region in the early 1940s, see Selden, *The Yenan Way*, pp. 229–67.

Kuomintang, though not abandoned, were modified by an energetic campaign to secure the reduction of excessively high rents and by the encouragement of mutual aid teams and other elementary forms for the pooling of labour during limited periods, already practised by the peasants in the Border Region. Cooperatives, at first of consumers or of handicraft producers, also developed to include small-scale industry. An important contribution to the effort to increase production, in order to make the Border Region as self-sufficient as possible in the face of the Japanese and Kuomintang blockade, was furnished by the army. These activities were once again characterized by a slogan drawn from the past, that of the *t'un-t'ien* or 'camp-field' system which had been known for some two thousand years in one form or another. The economic work of the model 359th Brigade at Nanniwan was explicitly linked, in Mao's own account of its achievements, to this historical precedent.[1]

In the cultural sphere, experiments were conducted in popular education with the dual aim of making education more relevant to the needs of the peasants, and of giving the population at the village level some experience in the management of schools.[2] As for culture in the narrower sense, Mao Tse-tung called, in his speeches of May 1942 to the Yenan Forum on Art and Literature, for a 'two-front struggle' in which the aims of 'popularization', or making art and literature accessible to the workers, peasants and soldiers, and 'raising standards' would be pursued simultaneously.[3]

Without a doubt, this set of interrelated policies can be seen as the fountainhead of many more recent developments. This does not, however, justify blurring the differences between the successive stages of the Chinese Revolution. It is a contradiction in terms to speak, as does Mark Selden, of 'agrarian revolution (in the guise of rent reduction)' in Yenan. It is perfectly true that, as he points out,

[1] Mao Tse-tung, *Ching-chi wen-t'i yü ts'ai-cheng wen-t'i* (*Economic and Financial Problems*) (Hong Kong, Hsin Min-chu ch'u-pan-she, July 1949), p. 132. Of the many works discussing this concept, and more broadly the relations between the soldiers and the peasants, Mao had certainly read those of the early Ch'ing philosopher Wang Fu-chih. (See especially the *E meng* and *Ts'un chih*.)

[2] Selden, *The Yenan Way*, pp. 267–74, and Peter J. Seybolt, 'The Yenan Revolution in Mass Education', *The China Quarterly*, 48 (October–December 1971), 641–69.

[3] *Selected Works*, III, pp. 69–98, especially pp. 80–1, 89–90.

the campaign for the reduction of rent sometimes went beyond the limits set by Mao's January 1942 directive on the subject, even to the extent of liquidating large landlord holdings entirely, and that it was thus 'a step towards a more radical class position which reached its culmination in 1946 in full-scale agrarian revolution'. Nevertheless, Mao's directive, while calling for a reduction in 'feudal exploitation' by landlords, also demanded that the landlords be guaranteed their 'civil liberties, political, land and economic rights'.[1] Moreover, in his report of December 1942, on the economy, Mao hailed two early labour heroes among the rural population who had become 'very good rich peasants', and in general stressed the importance of material incentives in developing agricultural production.[2]

Much closer to subsequent experience are aspects of the Yenan model such as self-reliance, decentralization, and involving the masses directly in all aspects of social activity, including production, education, and culture. In any case, when Mao later looked back at this period, there were ideas and to spare on which he could build. To mention only one, his report of December 1942 on economic and financial problems ends with a brief section on preventing waste, especially of foodstuffs, in which he notes that the replacement of individual cooking by 'collective eating' in one institution had diminished the consumption of food by one-third, a 'startling figure'.[3] One could easily see here a prefiguration of the mess halls of 1958. But the lasting significance of such 'sprouts of socialism'– as Mao called the Yenan mutual aid teams in 1958,[4] must be evaluated primarily in terms of how they later grew and developed.

As even the foregoing schematic and oversimplified account suffices to show, the political and ideological heritage of the Chinese Communists when they assumed power was made up of several contrasting strands: Leninist elitism and popular participation, patient realism and millenarian hopes of immediate revolutionary achievement. If the balance between these factors has varied from time to time, the explanation should not necessarily be sought in the competing influences of one leader or another, for the different ele-

---

[1] Selden, *The Yenan Way*, pp. 231–3.

[2] *Ching-chi wen-t'i yü ts'ai-cheng wen-t'i*, pp. 13–14.

[3] *Ibid.* p. 216.

[4] In his speech of 22 March 1958 at Chengtu. *Mao Tse-tung Unrehearsed*, Text 40.

ments coexist in all of them.[1] Nevertheless, there were clearly differences of personality, outlook and experience separating Mao Tse-tung from many of his comrades in the leadership of the Chinese Communist Party. In analysing these, it is convenient to follow Mao's example, and to take Liu Shao-ch'i as the symbolic incarnation of views differing from those of the Chairman not because he was from the beginning the chieftain of some black gang or other, but precisely because Mao retained, for so long, such a great measure of confidence in him. According to Mao himself, only in January 1965 did he decide that 'Liu had to go'. Edgar Snow, to whom this revelation was made in December 1970, concluded that it was a case of 'non-antagonistic contradictions' between the two men 'gradually becoming antagonistic' and that Mao 'apparently did not finally give up hope of winning Liu around...until much later than many supposed'.[2] If this is indeed the case, and if Mao continued, down to the end of 1964, to see Liu not as a traitor to the revolution, but as a comrade whose merits outweighed his faults, his views take on even more weight as the expression of the range of opinion within the ranks of the revolutionaries.

If we compare Liu's interpretation of democratic centralism with that of Mao, we find that there is not a great deal of difference in the relative importance they attach to the two aspects of this principle. Liu Shao-ch'i stressed rather heavily, in his lectures of 1941 on organizational and disciplinary self-cultivation, the centralist component,[3] but as we have seen, Mao has commonly done so too. In 1957 he declared that democracy was 'only a means', which served

---

[1] To take only one example, Mao Tse-tung, whose approach to the land question prior to 1949 is sometimes assumed to have been consistently moderate, distinguished himself on more than one occasion by his radicalism in this domain. On first ascending the Chingkangshan in 1928, he adopted an agrarian policy involving the confiscation and redistribution of all land without exception which he himself later characterized as marked by leftist errors. (See *Selected Works*, I, p. 104, note 17, referring to a passage in 'The Struggle in the Chingkang Mountains'.) After a long interval in which he was effectively identified with more prudent policies, he once more supported the radical line of 1947, for which the blame is now placed on Liu Shao-ch'i. (See his enthusiastic comment of 25 July 1947 on Liu's letter to Shansi-Suiyuan comrades, *T'u-ti wen-t'i chih-nan* (Hsi-pei-chü hsüan-ch'uan-pu, 24 Oct. 1947), p. 41.

[2] Edgar Snow, *The Long Revolution* (New York, Random House, 1972), pp. 15–20.

[3] For a brief account of his ideas as expounded in this text, see *The Political Thought of Mao Tse-tung*, pp. 94–5, and S. Schram, 'The Party in Chinese Communist Ideology', in John Wilson Lewis (ed.), *Party Leadership and Revolutionary Power in China* (Cambridge, Cambridge University Press, 1970), pp. 174–7.

the economic base.[1] And yet a significant nuance does appear to separate the views of the two men on this issue.

Liu Shao-ch'i referred in 1941 to democracy and centralism as 'two contradictory concepts',[2] and the whole record of his speeches and policies tends to suggest that he regards this contradiction as inherently irreconcilable. Mao also perceives a contradiction between 'democracy and centralism', but he treats it as something which still survives in China, rather than something inherent in the logic of the two concepts themselves.[3] The real hallmark of his thinking is perhaps the conviction that in the last analysis it is not necessary to choose between the two.

Growing logically out of this difference in basic approach is a greater emphasis on Liu's part on the need for organization and centralized guidance. This point emerges repeatedly in his writings and in his style of work. Thus, in 1948, Liu declared: 'The revolutionary situation is now developing very fast – faster than we had imagined. At present, what we need fear is not that it will go too slowly, but that it will go too fast. If it goes too fast, we will have many difficulties. It is better if it goes a bit slower, so that we can make thorough preparations.'[4] In other words, it is essential not to let things get out of control. A similar concern was even more emphatically expressed by Liu in his report of June 1950, on land reform, in which he stated that, if 'chaotic conditions' should occur in some areas after the start of the agrarian reform, the whole process should be 'held up in these areas in order that the deviations may be corrected and further preparations made to carry out agrarian reform next year'. 'Agrarian reform', he added, 'must be carried out under guidance, in a planned and orderly way...'[5]

Mao Tse-tung, too, held in 1950 that 'the work of agrarian reform

[1] 'On the Correct Handling of Contradictions among the People', *Selected Readings*, p. 354.
[2] Liu Shao-ch'i, *Lun tang* (Dairen, Ta-chung Shu-tien, 1947), p. 142.
[3] *Selected Readings*, p. 352.
[4] *Kuan-yü Liu Shao-ch'i tang-an ts'ai-liao hui-pien-chi* (*Compilation of materials regarding the Liu Shao-ch'i Party affair*). (Tientsin, Wu-ch'an-chieh-chi chuan-cheng ko-ming tsao-fan ta-tui, April 1967), p. 13.
[5] *The Agrarian Reform Law of the People's Republic of China*, together with other relevant documents, third edition (Peking, Foreign Languages Press, 1952), p. 74. Liu should not be turned either into a one-dimensional figure. His line of 1947 attributed crucial importance to the 'spontaneous movements' (*tzu-fa yün-tung*) of the masses. *T'u-ti wen-t'i*, pp. 42–8.

should be carried forward by stages and in an orderly manner', and he likewise declared: 'Blindness and anarchy in the economic field should be gradually eliminated in line with the principle of unified planning.'[1] He was, however, more inclined, as subsequent events were to show, to let a situation develop in accordance with initiatives from below, and then to endeavour to shape it in such a way as to produce a reasonable degree of order, whereas Liu Shao-ch'i preferred to keep a tight rein on things from beginning to end. He also accepted, more wholeheartedly and enthusiastically than Mao, the Leninist axiom of working-class leadership.[2]

Thus, from the level of general organizational principles to their concrete expression in methods of leadership and of economic development, one can discern from the outset differences in approach between Mao and Liu Shao-ch'i. Mao cannot have been unaware of this contradiction within the Party, but he may well have regarded it not only as 'non-antagonistic', but as positively useful in coping with the wide range of problems facing the leadership. The 'correct handling' of these contradictions became, however, progressively more difficult as China started to move away from the Soviet model.

As we have already seen, Mao Tse-tung himself dated the explicit abandonment of 'copying the Soviets' from the Great Leap Forward of 1958. Indications pointing in this direction were, however, visible as early as 1953, though few Western analysts interpreted them correctly at the time. The most crucial single issue involved, both in terms of its symbolic importance and in terms of the central place it occupied in the economy, was that of the relation between technological and social change in the countryside.

A convenient starting point for the discussion of this problem is provided by Liu Shao-ch'i's report of June 1950 on land reform. Justifying the policy (endorsed by Mao at the time[3]) of preserving a rich-peasant economy in order to foster the restoration of agricultural

---

[1] Mao Tse-tung, 'Fight for a Fundamental Turn for the Better in the Financial and Economic Situation in China' (Report delivered to the Third Plenum of the Central Committee of the Chinese Communist Party on 6 June 1950), in *New China's Economic Achievements 1949–1952* (Peking, China Committee for the Promotion of International Trade, 1952), pp. 6–7.

[2] See, for example, his speech of May 1944 to factory representatives in the Yenan Border Region, *Collected Works of Liu Shao-ch'i 1923–1944* (Hong Kong, Union Research Institute, 1969), pp. 450, 453.

[3] *New China's Economic Achievements*, p. 6.

production, Liu characteristically put the emphasis on technical factors: 'Only when the conditions are mature for the extensive application of mechanized farming, for the organization of collective farms and for the Socialist reform of the rural areas, will the need for a rich-peasant economy cease, and this will take a somewhat long time to achieve.'[1]

In thus subordinating collectivization to mechanization, Liu Shao-ch'i was, of course, wholly faithful to Lenin's theory and Stalin's practice. There is no evidence that Mao took exception to his formulation at the time, but in the long run such a position proved incompatible both with his longstanding conviction that men were more important than weapons and machines, and with his faith in the revolutionary potential imminent in the Chinese countryside. Moreover, if the Red Guards can be believed, Liu put his views, in the early 1950s, in a form deliberately calculated to be offensive to Mao. After asserting once again that industrialization was a necessary precondition to collectivization and the establishment of socialism in the countryside, he is reported to have said in June 1951: 'There are some comrades who hold that the countryside, relying on mutual aid teams and cooperatives...can carry out the collectivization of agriculture, the socialization of agriculture. This is a kind of utopian agarian socialism. It is erroneous.'[2]

In July 1955, Mao Tse-tung expressly rejected the Liuist position, declaring in his speech on cooperatives that because of economic conditions in China, the technical transformation of agriculture would take longer than the social.[3] This by no means implied that he underestimated the importance of technology in increasing agricultural production. His intention was rather to promote the social revolution and the technological revolution simultaneously, and also to stress that mechanization was only one aspect of the necessary application of modern techniques to Chinese agriculture. Nevertheless, this speech did constitute the first step toward the revival of Yenan-style 'mobilization' policies.

There is little doubt that the responsibility for initiating this trend

---

[1] *The Agrarian Reform Law of the People's Republic of China*, p. 88.

[2] *Liu Shao-ch'i tui-k'ang Mao Tse-tung ssu-hsiang san-pai li* (*Three hundred examples of Liu Shao-ch'i's opposition to Mao Tse-tung's thought*) (Hung-tai-hui Pei-ching t'ieh-tao hsüeh-yüan hung-ch'i kung-she she-hui tou-p'i-kai lien-lo-tien, 11 April 1967), p. 18.   [3] *Selected Readings*, p. 335

lies essentially with Mao – despite his later statement that he had retreated, immediately after the establishment of the Chinese People's Republic, to the 'second line', and thus did not 'take charge of day-to-day work'.[1] As might have been expected, the Chairman's real power was very great indeed, when he chose to exert it. One of the best known instances is precisely that of his cooperativization speech of 31 July 1955, which directly contradicts the provisions of the Five-Year Plan adopted only the day before by the National People's Congress regarding the tempo of collectivization.[2] Since the plan had presumably already received the assent of the Central Committee of the Chinese Communist Party, Mao thus showed himself able – and willing – to overturn the collective decisions of the highest Party bodies in a speech to an *ad hoc* meeting of local and provincial Party secretaries. There were, to be sure, solid economic arguments in favour of more rapid collectivization, revolving mainly around the disequilibrium between industry and agriculture, and the need to provide jobs in the countryside for a large proportion of China's population.[3] Mao himself made these points in his speech. It is nevertheless evident that in taking the decision he did, Mao was moved not merely by economic calculation, but by instinctive reasons deeply rooted in his own experience and political style. He saw a great revolutionary movement in progress at the grass roots, led by the rural cadres, and it appeared to him intolerable that this splendid and exciting revolutionary conflagration should be damped down by bureaucratic timidity, or a concern that things would get out of control.

The rapidly-changing situation in China during the winter of 1955–6 is vividly mirrored in Mao Tse-tung's own utterances. In the notes to the compilation of materials on the 'high tide' of cooperativization in the countryside which he edited in the closing months of 1955, Mao put the emphasis on struggle, and on conscious action. In

[1] See, in particular, his talk of 25 October 1966, *Mao Tse-tung Unrehearsed*, Text 21. This situation, he said, was rectified only after the Eleventh Plenum, i.e. in August 1966.

[2] For the provisions of the plan, which called for cooperativizing a third (rather than half) of China's peasant households by the end of 1957, see Li Fu-ch'un, *Report on the First Five-year Plan for Development of the National Economy* (Supplement to *People's China*, 16 August 1955), p. 27.

[3] See, in particular, the excellent analysis of Kenneth R. Walker, 'Collectivization in Retrospect: the "Socialist High Tide" of August 1955–Spring 1956', *The China Quarterly*, 26 (April–June 1966), 2–4.

China, he wrote, '1955 was the year of decision in the struggle between socialism and capitalism'. The first half of the year, he said, had been 'obscured by dark clouds', but the atmosphere changed completely in the second half (i.e. after his speech of 31 July), when 'tens of millions of peasant households swung into action' to form cooperatives. 'It is as if a raging tidal wave has swept away all the demons and ghosts', he commented, introducing neither for the first nor for the last time this metaphor from Chinese folklore. At the same time, he refurbished the Leninist axiom that 'political work is the lifeline of economic work'. And he saw 'many more battles' ahead.[1]

In January 1956, after consultations with 'responsible comrades from various provinces', Mao drew up a 'Draft National Programme for Agricultural Development (1956–1967)', in forty points, which was discussed at a meeting of some 1,375 people from various fields called by the Central Committee, and then presented to a meeting of the Supreme State Conference on 25 January 1956.[2] This document, like so many other policy papers of the years 1954–7, contained partially contradictory stipulations reflecting its origins in a period of transition. Thus, on the one hand, it put forward extremely ambitious and optimistic targets for grain production, which was to increase by more than two and a half times in twelve years, largely as a result of increased yields per acre. On the other hand, it stressed material rather than ideological incentives, and also adopted a relatively flexible attitude toward former landlords and rich peasants, who were to be accepted to a considerable degree as members of the cooperatives. Mao himself, who had emphasized the sharpness of class struggle in the countryside in his utterances of only a few months previously, now came forward with the view that the successes already achieved made it possible to carry forward the socialist revolution 'by peaceful means'.

Precisely one month after the adoption of Mao's forty-point programme for agricultural development, on 25 February 1956,

[1] *Socialist Upsurge in China's Countryside* (Peking, Foreign Languages Press, 1957), pp. 159–60, 302. Mao's preface to this work, of which the original three-volume Chinese edition appeared in early 1956, is dated 27 December 1955.

[2] See *The Draft Programme for Agricultural Development in the People's Republic of China, 1956–1967* (Peking, Foreign Languages Press, 1956). Mao's introductory speech on 25 January appears on pp. 3–5 of this pamphlet (also in *Marxism and Asia*, pp. 291–3).

Khrushchev delivered his secret speech denouncing Stalin's crimes and blaming them on the 'cult of the individual'. The first official Chinese reaction appeared on 5 April, in a *People's Daily* editorial entitled 'On the Historical Experience of the Dictatorship of the Proletariat'. In a speech likewise delivered during April, which became available only during the Cultural Revolution, Mao set forth his own reflections regarding methods of leadership, and more generally on the future pattern of the Chinese revolution.

This speech, entitled 'On the Ten Great Relationships', dealt with the whole range of economic, political, administrative, and cultural problems encountered in the task of transforming Chinese society.[1] The keynote is the need to avoid at all costs a one-sided approach to any problem whatsoever. Enumerating the ten relationships he proposed to discuss, which included such fundamental dichotomies as industry and agriculture, the Centre and the regions, and China and other countries, Mao observed: 'These relationships are all contradictions. Contradictions are everywhere in the world. Without contradictions there would be no world.' In other words, for him contradictions were not merely, as for Hegel, the motor of change; they were the very stuff of life itself. Any view of reality which failed to hold both aspects of each of these contradictions in creative tension would in his opinion be undialectical and erroneous, and policies based on such an undialectical view could only lead to failure.

As for the substance of Mao's ideas, the most remarkable thing about them is that the aspects of reality which he exhorts his comrades not to neglect do not fall into a consistent pattern favouring, in a nutshell, either 'democracy' or 'centralism', though, in the course of his speech, he evokes most of the paired elements which are commonly regarded as symbolic of one or the other.[2] In a majority of cases he comes down rather on the side of decentralization and local initiative, no doubt because he was trying to correct the Soviet-type emphasis of the First Five-Year Plan on heavy industry and centralized planning. In one important instance, however, that of

[1] All quotations below are from the translation in *Mao Tse-tung Unrehearsed,* Text 1.

[2] These have been most systematically and imaginatively explored by Franz Schurmann in his monumental work *Ideology and Organization in Communist China* (Berkeley, University of California Press, 1966). His view of the problem is summed up in the table on pp. 102–3.

relations between industry in the coastal regions and industry in the interior, he was concerned rather to prevent an error in the opposite direction: undue neglect of industry in the great coastal cities. Throughout the speech, the pattern of reasoning is the same: we must, to be sure, get our priorities right, but unilateral emphasis on one half of any contradiction will be self-defeating.

Thus, in the case of the relationships between heavy industry, light industry and agriculture, he recognized that heavy industry was 'the key sector which must be given priority', but noted at the same time that 'some socialist countries' had committed 'mistakes' by putting 'undue emphasis on heavy industry' and neglecting the other sectors. 'As a result,' he added, 'they have not enough goods on the market, daily necessities are in short supply, and their currency is unstable.' China, he said, had not committed these errors, but it was nevertheless essential to put even more emphasis on light industry and agriculture, precisely in order to achieve the goal of the priority development of heavy industry. If you really want heavy industry 'badly' (*li-hai*), then you will pay attention to the development of light industry and agriculture. 'This will result in more daily necessities, which in turn will mean more accumulation, and after a few years still more funds will be invested in heavy industry.'

A second point, in addition to the call for a many-sided development strategy, which emerges with great force from the lengthy discussion of economic issues in this speech is that Mao still attached great importance at this time to material incentives. 'The experience of some socialist countries', he declared, 'proves that even where agriculture is collectivized, where collectivization is mismanaged it is still not possible to increase production. The root cause of the failure ...is that the state's policy toward the peasants is questionable. The peasants' burden of taxation is too heavy while the price of agricultural products is very low, and that of industrial goods very high.' Returning to this point in the section on the relationship between the state, the units of production, and the individual producers, Mao added: 'The collective needs accumulation, but we must be careful not to make too great demands on the peasants. We should not give them too hard a time (*wa-te t'ai k'u*). Except where we meet with unavoidable natural disasters, we should enable the peasants' income to increase year by year on the basis of increased agricultural production.' The workers, too, he described as maintaining a 'high level of enthusiasm' because prices were 'low and stable', life was secure, and in general they enjoyed a higher standard of living than before Liberation.

The section of Mao's speech bearing most directly on the structure of the political system was that on the relationship between the Centre and the regions. Here, too, his views were most carefully balanced between the claims of democracy and centralism. In a passage which deserves to be quoted at some length, he said:

> The relationship between the Centre and the regions is also a contradiction. In order to resolve this contradiction, what we now need to consider is how to arouse the enthusiasm of the regions by allowing them to run more projects under the unified plan of the Centre.
>
> As things look now, I think that we need a further extension of regional power. At present it is too limited, and this is not favourable to building socialism. It is laid down in our Constitution that the regions do not have legislative powers, and that these are concentrated in the hands of the National People's Congress. But where the situation...demands it, the regions should also make rules and regulations, provided they do not conflict with the policies of the Centre, and that they fall within the limits sanctioned by the law. The Constitution does not prohibit this.

Once more, Mao drove home his point with a paradox: 'If we are to consolidate the leadership of the Centre, then we must attend to the interests of the regions.' He then proceeded to a rather detailed discussion of the problems of management at the local level resulting from the application of the branch system, which had been emphasized in the plan. The solution he recommended was to replace vertical rule by dual rule. This was, as we have seen, the pattern adopted in Yenan, and it was also to be that of the Great Leap Forward.

Politics being indeed, as Mao has put it, the lifeline or guiding thread of economic work, the section of his speech of April 1956 on the relationship between the Centre and the regions gives us not merely his view on administrative questions, but the most cogent formulation of the assumptions underlying his economic policies. 'If heavy and light industries are to develop', he declared, 'then markets and raw materials are needed, and to achieve these you must arouse the enthusiasm of the regions.' At present, he noted, there are 'dozens of hands meddling in regional affairs' – various ministries issuing orders in the name of the 'Centre' which have been approved neither by the Central Committee nor by the State Council, thus inundating the regions with a 'torrent' of statistics and reports. Mao's proposal for 'correcting' this method of work was 'a consultative mode of operation with the regions'. The Central Committee of the Party, he pointed out, never issued 'blind commands' to the regions without consulting them first. 'We hope that the various ministries at the Centre will take note of this and consult with the regions on all matters affecting them, and not issue any orders until after consultation has taken place.' Then followed the moral:

We want unity together with individuality. If local enthusiasm is really to be aroused, every place must have the individuality appropriate to its conditions. This individuality is. . .necessary in the interest of the whole country and to strengthen national unity. . .

There must be proper enthusiasm and proper independence. Provinces, municipalities, regions, counties, districts, and townships should all possess both. . .Naturally we must, at the same time, tell the comrades at the lower levels that they should not act wildly, that they must exercise caution. Where they can conform, they ought to conform. . .Where they cannot conform. . .then conformity should not be sought at all costs. Two enthusiasms are much better than just one. . .

In short, the regions should have an appropriate degree of power. This would be beneficial to the building of a strong socialist state.

In other words, as Mao was to put it in 1957 and in 1962, democracy is essential, but as a means to an end, the end being 'centralized unification'. To emphasize this point out of context would, however, be to distort and impoverish Mao's ideas. The enthusiasm generated by a policy allowing a proper degree of independence and initiative at the lower levels is not, for him, merely the indispensable cement of unity and motor of progress; it is very much what politics, and economics, are all about. The problem, of course, as the ensuing decade was to show, lies in defining what constitutes 'proper independence'.

It was also in his speech on the 'Ten Great Relationships' that Mao for the first time sketched out the idea that China can profit from the fact that she is 'poor and blank' and therefore resembles a blank sheet of paper on which anything can be written. At this time, he stressed not only the advantages of backwardness, which would allow the Chinese people to start afresh, but the need to study and learn from the experience of other countries in order to overcome backwardness. The Chinese, he said, must regain confidence in themselves after a century of semi-colonial humiliation, but they must not go to the opposite extreme and adopt an attitude of arrogant superiority toward others.

The carefully-balanced character of this speech, with its attempt to reconcile the claims of industry and agriculture, technical knowledge and political zeal, ideology and self-interest, efficiency and national dignity, suggests that Mao had set out deliberately to lay down a compromise line which might serve as a basis for a consensus among all the leading members of the Party, and thus avoid in China the misfortunes which had overtaken the Soviet Union as a result of internecine conflict. If such was indeed the case, he did not altogether achieve his end. As Mao himself later put it:

In 1956 three things were blown away: the general line of achieving greater, faster, better and more economical results, the promoters of progress, and the Forty Articles. There were three kinds of people with three kinds of reaction: distress, indifference, and delight...Of those exhibiting these three attitudes the ones in the middle were numerous, while the two extremes were small.[1]

The tempo of economic development was indeed slowed down in the autumn of 1956, and Mao's agricultural programme was quietly set aside, to reappear only a year and a half later. These developments may have had something to do with the fact that Mao's own position within the Party had been shaken by Khrushchev's revelations regarding the effects of one-man rule in the Soviet Union. The most obvious symbol of this was the removal, at the Eighth Party Congress in September 1956, of 'The Thought of Mao Tse-tung' from the place in the Party constitution which had been attributed to it in 1945. This is, of course, now blamed on Liu Shao-ch'i,

---

[1] Speech at the Chengtu conference, 22 March 1958 (*Mao Tse-tung Unrehearsed*, Text 4c). As we shall see below, the meeting at which Mao made this assessment marked the effective beginning of the Great Leap Forward, in which the things 'blown away' in 1956 once more came into their own.

though it was he who had proposed the adoption of Mao's thought as the official Party ideology at the previous congress.[1]

An idea put forward at the Eighth Congress which appears strikingly in conflict with Mao's recent thinking is to be found in the statements by both Liu Shao-ch'i and Teng Hsiao-p'ing to the effect that the class struggle, and even class differences, were rapidly dying out in China. But it is important not to assume as a matter of course that Mao was necessarily opposed at the time to such 'revisionist' notions. On the contrary, in October 1966, in the most radical phase of the Cultural Revolution, Mao was honest enough to admit his own responsibility. When K'ang Sheng, seeking to blacken his rivals, shouted during a meeting, 'The political report at the Eighth Congress contains the theory of the disappearance of classes', Mao replied abruptly: 'I read the report, and it was passed by the Congress; we cannot make these two [i.e. Liu and Teng] solely responsible.'[2]

Indeed, one can go farther, and suggest that in many respects there was still an effective alliance between Mao Tse-tung and Liu Shao-ch'i at this time. Though Liu, who had been reticent in the past regarding overly rapid collectivization, may well have concurred in the decision to slow down the pace of economic development, he appears to have agreed with Mao on the fundamental issue of the pattern of decentralization. In a perceptive passage written a decade ago, without the benefit of sources then unavailable, but with a vision likewise unclouded by recent polemics, Franz Schurmann summed up the evidence as follows:

During the Eighth Party Congress of September 1956, there was general agreement that greater emphasis must be given to 'democracy'. So far as state administration was concerned, this meant arousing the 'initiative and creativity' of administrative units below the central level. This could only be done by modifying the centralized systems of policy, planning,

[1] In his testimony of December 1966–January 1967 under detention, P'eng Te-huai confessed that he was the prime mover in this, as in so many crimes, but declared that Liu immediately agreed with him. 'In 1956, at the Eighth Party Congress, it was I who proposed to delete Mao Tse-tung's thought [from the Party constitution], but as soon as I had proposed it Liu Shao-ch'i gave me his approval. He said, "It is after all better to delete it!"', *The Case of Peng Teh-huai 1959–1968* (Hong Kong, Union Research Institute, 1968), pp. 119–20, 445.
[2] Talk at a report meeting, 24 October 1966 (*Mao Tse-tung Unrehearsed*, Text 20).

and control that had arisen during the First Five Year Plan...There was disagreement as to how centralism should be modified. One opinion group, headed by Ch'en Yün, then Minister of Commerce, argued for expanding 'democracy' at the production unit level, which ultimately would have led the country in the direction of a Yugoslav-type economy. Another opinion group, headed by Mao Tse-tung and Liu Shao-ch'i, argued for a different kind of decentralization, namely expanding the decision-making powers of regional administrative units, notably at the provincial level. The kind of decentralization finally adopted followed the Mao–Liu approach. Thus the resolution of the contradiction between centralism and democracy, and between centre and regions, took the form of a 'downward transfer of authority' to the regional level.[1]

If the Mao–Liu alliance was still in force, how did it come to break up? The 'Hundred Flowers' campaign, which had been under way since April 1956, revealed the usual nuances separating the thinking and style of work of the two men, but does not appear to have brought them immediately into opposition. The terms of the debate on this theme were radically altered by the events which took place in the autumn of 1956 in Poland and Hungary. Reflecting on the lessons of the Hungarian uprising, the Chinese leadership, in a *People's Daily* editorial clearly endorsed by Mao, declared that in this instance the 'counter-revolutionaries' had 'taken advantage of the discontent of the masses', and thus induced a 'section of the people' to revolt against the people's government. How was it possible for the counter-revolutionaries to succeed in this enterprise? On the one hand, 'the democratic rights and revolutionary enthusiasm of the Hungarian working people were impaired' as a result of errors by the leadership; on the other, 'the counter-revolutionaries were not dealt the blow they deserved', and Hungary 'had not yet made a serious enough effort to build up its dictatorship of the proletariat'.[2]

This editorial clearly reflected the two aspects of Mao's conception of democratic centralism, as he proceeded to formulate them once again in his speech of 27 February 1957 on contradictions among the people: the need to combine freedom and discipline. The conviction that, in China, the masses of the people understood the limits of the

[1] Schurmann, *Ideology and Organization*, p. 88.
[2] Editorial of 29 December 1956, translated in *The Historical Experience of the Dictatorship of the Proletariat* (Peking, Foreign Languages Press, 1959), p. 50.

freedom offered to them was the foundation of Mao's policy in the spring of 1957, when the 'Hundred Flowers' campaign reached its highpoint. His aim was, of course, not to encourage diversity as an end in itself, but rather to educate both communist and non-communist intellectuals through participation in debate. In the end, the Marxist position, being correct, would triumph. Meanwhile, the impact of criticism would stimulate the Marxists to re-think their own positions, and oblige them to abandon their bureaucratic airs.

There are good grounds for believing that the new and radical turn which Mao thus sought to give to the 'Hundred Flowers' campaign launched the previous year was opposed by many of his senior comrades. In opening wide the gates to criticism of the Party's work by people outside the Party Mao was, in their view, conjuring up a serious danger to the stability of the whole political system. (Subsequent events proved, of course, that they were right.) This conflict may well have been resolved temporarily on 26 April by a compromise in which Liu Shao-ch'i and other Party leaders accepted the principles of public criticism, and of physical labour by high-level cadres, provided offenders were not punished too harshly.[1]

The next day, on 27 April 1957, Liu Shao-ch'i delivered a speech to a meeting of Party cadres in Shanghai which showed that, while he did not actually oppose Mao's line, he certainly understood it in his own way. Thus, discussing the questions raised in Mao's February speech, he played down considerably the theme of class struggle, as compared to Mao's own emphasis. Whereas Mao had underscored the fact that the bourgeoisie still had a 'dual nature' and therefore had to be remoulded,[2] Liu stressed rather how much the capitalists had changed as compared to the past.[3] Mao declared that although 'the large-scale and turbulent class struggles of the masses characteristic of the previous revolutionary periods' had 'in the main come to an end', class differentiation continued to exist in Chinese society. Hence 'the class struggle between the proletariat and the bourgeoisie...and the class struggle in the the ideological field'

[1] These issues have been most thoroughly explored by Richard Solomon, *Mao's Revolution and the Chinese Political Culture* (Berkeley, University of California Press, 1971), pp. 268–329, especially pp. 304–9.
[2] *Selected Readings*, p. 369.
[3] *Liu Shao-ch'i tzu-liao hui-pien* (*A Compilation of Materials on Liu Shao-ch'i*), (Tientsin, April 1967), pp. 94, 96–7.

would continue to be 'long and tortuous' and at times even 'very acute'.[1] Liu, for his part, while indicating that struggle would on occasion be necessary, added that the Communist Party was 'by no means enamoured of struggle', and resorted to it only when certain contradictions, being antagonistic, could not be resolved otherwise.[2]

Liu's lack of enthusiasm for struggle is obviously related to the concern with order, discipline, and a sense of proportion which has marked his thinking from the beginning. In a speech of May 1957 to graduates of the Peking Institute of Geology, he declared, in a vein very far removed from that of Mao: 'As zeal is essential, so is sobriety. When zeal rises high, it is necessary to see that it does not go too far. Life is a long way to go, and there is no need for haste. Hastiness leads to trouble.'[3] The same basic cast of mind is apparent in his approach to the problem of bureaucracy, which he regarded, like Mao, in the spring of 1957 as one of the main causes of 'contradictions among the people'. In combating it, he declared, 'limited democracy' (*hsiao min-chu*) was a better method than 'extensive democracy' (*ta min-chu*). In other words, there should be criticism and self-criticism, but within a limited circle, rather than by mobilizing the masses to attack the cadres.[4] He advocated rectifying the work style of cadres solely by the method of 'light breezes and sweet showers'.[5] His preference for such methods was inspired not only by a distaste for violence, but by what might be described as a certain scepticism regarding the perfectibility of man. Thus, in his speech to the geology graduates, Liu denounced 'this weakness which has been in evidence for thousands of years' in the intellectuals, namely a contempt for manual labour. 'This weakness is also in you', he told these future cadres, adding that it could lead to bureaucracy. Bureaucracy, he stressed, had to be constantly combated. 'If we do not fight it', Liu said prophetically, 'it may become more and more serious until one day we will have to mount a big drive against it.' (Naturally he did not foresee that a decade later he himself

---

[1] *Selected Readings*, pp. 361, 375.

[2] *Liu Shao-ch'i tzu-liao hui-pien*, p. 101.

[3] *Collected Works of Liu Shao-ch'i 1945–1957* (Hong Kong, Union Research Institute, 1969), p. 426.

[4] *Ibid.* p. 424, and *Liu Shao-ch'i tzu-liao hui-pien*, pp. 96, 101.

[5] *Liu Shao-ch'i tzu-liao hui-pien*, p. 101. Mao proposed to combine such gentle methods with tempering in 'great storms'. *Selected Readings*, pp. 394, 400.

would become the principal victim of such a drive.) But at the same time he indicated that it was impossible to liquidate bureaucracy completely.[1]

One passage in Liu's speech of April 1957 in Shanghai was presumably directed likewise at bureaucratic attitudes, but could also be interpreted retrospectively as a veiled allusion to the Chairman. Some people, he said, hold that the principal contradiction in our country today is that between proletarian and non-proletarian thought:

I think...this way of putting it is correct...But what is proletarian thought? What is non-proletarian thought, and where is it to be found? ...I should guess that those comrades who put forward these ideas look at things more or less as follows: the masses, the workers, the students have non-proletarian thought, whereas we Communist Party members, we cadres, we leaders, we factory managers, we directors of schools, we responsible government workers have proletarian thought.[2]

When, in the spring and summer of 1957, the criticism unleashed by Mao's February speech went beyond the denunciation of particular abuses, and called into question the very existence of a socialist state in China, Mao was led to put the emphasis on the other half of his formula for avoiding a Hungarian-type uprising in China – on discipline rather than on freedom, and on strengthening the 'proletarian dictatorship' rather than on 'getting rid of the root causes of disturbances' by stamping out bureaucratic abuses. And yet, in Mao's own view, there was no real contradiction or rupture between his approach in early 1957, when he was encouraging flowers to blossom freely, and his policy during the latter half of the same year, when many a flower was re-classified as a 'poisonous weed' and suppressed. It was merely a matter of a shift in emphasis within a framework which he defined as follows in July 1957:

Our aim is to create a political situation in which there is both centralism and democracy, both discipline and freedom, both unity of purpose and personal ease of mind and liveliness, in order to facilitate the socialist revolution and socialist construction and make it easier to overcome difficulties, so that we can build more quickly a modern industry and agriculture in our country, and the Party and the state will be consolidated

[1] *Collected Works of Liu Shao-ch'i, 1945–1957*, pp. 423–4.
[2] *Liu Shao-ch'i tzu-liao hui-pien*, p. 95.

and better able to weather storms...A communist must be good at discussing things with the masses, and must at no time be divorced from the masses. The relationship between Party and masses is exactly like that between fish and water...[1]

Thus, Mao saw the 'strengthening of discipline' through 'sending down' to the countryside all those who had not yet grasped the true meaning of the revolution as a way of bringing their thinking in harmony with the masses, and thus helping them to enjoy true freedom. This is one more illustration of Mao's continuing attempt, over the past half century, to combine spontaneity and initiative from below with obedience to a correct line laid down from above. It is symbolic of the extraordinary constancy of this basic preoccupation, throughout many shifts in the policies by which Mao pursues his aim, that the first three lines of the above quotation have been incorporated, almost without changing a word, into the new Party Constitution adopted in April 1969.[2]

In the autumn of 1957, simultaneously with the anti-rightist campaign, Chinese economic policy began to take a new and radical direction. Though China had been moving to some extent away from the Soviet model since 1955, the great dividing line in the history of the Chinese People's Republic must be situated, in accordance with Mao's own periodization, in the winter of 1957–8.[3] Humiliated by the 'lack of creativity' which had been displayed in the early years, when China perforce copied Soviet methods, Mao was resolved to put an end to this unpleasant expedient. The policies he devised to this end had their roots in his own experience, and especially in the 'Nanniwan' model of Yenan days, but they went significantly beyond the precedents of the past.

The resulting approach to economic development, designated by the slogan of the 'Great Leap Forward' was spelled out in Mao Tse-tung's speech of 28 January 1958 to the Supreme State Conference,[4] and especially in a draft directive, the 'Sixty Articles on

---

[1] *Current Background* (Hong Kong, U.S. Consulate-General), no. 891, p. 25 (Hereafter *CB*).

[2] *Peking Review*, no. 18, 20 April 1969.

[3] In his 7,000-cadres speech of January 1962, Mao declared: 'Since the founding of the Chinese People's Republic, twelve years have already gone by. These twelve years can be divided into a first period of eight years and a second period of four years' (*Mao Tse-tung Unrehearsed*, Text 8). There follows the passage, quoted earlier, about putting an end to copying from the Soviet Union.   [4] *Mao Tse-tung Unrehearsed*, Text 3.

Work Methods', signed by Mao and dated 31 January 1958.[1] In both
of these documents, Mao called for a further acceleration of China's
economic progress and declared that such a speed-up was possible,
thanks to the remarkable upsurge of revolutionary enthusiasm
among the masses.

To be sure, Mao saw not only the strengths but the weaknesses of
his compatriots. 'Our country has such an enormous population',
he declared in his speech of 28 January, 'it has such a vast territory,
abundant resources, so many people, four thousand years of history
and culture...We have bragged so much about this, yet we cannot
compare with a country like Belgium. In short, we are an outstanding
people with a very long history, yet our steel output is so low.' Adding
that grain output was also inadequate, and there were many illitera-
tes, Mao nevertheless expressed confidence that the positive outweighed the negative: 'We cannot compare with Belgium on any of
these counts. Yet we have great drive and we must catch up. We
shall catch up with Britain in fifteen years.'

Putting forward the slogan of overtaking England in fifteen years
(in total, not *per capita*, output of the principal industrial products),
which was to be one of the main themes of the next two years, Mao
justified it in the first instance by the zeal and capacity for strenuous
effort of the Chinese people. It was in this context that he employed
the metaphor of thermonuclear energy, quoted earlier, to conjure up
an image of the mighty forces latent in the Chinese people. Mao's
'atom-smasher' for releasing this energy was, of course, political
consciousness. Such consciousness could be achieved in part by
'getting rid of bourgeois ideology' – a task in which China was
already ahead of the West.

Mao did not imagine that the economic development vital to
China's future could be achieved by zeal alone. On the contrary, he
declared that, beginning on 1 July 1958, the emphasis in the Party's
work should be shifted from the 'political and ideological revolution' exemplified in the rectification campaign begun in the previous year to the 'technical revolution'. Mao was well aware that, as
he had declared in 1949, this meant the leaders of the revolution
would have to acquire new skills. He was clearly nettled by the sug-

[1] Translated in *CB* 892, pp. 1–14, and also in Jerome Ch'en, *Mao Papers* (London,
Oxford University Press, 1970), 57–76.

gestion, voiced during the 'Hundred Flowers' period, that he and his comrades were ignorant bumpkins incapable of mastering the complexities of the modern world, and he declared in no uncertain terms that they *would* do so:

The rightists say that we are petty intellectuals, incapable of leading the big intellectuals. There are also people who say that the old cadres should be bought off, that they only know how to fight and to carry out land reform. We must definitely study and carry through this great technical revolution bestowed on us by history...In the past, we had the capacity to fight and carry out the land reform, but now it is not enough to possess these capabilities alone. We must learn new skills, we must truly understand professional work (*yeh-wu*), we must understand science and technology; otherwise, we will not be able to exercise good leadership.

Even as he stressed thus the need to master technical skills, Mao went on to declare, in a long discussion of the problem of combining 'redness' and 'expertise', that ideology and politics must remain the 'supreme commander' and the 'soul' of all the Party's work. Cadres with no knowledge of economic and technical problems he stigmatized as 'empty-headed politicans', merely pseudo-red; but those who paid no heed to politics and ideology and busied themselves all day with their professional tasks ran the graver danger of losing their sense of direction and going astray. The correct solution, in Mao's view, lay in the union of politics and technology in the man who was both 'red' and 'expert'.

A highly suggestive reflection of Mao's attitude at this moment, out of which the Great Leap Forward was soon to emerge, is to be found in his conception of 'disequilibrium' as a universal objective law. 'There is disequilibrium between one enterprise and another, between one workshop, one work group, and one individual and another within an enterprise', he declared in the 'Sixty Articles', 'Disequilibrium is constant and absolute; equilibrium is temporary and relative.' At first glance, Mao's enthusiasm for 'disequilibrium' would seem to imply the negation of all planning. Such a conclusion would be too sweeping, but the logic of the Great Leap Forward did indeed rule out rigid, centralized planning on the Soviet pattern. Mao proposed to substitute a more flexible system combining some central control with a substantial degree of local initiative. There were to be three sets of plans. The first was the published plan, containing minimum national targets which must be achieved. The second was a nation-wide plan containing higher targets which were expected to be fulfilled; these higher targets, regarded as desirable by the central authorities, were to be taken as binding on the local administration of each area. Finally, each local administration was to have a further plan containing targets higher still, which the authorities expected could be achieved within the area for which they were responsible. It was further laid down that the basis for appraisal and comparison should be the second of these three sets of plans. (See point 9 of the 'Sixty Articles'.) Thus any attempt to check the compatibility of all the various inputs and outputs involved would not extend to the third and highest set of targets. As a result, when a climate developed in which each and every economic unit felt itself bound to increase production as rapidly as it could, so that the third plan became in fact the operative plan – at least in terms of expectations, if not of performance – 'disequilibrium' effectively arose, to such an extent that even Mao was taken aback.

The attitude of enthusiasm and impatience which characterized Mao's thinking on the eve of the Great Leap Forward found its most general theoretical expression in the concept of the 'permanent' or 'uninterrupted' revolution,[1] which he developed at some length in the twenty-first of the 'Sixty Articles', and expounded more succinctly and rather more picturesquely in his speech of 28 January 1958. On this later occasion, after stating that he was a partisan of 'the theory of the permanent revolution' (not to be confused, he emphasized, with Trotsky's theory of the same name), Mao went on to define his conception of permanent revolution as 'striking while the iron is hot', so that one phase followed another and the revolution advanced without interruption. He also illustrated his idea of the theory with a Hunanese folk saying: 'Straw sandals have no pattern;

[1] This theory was never publicly expounded by Mao at the time of the Great Leap, but it was the subject of a large number of articles by authorized interpreters of his thought, in 1958 and 1959. For a selection of these – which now turn out to be in large part simple paraphrases of what Mao had written in the 'Sixty Articles' – and for a discussion of the concept *pu-tuan ko-ming* and my reasons for translating it 'permanent revolution' rather than 'uninterrupted revolution', see my monograph, *La 'révolution permanente' en Chine* (Paris, Mouton, 1963). I have endeavoured to bring my interpretation up to date, in the light of the fragments by Mao himself that have recently become available, in 'Mao Tse-tung and the Theory of the Permanent Revolution, 1958–1969', *The China Quarterly*, 46 (April–June, 1971), 221–44.

they shape themselves in the making.' In other words, the China of the future would be shaped by the ceaseless and tireless endeavour of the present. Above all, it was necessary to do one's utmost each day. In a single sentence commenting on the slogan of overtaking England in fifteen years, Mao summed up what was and has remained his philosophy of revolution: 'These fifteen years depend on the first five. The first five depend on the first three, the first three depend on the first one, and the first one depends on the first month.' *Carpe diem!*

In this speech, Mao once more noted, as he had in April 1956, that it was easy to re-shape the Chinese people because they were 'poor and blank'. Mao's January 1958 speech, like that of April 1956 on the 'Ten Great Relationships', was not published, but he developed the same theme at length in an article written in April 1958, on the eve of the Second Session of the Eighth Party Congress:

Apart from their other characteristics, China's 600 million people have two remarkable peculiarities: they are, first of all, poor and secondly, blank. This may seem like a bad thing, but it is really a good thing. Poor people want change, want to do things, want revolution. A clean sheet of paper has no blotches, so the newest and most beautiful words can be written on it, the newest and most beautiful pictures can be painted on it.[1]

When Mao had first expounded this idea two years earlier, he had carefully weighed against one another the advantages and disadvantages of this condition. Now he saw the negative aspects – the fact that, as he had put it in 1956, China had 'not much industry' and a rather low cultural and scientific level – as merely a seeming handicap compared to the revolutionary energy generated by poverty and the moral purity and malleability resulting from the 'blankness' of China's rural masses. Thanks to these qualities, Mao concluded that China 'might not need as much time as previously thought to catch up with the big capitalist countries in industrial and agricultural production'.

Meanwhile, steps toward the implementation of Mao's radical new line had been taken at a gathering of Party leaders held in March 1958 in Chengtu. In the context of the blueprint laid down in the 'Sixty Articles' for a planning system combining central control and local initiative, a large part of the proceedings was devoted to the pro-

[1] *The Political Thought of Mao Tse-tung*, p. 352.

blem of encouraging innovation and improvement in agricultural implements, under grass-roots control. In particular, we are told that at Chengtu Chairman Mao restored the double-wheeled and double-bladed plough, which he had been promoting for some time, 'to its original fame'. In January 1958, Mao had singled out this implement (in fact, a Soviet model ill-adapted to Chinese conditions) for mention once more in the 'Sixty Articles'. (Characteristically, he had cited in this context the original January 1956 version of his 'Twelve-Year Programme for Agricultural Development', which specifically referred to such ploughs, and not the version adopted in the autumn of 1957, which spoke only in general terms of improvements in agricultural technology. Clearly, he regarded as null and void any tinkering with his ideas by Party and government organs.) Finally, steps were taken to encourage the fusion of several cooperatives into one large coop, with larger financial and human resources for irrigation and other necessary tasks. These were not yet communes, for they did not assume political and military as well as economic functions, but they marked a step toward the communes.

Recent accounts of the Chengtu Conference stress Mao's role in promoting all these ideas, and it can be assumed that he made one or several speeches on economic matters, but that the only speech available at the time of writing deals with problems primarily of literary and educational policy.[1] The gulf between these two domains was not, however, by any means so wide as might at first glance appear. For the guiding spirit of the new policies now taking shape in every domain was summed up in the slogan 'Politics takes command' (*cheng-chih kua-shuai*). This formula, which derives directly from Mao's characterization, in the 'Sixty Articles' of politics as the 'supreme commander' and the 'soul', meant Party control at all levels. But it also carried wider implications, harking back to Yenan days, regarding the priority of men over machinery, and of a correct ideological orientation over technical competence. And in this context, Mao's Chengtu speech on cultural and ideological problems, with its ringing proclamation of the superiority of youthful enthu-

---

[1] Two more speeches became available in the summer of 1973; see *Mao Tse-tung Unrehearsed*, Texts 4a and 4b. For Cultural Revolution discussions of the conference, see *Survey of China Mainland Magazines* (Hong Kong, U.S. Consulate-General), no. 610, pp. 19–20, no. 632, pp. 13 and 21, and no. 633, *passim*, especially pp. 7, 12, 14, 23 etc.

siasm over the knowledge of tired and conservative old men, amounted in fact to a statement of his economic philosophy as well.

Mao's Chengtu speech of March 1958 also illustrates the persistent concern with education which constitutes another important element of continuity between the Chinese revolution as it has developed under his leadership, and the China of yesterday. Talking to Edgar Snow in December 1970, Mao said that he wished to be remembered by only one of the four titles given to him in the early stages of the Cultural Revolution ('Great Teacher', 'Great Leader', 'Great Supreme Commander', and 'Great Helmsman'), that of teacher. He had, he recalled, been a primary-school teacher in his youth.[1] At first glance, this would seem to be merely a gesture of modesty. Yet there is a sense in which a concern with education stands at the centre of Mao's career. As we have already seen, his approach to revolution stresses the importance of cultural change, and education, in the broadest sense, is the instrument by which he seeks to create new men and women.

One can discern three strands in Mao's conception of education. Education, to be effective, must break with traditional patterns of rote learning, scholasticism, and meek submission of the pupil to the authority of the teacher; it must be linked to practice, and specifically to production; it cannot be separated from class struggle. Consequently, formal academic training is not, in his view, the only kind of education, or even the most important kind of education. At Chengtu Mao went even farther than he had in Yenan in 1942 in downgrading the value of book learning. The young, he declared, are always superior to the old, and those with less learning always overthrow those with more learning. This criticism of the fetishism of learning was coupled not only with praise for youthful vitality, but with an evident nostalgia for Mao's own youth at the time of the May 4th era, which evokes even more strongly the climate at the beginning of the Cultural Revolution:

From ancient times the people who have created new schools of thought have always been young people without great learning. Confucius started at the age of twenty-three; and how much learning did Jesus have? Sakyamuni founded Buddhism at the age of nineteen; his learning was

[1] Edgar Snow, *The Long Revolution*, p. 169.

only acquired gradually later on...Marx also was very young when he created dialectical materialism...

Of course some things can be learnt at school: I don't propose to close all the schools. What I mean is that it is not absolutely necessary to attend school. The main thing is whether your direction is correct or not and whether you come to grips with your studies. Learning has to be grasped. As soon as they have grasped the truth the young founders of new schools embarked on discoveries, scorning the old fogies. Then those with learning oppressed them. Isn't that what history is like? When we started to make revolution, we were mere twenty-year-old boys, while the rulers of that time, like Yüan Shih-k'ai and Tuan Ch'i-jui, were old and experienced. They had more learning, but we had more truth.[1]

Mao's educational philosophy as expounded at Chengtu was not, in some respects, far removed from the views which Liu Shao-ch'i had put forward in May 1957, in talking to the geology graduates. On that occasion, Liu had even resuscitated the term 'semi-intellectual', which, as we have seen, had been used by Mao during the Yenan Rectification campaign of 1942 as a derogatory epithet for those with only book learning.[2] One passage of Mao's Chengtu speech, however, highlights the continuing differences of style and temperament between Mao and Liu, as well as the change in climate since the previous year. Liu had called, in the spring of 1957, for resolving disputes within the Party by persuasion, and by the method of 'light breezes and sweet showers' (*ho-feng hsi-yü*). Mao had agreed in part, but now declared:

This conference is a rectification conference. But we do not talk about ideology or fulfil our pledges. Isn't there a contradiction here? We have neither been carrying out struggles nor identifying rightists, but talking in gentle tones like light breezes and sweet showers...My purpose is to get people to dare to speak out with vigour and invincible force, like Marx or Lu Hsün...

When, in the course of the summer, 'people's communes' began to be formed on an experimental basis, Mao set off for the countryside to inspect them, and threw the weight of his authority behind this development. During the second half of August an enlarged meeting of the Politburo at Peitaiho gave official sanction to the

---

[1] *Mao Tse-tung Unrehearsed*, Text 4c.
[2] *Collected Works of Liu Shao-ch'i, 1945–1957*, p. 421.

establishment of communes, and announced wildly exaggerated results for the Great Leap Forward policies, including a 100 per cent increase in agricultural production between 1957 and 1958.[1] Returning from another trip at the end of September, Mao declared that, in order to achieve a leap forward in agriculture even greater than that which had been accomplished in 1958, it was necessary to extend the system of people's communes throughout the whole country. At the same time, he defended the programme for making steel in 'backyard furnaces' in terms which strikingly reveal his state of mind at the time:

During this trip, I have witnessed the tremendous energy of the masses. On this foundation, it is possible to accomplish any task whatsoever. We must first complete the tasks on the iron and steel fronts. In these sectors, the masses have already been mobilized. Nevertheless, in the country as a whole there are a few places, a few enterprises, where the work of mobilizing the masses has still not been properly carried out...There are still a few comrades who are unwilling to undertake a large-scale mass movement in the industrial sphere. They call the mass movement on the industrial front 'irregular' and disparage it as a 'rural style of work' and a guerrilla habit'. This is obviously incorrect.[2]

It is not surprising that Mao should have objected to the criticism of his policies for economic development through mass mobilization as a hangover from the guerrilla days of the past. Those 'few comrades' who took this view may well have included among their number Liu and other leading figures in the Party who supported rapid development, but feared disorder. Mao subsequently brought home to them in the Cultural Revolution his conviction that their attitude was incorrect.

The Great Leap Forward, though it was not the utter catastrophe it has sometimes been made out to be in Western accounts, did encounter, as Mao himself subsequently recognized, very serious difficulties. In politics, as in war, a victorious advance tends to unite people, whereas retreat gives rise to recrimination and dissension. It was therefore natural that the increasingly grave economic

[1] For the text of the resolution adopted on 19 August regarding the people's communes and other developments in the countryside, see *Communist China 1955 - 1969: Policy Documents with Analysis* (ed. R. R. Bowie and J. K. Fairbank) (Cambridge, Mass., Harvard University Press, 1962), pp. 454–6
[2] *The Political Thought of Mao Tse-tung*, pp. 352–3.

and administrative problems encountered in China in 1959 and 1960 should encourage the emergence of sharply opposed viewpoints, and ultimately of hostile factions (or, in Mao's own vocabulary, of rival 'headquarters') within the leadership. There are good reasons to believe that Mao's ideas regarding the cieative role of 'disequilibrium' in economic development had aroused from the beginning considerable reservations on the part of Party and state officials, especially the planners.[1] The opposition of this group to Mao's 'guerrilla' methods was naturally intensified as the consequences of inadequate coordination between the ouputs of various units and sectors became increasingly and graphically apparent. Nevertheless, the Lushan Plenum of July–August 1959 showed clearly that both Mao and his critics within the Party wished to avoid the consequences of a split. Thus Liu Shao-ch'i and most of the other major figures in the leadership refrained from supporting openly the all-out attack on the Great Leap policies launched by P'eng Te-huai, then Minister of Defence.[2] For his part, Mao went rather far in his self-criticism on this occasion, taking full responsibility for the mass steel-smelting campaign, which he said had led to considerable waste of resources, and accepting a share of the blame for the general economic chaos in late 1958. Suddenly, at the Peitaiho meeting, he said, the Planning Commission decided not to concern itself any more with effective planning:

By doing away with planning, I mean that they dispensed with overall balances, and simply made no estimates of how much coal, iron and transport would be needed. Coal and iron cannot walk by themselves; they need vehicles to transport them. This I did not foresee. I and...the Premier did not concern ourselves with this point. You could say that we were ignorant of it. I ought not to make excuses, but I shall too, because I am not the head of the Planning Commission. Before August of last year my main energies were concentrated on revolution. I am a complete outsider when it comes to economic construction, and I understand nothing about industrial planning...But comrades, in 1958 and 1959 the main responsibility was mine and you should take me to task.[3]

---

[1] For a summary of some of the evidence on this point, see my article, already cited, in *The China Quarterly*, 46 (April–June 1971), 232–6.
[2] Most of the principal documents regarding Mao's confrontation with P'eng Te-huai at Lushan and its antecedents are translated in *The Case of Peng Teh-huai*.
[3] Speech at Lushan, 23 July 1959, *Mao Tse-tung Unrehearsed*, Text 6.

This is a far cry from Mao's resounding eulogy of the 'mass movement in the industrial sphere' only ten months earlier. Indeed, Mao was far harsher on himself and his economic policies as a whole than P'eng Te-huai had ventured to be. But although he was willing to recognize that he knew little about industrial production or planning techniques, one thing he *was* sure he understood: the Chinese countryside, and the revolution required to transform it. It was against this aspect of the Great Leap policies that P'eng had directed the brunt of his criticism, and therefore P'eng must go – not only because he had offended Mao, but because in Mao's eyes this was the foundation of all the rest. If, as P'eng and others demanded, the errors committed in the rural areas were extensively publicized, morale would be shattered. 'Our state would collapse and even if the imperialists didn't come, the people would rise up and overthrow us.'

Mao therefore insisted on a formal condemnation of P'eng Te-huai, which was pronounced in a resolution adopted by the Central Committee on 16 August. This document denounced P'eng for having 'negated the victory of the general line and the Great Leap Forward, and opposed the high-speed development of the national economy' and declared that he had 'brazenly slandered as "petty bourgeois fanaticism" the revolutionary zeal of the Party and of hundreds of millions of people.'[1] He was also accused of slavishness toward the Soviets. In a speech of 11 September 1959 before the Party's Military Affairs Committee, Mao Tse-tung declared: 'It is absolutely impermissible to go behind the back of our fatherland to collude with a foreign country.'[2] The domestic and foreign aspects of this affair were, of course, closely linked, since P'eng Te-huai's worst crime, in Mao's eyes, was his criticism of the communes, which Khrushchev had likewise ridiculed publicly.

Formally speaking, Mao had obtained a complete victory at Lushan, but regarding the substance of policy the situation was much less clear cut. An official communiqué issued at the end of the Lushan Plenum declared that the figures previously published for economic achievements during the first year of the Great Leap were exaggerated by 40 or 50 per cent. To be sure, Mao himself acknowledged that there had been considerable over-optimism in the early stages of the

[1] *Peking Review*, 34 (1967), 8.   [2] *Mao Tse-tung Unrehearsed*, Text 7.

Great Leap, and in a speech of 2 August he had called for a revision of the output figures. 'The high targets', he declared, 'are Buddhist idols which we set up for ourselves to worship. Now we must smash them – smash the unrealistic targets for steel, coal, grain, cotton, etc.'[1] This downward revision of targets and production figures soon proved, however, to be only the entering wedge of a growing trend towards economic methods flagrantly in contradiction with his ideas. The majority of the Central Committee had not been willing to associate itself with an open disavowal of Mao's policies – and by implication of his leadership. P'eng Te-huai had paid the price for his boldness in this respect. But at the same time many influential figures among Mao's colleagues had no intention of allowing him to have his way in the economic domain – about which he had just admitted he knew little or nothing. So, while safeguarding the shadow of his prestige, they set about depriving him of the substance by re-establishing order and discipline in the economy, and exalting the role of material incentives.

Mao Tse-tung himself soon accepted the fact that withdrawal from the more extreme policies of the Great Leap Forward was inevitable as the price of his tactical victory at Lushan. He was, however, resolved that this retreat should be carried out in good order, and that he should remain in control of it. In his speech of 11 September 1959 he asserted that the erroneous views of P'eng and the others were shared only by a minority of one, two, three, four, or five per cent of the Party, whereas his own correct line enjoyed the support of the familiar and symbolic figure of 95 per cent. P'eng and his allies had plotted to split the Party, thus showing their ignorance of the fact that a Marxist political party must have 'iron discipline'. Such discipline, in Mao's view, was not merely a principle of Leninism; it was also indispensable to China's renaissance as a great power:

The banner of unity is exceedingly important...If you want unity, you must have discipline...The present task is for the people of the whole country, together with the whole Party, to build a strong country within the space of a few five-year plans. For this iron discipline is needed, it cannot be done without it, so we must unite. I ask you, how can we achieve this aim otherwise? Is it possible to build a great socialist country within the

[1] *The Case of Peng Teh-huai*, pp. 27, 413.

space of a few five-year plans?...Without discipline nothing is possible.[1]

Unity, for Mao, meant, of course, unity under his leadership, but he fully understood that a display of flexibility on his part would help to re-establish the cohesiveness of the Party. As usual, having decided to do a thing, he threw himself into it wholeheartedly, and drafted an extraordinarily far-reaching circular letter which, in fact called for the abrogation of many of the policies and attitudes he himself had been advocating for the past two years, and the adoption of some at least of the proposals of P'eng Te-huai and his 'Anti-Party Group'.

Mao's letter of 29 November 1959[2] was addressed in the first instance to production team leaders, though it was also directed to comrades of all levels from the province down to the *hsien*, the commune, and the production brigade. This fact in itself was extraordinarily significant, for it already foreshadowed the decentralization of ownership and effective control over production in the communes to the lowest level, that of the team – a measure which was to be formally announced only in November 1960, and implemented still later. (The Lushan Plenum had introduced a three-tier system of ownership, with the emphasis on the intermediate level of the brigade.)

'I want to discuss with you comrades a few questions, all of which concern agriculture', Mao began.

The first is the question of fixing output quotas...Output quotas must definitely be translated into reality, you must pay absolutely no attention to the directives from a higher level, you must pay no attention to them, you must pay attention only to the real possibilities. For example, the per *mou* yield in fact amounted only to 300 catties last year, and it will be excellent if we can increase it by 100 or 200 catties this year. It is nothing but boasting to say that the yield will amount to 800 catties, 1000 catties, 1200 catties or even more. This really can't be done, so what is the use of such boasts?

Production brigades and teams were told to decide on norms themselves, paying no attention to 'rigid orders from above'.

As for the vital problem of mechanization and the introduction of more modern farm implements, Mao continued to hold that 'the

[1] *Mao Tse-tung Unrehearsed*, Text 7.
[2] *CB* 891, pp. 34–5. Recently available materials indicate that this letter should be dated April 1959, and the chronology of the retreat from the Great Leap revised accordingly.

fundamental way for agriculture lies in mechanization'. But instead of calling, as he had done in the January 1956 draft of the Twelve-Year Programme for Agricultural Development, for a revolution in this domain in three to five years, he declared that at least ten years would be required. There was no mention of the notorious double-wheeled and double-bladed ploughs; instead Mao advocated the gradual improvement of existing farm implements.

No doubt Mao sincerely felt that the policy line laid down in his letter of November 1959 was the one best adapted to the needs of the Chinese countryside under the existing circumstances. At the same time, he can hardly have been unmindful of the tactical utility of such a letter in strengthening his hand vis-à-vis the other Party leaders. Had he left it to Liu Shao-ch'i or someone else to write this directive, those Party cadres and ordinary peasants who felt that the Great Leap policies had gone too far – very likely a majority at this stage – would have been tempted to say to themselves: 'The Chairman got us into this mess; the sensible people in the Party leadership are showing us the way out of it.' By grasping the nettle firmly, Mao could hope to reap praise for himself and to put the blame for past mistakes on others.

His point made, Mao appears to have withdrawn to a large extent from the affairs of the Party. On the one hand, he was clearly turning his attention at this time to the polemics with the Soviets, and to the encouragement of revolutionary movements in Asia, Africa and Latin America. But there are likewise grounds for believing that, as early as the end of 1959 or the beginning of 1960, Mao Tse-tung had begun to doubt the possibility of securing really whole-hearted support from the Party leadership, and had consciously set out to make of the People's Liberation Army a bastion of his influence and the most important instrument for propagating his thought.

Lin Piao, who succeeded P'eng Te-huai as Minister of Defence in September 1959, had distinguished himself as early as June 1958 by his eloquent praise for Mao's contribution to military thought, declaring:

in military science, in problems of strategy, we have our own fully-developed system. Lenin died too early. He did not have time to attend to this question. Stalin had no developed system. We do not have to learn from the Soviet Union. As regards tactics, we can learn half and leave half. Their tactics are questionable both ideologically and as regards their attitude to the masses. The half we learn would consist of the use of naval and air forces and the coordination of the services. As for the half we don't learn, such as tactical thinking, we have Chairman Mao's, so we don't need to learn theirs.

Lin also wholeheartedly agreed with Mao's emphasis on the value of China's own tradition. In his speech of 28 June 1958, Mao declared: 'Li Shih-min [the second emperor of the Tang Dynasty], Ts'ao Ts'ao [Emperor Wu, the founder of the Wei Dynasty], etc., all knew how to fight wars. China's past has quite a lot to offer. When Mao went on to criticize a comrade who said there was no Marxism in the writings of China's celebrated ancient military thinker Sun Tzu, although manifestly he had not read them, Lin Piao interjected: '*Sun-tzu ping-fa* [Sun Tzu's Art of War] does contain both materialism and dialectics.'[1]

Although Lin Piao was a fervent admirer of Mao's military policies, it was only in the autumn of 1960, a year after he had taken charge of the Ministry of Defence, that he was at last ready to begin turning the People's Liberation Army into a 'great school of Mao Tse-tung's thought'. By this time, production had declined, under the triple impact of the brusque withdrawal of Soviet technical assistance, the disorganization engendered by the Great Leap, and the effect of natural calamities, to a point where the food supply was barely above the starvation level.

Certain regions of the country were, in fact, referred to officially as 'disaster areas', and in these places there occurred significant numbers of deaths attributable to malnutrition and the resulting lack of resistance to infectious diseases. Even the soldiers of the People's Liberation Army, who were better fed than the population as a whole, suffered in many cases from oedema, which reached its peak in December 1960. The PLA *Work Bulletin* published, in the early months of 1961, graphic accounts of these problems, and of the negative attitudes they engendered among the population. The widespread discontent which existed at this time in the country was of direct concern to the PLA both because of the effect on morale of letters from relatives in the disaster areas, and because it was the task of the army to intervene when, as happened in certain cases, peasant discontent led to actual armed uprisings. But although force

[1] *Mao Tse-tung Unrehearsed*, Text 5.

was used when necessary, the directives of the PLA General Political Department called for emphasis on explanation and persuasion.[1]

Despite isolated instances of rebellion, the army, and the population at large, responded to these difficult conditions with admirable courage, and with remarkable ingenuity in developing supplementary food resources, from hunting and fishing to the production of duck-weed protein.[2] But all these practical measures were put into effect in the context of a vast campaign, within the People's Liberation Army, for the study of Mao Tse-tung's thought.

In September 1960, Lin Piao presented to a meeting of the Military Affairs Committee a report on what he called the 'four relations', shortly to be reformulated and re-baptized as the 'four firsts': priority of men over weapons, of political work over other work, of ideological work over routine political work, and of living ideology over ideas from books.[3] These points were developed in the resolution adopted by the Military Affairs Committee on 20 October 1960, entitled 'On Strengthening Political and Ideological Work in the Army.'

This document was to play a decisive role in Chinese politics during the ensuing decade. It was revised by Mao Tse-tung himself before being adopted by the Military Affairs Committee, and subsequently approved by the Central Committee of the Chinese Communist Party on 21 December 1960.[4] Mao's role in drafting this text lends weight and piquancy to the fact that it is devoted almost exclusively to the glorification of his thought. Moreover, the very language employed was to serve as a model for the writings on the

[1] *The Work Bulletin* (*Kung-tso t'ung-hsün*) was a secret periodical for PLA cadres at the regimental level and above, of which 29 issues for the period January–August 1961 fell into the hands of the U.S. Government and were subsequently made available through the Library of Congress. A complete English translation has also been published: J. Chester Cheng (ed.), *The Politics of the Chinese Red Army* (Stanford, Hoover Institution, 1965). Regarding the army's role in putting down unrest, see in particular the directive of 9 November 1960 on the suppression of counter-revolution published in issue no 1 (*ibid.* p. 27). On the gravity of food and morale problems, see issues nos. 1–11 *passim*, especially pp. 15–19, 209–13, 277–301.

[2] Cheng, *The Politics of the Chinese Red Army*, *passim*, especially the decision of the Chinese Communist Party on substitute food, p. 270.

[3] *Ibid.* p. 66.

[4] The text of the resolution, with the Central Committee's endorsement, appears in *ibid.* pp. 66–94. On p. 33 of the same volume it is stated that Mao himself revised the draft.

same theme in the course of the Cultural Revolution. Thus, the whole first paragraph of the Foreword to *Quotations from Chairman Mao* signed by the General Political Department of the PLA and dated 1 August 1965, which appeared in all Chinese editions of the little red book down to the end of 1966, was lifted bodily, with only very minor changes and the addition of a single sentence, from the resolution of 20 October 1960. Mao was thus personally responsible for the proclamation as authoritative doctrine of sentences such as these:

Comrade Mao Tse-tung is the greatest Marxist–Leninist of our era. Mao Tse-tung's thought is the application of the universal truths of Marxism–Leninism in the era in which imperialism is heading for collapse and socialism is advancing to victory, in the concrete practice of the Chinese revolution, in the collective struggles of the Party and the people; it is Marxism–Leninism creatively developed. Mao Tse-tung's thought is the guiding principle for the Chinese people's revolution and socialist construction, it is a powerful ideological weapon for opposing imperialism and for opposing revisionism and dogmatism...We must carry out propaganda calling on everyone to study Chairman Mao's writings, follow his teachings, act according to his instructions, and be his good fighters.[1]

The essence of this very long resolution was an exhortation to comrades in the army to 'transform themselves thoroughly', taking Chairman Mao as their model. Henceforth, Mao Tse-tung's writings, (including Volume IV of his *Selected Works*, which had just appeared) were to constitute the main content of theoretical study by all cadres, though persons with a sufficiently high cultural level could also study the works of Marx, Engels, Lenin and Stalin. This aspect of the resolution is summed up in a single lapidary phrase: 'Politics in command means putting Mao Tse-tung's thought in command (*cheng-chih kua-shuai, yeh chiu shih yung Mao Tse-tung ssu-hsiang kua-shuai*).' The 'red and expert' slogan was again put forward, with emphasis not merely on redness, but on expertise, on the need to master new skills in order to function effectively in a 'modernized' army. But, ultimately, the decisive stress was placed on 'living ideology', that is, on 'Mao Tse-tung's thought in command'. A

---

[1] In order to make clear the extent of the borrowing from the language of the 1960 resolution in the Foreword to the little red book, I have used here the translation which I made for the Bantam/Corgi Books edition of *Quotations from Chairman Mao* (New York and London, 1967), p. xxvii, modifying it only where there are differences in the Chinese.

correct political attitude based on Mao's thought was described, in a phrase repeated by Lin Piao in a directive of 17 December 1960, and which subsequently became a cliché, as 'a spiritual atomic bomb'.[1]

The glorification of Mao Tse-tung and his thought had, of course, reached impressive proportions in the years of the Great Leap Forward. Beginning in 1960, however, statements of this kind had become increasingly rare in the periodicals controlled by the Party. If one compares the PLA *Work Bulletin* in early 1961 with the issues of *Hung ch'i* for the same period, the contrast is startling. Mao's name is rarely mentioned in the Party organ, and then only in rather perfunctory fashion. His increasing reliance on the army is therefore entirely understandable, especially as the lack of reverence for his name displayed by the Party organs was accompanied by the progressive dismantlement of even the irreducible core of the Great Leap Forward policies which he thought could and should be salvaged.

What was Liu Shao-ch'i's role in these developments? In September 1959, while reasserting in general terms the validity of the Great Leap policies, he came out in effect against Mao's economic philosophy of disequilibrium. 'Balance', he said, in an article written on the occasion of the Tenth Anniversary of the Chinese People's Republic, 'can and should be achieved while developing our economy at high speed.'[2] It may be that at this time, Liu was not so much repudiating Mao's approach to economic development completely as suggesting that it should be tempered with realism and not applied in too implacable a spirit. Such is the implication of the slightly facetious remarks he is reported to have made at the September 1959 meeting of the Party's Military Affairs Committee. 'In guiding the Party's policy', he declared, 'it is necessary to go to the left for a while, and then to the right for a while. Just as in flying an airplane, this is the only way to reach one's goal.'[3] This hardly squares with Mao's speech before the same forum, in which he stated that in recent weeks 'quite a few high cadres' had been exposed as 'right-opportunist elements and trouble-makers', adding

[1] Cheng, *The Politics of the Chinese Red Army*, pp. 9. 67. This metaphor can perhaps be traced back to Mao's reference, in January 1958, to the 'thermonuclear energy' inherent in the Chinese people.
[2] *Collected Works of Liu Shao-ch'i, 1958–1967*, pp. 47–72, especially pp. 66–7.
[3] *Kuan-yü Liu Shao-ch'i . . .*, p. 24.

that it would be 'very difficult for this small minority of people to enter Communism'.[1]

By early 1960, in any case, Liu was clearly voicing ideas which went against the grain of Mao's whole approach to economic development. Not only did he stress material incentives, as Mao, after all, has often done himself, but he declared that in training specialists, there was no real need to force them to join the Party or to engage in political work.[2] Most significant and most characteristic of all, he returned to his habitual theme of doing things in an orderly manner. On 31 January 1960, speaking to members of his family, he quoted the Great Leap 'general line' of 'going all out and aiming high to build socialism more, faster, better and more economically', and then proceeded to elucidate it as follows: 'For the Chinese people to "go all out" (*ku-tsu kan-ching*) does not mean stimulating them in any old way (*luan-ku*), it means going all out under the leadership of the Party.'[3] And in a talk of 5 May 1960, he declared: 'We must set up a suitable system of rules, we must organize production in a suitable manner, for it is only thus that the activism of the masses can be called forth. If there is no system, the masses will pay no attention to production.'[4]

It is hardly necessary to emphasize the contrast between this approach and that of the Great Leap Forward – and of the Cultural Revolution. In Mao's view, the contribution of the masses to building socialism will be maximized if they are allowed to exercise initiative, and their enthusiasm is thereby aroused. In Liu's view, people will work hard if everyone knows his place.

In January 1962, when the retreat from the Great Leap had gone much further, it is thus entirely credible that Liu Shao-ch'i should have launched, as the Red Guards claim, a sharp attack on the policies of 1958. Mao, though he had made a self-criticism in June 1961, and made another in very strong terms, at the 7,000-cadres meeting of January 1962, devoted himself mainly, on the latter occasion, to a defence of the basic pattern of the Great Leap policies, whatever errors of detail had been committed.[5] Liu Shao-ch'i, on the other hand, judging from the scattered but rather lengthy

---

[1] *Mao Tse-tung Unrehearsed*, Text 7. [2] *Liu Shao-ch'i tui-k'ang Mao...*, p. 51.
[3] *Liu Shao-ch'i tzu-liao hui-pien*, p. 109. [4] *Kuan-yü Liu Shao-ch'i...*, p. 24.
[5] *Mao Tse-tung Unrehearsed*, Text 8.

extracts from his speech at the same meeting to be found in Red Guard sources, adopted a very different tone. The economic difficulties encountered following the Great Leap were, he said, 30 per cent the fault of nature, and 70 per cent the fault of men. The general line, he declared, was incomplete, and should be spelled out (as he had done in private conversation two years earlier) by adding the words: 'stimulate the subjective capacities of the masses in full measure, under the centralized and united leadership of the Chinese Communist Party'. Most significantly of all, he is claimed to have asserted: 'The Great Leap Forward was carried out somewhat too fast, for equilibrium was destroyed, so that after three years of leaping, it will take eight to ten years, starting from the present, to put things in order. This doesn't add up.' He summed up his view of the situation in a frequently-quoted remark: 'When the chairman says the situation is very good, he is referring to the excellence of the political situation. One can't say the economic situation is very good; on the contrary, it is very ungood.'[1]

These quotations *must* have been taken out of context, for Mao himself, in his speech to the 7,000-cadres meeting, summarized Liu's report, which had been made a few days earlier, as follows: 'Comrade Liu Shao-ch'i said in his report that in the past four years our line was correct, and that our achievements were the main feature; we made some mistakes in our practical work and suffered some hardships, but we gained experience; therefore we are stronger than before, not weaker. This is how things actually are.'[2] Most likely Liu made a balanced presentation, including the critical remarks noted above, but ending (or beginning) with the overall judgement summarized by Mao. In the political context of the time, Mao chose to ignore the barbs and to stress Liu's basic agreement with his policies; later, during the Cultural Revolution, extracts from his speech were selected by the Red Guards in such a way as to emphasize rather Liu's disillusionment with the Great Leap approach.

Mao, for his part, although he referred in January 1962 to the need

[1] See especially *Kuan-yü Liu Shao-ch'i...*, pp. 26–8; also *Liu Shao-ch'i tui-k'ang Mao...*, pp. 18–23, 43; *Liu Shao-ch'i fan-ko-ming tsui-o shih* (*A History of Liu Shao-ch'i's counter-revolutionary crimes*), [Peking], Cheng-chao-hsi chan-tou-tui, n.d. (preface dated 30 May 1967), pp. 38–40.
[2] *Mao Tse-tung Unrehearsed*, Text 8.

for discipline, spoke at greater length of the importance of democracy as a means to achieve the end of 'centralized unification'. His general theoretical discussion, quoted earlier, of the concept of democratic centralism, was followed by a denunciation in very concrete terms of those Party cadres who did not understand the importance of listening to the masses, and confused 'Party leadership' with their own leadership: 'Those of you...who do not allow people to speak, who think you are tigers, and that nobody will dare to touch your arse – whoever has this attitude, ten out of ten of you will fail. People will talk anyway. You think that nobody will really dare to touch the arse of tigers like you? They damn well will!'

By this time, Mao Tse-tung had very drastically revised the optimistic time scale for China's economic development symbolized by the slogan 'Overtake England in 15 years!' In January 1962, he declared:

In the 17th century, a number of European countries were already in the process of developing capitalism. It has taken over 300 years for capitalist productive forces to develop to their present pattern. Socialism is superior in many respects to capitalism, and the economic development of our country may be much faster than that of the capitalist countries. But China has a large population, our resources are meagre, and our economy backward, so that in my opinion it will be impossible to develop our productive power so rapidly as to catch up with and overtake the most advanced capitalist countries in less than one hundred years. If it requires only a few decades, for example only fifty years as some have conjectured, then that will be a splendid thing, for which heaven and earth be praised. But I would advise, comrades, that it is better to think more of the difficulties and so to envisage its taking a longer period. It took from three to four hundred years to build a great and mighty capitalist economy; what would be wrong with building a great and mighty socialist economy in our country in about fifty or a hundred years?[1]

If Mao had thus become more cautious as to the speed of socialist construction in China, he was still resolved that it should take place in accordance with the characteristic pattern which had emerged in the late 1950s. There is hardly any doubt that Liu Shao-ch'i came to differ sharply with Mao over many crucial questions of internal policy in the years 1962–5, but it is not easy to pinpoint these differ-

[1] *Ibid.*

71

ences with precision. Perhaps the best starting point is Mao Tse-tung's speech to the Tenth Plenum of the Central Committee in September 1962, which marks the explicit emergence of many of the themes which were to culminate in the Great Proletarian Cultural Revolution. On this occasion, Mao summed up the conclusions which had been reached in the course of nearly two months of informal discussions among the top leadership, first at the seaside resort of Peitaiho, and then in Peking, and which should, in his view, be embodied in the decisions of the formal Plenary Session about to begin. At Peitaiho, he recalled, he had raised three pro-blems: 'those of class, the situation, and contradictions'. He then proceeded to discuss all three both in the international and in the Chinese context. In the world as a whole, the problem of class had not been solved either in the imperialist countries or in many parts of Asia, Africa, and Latin America, where it was necessary to decide with whom to unite. As for conditions within China, Mao reiterated the view, which he had consistently expounded since 1956, that classes and class struggle persisted under socialism. He took, however, a somewhat more relaxed view of this phenomenon than he was to adopt a year or two later. While noting the 'possi-bility of the restoration of reactionary classes', and calling for an increase in vigilance and for the proper education both of young people and of cadres, without which a country such as China could 'still move toward its opposite', he added: 'Even to move toward its opposite would not matter too much because there would still be the negation of the negation...If our children's generation go in for revisionism and move towards their opposite, so that although they still nominally have socialism it is in fact capitalism, then our grandsons will certainly rise up in revolt and overthrow their fathers.' Nevertheless, he added that 'from now on we must talk about this [i.e. about the persistence of class struggle] every.year, every month, every day'.

Turning to the 'situation', first within China, Mao acknowledged once again that 'in 1959 and 1960 a number of things were done wrongly', because of lack of experience. The most serious faults were 'excessive requisitioning' of grain, and the issuance of 'blind commands' in both industry and agriculture. The rectification of these errors, though begun in October 1958, had really got under way in the second half of 1960, though progress had been impeded because 'our attention was diverted to opposing Khruschev'.

As for contradictions, as they emerged from the situation in general and the survival of hostile classes in particular, Mao declared that the primary one on the international scene was that between 'the people of the whole world and imperialism'. Internally, he declared in an apparently innocuous but in fact very weighty sentence: 'I think that right-wing opportunism in China should be renamed: it should be called Chinese revisionism.' In other words, the errors of those in the Party who opposed Mao's policies were in danger of accumulating to the point where they would make the qualitative leap from a socialist to a capitalist position, and become defenders of 'bourgeois ideas'. Mao's proposals for dealing with this problem were, for the moment, relatively moderate. The 'line of the Rectification Campaign of 1942–1945', with its emphasis on 'curing the sickness in order to save the patient', should, he said, be followed. In accordance with the principle, 'unity–criticism–unity', he promised to 'unite with you comrades who have made mistakes, provided that you recognize your errors and return to a Marxist stand-point', and he emphasized the need to avoid excessive severity in punishing even those who had conspired against the Party, provided they confessed their crimes. Finally, he emphasized that 'work and the class struggle should proceed simultaneously', with the first place going to work. 'We have to engage in the class struggle', he added, 'but there are special people to take care of this kind of work. The security departments are specially charged with carrying on the class struggle.'[1]

Out of the Tenth Plenum of September 1962, and of the ideas propounded there by Mao Tse-tung, there emerged the 'Socialist Education Campaign' which, in various guises, was to continue until, at the end of 1965, it merged into the opening phase of the Cultural Revolution. These events have been the subject of several monographic studies,[2] and I shall not therefore attempt to sum-

---

[1] *Mao Tse-tung Unrehearsed*, Text 9.

[2] The most important contributions are those of Richard Baum. See, in particular, his unpublished doctoral dissertation, 'Revolution and Reaction in Rural China: the "Struggle between Two Roads" during the Socialist Education Movement (1962–1966) and the Great Proletarian Cultural Revolution (1966–1968)' (University of California, Berkeley, 1970); also R. Baum and F. C. Teiwes, *Ssu-ch'ing: The Socialist*

marize the facts here even rather briefly. It is, however, indispensable to spell out very clearly the issues at stake in the controversies as to how this movement should be carried out, for it is almost certain that disagreement on this score was the most important single cause of the final break between Mao Tse-tung and Liu Shao-ch'i.

The overall policy context in the countryside, as contained in the 'Resolution on the Strengthening of the Collective Economy of the People's Communes and Expanding Agricultural Production',[1] was made up in large part of quotations and paraphrases from Mao's statements regarding these matters since his cooperativization speech of 1955. While stressing the basic importance of the collective economy in the countryside, this resolution, and the revised draft regulations regarding the organization of the people's communes adopted at the same time, confirmed the decision to make the production team the basic accounting unit (stipulating that there should be no change in this respect for at least thirty years), and laid it down that commune members were not only 'permitted' but 'encouraged' to cultivate private plots and to carry on other subsidiary domestic enterprises. It demanded the implementation of democratic centralism, quoting in this context the key passage from Mao's 7,000-cadres speech of the previous January, calling for more extensive democracy, in order to achieve the centralized leadership indispensable to building a socialist economy.

When this and the other documents of the 10th Plenum were translated into more concrete terms at the provincial and *hsien* level, the results frequently followed very closely the spirit and even the letter of Mao's speech of 24 September, though the emphasis varied from one local Party secretary to another.[2] In May 1963, after

Education Movement of 1962–1966 (Berkeley: Center for Chinese Studies, 1968), and R. Baum, 'Revolution and Reaction in the Chinese Countryside: The Socialist Education Movement in Cultural Revolutionary Perspective', *The China Quarterly*, 38 (April–June 1969), 92–119.

[1] This resolution was kept secret at the time; a copy was obtained in 1964 in the course of a Nationalist commando raid on Lien-chiang, in Fukien Province, and is translated in C. S. Chen (ed.), *Rural People's Communes in Lien-chiang*. Documents Concerning Communes in Lien-chiang County, Fukien Province, 1962–1963 (Stanford, Calif., Hoover Institution Press, 1969), pp. 81–9.

[2] For example, a report of late 1962 on the implementation of the resolution 'On Strengthening the Collective Economy' considers the problems involved under the same three headings used by Mao in his speech of 24 September, though in a slightly

half a year of experimentation, the way in which the 'education' of the masses and of the cadres for which Mao had called in September should be carried out was stipulated for the first time in a draft directive, the so-called 'Early Ten Points'. It is generally accepted that this document was composed by Mao Tse-tung, or under his direct supervision, and that it reflected his views.[1]

The directive began with a passage, later officially published as a philosophical essay under the title 'Where do Correct Ideas Come From?' summarizing Mao's theory of knowledge.[2] The concrete instructions to basic-level cadres contained in the directive were relatively narrow in focus; the 'Socialist Education Movement' in the countryside was to take the form of the 'Four Clean-ups', i.e. of a checkup on the handling of accounts, warehouses, properties and work-points in the course of the past year. The aim, however, was much wider: to detect, in this way, the misdeeds of elements from hostile classes (including not only former landlords and rich peasants, and the 'old bourgeoisie' in general, but 'new bourgeois elements who have become rich by speculation'), and to mobilize the masses for a 'socialist revolutionary struggle that will deal a smashing blow to the frenzied attack of the capitalists'. Hence the long introduction setting forth Mao's ideas, as expounded at the Central Committee meetings of August and September 1962, regarding the persistence of classes and of class struggle under socialism. In February 1963, at another gathering of the Central Committee, Mao was reported to have drawn the moral, in a lapidary and characteristic sentence: 'Once class struggle is grasped, miracles are possible.'

The first step in this campaign was 'to set the masses in motion', and the directive likewise provided for setting up 'poor and lower-middle peasant associations' for 'assisting and overseeing' the work of the commune and brigade administrative committees. The importance of cadre participation in productive labour was once more

different order: the situation, classes, and contradictions (*ibid.* pp. 90–110). It places strong emphasis on 'centralization' as the most important aspect of democratic centralism – but this is compatible with Mao's own presentation at the 7,000-cadres meeting. *Hsien*-level documents of January and February 1963 stress class struggle more heavily, and translate it already into the struggle between the 'two lines' of socialism and capitalism (*ibid.* pp. 149–53, 199–208).

[1] For the text, see Baum and Teiwes, *Ssu-ch'ing*, pp. 58–71.
[2] *Selected Readings*, pp. 405–6.

proclaimed, and Mao expressed the hope that one-third of all rural Party cadres could participate in this in the course of the first year. At the same time, the importance of leadership was clearly recognized. The poor and lower-middle peasant associations should 'not be allowed to take over the day-to-day affairs of the commune and brigade', and the ultimate aim was to unite 'more than 95 percent of the cadres for the struggle against the class enemy and nature'.

The movement as a whole was thus a characteristic Maoist effort to educate both cadres and masses through participation in struggle, as well as through study. The aims were summed up at the end of the directive in a long quotation from Mao himself. Negatively, it would prevent China's 'Marxist–Leninist Party' from turning into a 'revisionist party or a fascist party'. Positively, it would produce cadres who were red as well as expert, and who were therefore 'no longer bureaucrats and overlords, no longer divorced from the masses', but rather 'truly good cadres supported by the masses'. When the movement was completed, there would 'emerge throughout the nation a new climate for progress into greater prosperity'.[1]

The phases in this movement between the spring of 1963 and the beginning of 1965 have been dealt with extensively elsewhere. I shall therefore limit myself to a few comments on the ideological formulations contained in the so-called 'Later Ten Points' of September 1963, and 'Revised Later Ten Points' of September 1964, and their possible relevance to the sharpening conflict between Mao and the Party bureaucracy. This document, in its two successive guises, was entitled 'Some Concrete Policy Formulations of the Central Committee of the Chinese Communist Party in the Rural Socialist Education Movement'. It was put forward ostensibly as a complement to rather than a replacement of Mao's own directive of May 1963, intended merely to spell out in more detail how the movement should be carried out. While some such explanations would probably have been useful to basic-level cadres, there is no doubt that the 'Later Ten Points' in fact departed considerably from the spirit of the earlier directive.

The crucial issue is precisely the one which I have stressed throughout this introduction as distinguishing Liu Shao-ch'i's

---

[1] All quotations from the May 1963 directive are from Baum and Teiwes, *Ssu-ch'ing*, pp. 58–71, *passim*.

outlook from Mao's: the need for the cadres to keep things under control. While paying lip-service to the need to 'mobilize the masses', and recognizing that the Socialist Education Movement was 'a large-scale mass movement even more complicated than land reform', which would result in 'a very sharp struggle', the September 1963 directive called for the organization, at higher levels of the Party, of 'work teams' which would be sent to guide the movement at the grass roots. To be sure, these teams were to carry out their task by 'relying on the basic organizations and basic cadres', serving as the 'staff' of the latter, and 'enlightening' them, rather than thrusting them aside and doing the work in their place. It was laid down, however, that with the consent of the *hsien* Party committee local leadership could be ousted in communes and brigades controlled by 'landlords, rich peasants, counter-revolutionaries, and undesirable elements', or by 'degenerates', and replaced by the work teams. Moreoever, there was implied in the work team concept a degree of tutelage over basic-level cadres. The philosophy which informed the whole directive was summed up in the remark, 'to consolidate over 95 per cent of the cadres is a prerequisite to the consolidation of over 95 per cent of the masses'. In other words, the success of our revolutionary work depends in essence on the quality of the Party organization. This corresponds to Stalin's view, epitomized in the slogan, 'Cadres decide everything.' It does not correspond to Mao's view, though he has on occasion used the same slogan as Stalin. This emphasis was carried through in the paragraph of the September 1963 directive dealing with Party rectification, which stipulated that the process should be carried out essentially within the Party, though at the end 'active elements' from the poor and lower-middle peasants should be asked to participate in criticism and self-criticism sessions.[1]

The 'Later Ten Points' of September 1963 appear to have been drafted by the Party's Secretary General, Teng Hsiao-p'ing. It was on the basis of this directive that the Socialist Education Campaign got under way on an even larger scale during the winter of 1963-4.[2] The first half of 1964 was, in fact, marked by a whole series of

[1] For the text of this directive, see Baum and Teiwes, *Ssu-ch'ing*, pp. 72-94.

[2] The Socialist Education Campaign, called *ssu-ch'ing* or 'four clean-ups' in the countryside, was known as the *wu-fan* or 'five antis' in the cities. In contrast to the

extremely important developments, of which the outside world was only partially aware at the time, affecting both the temper of Chinese society and Mao Tse-tung's role in shaping events. These included the campaign to 'learn from the People's Liberation Army', the 'Spring Forum on Education' convened by Mao in February 1964, Chiang Ch'ing's efforts to reform Peking Opera, and the campaign, in the summer of 1964, for 'bringing up successors' to the revolutionary cause. In this context, Liu Shao-ch'i personally took a hand in reorienting the Socialist Education Movement. His 'Revised Later Ten Points' of September 1964 appear at first glance to be more revolutionary and less bureaucratic in spirit than the directive issued a year earlier. There are repeated exhortations to 'boldly mobilize the masses', and the priority of consolidating over 95 per cent of the cadres is even stood on its head: 'To consolidate over 95 per cent of the rural cadres', the directive states, 'we must first consolidate over 95 per cent of the peasants.'[1] The essential content of the movement is stated to be 'the reform of the Party's basic-level organizations'. Whereas work teams were specifically warned against replacing local cadres in the directive of September 1963, the revised draft took a very pessimistic view of the integrity and political awareness of cadres at the grass roots, and therefore decreed: 'The whole movement should be led by the work team.'[2]

This approach was subsequently characterized by Mao and his supporters as 'hitting at the many in order to protect the few' – in other words, as blaming everything on the lower-level cadres in order to distract attention from the far worse bureaucratic vices of those at the top.[3] Liu's view of the situation in the countryside had been substantially influenced by the experience of his wife, Wang Kuang-mei, who had gone, in accordance with the policy of 'squatting at a point' by higher-level cadres, to observe conditions for

urban campaign of the same name in the 1950's, this movement is relatively little known, and has been the subject of far less research than the rural *ssu-ch'ing*. The reason lies, perhaps, in the fact that it had difficulty making headway in the immediate shadow of the top Party bureaucracy, so that there is really little to be said about it.

[1] This did not prevent the Red Guards, at a time when everything was being blamed on the symbolic figure of Liu Shao-ch'i, from attributing Teng's formulation to him. See *Liu Shao-ch'i tui-k'ang Mao* . . ., pp. 3, 4; *Kuan-yü Liu Shao-ch'i* . . ., p. 32.

[2] For the text of this directive, see Baum and Teiwes, *Ssu-ch'ing*, pp. 102–17.

[3] See, for example, 'Struggle between the Two Roads in China's Countryside', translated in *Peking Review*, 49 (1967), 11–19.

herself in the 'Peach Garden' Brigade in Hopei Province. Her verdict to the effect that the 'four uncleans' existed 'universally' among the basic-level cadres, all of whom, 'big or small', 'have problems and cannot be trusted' led to a sharp intensification of the rural struggle which ultimately resulted in the dismissal of from $1\frac{1}{4}$ to $2\frac{1}{2}$ million basic-level cadres.[1]

It is difficult to state definitely whether Liu Shao-ch'i was concerned primarily to 'protect the handful' (including himself), or whether he was rather seeking a compromise between Mao's insistence on class struggle and the maintenance of what he regarded as an acceptable degree of centralized control. No doubt, for him, the two goals were inseparable. His desire for a compromise is symbolized by his reported habit of lumping together Mao's directive of May 1963 and his own 'Revised Later Ten Points' of September 1964, and calling them the 'Double Ten Points' (*shuang shih-t'iao*).[2] Whatever Liu's intentions at this time, Mao Tse-tung had clearly come to the conclusion that no further compromise was possible. He therefore put forward his own new 23-point directive, explicitly repudiating a number of the views advanced by Liu Shao-ch'i, and specifying that henceforth the spearhead of the movement should be directed against 'those people in authority within the Party who are taking the capitalist road'. But before considering this document and the struggle regarding its adoption, it is necessary to review some of the other developments which had taken place during 1964.

The activities in which Mao was involved at this time, enumerated above, may appear at first glance somewhat disparate, but they are in fact all closely tied together and related to a single overriding concern: to ensure that the 'superstructure' of Chinese society, and especially the quality of the human beings composing it, did not lag behind the economic basis, and ultimately drag the latter, as Mao had suggested in May 1963, back toward 'capitalism', or even 'fascism'. 'To look at things and not people', Mao was quoted as saying early in 1963, 'is to do an ineffective job.'[3] In a sense, this

---

[1] Baum, 'Revolution and Reaction', pp. 110–42, *passim*.

[2] *Liu Shao-ch'i ts'ai-liao hui-pien*, p. 41. This is, of course, described as a plot aimed at replacing, in the long run, Mao's directive with his own. As already indicated, the two directives were in any case supposed to complement one another. We now know that Mao himself used the expression 'Double Ten Points' in 1963–4.

[3] Baum and Teiwes, *Ssu-ch'ing*, p. 52.

STUART R. SCHRAM

statement sums up his entire philosophy, and the difference in outlook which separates him from the Party bureaucracy.

The 'Spring Forum on Education', the reform of the Peking
Opera, and the campaign for training successors were all obviously
and directly connected with this aim of re-shaping the attitudes and
outlook of human beings. The 'Learn from the PLA' campaign,
formally launched in February 1964, reflected other concerns as well,
including Mao's desire to strengthen his position in the showdown
with other Party leaders by increasing the role in society of an organization which had been turned by Lin Piao into a bastion of his influence. This is particularly evident in view of the fact that the movement involved the setting up, in industrial enterprises, schools, and
other types of unit, of 'political departments' which were not only
patterned on that of the army, but were commonly staffed by PLA
personnel. And yet, as Mao's directive endorsing these developments
made plain, they were concerned not only with political control,
but with matters of ideology and attitude:

The whole country is now learning from the Liberation Army...and
schools must learn from the PLA too. The Liberation Army is good
because it is good in political ideology...

There are now people in all sectors of state industry advocating that
all levels from the highest to the lowest (i.e. from the ministries to the
factories and mines) should learn from the Liberation Army, set up
political departments...and political instructors, and carry out the 'four
firsts' and the 'three-eight work style'. It appears that unless this is done,
it is impossible to rouse the revolutionary spirit of the millions of cadres
and workers...[1]

Thus the political vocabulary of the PLA, as it had been fixed in
the autumn of 1960 under Mao's direct guidance, entered the common parlance of the Chinese people as a whole, in which it continued
to flourish prominently until the fall of Lin Piao in 1971. Why Mao
regarded the PLA as the ideological mentor of society, as well as the
link between this idea and his educational philosophy in general, he
stated forcefully in a conversation of July 1964 with his nephew, Mao
Yüan-hsin, a student at the Harbin Military Engineering Institute:

The whole country is engaged in learning from the People's Liberation
Army on a vast scale. You are members of the PLA; why aren't you

[1] *CB*, no. 891, p. 48.

learning from it? Does the Institute have a political department? What is it doing?...(Mao Yüan-hsin explains the way political training is carried out at the Institute.) All this is nothing but attending classes and discussing things, what is the use of it? You should go and study reality...

The most fundamental defect of your Institute is that you have not applied the 'four firsts'....How much can you learn merely by relying on listening to lectures? The most important thing is to go and learn from practice. (Comrade Mao Yüan-hsin said: 'A faculty of science and engineering and a faculty of letters are different; [the former] doesn't provide for so much time to go and enter into contact with society.') That is wrong; the class struggle is your most important subject, and it is a compulsory subject...[You] should go down to the countryside to carry out the 'four clean-ups'...also...to a factory and spend half a year carrying out the 'five antis'...If you don't carry out the four clean-ups, you won't understand the peasants, and if you don't carry out the five antis, you won't understand the workers. Only when you have completed such a course of political training can I consider you a university graduate ...If you don't even know about the class struggle, how can you be regarded as a university graduate?[1]

At about this time, in the spring of 1964, Mao Tse-tung put forward five requirements for 'worthy successors to the revolutionary cause of the proletariat', which were first published in mid-July in the editorial entitled 'On Khrushchev's Phoney Communism and its Historical Lessons for the World'.[2] Such successors must be 'genuine Marxist-Leninists and not revisionists'; they must be 'revolutionaries who wholeheartedly serve the majority of the people of China and the whole world'; they must be 'proletarian statesmen capable of uniting and working together with the overwhelming majority'; they must be 'models in applying the Party's democratic centralism', and must master the 'mass line' method of leadership; they must be 'modest and prudent and guard against arrogance and impetuosity'. Commenting on these five criteria, Mao said to his nephew: 'These five requirements are linked to one another. The first is theory, or also orientation; the second is the aim – i.e., when you come right down to it, whom do you serve; this is the most important. When you have mastered this condition, you can do

[1] *Mao Tse-tung Unrehearsed*, Text 15.
[2] *Peking Review*, 29 (1964), 7–27. (The 'five requirements' quoted below appear on pp. 26–7).

anything. The third, fourth and fifth conditions relate to questions of methodology.'

If, for Mao, educated young people had even greater need for a correct ideological outlook, and above all for a correct class stand, than youth as a whole, this was because of the perverse effects of book learning. His approach to education in the narrow sense remained what it had been in 1958. Teaching should be primarily by discussion and independent work, rather than by 'inculcation', which even bourgeois educators had rejected at the time of the May 4th Movement. It is because the teachers 'can do nothing without their lecture notes', and are afraid of discussion because they may be asked questions they cannot answer, that the problem of educational reform is, as he told Mao Yüan-hsin, 'primarily a problem of teachers'. Both in this talk, and in his remarks at the spring festival on education in February 1964, Mao stressed once again, as he had at Chengtu in 1958, that those who had come first in the imperial examinations were often of little account. 'Only two of the emperors of the Ming dynasty did well', he declared, 'T'ai-tsu and Ch'eng-tsu. One was illiterate and the other only knew a few characters. Yet afterwards in the Chia-ch'ing reign when the intellectuals had power, things were in a bad state. . .to read too many books is harmful.' As for Marxist books, one should read them, but 'not too many either. It will be enough to read a dozen or so. If we read too many we can move towards our opposites, become bookworms, dogmatists, revisionists.'[1]

One can hear in these statements clear echoes of Mao's conflict, thirty years earlier, with those in the Chinese Communist Party who thought that they would make 'good emperors' because they had read many Marxist books. Mao's views on education reflect, however, not so much his own personal experience as his analysis of the needs of Chinese society. In the bleak days of 1961, he reaffirmed, in a letter to the Kiangsi Communist Labour University, his faith in the pattern of part-work part-study which he had promoted at the time of the Great Leap. Such schools, he emphasized, do not cost the state a cent; he hoped the example of Kiangsi would be more widely emulated.[2] Shortening the period of study and combining education with productive labour appealed to him on the

---

[1] *Mao Tse-tung Unrehearsed*, Text 10.   [2] *CB*, no. 891, p. 36.

triple grounds that it would be better for the health of the students, save money and inject young people more rapidly into the productive process, and prevent them from becoming divorced from reality and taking on the airs of scholars.

These views were clearly not embodied in the educational system prevailing in China in the early 1960s.[1] This fact, like so many others of this period, is not easy to evaluate, for Mao had explicitly welcomed, in January 1962 at the 7,000-cadres conference, the imminent issuance of the directives of 1963 on which the system now stigmatized as revisionist was based. Moreover, Liu Shao-ch'i had enthusiastically hailed on a number of occasions the advantages of part-work part-study schools. It does seem, however, that he saw these as a cheap form of education for the average child, full-time schools being reserved for the specially gifted (or the specially privileged), whereas Mao wanted to make this the mainstream of the Chinese educational system.[2]

Such were some of the issues outstanding between Mao and the Party leadership at the end of 1964. The decisive moment came when Mao presented for adoption his new and radical directive for the conduct of the Socialist Education Campaign. In December 1964, Liu Shao-ch'i had proposed at a meeting of the Supreme State Conference (of which he had been Chairman since he succeeded Mao in 1959 as Head of State) that his own Revised Later Ten Points be officially adopted and openly published.[3] In a report regarding the Socialist Education Movement presented in late 1964 before members of the Central Committee and of the Peking Party organization, he is reported to have said that the aim of the 'four clean-ups' was to solve the contradiction between the 'four cleans' and the 'four uncleans', as well as 'the overlapping of contradictions within and without the Party, and the overlapping of contradictions between the enemy and ourselves, and contradictions among

[1] For a general survey of the problem, see John Gardner, 'Educated Youth and Urban-Rural Equalities, 1958–66', J. W. Lewis, ed., *The City in Communist China* (Stanford, Stanford University Press, 1971), pp. 235–86. For a translation of the directives on secondary education in force in the years 1963–6, and a perceptive analysis of its consequences in practice, see the article by Susan Shirk in *The China Quarterly*, 55 (July–September 1973).

[2] See, for example, *Chiao-hsüeh p'i-p'an*, no. 1 (Peking, Pei-ching kung-yeh ta-hsüeh tung-fang-hung kung-she, July 1967), pp. 32–4.

[3] *Kuan-yü Liu Shao ch'i...*, p. 32; *Liu Shao-ch'i fan-ko-ming tsui-o shih*, p. 48.

the people'.[1] Mao's new directive specifically stated that these formulations of Liu's 'do not refer to what society the contradiction between the "four cleans" and "four uncleans" arises in', 'could be applied to any historical period', and were therefore 'not Marxist–Leninist methods of looking at things'. The only correct way of defining the movement was, in his opinion, as 'the contradiction between socialism and capitalism'. In other words, as he had hinted in his speech to the Tenth Plenum more than two years earlier, those within the Party who adopted wrong attitudes were in fact taking a stand on the side of the bourgeoisie. The key point of the movement was to rectify such 'people in positions of authority within the Party who take the capitalist road', who were to be found at all levels from the grass roots up to the Central Committee. As to methods, the Party must 'boldly unleash the masses'. Repeating a metaphor he had already employed in his cooperativization speech of 1955 – likewise devoted to a denunciation of bureaucratic cadres within the Party who lagged behind the masses – he declared: 'we must not be like women with bound feet'. As for the replacement of seriously erring cadres, 'authority must be seized, first by struggle' – by implication, from below. 'Cadres', the directive also stated, 'must be supervised both from above and from below. The most important supervision is that which comes from the masses.' Finally, in what appears as a parting shot against Liu (who had said that the masses would work hard only if there were appropriate rules), the directive stated: 'To spend one's time...compiling great quantities of rules and regulations is scholasticism.'[2]

It is not surprising that Liu Shao-ch'i should have refused to give his willing approval to such a document, which not only weakened Party control over the Socialist Education Movement to a degree he could only regard as dangerous, but at the same time broadened the scope of the movement immeasurably by re-defining the 'four cleans' no longer in terms of honest accounting and respect for collective property, but as 'clean politics, clean economics, clean organization, and clean ideology'. This definition – which was to be applied in the cities as well as in the countryside – amounted in fact to an invitation

[1] *Liu Shao-ch'i tui-k'ang Mao...*, p. 25.
[2] For the text of Mao's 23-article directive, see Baum and Teiwes, *Ssu-ch'ing*, pp. 118–26.

to attack anyone at any time for what was perceived as an incorrect political orientation. Thus, although in a formal sense the Socialist Education Movement and the Great Proletarian Cultural Revolution are, as Richard Baum has made clear, entirely separate, the latter having superseded the former,[1] the 23-article directive contained in effect the germs of much that came after. It is no doubt in this sense that Mao Tse-tung called the document he 'put before the Politburo' in January 1965, and which Liu 'strenuously opposed' a 'programme for the coming cultural revolution'.[2]

III. THE CULTURAL REVOLUTION AND AFTER

The Cultural Revolution, as everyone now recognizes, was both a struggle for power and a confrontation as to which road the Chinese revolution should follow. The course of Mao's struggle against Liu Shao-ch'i and the Party bureaucracy in the years 1965–9, and of its epilogue leading to the fall of Lin Piao and of the 'ultra-leftists' headed by Ch'en Po-ta, is obviously not without its implications for the deeper changes which were in progress simultaneously. On the other hand, these events are of such complexity that it would be futile to attempt to summarize even the essential facts here. Fortunately, although it is as yet too early for a definitive history of the Cultural Revolution, the principal episodes have been chronicled in immense detail, day by day and even hour by hour.[3] For my part, I shall therefore limit myself, in seeking to provide a chronological framework for the discussion of the movement's impact on the life of the Chinese people, to a survey of the evolution of Mao Tse-tung's thinking about some aspects of the pattern he was striving to create.

Mao's aim, clearly, was twofold: to change the structure of power in society, and to carry out an irreversible transformation in the patterns of thought and behaviour of the Chinese people. The second point is intimately related to the first, since Mao's attempt to limit the dependence of the masses on the Party elite implies that the

[1] Baum, article cited, *The China Quarterly*, 38 (April–June 1969).
[2] Snow, *The Long Revolution*, p. 17; see also p. 84.
[3] Two recent Mao-centred overall accounts are those of Stanley Karnow, *Mao and China: from Revolution to Revolution* (New York, Viking Press, 1972), and Edward Rice, *Mao's Way* (Berkeley, University of California Press, 1972).

masses will be prepared to act with initiative – in other words, that they will have undergone a cultural revolution in the narrow sense. This second dimension of the problem is the more important in Mao's eyes, for progress here is the only guarantee that any changes in the political system will be lasting ones, and that the leaders will not relapse into bureaucracy, and the led into passivity. Changes in attitudes and behaviour are also, however, the most difficult to define, and only become perceptible over time. The chapters in this book (with the exception of Jack Gray's historical survey of the emergence of the two lines) have all endeavoured to come to grips with this aspect of reality, and I shall return to it by way of conclusion, in the light of their findings. But first it is necessary to look briefly at Mao's attempts to change the system, which provide the context for his attempt to 'change men's souls'.

The crucial problem here is that of the leading role of the Party – or, more broadly still, of the acceptance of leadership as a specialized function which should properly be exercised by a limited group of people on a relatively long-term basis. Leadership, and especially Party leadership, has been increasingly reasserting itself in China. To what extent does this correspond to Mao's original long-term strategic plan in launching the Cultural Revolution, and to what extent does it represent a compromise with reality? A review of the positions successively adopted by Mao on these issues will perhaps provide the basis for an answer.

In July 1966, on the eve of the first great outbreak of Red Guard violence directed against Party cadres, Mao declared: 'To use the excuse of distinguishing between "inner [Party]" and "outer [Party]" is to fear revolution.'[1] That is to say, Party members should not regard themselves as qualitatively different from the masses and superior to the masses. When Mao then proceeded to give tacit approval to the big-character posters penned by Red Guards at Tsinghua University Middle School, in which the slogan (coined by Mao himself in 1939) 'to rebel is justified' was used, in effect, to signify that authority existed only in the eye of the beholder, it appeared that he was not merely re-defining the content of 'demo-

[1] 'Talk to Leaders of the Centre', 21 July 1966, *Mao Tse-tung Unrehearsed*, Text 16.

cratic centralism', but abandoning Leninist organizational principles altogether.[1]

Those who arrived at this conclusion – some of them with enthusiasm, others with consternation, still others (myself included) with perplexity – were, we now know, committing the most natural, but at the same time, the most inexcusable, error into which one can possibly fall in interpreting Mao's thinking: taking at face value the one-sided actions or statements into which he is constantly led by his passionate and impulsive temperament, and forgetting that somewhere in the background there is surely lurking an antithesis which will bring the picture into focus again. In fact, even before Mao gave the Red Guards his blessing at the time of the Eleventh Plenum, he had written to the authors of the Tsinghua University Middle School posters making plain the limits to his endorsement of rebellion. Replying to a letter transmitting these texts to him, he subtly transmuted the slogan 'to rebel is justified' to read: 'It is right to rebel against reactionaries.'[2] In other words, rebellion is *not* justified merely as a form of self-expression, directed against anyone and everyone in authority; it is legitimate only when it serves politically correct ends.

For the moment, Mao did not make public his reservations about the open-ended rebellion of the Red Guards, because he hoped, as everyone knows, to channel their energies into breaking the grip of the Party bureaucracy. 'To oppose', Mao said on 21 July 1966 in a talk to the leaders of the Centre, 'especially to oppose "authoritative" bourgeois ideology, is to destroy. Without this destruction, socialism cannot be established, nor can we carry out first struggle, second criticism, third transformation.'[3] By October 1966, however, he was obliged to recognize that, in calling forth the Red Guard movement, he had not realized how shattering its impact might be. 'Since it was I who caused the havoc', he said, 'it is understandable if you have some bitter words for me.'[4] He also began to stress the

---

[1] For the texts of these Red Guard posters, see *Peking Review*, 37 (1966), 2–21. For Mao's original statement, in 1939, that 'to rebel is justified' (then attributed to Stalin), see *The Political Thought of Mao Tse-tung*, pp. 427–8.

[2] Letter of 1 August 1966, *Mao Tse-tung Unrehearsed*, Text 18.

[3] *Ibid*. Text 16.

[4] 'Talk at the Central Work Conference', 25 October 1966, *Mao Tse-tung Unrehearsed*, Text 21.

way in which Party cadres should learn from the Red Guards and correct their work style, rather than the role of the Red Guards themselves. After all, he said, you have had only five months' experience of the Cultural Revolution, as compared to twenty-eight years of the democratic revolution and seventeen years of the socialist revolution – no wonder if you have still not thoroughly understood everything:

That which you never dreamed of has come to pass. What's come has come. I think there are advantages in being assailed. For so many years you had not thought about such things, but as soon as they burst upon you, you began to think. Undoubtedly you have made some mistakes. . . but they can be corrected, and that will be that! Whoever wants to overthrow you? I don't, and I don't think the Red Guards do either. . .

You find it difficult to cross this pass, and I don't find it easy either. You are anxious and so am I. I cannot blame you, comrades, time has been so short. Some comrades say that they did not intentionally make mistakes, but did it because they were confused. This is pardonable. Nor can we put all the blame on Comrade Shao-ch'i and Comrade Hsiao-p'ing. They have some responsibility, but so has the centre.[1]

This was said, as the penultimate sentence indicates, at a time when Mao had not yet openly singled out 'China's Khrushchev' as the main culprit to be attacked. In this context, the promise that his listeners would not be overthrown could have been partly a tactical manoeuvre, aimed at calming their anxieties and disarming the opposition. In any case, despite Mao's soothing remark about the intentions of the Red Guards, it is evident that many of them were bent precisely on destroying Party authority as such. Other elements within the Party itself, while not proposing to abolish their own role, did look toward a radical re-structuring of the entire Chinese polity, along the lines which they felt to be indicated by the reference to the Paris Commune in the Decision of the Eleventh Plenum concerning the Great Proletarian Cultural Revolution.[2]

The letter of the August 1966 Decision ruled out, in fact, any such interpretation. The 'system of general elections like that of the Paris Commune', including the right of recall, was to apply only to the 'cultural revolutionary groups, committees and congresses'

[1] *Ibid.*
[2] For the text, see *Peking Review*, 33 (1966), 6–11.

which had sprung up in recent months. These were described as 'excellent new forms of organization whereby under the leadership of the Communist Party the masses are educating themselves', and as an 'excellent bridge to keep our Party in close contact with the masses'. Both here, and in the directive as a whole, the axiom of Party predominance was clearly reaffirmed; for example, it was laid down that criticism of anyone by name in the press should be decided 'after discussion by the Party committee at the same level, and in some cases submitted to the Party committee at a higher level for approval'. In his speech at the closing session of the August Plenum, Mao had hailed the fact that 'our decisions are welcomed by the masses', and that 'the broad masses of students and revolutionary teachers support us and resist the policies of the past'. The decision concerning the Cultural Revolution, he declared, 'was based on their resistance to past policies'. But at the same time he added quite clearly, 'whether this decision can be implemented will ultimately depend on the action of leaders at all levels, including those present today and those who are not'. He also stated that 'adjustments in the full and alternate membership of the Politburo, in the Secretariat and in the membership of the Standing Committee' guaranteed that this time (as contrasted, perhaps, with the Tenth Plenum) the decisions of the Central Committee would be carried out.[1] In other words, leadership of the movement he had launched rested with the Party, and ultimately with the Party summit.

Though such was the initial design, the direction in which events had moved during the last four months of 1966, and Mao's tacit encouragement to the action of the Red Guards in taking things into their own hands, led many people, both in China and outside, to conclude by early 1967 that for Mao, the Leninist letter of the August directive was less important than the spirit which informed it. Even today, the evidence as to his real intentions, prior to February 1967, is contradictory and difficult to decipher. He was unquestionably resolved to break the power of a certain number of Party leaders in positions of authority, and he was quite prepared to accept the temporary paralysis of some Party organs as the price of such a

---

[1] 'Speech at the Closing Ceremony of the 11th Plenum of the 8th Central Committee' *Mao Tse-tung Unrehearsed*, Text 19.

victory. Thus, in late August 1966, he said: 'I am firmly persuaded that a few months of confusion (*luan*) will be mostly for the good... Even if there are no provincial Party committees, it doesn't matter; aren't there still district and *hsien* committees?'[1]

Here the pre-eminence of the Party organization is implicitly re-affirmed, even though it is recognized that portions of it may be, for the moment, unable to function. The picture changed, however, in the critical weeks preceding Mao's call of January 1967 to 'Seize power!' which amounted in fact to a declaration of war on the Party bureaucracy as a whole, as well as on its chiefs Liu Shao-ch'i and Teng Hsiao-p'ing. The Central Committee directive of 15 December 1966 on the Cultural Revolution in the rural areas proclaimed that the 'authoritative organs' leading the movement would be democratically-elected 'cultural revolution committees of poor and lower-middle peasants', and made no reference to the subordination of these bodies to the Party.[2] Despite this omission, the directive could have been taken as a characteristic Maoist effort aimed at tempering the Party by challenging it from below. It had, to some extent, been foreshadowed by Mao's directive of January 1965 regarding the Socialist Education Movement, which stipulated that in places where basic-level Party organizations had 'atrophied or become paralyzed', it would be proper, until a 'new leadership nucleus' had been formed, to implement the policy of 'all power to the poor and lower-middle peasants' associations'.[3]

Events in early January 1967 suggested that Mao might be moving in a far more radical direction. A New Year's Day editorial called for the establishment of 'extensive democracy' (*ta min-chu*) as the 'best way for the masses to educate and liberate themselves'. At the same time, Mao's 1957 statement that democracy is 'only a means' was quoted once again, the end being given as the consolidation of the dictatorship of the proletariat.[4] On 4 January, the conflict between

[1] *CB*, no. 891, p. 68. (Translation slightly revised after comparison with Chinese text.)

[2] *CCP Documents of the Great Proletarian Cultural Revolution 1966–1967* (Hong Kong, Union Research Institute, 1968), pp. 137–42; see also the analysis of R. Baum, 'Elite Behaviour under Conditions of Stress', in Robert A. Scalopino (ed.), *Elites in the People's Republic of China* (Seattle, University of Washington Press, 1972), esp. pp. 561–2.

[3] Baum and Teiwes, *Ssu-ch'ing*, pp. 124–5.

[4] 'Carry the Great Proletarian Cultural Revolution through to the End.' *Jen-min jih-pao* and *Hung-ch'i* joint editorial published on 1 January 1967; translated in *Peking Review*, 1 (1967), 8–15.

the established Party authorities in Shanghai and the Maoists, which had been escalating for more than a month, finally erupted in a 'seizure of power' by a coalition of radical organizations led by the Workers' Revolutionary Rebel General Headquarters. The leading Shanghai newspaper *Wen-hui pao*, which had been taken over by the insurgents, published next day a 'Message to All Shanghai People' presenting their action as an initial victory in the 'general attack on the handful of persons within the Party who are in authority and are taking the capitalist road' predicted in the New Year's Day editorial.[1] At a meeting of the Central Cultural Revolution Group on 9 January, Mao reacted with enthusiasm. The *People's Daily*, he said, should reprint the Shanghai 'Message' – as was in fact done that very day – and the radio stations should broadcast it. 'Internal rebellions are fine', he continued. 'This is one class overthrowing another. This is a great revolution.' After stressing the importance of newspapers as moulders of public opinion, the question being 'by whom they are brought out', Mao made a series of remarks which appeared to reflect unstinting support for rebellion from below:

There are many things which the Propaganda Department and the Ministry of Culture were unable to cope with. Even you (pointing to Comrade Ch'en Po-ta) and I could not cope with them. But when the Red Guards came they were immediately brought under control.

The upsurge of revolutionary power in Shanghai has brought hope to the whole country. It cannot fail to influence the whole of East China and all provinces and cities in the country...

We must speak of grasping revolution and promoting production. We must not make revolution in isolation from production. The conservative faction do not grasp production. This is a class struggle.

You must not believe that 'When Chang the Butcher is dead, we'll have to eat pork bristles and all,' or that we can do nothing without them. Don't believe that sort of rubbish.[2]

The earthy proverb quoted in the last paragraph implied a sweeping rejection of the notion that experts – whether it be technical specialists expert in production, or Party cadres expert in running the administration – were indispensable to the efficient functioning of the country. On 11 January, an official message of greetings

[1] *Peking Review*, 3 (1967), 5–7.
[2] *Mao Tse-tung Unrehearsed*, Text 22.

was sent to the Shanghai Workers' Revolutionary Rebel General Headquarters in the name of the Central Committee hailing the achievement of this body in bringing about 'a great alliance of the proletarian revolutionary organizations', and declaring that it had taken firmly into its hands 'the destiny of the proletarian dictatorship'. 'Party, Government, Army and civilian circles' – including workers, peasants, revolutionary students, and revolutionary cadres – throughout the country were called upon to 'learn from the experience of the revolutionary rebel groups in Shanghai'.[1] The issue of *Hung ch'i* published on 16 January contained an authoritative article characterizing the 'great revolution in Shanghai' as the 'embodiment of the leading role and initiative of the working class', of their 'sense of revolutionary organization and discipline', which had enabled them to 'develop extensive democracy', and at the same time to strengthen the dictatorship of the proletariat. For the first time, the call was put forward: 'Resolutely seize power from the handful of people within the Party who are in authority and are taking the capitalist road!'[2]

And yet, even as the Shanghai model was being thus held up for emulation, on Mao's personal instructions, a power seizure of a distinctly different type was under way in Shansi Province, where on 12 January a Revolutionary Committee was set up on the basis of a 'three-way alliance' of 'revolutionary masses', PLA representatives, and Party and state cadres. In this instance, 'The People's Liberation Army units...unequivocally and wholeheartedly backed the proletarian revolutionary rebels in the crucial moment of their seizure of power.'[3] Thus the backbone of the new organ of power was provided not by the 'sense of organization' of the workers, but by the army.

These events were announced only on 25 January. Meanwhile, Mao Tse-tung had written on 21 January to Lin Piao cancelling his

[1] Translated in *Peking Review*, 4 (1967), 5, followed by a number of other documents issued about the same time by the Shanghai rebels, including (pp. 7–9) their 'Urgent Notice' of 9 January. On the situation in Shanghai at this time, see especially Neale Hunter, *Shanghai Journal: An Eyewitness Account of the Cultural Revolution* (New York, Praeger, 1969).

[2] 'Proletarian Revolutionaries, Unite!', translated in *Peking Review*, 4 (1967), 15–17.

[3] *Jen-min jih-pao* editorial of 25 January 1967, translated in *Peking Review*, 6 (1967), 19. See also Karnow, *Mao and China*, pp. 288–9.

previous instructions to the effect that the People's Liberation Army should not intervene in the Cultural Revolution, and asking him instead to 'send the Liberation Army to support the broad masses of the Left'.[1] On the 22nd, a *People's Daily* editorial called on all 'proletarian revolutionaries' to 'form a great alliance to seize power from those in authority who are taking the capitalist road', though the nature of the 'great alliance' was not spelled out.[2] On the 23rd, Lin Piao effectively issued the order to the PLA to intervene,[3] as it shortly proceeded to do in Heilungchiang Province.[4]

This bare chronology suffices to make clear that in the middle of January 1967, China moved decisively away from the model of the Paris Commune. It does not really enlighten us, however, as to what went on in Mao's own mind. Had he, as some believe, been dreaming anarchist dreams which he had only abandoned under pressure from his own supporters, and in the face of imminent chaos? Or had the whole phase of incitement to 'rebellion' been nothing but a cynical manoeuvre from beginning to end, in which the Red Guards were used to smash the Party bureaucracy, with the full intention of casting them aside, in Stalin's phrase, like squeezed lemons, once the job had been done?[5]

Perhaps the alternative should not be put quite so starkly. Mao's response of August 1966 to the Red Guards, the reference in the 1 January 1967 editorial to democracy as a means, and many other indications illustrated the basic continuity of his thinking, and showed that he had not been converted, at this late stage, from Leninism to anarchism. At the same time, he may have hoped, even in mid-January, that within the framework of democratic centralism it would be possible to encourage the blooming of a greater degree of 'extensive democracy', under less military supervision, than ultimately proved to be the case. Editorial comment in early February,

---

[1] *CB*, no. 892, p. 50. The date is given in Rice, *Mao's Way*, p. 309, on the basis of a wall poster.

[2] Translated in *Peking Review*, 5 (1967), 7–9.

[3] *CCP Documents*, pp. 195–7.

[4] See *Peking Review*, 7 (1967): 12–14 and 8, pp. 15–19.

[5] The former view was put forward in an early analysis by Phillip Bridgham, 'Mao's Cultural Revolution in 1967: the Struggle to Seize Power', *The China Quarterly*, 34 (April–June 1968), 6. It is also that of Stanley Karnow (*Mao and China*, p. 286). Edward Rice sees rather a Mao torn by contradictions, following a flexible strategy constantly adapted to changing circumstances; see *Mao's Way*, especially pp. 298–317.

while revealing clearly which way the wind was blowing, appeared to reflect considerable inner conflict. The Paris Commune was still referred to, and the moral which Marx had drawn from these events was applied to China. In those units where Party persons in authority taking the capitalist road had been 'exercising bourgeois dictatorship', the 'Marxist principle of smashing the existing state machine must be put into practice in the struggle for power'. The current seizure of power was 'not effected by dismissal and reorganization from above, but from below by the mass movement called for and supported by Chairman Mao himself'. This experience would 'open a new era in the international history of proletarian revolution', and 'greatly enrich and develop the experience of the Paris Commune'. But at the same time, it was heavily underscored that, as Engels had said, 'a revolution is the most authoritarian thing there is'. Thus, while 'ignoring' Party discipline as exercized by reactionary superiors, the 'provisional organs of power' set up by the 'proletarian revolutionaries' should enforce 'revolutionary discipline', combining 'the most extensive democracy' with 'the highest degree of centralism'. The Paris Commune, it was recalled, 'was too restrained in the use of its authority'. The ultimate source of authority was 'the proletarian revolutionary line represented by Chairman Mao'; the provisional organs exercising it must be set up on the basis of the 'three-way alliance', with the active participation of the PLA.[1]

In the light of these events and policy statements, the establishment on 5 February of a Shanghai People's Commune appears as an anachronism. Did the leaders of this organ, Chang Ch'un-ch'iao and Yao Wen-yüan, imagine that the commune formula still enjoyed Mao's support – or did they hope to force his hand by creating a *fait accompli*? In any case, Mao made his position abundantly clear when he summoned them to Peking for discussions on 12 February. They stayed in the capital for a week, and met with the Chairman on

[1] See the two editorials, 'On the Proletarian Revolutionaries' Struggle to Seize Power' and 'On Revolutionary Discipline and Revolutionary Authority of the Proletariat', translated in *Peking Review*, 6 (1967), 10–15, and 7, pp. 17–19. It would appear that the contradictions in these texts were in fact internal to Mao himself. According to Red Guard sources, Mao personally added the passage in the first of these two editorials stressing the need to make use of experienced cadres, but nevertheless gave his approval to the references to the Paris Commune; afterward, he repented of this. See Rice, *Mao's Way*, pp. 326–8.

three occasions.[1] According to the summary record of the conversations, Mao began by asserting that 'for the purpose of seizing power the three-way alliances were essential'. Holding up as a model the committee formed in Shansi, which included 53 per cent revolutionary masses, 27 per cent army, and 20 per cent cadres from various organs, he declared: 'Shanghai ought to learn from them.' And he continued:

The slogan of 'doubt everything and overthrow everthing' is reactionary. The Shanghai People's Committee demanded that the Premier of the State Council should do away with all heads. This is extreme anarchism, it is most reactionary. If instead of calling someone the 'head' of something we call him 'orderly' or 'assistant', this would really only be a formal change. In reality there will still always be 'heads'. It is the content which matters. There is a slogan in Honan, 'The present-day proletarian dictatorship must be completely changed.' This is a reactionary slogan.

As the last sentence made plain, the language in the editorials published on 3 February about 'smashing the bourgeois state machine' was meant as an invitation to demolish individual organs in various domains and at various levels whose leaders had refused to join the Maoist camp; it was not intended to negate the legitimacy of the state and Party apparatus as a whole. This point had already been made even more graphically by a concrete symbol: the fact that, in the model province of Shansi, the newly-formed Revolutionary Committee was presided over by the former provincial Party secretary. The first sentence of the above quotation is likewise a repudiation of the tendency to be excessively suspicious of experienced cadres.

Turning to the Shanghai People's Commune itself, Mao declared:

With the establishment of a people's commune, a series of problems arises and I wonder whether you have thought about them. If the whole of China sets up people's communes, should the People's Republic of China change its name to 'People's Commune of China'? Would others recognize us? Maybe the Soviet Union would not recognize us, whereas Britain and France would.

After these rather whimsical observations, Mao came to the essentials. The Centre, he said, had issued an order that no place apart

[1] The quotations below are from 'Chairman Mao's Talks at Three Meetings with Comrades Chang Ch'un-ch'iao and Yao Wen-yüan', *Mao Tse-tung Unrehearsed*, Text 23.

from Shanghai might set up People's Communes, and Shanghai itself should 'make a change and transform itself into a Revolutionary Committee or a City Committee'. By way of justification, he remarked: 'Communes are too weak when it comes to suppressing counter-revolution', thus emphasizing once again his awareness of the limits of government by committees, and echoing his remark at the Tenth Plenum about there being special organs for this sort of thing.

On 24 February Shanghai proceeded to fall into line, and to establish a 'Revolutionary Committee' based on the 'three-way alliance', with the participation of the PLA.[1] Mao's talks with Chang and Yao, the substance of which rapidly became known in Red Guard circles throughout China, appeared to mark a definite break on his part with all those interpreters of 'extensive democracy' who imagined that the masses, under the guidance of correct ideology, could do without leadership. Indeed, his confrontation with the leaders of the Shanghai Commune was perceived at the time by many of this persuasion as marking the betrayal of their hopes. The situation as a whole was by this time so unstable and confused that it was nearly two years before 'ultra-leftism', even in its more extreme and obvious manifestations, was eliminated from the scene, but there is no indication that Mao Tse-tung ever again wavered after February 1967 in his attitude toward the abolition of 'heads'. In April 1969, the wheel came full circle, and he reasserted at the First Plenum of the new Ninth Central Committee the orthodox Leninist doctrine of the vanguard party: 'You are Communists, you are that part of the masses which is more conscious, you are that part of the proletariat which is more conscious.' The brief phase when he had regarded it as reactionary to distinguish between inner-Party and outer-Party had long since been buried.[2]

Intimately related to the question of the balance between democracy and centralism, and of Party control, is that of the role of youth, since the first and most characteristic force by which Mao challenged the Party from outside was an organization of young people: the Red Guards. As regards this problem, too, Mao's attitude is less unorthodox than has sometimes been imagined. We have noted his emphasis, from the Great Leap onwards, on the superio-

---

[1] *Peking Review*, 10 (1967), 10–17.
[2] Speech of 28 April 1969, *Mao Tse-tung Unrehearsed*, Text 25.

rity of young people who have grasped the truth over the 'old fogies', but he is also aware of the fact that old people after all do have experience, which young people lack. This point, which he had made in the 1930s,[1] Mao re-affirmed in 1966, on the eve of the Cultural Revolution. Talking once again to his nephew, Mao Yüan-hsin, he said:

Formerly, I was principal of a primary school, and a teacher in a middle school. I am also a member of the Central Committee, and was once a Department chief for the Kuomintang. But when I went to the rural areas and spent some time with the peasants, I was deeply struck by how many things they knew. I realized that their knowledge was wide, and I was no match for them, but should learn from them. To say the least, you are not a member of the Central Committee, are you? How can you know more than the peasants?[2]

This passage expresses Mao's conviction that all Chinese revolutionaries have something to learn in the countryside – a point to which I shall return in a moment. But it also sheds light on his view of the relations between seasoned revolutionaries such as himself, and callow young men. The record of his talks during the Cultural Revolution shows him moving from an initial emphasis on the virtues of youth back to a stress on the need to educate young people. On 21 July 1966, when he made his famous statement about not distinguishing between 'inner Party' and 'outer Party', he identified a positive attitude toward the Red Guards as the touchstone of a true revolutionary, likening those who suppressed the student movement to the Pei-yang warlords of the 1920s. 'It is anti-Marxist for Communists to fear the student movement', he added.[3]

The decisive turning point here, too, came at the February meetings with Chang Ch'un-ch'iao and Yao Wen-yüan. In late 1966 and early 1967, the Red Guards had made extensive use of a quotation from an article written by Mao Tse-tung during the May 4th Movement: 'The world is ours, the nation is ours, society is ours.'[4] In the course of his conversations with Chang and Yao, the Chairman said he didn't altogether remember these words, and they shouldn't be used any more. The implication was clearly that today's

---

[1] *The Political Thought of Mao Tse-tung*, p. 353.
[2] *Mao Tse-tung Unrehearsed*, Text 15.   [3] *Mao Tse-tung Unrehearsed*, Text 16.
[4] This quotation is from Mao's article 'The Great Union of the Popular Masses', cited earlier. The sentence in question appears on p. 84 of my translation in *The China Quarterly*, 49 (January–March 1972).

young people were taking too seriously their re-enactment of the glorious days of Mao's youth, and beginning to imagine that the world belonged to *them*, rather than to the Party cadres – or perhaps even to them rather than to the Chairman himself.[1]

This evolution found its logical culmination in Mao's directive of December 1968 according to which educated young people should go to the countryside to be 'recducated by the poor and lower-middle peasants'.[2] Although this measure was inspired in part by a desire to get undisciplined elements among the Red Guards out of the cities, where they had been fighting bloody battles with one another, it was also in complete harmony with Mao's deep-seated conviction that the education required by the younger generation cannot be merely book learning, but must be linked to reality, especially to rural reality. 'To get some experience of class struggle – that's what I call a university', he said in 1965 to Ch'en Po-ta and K'ang Sheng. 'They argue about which university is better, Peking University or People's University. For my part, I am a graduate of the university of the greenwoods (*lü-lin ta-hsüeh*).'[3]

The 'greenwoods' in Chinese parlance, as in English, evokes the habitat of heroic outlaws in revolt against an unjust society. Mao is here referring, of course, to his years of guerrilla warfare in the countryside, in the days of Chingkangshan and Yenan, the emphasis being on the lessons he learned from the guerrilla experience. But he also attributes crucial importance to the locus of that experience – the Chinese countryside and the world of the peasants who inhabit it. Though he had declared, on the eve of taking power, that henceforth the relation between the cities and the countryside in the Chinese revolution would be reversed, and the cities would lead the villages, he remained strongly marked by the populist morality inculcated into him as a young man by Li Ta-chao. In 1929, he had denounced the tendency toward 'pleasure-seeking' among his soldiers in terms which clearly reflect his attachment to the moral purity of the countryside:

In the Red Army there are also quite a few people whose individualism finds expression in pleasure-seeking. They always hope that their unit will

---

[1] *Mao Tse-tung Unrehearsed*, Text 23. How necessary it was for Mao to make plain his wishes is shown by the fact that this quotation was used in *Peking Review* as late as 3 February 1967 (no. 6, p. 11).
[2] *Peking Review*, 52 (1968), 6–7.   [3] *Mao Tse-Tung Unrehearsed*, Text 14.

march into big cities. They want to go there not to work, but to enjoy themselves. The last thing they want is to work in the Red areas where life is hard.[1]

Mao's belief in the continuing relevance of such ideas was shown by the inclusion of the passage just quoted in the chapter of *Quotations from Chairman Mao* on 'ideological self-cultivation'.[2] That it was not merely Lin Piao and the General Political Department of the People's Liberation Army who, in the mid-1960s, felt such a nostalgia for the simplicity of bygone days, is eloquently demonstrated by Mao's remarks on this theme at the First Plenum of the new Central Committee in April 1969:

For years, we did not have any such thing as salaries...We had only a fixed amount of food, three mace of oil and five of salt. If we got one and a half catties of millet, that was great. As for vegetables, how could we get vegetables everywhere the army went? Now we have entered the cities. This is a good thing. If we hadn't entered the cities Chiang Kai-shek would still be occupying them. But it is also a bad thing, because it caused our Party to deteriorate.[3]

We have seen that at this same Plenum, Mao enunciated a wholly orthodox view on the role of the vanguard party. The ideas just quoted regarding the corrupting influence of the cities appear, on the other hand, the reverse of orthodox. Perhaps we can make of this contradiction the guiding thread for a discussion of the logic and consequences of the Cultural Revolution.

In a word, the view I propose to put here is that China today is groping toward a synthesis between certain elements of Leninism and the demands of a national reality which will have its centre of gravity in the countryside for a long time to come. But before developing this idea it is necessary to sketch very briefly changes in the predominant view of the nature of authority in China over the past six years.

Early in 1967, as we have seen, Mao explicitly rejected a wholly 'inner-directed' notion of authority in favour of a three-pillared conception symbolized by the 'three-way alliance'. Authority, in

---

[1] *Selected Works*, I, p. 113.
[2] *Quotations from Chairman Mao Tse-tung* (Peking, Foreign Languages Press, 1966), p. 244; *ibid*. Bantam/Corgi Books edition, p. 137. The chapter title quoted above is that of the first edition; from 1967 onwards, it was replaced by 'Correcting Mistaken Ideas', in order to eliminate Liu Shao-ch'i's term of 'self-cultivation' (*hsiu-yang*).
[3] *Mao Tse-tung Unrehearsed*, Text 25.

this view, flowed from Mao and his thought, from the PLA, and from the Party organization. Editorials published in February 1967 reflected this approach. On the one hand, the existence of authority derived from a correct perception of Mao's thinking was explicitly proclaimed:

Marxism–Leninism, Mao Tse-tung's thought, is the highest authority of the proletariat. The proletarian revolutionary line that Chairman Mao represents is the highest authority in the great proletarian cultural revolution. All provisional organs of power that carry out this correct line in directing the struggle to seize power should have authority and do have it as a matter of course...This is the authority of the proletariat.[1]

The PLA, 'the revolutionized force of the proletariat created and educated by Chairman Mao himself', was characterized at the same time as 'the firm and solid cornerstone of the dictatorship of the proletariat and the most reliable guarantee of complete victory in the present struggle to seize power'. The participation of PLA representatives in the provisional 'three-in-one' organs of power would, in particular, make it easier 'to suppress the counter-revolutionaries firmly'.[2] Finally, the 'revolutionary leading cadres' who had joined the seizure of power were described as 'more experienced in struggle', 'more mature politically', and possessed of 'greater organizational skill'. They should therefore be included in the 'core of leadership'.[3]

Since the Party organization as a whole was, for the moment, largely unable to function, the main sources of authority in China, in the years 1967–9, were the first two indicated above. Indeed, the position of the 'revolutionary leading cadres' might be seen as deriving rather from the first type of authority than from the third; they were included in the 'leadership core' not because of their status in the Party, but because they correctly interpreted Mao Tse-tung's thought and enjoyed the confidence of the masses.

It was already implicit in Mao's remarks of February 1967 to Chang Ch'un-ch'iao and Yao Wen-yüan, and became increasingly evident in the course of the ensuing months, that because Mao either

[1] 'On Revolutionary Discipline', *Peking Review*, 7 (1967), 19.
[2] 'A Good Example in the Struggle by Proletarian Revolutionaries to Seize Power', *Jen-min jih-pao* editorial of 10 February 1967, translated in *Peking Review*, 8 (1967), 18.
[3] 'On the Proletarian Revolutionaries' Struggle', *Peking Review*, 6 (1967), 12.

had never believed in, or had finally despaired of, the capacity of the masses to discipline themselves – even with the guidance of his thought – ultimate authority must come to rest, at least in the short run, with the PLA. Thus, by the spring of 1968, the army was explicitly recognized as 'the main pillar of the dictatorship of the proletariat'. Though the importance of 'direct participation by the revolutionary masses in the running of the country and the enforcement of revolutionary supervision from below over the organs of political power at various levels' was still emphasized, 'revolutionary leading cadres' were now described as 'the backbone of the "three-in-one" organs of power'.[1]

In the chaotic and violent conditions prevailing in China during 1967 and 1968, the 'main pillar' was necessarily more important than the 'backbone'. Now the balance has swung back to the Party. Nevertheless, the current situation is inevitably still influenced by the experience of the period of military predominance.[2]

The People's Liberation Army is the incarnation and the symbol of two essential elements in the Chinese revolution as perceived by Mao: the role of the countryside and of the peasantry, and the importance of struggle, especially of armed struggle. To the extent that the Cultural Revolution aimed to exalt these two aspects of the Chinese experience, the intervention of the army was more than simply a response to a situation in which every other force capable of maintaining order had broken down. The PLA is, of course, a symbol of China's rural reality for the obvious reason that it is an army of peasants. More important, perhaps, is the fact that its traditions were shaped by a long period of schooling in what Mao Tse-tung has called the 'university of the greenwoods'. It was tempered in struggle, and in struggle which took place in the countryside.

[1] 'Revolutionary Committees Are Fine', joint editorial of *Jen-min jih-pao*, *Hung ch'i*, and *Chieh-fang-chün pao*, 30 March 1968, translated in *Peking Review*, 14 (1968), 6–7.

[2] This schematic outline of developments leaves out of account both the extensive interpenetration which has existed between military and political elites in the history of the Chinese Communist movement since 1927, and the fact that the PLA is, and has been in recent years, by no means a monolith intervening as such in the political arena. These questions, vitally important in the analysis of the Chinese political system as a whole, are not directly germane to the ensuing brief discussion of the significance of a period during which the army, whatever its divisions, played a decisive role in the Cultural Revolution.

One might even go further, and suggest that the particular *kind* of politico-military struggle which constitutes the matrix, both of the People's Liberation Army and of the victory of the Chinese revolution as a whole, can take place only in the countryside. This is so, not simply because in the China of the 1930s and 1940s the cities were strongly held by the Japanese, the Kuomintang, and/or foreign imperialist forces. Only in the countryside, where economic activity is simple, decentralized, and directly concerned with the supply of the means of subsistence, is it possible to combine fighting and production, and thereby to create enclaves of an alternative society inside the old.[1]

The view expressed by most of the contributors to this book is that, while the patterns of organization emerging in China today resemble, in many respects, those before the Cultural Revolution, the spirit which informs them is significantly different. The system now taking shape might be described as a combination of Leninism and the guerrilla heritage. Another way of putting it would be to say that China today bears the imprint of both Party and army styles of leadership. Is it possible to forge a true synthesis of two such disparate elements? One's answer to this question will no doubt depend to a considerable extent on an evaluation of the nature and impact of PLA leadership in China.

As I have suggested repeatedly throughout this introduction, Mao's approach to revolution is characterized by a dialectical conception of the relation between social change and cultural change. On the one hand, by transforming men's thinking through study and thought reform, it is possible to change their class nature and thereby to influence reality. On the other hand, and more importantly, participation in struggle is the most potent instrument for awakening revolutionary consciousness. Mao sees in war the strongest manifestation of man's 'conscious activity', and thus, *a fortiori*, the supreme form of struggle.[2] The People's Liberation Army, which is adept at this form of conscious activity, is therefore an ideal mentor for guiding people in the acquisition of an ethos of resolute struggle

[1] For this reason, 'urban guerrilla' is really a contradiction in terms. Terrorist activity in the cities can prevent the functioning of a complex productive or administrative machine; it cannot create an alternative.

[2] See the extract from 'On Protracted War' in *The Political Thought of Mao Tse-tung*, p. 284.

– especially in a country such as China where a core value of the traditional culture has always been the avoidance of conflict.

And yet, Mao was not prepared to countenance the substitution of the army for the Party – or even the continued pre-eminence of the army in the context of the 'three-in-one' combination. After a period of three or four years, during which the PLA had played a central role both in the political system and in economic work, it therefore receded once more into the background, following the fall of Lin Piao, leaving individuals at the grass roots in the presence of a leadership increasingly dominated by the Party. This development was obviously not unrelated to the emergence of a sharp conflict between Mao Tse-tung and Lin Piao. The explanation must, however, be sought not only in these immediate circumstances, but in the pattern of Mao's political thinking as a whole. In Mao's eyes, China's military men have many precious qualities, such as their lack of bureaucratic airs and their spirit of struggle and self-sacrifice, but they also have shortcomings – notably a tendency to take charge and to do things for people instead of letting them learn by doing for themselves.[1] In any case, however unorthodox his Leninism, Mao Tse-tung has proved to be too deeply committed to the axiom of Party leadership to envisage a political system run in any other way.

For a brief season, those who had still not given up hope that something could be salvaged from the utopian visions of early 1967 had imagined that the Revolutionary Committees, on which (side by side with effective control by the PLA) the new revolutionary activists enjoyed considerable representation, might provide an alternative to Party control. By the end of 1971 it was plain, and it has since become even plainer, that the whole network of political and economic authority at all levels would be effectively subordinated to the Party, not only in theory but in fact. Simultaneously with these developments the cult of Mao was progressively dismantled. The two trends were, of course, logically interrelated. Mao himself explained to Edgar Snow that he had only promoted the cult as a

---

[1] Mao has also suggested, in his private talks to provincial leaders of August–September 1971, that the Chinese army suffers from a defect not unknown in armies elsewhere: a tendency to over-simplify complex problems, and to act on that over-simplified understanding. 'I approve of the traditional army style of quick and strict implementation,' he said, 'but not where it concerns questions of ideology. Facts must be laid on the table and reasoning adopted.' *Chung-kung yen-chiu* (Taipeh), 9 (1972), 93.

weapon against a Party bureaucracy which had slipped from his control, and that, with the overthrow of Liu Shao-ch'i and those who formerly dominated the apparatus, it had lost its usefulness.[1]

In recent months, it has also been claimed that the exaggerated worship of Mao and his thought was promoted by Lin Piao for his own purposes. Such is, in particular, the lesson meant to be drawn from Mao's letter dated 8 July 1966 to Chiang Ch'ing, circulated for study in China since the middle of 1972.[2] But this document, too, reiterates implicitly the point that Mao himself regarded the cult as an indispensible weapon against Liu Shao-ch'i and the Party bureaucrats. To make public in 1966 what he had written deprecating Lin Piao's praise of himself as a 'genius' would, he said, discourage the leftists, and thus 'help the rightists'.

Quite apart from the tactical aims which Mao may have been pursuing in disseminating this letter, and the excerpts from his 1971 talks, or from the question of the authenticity of either of these documents, they pose suggestively the problem of the relation between ultra-leftism and the exaltation of individual leadership. In my own view, authoritarianism and anarchism are two maladies of the political process which engender one another. At the risk of being accused of substituting my own thinking for Mao's, I would suggest that Mao Tse-tung has been struck by this truth, and that he has come to doubt whether the blind worship of his 'genius', and the rote learning of a few precepts drawn from his works, can really liberate the Chinese people to pursue the 'conscious action' which he has always taken as his goal. So much is implied by his linking, both in the 1971 talks and in the letter to Chiang Ch'ing, of the popularization by Lin Piao of the 'magical power' inherent in the little red book, and Lin's plans for a *coup d'état*, and/or Ch'en Po-ta's ambition to establish his own prestige. The moral is clearly that 'study' of the kind which flourished during the early stages of the Cultural Revolution does not arm the individual with any real basis for political judgement and independent decision, and thus leaves him open to the tricks and manipulation of whatever 'swindler' comes

[1] Snow, *The Long Revolution*, pp. 18–19, 169. It is hard to believe that Mao did not also derive some personal satisfaction from the adulation he received, but no doubt the utilitarian explanation he put forward in 1970 is also valid.

[2] See, e.g., *Hsing-tao jih-pao* (Hong Kong), 4 November 1972.

along. In a word, fervour is no substitute for knowledge on the part of the citizens; hence the recent doubts about 'touching people's souls'.[1]

As an alternative to the notion of authority derived from an inner light, which had led both to factional fighting and to rivalry for the succession among his authorized interpreters, Mao could find no other solution than to restore the Party as the source of truth and authority. The main burden of his talks of August–September 1971 was the avoidance of a split within the leadership; the necessary unity, he emphasized, could only be assured on the basis of a correct ideological and political line. This sounds at first like an echo of the ideas put forward in 1966–1967 about 'Mao Tsetung Thought' as the source of 'proletarian' authority, but Mao added that such a correct line could not come from an individual: 'Genius does not come from a single person, but from several persons and from the Party, which is the vanguard of the proletariat. Genius is dependent on the mass line and mass wisdom.'

Despite the evolution back toward orthodoxy in the structures of power, it can be argued that there has not been simply a return to the *status quo ante*. The difference, as already suggested, lies rather in attitudes than in institutions. The ritual humbling of the Party cadres, during the early and violent stages of the Cultural Revolution, constituted an instance of the educational use of terror not without analogies to the public trials of landlords at the time of the land reform. Unlike the landlords, the cadres who had undergone this experience were not shot, or condemned to live in the margin of society, but re-educated through participation in productive labour, in May 7th Cadre Schools or elsewhere, and then re-integrated for the most part into leading positions. As a result of this process, and of the other side of the same coin, which was the assumption of a substantial degree of responsibility on the part of groups at the basic level for running their own affairs, at a time when Party control had largely evaporated, relations between the leaders and the led, especially in the countryside, but also in the factories and other urban institutions, underwent a qualitative change.

It is in the economy that the cumulative effect can best be

[1] It is worth noting in passing that this slogan, though associated with Lin Piao, was also used by Chou En-lai. See, for example, his speech of 12 November 1966, *Peking Review*, 47 (1966), 11.

evaluated. The development strategy which took shape when order was restored in 1968–9 was in many ways similar to that of the Great Leap, but the results, it is widely agreed, were far more satisfactory. The reasons, as pointed out by Marianne Bastid, are three-fold: an increase in the available skills and resources; the consolidation of the basic administrative framework of communes, brigades, and teams, so that the effort to increase production did not take place simultaneously with a radical re-structuring of the pro-ductive units; and finally, a more clearly established hierarchy of responsibility. One might well ask whether the third of these points corresponds to a tidying-up of the Great Leap approach, and the attenuation of some of its excesses, or rather to the negation of the Great Leap. Such doubts seem even more justified in view of the fact that the past two or three years have seen a further reflux of the emphasis on mass mobilization as the key to increased production, a degree of retrenchment and consolidation in local industry, and the increasing valorization of technical expertise. This last development is symptomatic both of the changing political context, marked by a heightened sense of hierarchy, and of a new emphasis on certain types of economic rationality, leading to the conclusion that the misallocation of trained manpower represents a waste of resources. This trend in economic thinking, as Christopher Howe has shown, is linked to the reassertion of the respectability of material incentives in general, which has found its most striking expression in the first large-scale wage increase in a decade and a half. There do appear, however, to have been irreversible achievements: the steady accre-tion of human and technical resources as a result of the vertical and horizontal transfers of technology analysed by Jon Sigurdson; the rationalization and refinement of the administrative structure dis-cussed by Marianne Bastid; and a tendency, noted by Christopher Howe, toward the adaptation of systems of management and remu-neration to the size and character of the enterprises.

The changes in the texture of social relationships are far more diffi-cult to grasp. Has Mao truly achieved a synthesis of effective organi-zation with the enthusiasm which he has long regarded as the motor of progress? And even if he has achieved it momentarily, will it prove durable? Visitors to China in 1971 and 1972 generally agreed that, while there had unquestionably been a re-affirmation of the authority of those exercising political and economic leadership at all levels, the ordinary peasant or worker ventured to speak his mind and criticize those in authority as he rarely did a decade ago. But can this absence of awe for one's hierarchical superior survive, once hierarchies themselves are re-established, especially in a society where the habit of obedience has such deep roots in the past?

The hope that, in this domain, the effects of the Cultural Revolution will prove positive and durable resides partly in the fact that the average man now has both knowledge and self-confidence that he did not have a decade ago, and therefore will not be so easily turned once again into a 'docile tool'. But it lies also, and perhaps more importantly, in changing attitudes at the top. It is hard to believe that Mao's successors will risk playing the role of sorcerer's apprentices by launching mass campaigns of the magnitude of the Cultural Revolution, or that they would be able to control them if they did. It is possible, however, that they will accept his revision of the logic of Leninism in two important respects: the importance of people rather than things, and of the countryside as compared to the cities.

Both the emphasis on human and moral factors, and the recognition of the dignity of agriculture, are of course in conformity with the Chinese tradition, though Mao's understanding of these two points is radically different from that of the literati. I suggested earlier that the guiding thread for an interpretation of the Cultural Revolution might be found in the contrast between Mao's wholly orthodox statement of April 1969 regarding the Party as the bearer of consciousness, and his distinctly unorthodox suspicion of the cities. As is obvious from his repeated calls to increase production and catch up with the West, his reminder, on that occasion, of the austerity which prevailed in the heroic days when the Red Army was operating in the countryside should not be taken as the expression of some philosophy of economic stagnation, in the manner either of the Confucianists of yore, or of certain thinkers today. No Chinese leader, it can be asserted categorically, wants economic development more than Mao – but, to use his own language of 'On the Ten Great Relationships', if you really want economic development badly, you must not forget man.

It is here that the heritage of the Chingkangshan and of Yenan, which led to near-disaster when too hastily and literally applied at the time of the Great Leap, may provide a valuable complement to those elements of the Soviet model which still survive in China. Not to rely, as Lenin recommended, on exposure to technology and to large-scale organization as the main instrument for creating a socialist man; not to concentrate on economic development in the cities, on the assumption that the effects will ultimately percolate down to the countryside, as the Indians and many other Asian and African peoples have been all too prone to do – these are the lessons which Mao has drawn from half a century of making revolution in a peasant country. Many of his comrades have undoubtedly come to accept them, not only because of the Chairman's prestige, but because they correspond to Chinese reality, and to the Chinese way of looking at things. To redress the one-sided balance of the Leninist approach does not mean to stand Marxism on its head, by subordinating the cities to the countryside. Such an excessive valorization of rural reality would merely condemn the peasants indefinitely to the role they occupied in the Confucian scheme of things: that of the 'foundation' of the state, upon which rested the whole burden of supporting the rest of society. The intuitions Mao has drawn both from the past and from his own experience could serve rather as the starting point for the elaboration and implementation of a pattern of development which endeavours to narrow the gap between the rural world and the urban world by working from both sides at once.

They could serve this purpose – but will they? Here we return to the dilemma of Chang Chih-tung. Is it possible to borrow the techniques of Leninism, without accepting at the same time the elitism and the technocratic bias which so deeply impregnate the Leninist approach to politics and to economic development? Will the new spirit which has been abroad in Chinese society in recent years permeate and transmute the resurgent Leninist structures? Or will the well-oiled and finely articulated administrative machine, once more under the control of a Party which may relapse again into the bureaucratic ways of the past, squeeze out these impulses from below, and extinguish the hope of change? This is the question which hangs over China today – as Mao Tse-tung, more than anyone, must be keenly aware. The essays in this book cannot give us the answer, which lies in the future, but they may at least help to formulate the problem more clearly.

I

THE TWO ROADS:
ALTERNATIVE STRATEGIES
OF SOCIAL CHANGE
AND ECONOMIC GROWTH IN CHINA

Jack Gray

The purpose of this article is to examine the history of the policy controversies in China which underlie the emergence of the 'two roads'. The paper falls into four parts. In the first, I examine the Maoist view of the relationships between economic development, the development of political consciousness, the transformation of social institutions, and cultural change. In the second, I examine policy controversies as they appeared in the public documents of the time, excluding for the moment the revelations made during the Cultural Revolution. Third, I examine some of these issues in greater depth in the light of the revelations during the Cultural Revolution, before attempting to reconstruct a Liuist model which the so-called 'capitalist roaders' might have adopted if they had ever had the power to do so – concluding with a consideration of the essential elements of the conflict between the two roads.

The Maoist model is (as I argue below) the result of the unique experience of the Chinese Communist Party in the wartime Border Regions before the achievement of national power. To understand its full significance, however, and to isolate what is specific to the Chinese situation in the Maoist model, a brief comparative introduction is necessary.

China began her intensive planned economic growth in the decade after the Second World War, at a time when many other countries, independent or ex-colonial, were also beginning to attempt planned growth. During the 1950s and 1960s, increasing practical experience of the problems of development led to changes of attitude and emphasis in all these countries in varying degrees, and revealed the necessity for sharp choices of direction and priority. It is no part of the purpose of this article to take sides on the issues involved, but it is necessary to state these issues as they were seen by those concerned.

The underdeveloped countries, on the whole, began with two different models of development in mind, essentially derived from two very different sources. The first was the classical idea of 'balanced growth', based on current and often fallacious interpretations of western industrial development, and incorporating the assumption that the course of economic growth in underdeveloped countries should be, in principle, the same. This, however, quickly came to be regarded as untenable for some obvious reasons. Few of the underdeveloped countries enjoyed conditions comparable to the conditions of the original British industrialization process. Their populations were generally much poorer, and the land/man ratio generally much worse and worsening. They could not enjoy the vast expansion of world trade in proportion to total world production which characterized the eighteenth and nineteenth centuries. They had not undergone a long preliminary development of proto-modern forms of enterprise which, in Britain had provided the climate for collective economic optimism as well as brisk entrepreneurship generations before the industrial revolution. Most of them lacked the effective national economic integration which Britain enjoyed and western Europe had gained. They suffered (and still suffer) from gross and often institutionalized inequalities which, in some respects, inhibit economic development, and which had been decisively diminished in Britain; they were unlikely to be able to innovate at a rate which would allow them even to overhaul western technology, far less to surpass it and enjoy the advantages of a superior technology. Finally, and perhaps most important of all, the political possibilities of destroying peasant farming in order to use agricultural resources freely for capitalist ends had been very much diminished.

As frustrations grew, there was a tendency to seek salvation through the alternative model presented by the experience of the Soviet Union – the industrial 'big push', with its emphasis on the creation as rapidly as possible, and at the sacrifice of other opportunities, especially in agriculture and light industry, of a heavy industrial base. Aspirations towards national economic independence were an important factor in the attractions of this strategy. However, in many cases, it proved inappropriate. The assumption that the very creation of heavy industry would automatically bring about an economic revolution through spread effects proved false. Lacking a large or an integrated home market and adequate physical or social communications; lacking the means of effective mobilization of capital on a national scale; lacking in entrepreneurship;[1] with a low level of relevant skills and with undeveloped popular education; crippled by inhibiting barriers to social mobility, and with *per capita* purchasing power very small in a population consisting mainly of semi-subsistence peasants – spread effects were not and could hardly be automatic.

The most pressing problems to which concentration upon urban, modern, and mainly heavy, industry gave rise was the problem of employment. It became obvious that no conceivable rate of growth of modern urban industry could provide employment for more than a small fraction of new entrants to the labour market, far less mop up the surplus of labour in the rural areas.

The case of India can illustrate the changes of thinking which followed. The stress on heavy modern industry in the Second Five-Year Plan was modified, under criticism from many quarters, to incorporate policies such as the promotion of light industry, the protection of handicrafts, attempts to organize locally based growth through community development schemes, and even, as a result, the encouragement of the communities not only to develop through agriculture and handicrafts but also through the creation of their own social overheads through the processing of their own crops and the manufacture of their own tools, and even the production of their own industrial raw materials by mining and metallurgy.

The course of change in Chinese thought was, in some respects, the

---

[1] The problem of effective entrepreneurship is the focus of the problems of attitudes and institutions. On this see J. Habakkuk, 'The entrepreneur and economic development' in I. Livingstone (ed.), *Economic Policy for Development* (London: 1971). The most eloquent case for the importance of these non-economic factors in economic development is G. Myrdal, *Asian Drama* (Harmondsworth: Penguin Books, 1968), p. 1190.

same. The Chinese began, of course, not from the idea of balanced growth through a market or a mixed economy but immediately with the Soviet Stalinist 'big push' heavy industry model. Though formally adopted in the First Five-Year Plan only in 1955, it had been effectively put into operation in 1953. By 1956 it was already under criticism as expressed in Mao Tse-tung's 'Ten Great Relationships'. In 1958, policies swung to an emphasis on local development to create employment and to increase purchasing power as the effective basis for the further growth of heavy industry, through community development. As in India (but of course in a drastic and hasty way), the stress was on local investment in agriculture, consumer goods production, crop processing and tool manufacture, and on local production of raw materials. There also occurred disillusionment with the idea that the crux of development policy was the manipulation of economic factors in and through the state sector, and there was a growing realization that, for the purpose of inducing the local community to undertake successful self-development, questions of social and psychological attitudes and of local institutions and political leadership were critical. In the Indian, as well as in the Chinese literature, 'Cultural Revolution' in the broadest sense was seen to be necessary.

The question of heavy industry versus light industry and agriculture, with all the social and political implications of the choice, had also a history of its own within the Communist tradition. A brief glance at the Soviet industrialization debates of the 1920s can cast further light on the policy choices in China. This debate was the first classical exposition of the opposing points of view. On the left was Preobrazhensky, who began as the uncompromising and eloquent defender of the industrial 'big push', and who was prepared to soak the private sector (in effect agriculture) by price manipulation, taxation, and even currency depreciation, as a means of securing the most rapid 'primitive socialist accumulation'. Against him was a group of men led by Bukharin who insisted that the fastest path to industrial growth was through agriculture. Shanin (one of that group) argued that the same resources passed through agriculture would, by stimulating investment in the agricultural sector (where relatively small investments could have a vast and rapid effect), produce a greater surplus to stimulate industry.

Bukharin insisted that industrial products should be priced as cheaply as possible in order to induce the peasants to sell the maximum on the market. He went further than this by insisting that industry, in its first phase of development, should directly serve agricultural needs; 'industry must be turned to face the village'. Bazarov, the ablest of those condemned as 'Rightists', deplored the prejudice which identified industrialization with urbanization, arguing that 'cheap electric current and cheap lathes' had made the grim industrial cities of nineteenth-century capitalism irrelevant. He looked forward to the creation of local economic communities in which all available resources would be co-ordinated. In the context of this proposed strategy, he showed himself very conscious that the obstacles to success were as much social and psychological as economic.[1]

The analogy between the ideas of the Soviet Right, especially of Bazarov, and some of Mao's attitudes, as expressed in the 'Ten Great Relationships', is obvious. Mao's insistence on low prices for industrial goods, his interest in the importance of peasant accumulation, his statement that 'if you are one hundred per cent sincere in wanting heavy industry...you will concentrate on light industry and agriculture', and his insistence on the decentralization of economic decision-making to the localities, all chime with the ideas of the condemned Bukharinists.

The difference however, is that Mao insists that collectivization must be the basis of local economic effort whereas, in the Soviet Union in the 1920s, the assumption of the Right Wing was that individual peasant agriculture would continue. But the close analogy between Mao's views and theirs points out strongly that Mao's purpose in collectivizing served ideas more akin to theirs than to the extractive ideas of Stalin and Preobrazhensky upon which the operation of Soviet collectivization was based.

The purpose of this comparison has not been to advocate one or other economic strategy for China, nor to show that Mao Tse-tung's economic ideas are merely derivative. My aim has been first to show

[1] For some of the main points made in the Soviet industrialization debate, see N. Spulber, *Soviet Economy* (New York: Norton Press, rev. ed. 1969); Alex Erlich, *The Soviet Industrialization Debate* (Cambridge, Mass.: Harvard University Press, 1960); E. Preobrazhensky, trs. B. Pearce, *The New Economics* (London: Oxford University Press, 1965. Original version, 1926).

that there is a basic choice which affects peasant countries seeking to modernize, whatever their political system or ideology. This choice is between emphasizing investment in modern industry in the hope of spread effects, and emphasizing investment in the economic improvement of local communities which would feed back into modern industry – what Shanin called pushing resources through agriculture. I have also sought to show that, if the second strategy is chosen, the necessary decentralization of economic decision-making must be accompanied by the removal of attitudinal and institutional obstacles to entrepreneurship and community action, involving policies across the whole board of social effort and social relations.

Mao Tse-tung has chosen the second alternative and he has accepted the social and political implications of this strategy.

THE MAOIST ECONOMIC STRATEGY

Having suggested reasons for expecting a divergence between modern Chinese and earlier non-Chinese patterns of economic growth, I wish to turn now to a consideration of the special characteristics of the Maoist solution to the problems of growth as faced in contemporary China – and indeed in some other countries at early stages of economic development. In the first place, it is clear that the choice of an economic strategy stressing local self-development implies certain specific types of social and political policies. It would be an over-simplification, however, to see the Maoist road in politics and in matters of social change as simply derived from economic policies. The social and political values which are associated with Maoist economic strategy represent values which exist in their own right, nor are the economic, social and political value systems separate entities which can be made, by a choice of policies, to complement each other more than they contradict each other. Their relationship is far more organic.

A recent article in the Chinese theoretical journal *Hung ch'i*, in discussing Marxist economic analysis, makes a distinction between 'political economy' and 'economics'.[1] Stripped of its particular

---

[1] Fang Hai, 'Learn some Political Economy', *Hung ch'i (Red Flag)*, No. 7, 1972, 35–42, English translation in *BBC Summary of World Broadcasts, Part III, The Far East, FE* 4055.

Marxist dress, the distinction is a simple one: political economy is the study of the economic implications of all relevant social relationships, and the implications of economics in turn *for* all these social relationships. Economics is the narrower business of the alternative allocation of resources. These resources are devoted to defined ends; and the ends are defined by society. They may be expressed largely through a market mechanism, or through the decisions made by the politicians who represent the community. In China, obviously, the relevant social relationships are seen as class relationships; the community which defines the economic ends is the working class and its peasant allies; the politicians who express these ends in their decisions are the Party. But the essential distinction made between political economy and economics is familiar enough in the liberal as well as the Marxist world.

The Maoist view of the relations of economics, politics, society, and culture seems to be as follows:

(i) Any successful increase of wealth will either serve the interests of the majority, or serve to increase minority privileges until a class system is re-asserted.

(ii) Each of these two trends will express itself in the form of appropriate laws and institutions.

(iii) Each will also express itself in a characteristic allocation of resources tending to confirm the prevailing trend.

(iv) Each will also express itself in political groupings and alliances, in which compatible interests are federated, with the probability that this political distribution will be bi-polar.

(v) Each will also have its intellectual expression, in a characteristic art, literature, and education.

This is all basic Marxism, but the Maoist view has some characteristic additional features. The first is a great stress upon consciousness. The main means of preventing the victory of creeping privilege is to make the masses – and also the members of the minority who, by their actions, are building up these privileges, but who are only half aware of what they are bringing into existence – fully conscious of the two opposing trends in all their economic, social, political and cultural manifestations.

The implications of this rationale, however, go beyond the mere creation of a critical consciousness. The method of creating this consciousness is of vital importance. Since 1927 and his experience in Hunan, Mao has believed (or acted as if he believed) that the first and decisive step to mass consciousness is the seizure of power. The realization of this in Hunan may be said to have been Mao's blinding light on the road to Damascus, which resolved in his mind once and for all the problems of 'education versus political action' which had inhibited and divided the May Fourth radicals. Only when the masses have seized power are they motivated to articulate their aspirations fully and to develop their own political perspectives; only then does a dialogue between leaders and led become truly feasible. Mao has applied this lesson not only in the establishment of revolutionary state power, but in the re-organization of Chinese life since 1949: in land reform, in collectivization, in education, in industrial management, in the commune movement, and finally in the Great Proletarian Cultural Revolution.

Mao further believes that consciousness – in this case consciousness of the antithetical Two Roads – can be a powerful motive for action and can help to drive development forward. The rationale of the Great Leap Forward expressed this idea in the assertion that the rectification campaign of 1957 and the Leap were one continuous process in which, beginning from criticism of the bureaucracy and the bourgeoisie, the masses achieved a level of consciousness which both prepared them and motivated them to 'seize power' and to create their own alternative, non-elite, society with its characteristic economy, and drag urban modern industry into its orbit. Thus, political consciousness becomes a pre-condition of economic development or, as Mao would put it, 'a great spiritual force becomes a great material force'.

This dialectic between politics and economics expresses itself over time as a dialectic between the productive forces and production relations,[1] in which increasing capacity to produce (by gradual mechanization of operations) induces a consciousness of the need for changes in social organization, which in turn makes possible the exploitation of other and better technologies. In this context,

---

[1] This is the main theme of Mao's 'On the Correct Handling of Contradictions Among the People'; it was the importance of this theme which made it possible to use 'Correct Handling' as the text of the Great Leap and the commune movement. Interpretations of the 'Correct Handling' in this sense are so numerous in late 1957 and 1958 that it would be pointless to attempt to list them here.

there is a good economic case for the encouragement of traditional skills and of intermediate technologies.[1] The spiral development which will be alluded to below, and which is basic to the 'Socialist Upsurge' of 1955 was meant to be at once a spiral of increasing technical modernization, increasing incomes and investment, increasing knowledge and confidence, and increasing readiness to accept higher levels of social organization – from the mutual aid team to the primary co-operative to the full collective; and (latterly) to the commune, the county federation of communes and then to full ownership by the whole people. This is still the Maoist perspective in 1973.

The success of community development in a poor peasant country depends on certain cultural and institutional changes. These requirements can be summed up in a sentence: the inculcation and implementation of the social and psychological concomitants of economic modernization. The psychological concomitants include the ability to apply rational calculation to the use of scarce resources; some simple appreciation of the idea of controlled experiment; readiness to accept change; the ability to recognize new opportunities; willingness to co-operate in communal improvement; the foresight necessary for long-range planning; the discipline to accept and carry out majority decisions, local and national; and the capacity for honest, diligent and economical administration. It must be emphasized that the successful inculcation of these qualities cannot be separated from the increase of production. The traits of dependence are the marks of poverty.

It is clear that psychological change and institutional change are mutually dependent. Specific new forms of political leadership sub-

[1] There is now a large literature on intermediate technology. For a brief summary of the arguments in favour of the encouragement of low capital cost techniques in poor countries, see E. F. Schumacher, 'Industrialization through Intermediate Technology' in R. Robinson (ed.), *Developing the Third World* (Cambridge: Cambridge University Press, 1971), pp. 85ff. There is also a growing appreciation of the continuing role of small-scale industry in the advanced economies; see B. Hoselitz, 'Small industry in under-developed countries' in *Journal of Economic History*, No. 19, 1959. For a perceptive study of small-scale industry in China, see two articles by Carl Riskin: 'Small industry and the Chinese model of development', *The China Quarterly*, No. 46 (April-June 1971), and 'Local industry and choice of technique in planning of industrial Development in Mainland China', in U.N. Industrial Development Organization, *Planning for Advanced Skills and Technologies* (Vienna, 1969).

stantially different from those which would suffice for the operation of a system which gave the highest priorities to centralized modern heavy industry must be created. Educational policies giving priority to secondary and higher education for the purpose of producing a limited number of highly trained scientists, technicians and administrators must give way to policies giving a high priority to the achievement of universal literacy and a simple education relevant to rural needs; that is an education based upon production. Health policy must take as its priority the development of hygiene, simple midwifery, the improvement of traditional medicine and the improvement of dietary habits in the rural areas, not only to relieve the hardship of chronic and almost universal bad health, but to minimize the consequent inefficiencies so that the population can get as much effective working energy as is possible out of a relatively low calory intake.

In achieving the changes, the quality of local leadership is of primary importance. This leadership must be able to mediate between national policies and local conditions and aspirations. It is not possible in a vast and varied country to lay down at the national level policies sufficiently detailed for their automatic application to be practicable. Two main tasks are therefore set for that critical level of local leadership at which the representative of the national government meets the citizens of the local community face to face. The first is to interpret the national directives in terms of actions which are practicable in local conditions. The second is to secure majority consent for, and community co-operation in, the actions proposed. In Maoist mass-line theory, of course, the two tasks are inseparable. The community is encouraged to participate in the practical interpretation, and in so doing commits itself to accepting it.

In solving these problems the local leaders must overcome the tendency inherited from the past to regard their official or Party position as one which gives them the duty of supervision but not the duty of labour. Everybody in China over 45 years of age knows that it was this assumption which emasculated the Nationalist administration at all levels.

The local leaders of community development must identify themselves with the interests of the poor majority of the local community. To the very extent that these leaders are a little better educated than average, have broader views, are more experienced in discussion and organisation, have a distaste for superstition, have a greater consciousness of hygiene, and have more contacts beyond the village, they inevitably tend to find that in many important respects they have more in common with the former elite of the village than with the majority. And while they may see themselves involved in a political struggle with the elite, in a community so small and a struggle so protracted, in their own community with its personal relationships cutting across class, one can assume that this local highly personalised class struggle will tend to become somewhat unreal. Class consciousness flourishes best where the relationships involved are totally impersonal, and is difficult to maintain where economic relationships are face-to-face, as in the Chinese village.

Mao's contribution to policies for rural self development has been based upon the idea of a spiral process starting with the use of the surplus labour of the village. This spiral was an essential constituent of the collectivization process, beginning with the mutual aid team. The community (or that part of it willing to participate) pledged itself to a specific plan of development; this was usually concerned with agricultural construction and used the available surplus labour co-operatively. The reclamation of land, its irrigation, or other improvements carried out in winter would, if successful, pay off at the autumn harvest. Any such construction would result in an increased demand for routine labour the following year, and this would begin to press very soon on the supply of labour at the busy seasons of agriculture. This new labour scarcity would create a demand for simple labour-saving devices, while the profits of the construction already completed would provide the means to purchase these. In the next year, with better equipment, enlarged construction could be undertaken, resulting in an increased further demand for better tools and, at the same time, new means to pay for them. Mao believed that this spiral could go on, working through agricultural construction, crop processing, tool production and the development of ancillary occupations, until agriculture was fully mechanized and fully modernized and the rural areas industrialized, with each step taken only in response to increasing labour scarcity. This idea has great significance in Mao's theory. It lay behind his insistence that, in Chinese conditions, the co-operativization of agriculture must proceed more rapidly than technical change, and was the first condition of successful technical change. The Great Leap can be seen, in one sense, as a speeding up and generalization of this process.

The pattern of institutional change pursued in China since 1949 has three main aims: increasing scale of operation, the gradual elimination of the private sector, and the gradual integration of collective organs with state organs. Cultural change was expected to proceed in a dialectic with economic development and institutional change. The institutional changes themselves would be one expression of cultural change, made possible by increasingly rational views of the possibilities of larger-scale social organization. The operation of this dialectic was assisted by several lines of policy.

Generally speaking, these policies have aimed to provide education on the basis of productive effort and motivated by productive effort. Collective agriculture and commune construction and industry were expected to create a consciousness of new educational needs which the rural communities would be helped to satisfy for themselves as this consciousness grew. This is why the creation of local schools, providing an education firmly based in agricultural needs, largely part-time, paid for by the community itself and more concerned to harness the new motivations than to work to academic guidelines, was so much encouraged, especially during the Great Leap. The first aim of these popular schools was to increase basic literacy.[1] Beyond that (but inseparable from it), the intention was to provide an introduction to new technical possibilities; to encourage the capacity to innovate together with high expectations as to the possibilities of innovation; to create a first-stage scientific consciousness largely through the operation of experimental plots; and to point the political moral and adorn the social tale of collective organization and effort. The education which these schools sought to give was above all an education in self-reliance, though this was the self-reliance of the group rather than of the individual.

[1] The campaign to re-create and spread the Border Region *min-pan* schools in relation to the Great Leap was associated with K'ang Sheng. See *New China News Agency* (NCNA), 15 February 1958.

Three more lines of policy must be mentioned. The first is the tremendous stress laid in China on the 'generalization of advanced experience', on trying to ensure the maximum of communication of successful new ideas and methods. The effort put into this is unique among all developing countries. The second is the attempt to induce large numbers of educated youths, and to direct experienced cadres, to settle in the countryside, in order to provide the villages with administrative and technical expertise. More recently, to this has been added the attempt to give the poor majority in the village control of selection of students for secondary education, so that they can promote those pupils who are likely to come back and serve the village. The third is that, in the operation of village leadership, as in the absorption of urban students and cadres by the villages, great stress is laid on cadres' participation in physical labour. This has been one of the most persistent features of left-wing policy in China. Its rationale is obvious. First, the Asian contempt for manual labour, strongly present in China, must be overcome. Second, it is argued, it is impossible for cadres to solve day-to-day problems of production and productive organization unless they are directly and intimately involved. Third, the cadre must be seen to 'share weal and woe' (the phrase, in origin, is Nationalist, not Maoist) with the poor majority. Fourth, at the village level, there is little need for full-time cadres, and it would therefore be uneconomic for them to be divorced from productive labour. A further probable reason, which is never explicitly given, is that when some peasants are reluctant to work regularly on the collective, the presence of the cadres acts both as an example and a means of supervision.

With these general views of the tendencies which have actually occurred in Chinese social and economic development since 1949, together with some thoughts on the crucial aspects of the Maoist view of the dialectical spiral needed to bring about economic growth, we have provided a background against which differences over policy amongst the Chinese leaders can be seen in better relief and the emergence of the 'two roads' of development strategy be better assessed. It is now time to move from the schematic to the chronological approach.

THE EMERGENCE OF THE TWO LINES

The history of policy controversies in the Chinese People's Republic is, to a very large extent, the history of discussion and experiment focussed upon the issues dealt with in the previous section. Indeed, in some relevant respects, the controversies of the Yenan Border Region period were concerned with some of the same issues, though in a very much simpler form, and provided experience in the 1940s which the Maoist section of the Party believed to be relevant in the 1960s.

Perhaps the first experience of the Chinese Communist Party which might be considered to have contributed to the later evolution of Chinese ideas of economic strategy was the experience of land reform in the Kiangsi Soviet. The Chinese Communist Party's first taste of territorial power proved to be a potent solvent of *a priori* ideas. The economic viability of the Soviet demanded that land reform must avoid antagonizing the middle peasants and must as far as possible avoid the disruption of existing units of production, while changing the existing units of ownership. It was carried through with considerable and sustained harshness in order to destroy the prestige of the former landlords and the danger which their continuing influence presented to guerrilla armies, dependent for their success on depriving the enemy of information. But the land reform itself was moderate. It took the form primarily of the abolition of tenure. This policy was the basis of the agrarian reform law of 1950, but only after controversies in 1947–9, in which Liu Shao-ch'i was associated with an attempt to redistribute all land equally to all consumers, against which Mao Tse-tung eventually reacted to demand the maintenance of the more moderate policy of abolition of tenure, carried through by representative village governments and only after such village governments had been duly formed.[1] In

[1] Mao Tse-tung, 'Speech to a Conference of Cadres in the Shansi-Suiyuan Liberated Area', (April 1948), in Mao Tse-tung, *Selected Works*, IV, 227. The association of Liu Shao-ch'i with the return to uncompromising egalitarianism which the October Land Law represents, contradicts the accusations made against him during the Cultural Revolution to the effect that he took a right-wing position over land reform. However, the history of land reform legislation between 1946 and 1950 suggests that the swings of policy over the extent of redistribution and the manner of execution of the reform, clearly bear a much closer relation to the changing problems which met the CCP successively in the varying local societies through which their conquest passed – from Yenan

Honan, in 1949, an elaborate process was worked out by which the creation of a village leadership and successive stages of agrarian reform were interwoven. This process was meant to ensure (ideally at least) that land reform was carried out on the basis of local knowledge, with the support of a majority of the population. The land reform campaign in Honan was a classical application of the mass line, a dialectic of political action, psychological change and institutional development, based on local conditions, operating on local knowledge and limited to what could be achieved with the sanction of a majority of the village. It created for the future a political method appropriate to the problems of inducing the village communities to pull themselves up by their own boot-straps in the collectivization campaign and the Great Leap Forward. It was subject to abuse and it was abused (indeed it may have existed more in aspiration than reality), but this does not destroy its interest and relevance to the problems under consideration in this paper.

In tracing the history of land reform policy, we have jumped over the Border Regions, to which we must now return. It now is widely accepted that conditions in the Border Regions created certain new political and economic predilections in the minds of the Communist leadership or, more precisely, among those leaders most closely associated with the Border Regions and the related guerrilla zones. The issues which emerged foreshadowed the controversies which were increasingly to split the CCP from 1955 onwards, and to culminate in the Great Proletarian Cultural Revolution.

Mark Selden's excellent article on the subject provides a useful starting point for the consideration of the issues involved.[1] Japanese counter-attacks after the 100-Regiments Offensive had by 1942 so reduced Communist territories in North China that the total population under Communist control had been reduced by half. Accompanying this was the Japanese policy of both blockading the guerrilla areas closely and attempting to disrupt their economy by dumping goods at low prices. At the same time, the New Fourth Army

to Manchuria to the North China plain, to the Yangtse – than to the personal predilections of leaders. See my unpublished paper, 'The Evolution of Land Reform Policy in China, 1928–1950'.

[1] Mark Selden, 'The Yenan Legacy: the Mass Line', in A. Doak Barnett (ed.), *Chinese Communist Politics in Action* (Seattle: University of Washington Press, 1969), p. 99.

incident not only destroyed the Red Army's southern flank, but brought retaliation from the Nationalists, who cut off the subsidies until then paid to Yenan.

In this desperate situation, the focus of policy inevitably became economic – how to maximize the resources of the Liberated Areas in order to maintain their defence. Political, ideological, and cultural changes clustered round an economic nucleus. It was in this situation that Maoism came of age, twenty-one years after the foundation of the CCP. The new theoretical statements of Mao Tse-tung on political leadership, on knowledge and the dissemination of know-ledge, on relationships within the Party, were in a historical sense (though not necessarily in a logical sense) ancillary to a swift re-organization of human resources for urgent economic ends. 'Make revolution to increase production', though a much later slogan, could well have been the slogan of the Rectification Movement; the mass-line, in this, its first sweeping application, served economic purposes.[1]

The re-organization of 1942 took the form of drastically reducing the now top-heavy administration of the Border Regions, and sending the surplus cadres down to the grass roots to organize a vast production campaign on co-operative lines. Anxieties over this dis-mantling of the state apparatus, the demoralization of demoted central government cadres, the new work style required by the new system of administration through local multi-purpose committees, the problems of liaison between young intellectuals and village leaders, and the necessity of guarding against the disintegration of policies in this thoroughly decentralized system by creating a tougher backbone of common ideology – these are the subject matter of Mao's theoretical generalizations.[2] These were the catalyst which crystallized his long suspended ideas.

The production drive involved two main types of operation, one in agriculture and the other in industry. In agriculture, mutual-aid

[1] The apparent necessity of resort to revolutionary action, as opposed to 'united front' action, in this crisis, suggests that nationalist motives alone were not considered enough to call forth the necessary popular effort and sacrifice. This would tend to weaken the Chalmers Johnson hypothesis that the CCP rose to power essentially, if not solely, through patriotic rather than revolutionary appeals.

[2] See my forthcoming contribution to the *Encyclopoedia Britannica*, 'China: Nation-alist and Communist Political Thought, to 1949', for an analysis of the relationship between the problems and policies of 1942–3 and the systemization of Maoism.

methods were used to increase the cultivated area, and within it the irrigated area. Central to this undertaking was the resettlement of refugees from the Japanese-held areas through co-operative land reclamation.[1] This experience was the source of Mao's confidence that the collectivization of Chinese agriculture could be achieved through the benefits of co-operative labour-intensive construction, based on mutual-aid teams – one of the key controversies of the mid-fifties.[2] In industry, co-operatives were created using simple or improvised technologies; and these co-operatives were pregnant for the whole future of China, for within them are the seeds of the Great Leap, the Communes, and much of the strategy of rural economic development which emerged in 1958.

It is worthy of note that the Yenan industrial co-operatives were part of the wider Chinese Industrial Co-operatives movement of the war period; indeed they owed more to Indusco than to Communist ideas of co-operative organization. The existing bureaucratic Party co-operatives were abolished in 1943,[3] and the only industrial co-ops which remained to act as models for a new co-operative movement were those which had been set up with Indusco help for which Mao Tse-tung expressed his gratitude.[4]

The history of Indusco has not been written, but we are fortunate in having an extensive description of the movement by Edgar Snow.[5] The movement was led by Rewi Alley and backed largely by contributions from American supporters of the Chinese resistance to Japan as well as by overseas Chinese. In 1940, it was running 2,300 co-operatives throughout free China, of which about 80 were in the Shen-Kan-Ning Border Region. By 1945, there were 882 in the whole Communist area. In Chinese rural conditions and with the use of simple technologies and local materials, the capital needed

---

[1] Mao Tse-tung, *Ching-chi wen-t'i yü ts'ai-cheng wen-t'i* (*Economic Problems and Financial Problems*) (Yenan, December 1942). (Republished Hong Kong: Hsin min-chu ch'u-pan she, 1949), pp. 19–26.

[2] Ch'en Po-ta's speech at Peking University on the 37th Party Anniversary, *Hung ch'i*, No. 4, 16 July 1958. Ch'en defended Mao's belief that collectivization in China could be carried through on the basis of the mutual-aid teams and emphasized the importance of Border Region experience in this respect. The opposing opinion seems to have been most clearly expressed (at least in the 1950s) by Liu Shao ch'i.

[3] Mark Selden, 'The Yenan legacy', p. 131.

[4] Mao Tse-tung, *Ching-chi wen-t'i yü ts'ai-cheng wen-t'i*, pp. 60–4.

[5] Edgar Snow, *Scorched Earth* (London: Gollancz, 1940), II, 213–27 and 309–16.

was extremely small, capital turnover very high, and the capacity of the co-operatives to accumulate capital so high as to match the apparently incredible figures given for similar operations in 1958 – figures upon which was based Maoist insistence that such simple local forms of industry represented the fastest way to accumulate capital for the creation of large modern plants.

These little firms often had to provide their own complementarities: their own source of power, their own transport, and their own raw materials. It was also necessary for the co-ops to provide their own clinics, elementary schools, and training schools; thus they were forced to be more than merely production units. There was a tendency for successful co-operatives to diversify their operations until they became virtually a new social unit which 'represented the savings and the surplus labour power of one or more entire villages mobilized for production'. The workers in these little plants seem to have seen their efforts in a perspective which was to be a part of the inspiration of similar efforts in 1958, confident of their power to improve their own technology, increase the scale of their operation and plough back their profits for this purpose.

The motivation involved in the creation of Indusco is reminiscent of the motives to which Great Leap propaganda appealed. The backbone of the movement throughout China consisted of technicians and workers and young intellectuals inspired by patriotism and by ideals of service, who were both economic entrepreneurs and political evangelists. Their material reward was a bare subsistence; they fed and lived with the other co-op members. They represented a voluntary *hsia-fang*.

The economic policy for the Border Regions was clearly parallel to Indusco in some respects. Not only Mao's instructions for the co-operative movement, but also the first *hsia-fang* of 1942, the popular local governments based largely on co-ordinated economic effort, the work-study, *min-pan*, schools and the principal of 'centralized leadership and dispersed management' equally clearly had marked similarities to some aspects of the operations of Indusco, whose motives and spirit chimed so well with Mao's own concepts of social organisation.

Thus the administrators of the Border Regions, with Mao as their spokesman, developed a view of economic growth which entertained high expectations of self-reliance and improvisation, of local initiative exercised by democratically organized communities, and of labour-intensive low-capital-cost production; and this view was backed by unique experience.

These Communist leaders had already faced and prescribed for the political and cultural problems involved in an economy based on induced self-help. They had developed these views, and faced and solved these problems, in a context which though a very special one – a garrison state in a sense – was in its characteristics not essentially different from the Chinese national context except in the degree of severity of the problems. In its economic constraints and possibilities, in the problems of creating a united leadership out of urban intellectuals and village leaders, and not least in the problems for radical politics which China's own heritage of political culture set, the Border Regions were a microcosm of China.

The relevance of this history to the issues which we examined in the first section of this paper, and to the policies with which Mao Tse-tung has been associated from the Great Leap onward, is obvious. With this background sketched in, we can now look at the controversies which took place over policy in the Chinese Communist Party, and the policy choices as they appeared to Chinese leaders.

The accusations made by the Maoists during the Cultural Revolution against members of the Party 'taking the capitalist road' make it seem probable that, by the early 1960s, the different points of view within the Party were fast becoming irreconcilable. These accusations, however, include so much muck-raking, quotation out of context, and palpable exaggeration that clearly they can be used as evidence only with the greatest caution. They attribute to individuals opinions which these individuals may never have held. They paint a black-and-white picture in which one clear-cut group within the Party faces another, and the positions which these two groups represent are so described as to emphasize that their policies and attitudes were contrasted at every point on the spectrum of Chinese economic, political and cultural issues.

It is perhaps better to take as our starting point what we already knew or strongly suspected concerning differences of opinion within the Chinese Communist Party before the Cultural Revolution began.

Put briefly and schematically, we had evidence arising from periodic changes of policy to suggest the following:

1. *Land reform.* Controversies during the formation of land reform policy have already been alluded to. The two poles of opinion were doctrinaire egalitarianism on the one hand and, on the other, a policy of limited land redistribution carried through with majority support in the villages and concerned with preventing the disruption of agricultural production.

2. *Socialization, 1951–6.* It was obvious at the time that the process of socialization, and especially of the collectivization of agriculture, was carried out amid constant discussion, re-assessment and adjustment. Mao's intervention in July 1955, with his 'old women with bound feet' speech,[1] seems sufficient evidence that the starts and stops in the process of collectivization expressed a tug-of-war within the Party. The chronology of events was as follows. Experimental collectivization at the first-stage co-operative level was effectively begun in the winter of 1951–2 on the basis of an intra-Party directive,[2] and was accompanied by a rapid development of mutual-aid teams. In early 1953, the number of mutual-aid teams was reduced but, by the end of 1953, the co-operativization of agriculture was again forging ahead. In June 1955, the movement was again subjected to criticism and limitation. In July 1955, however, Mao's speech, 'On the Question of Agricultural Co-operatives', silenced the opposition for the time being and produced a drastic speed-up in the whole process. In December 1955, Mao edited the original three-volume edition of the work subsequently translated in condensed form under the title *Socialist Upsurge in China's Countryside*, which gave an elaborate justification for the acceleration of the movement.[3] By summer 1956, virtually the whole of

[1] Mao Tse-tung, 'Question of Agricultural Co-operation, in R. R. Bowie and J. K. Fairbank, *Communist China 1955–1959. Policy Documents with Analysis* (Cambridge, Mass.: Harvard University Press, 1962), pp. 94–105.

[2] *Chung-kuo k'o-hsüeh yüan, ching-chi yen-chiu-so* (Academy of Sciences, Economic Research Institute) *Kuo-min ching-chi hui-fu shih-ch'i nung-yeh sheng-ch'an ho-tso tzu-liao hui-pien*, 1949–52 (*Collected Source Material on Agricultural Producers' Co-operatives during the Period of National Economic Reconstruction*), I, 3–14.

[3] *Chung-kuo nung-ts'un ti she-hui-chu-i kao-ch'ao* (*The High Tide of Socialism in the Chinese Countryside*) (Peking: Jen-min ch'u-pan she, 1956, 3 vols.). This constituted a vast elaboration of Mao's speech 'On the Question of Agricultural Co-operatives'. The English translation appeared in 1957. For analysis of this collection, see my

China's farmland had been collectivized, not merely at the level of the first-stage co-operative, but at the level of the full collective. Soon after, as a consequence of the condemnation of Stalinism at the 20th Congress of the CPSU in February 1956, there were the beginnings of protest in China, which included, as well as strikes and student riots, withdrawals from the collective farm organization.[1] The response was to limit the size of co-operatives, adjust procurement prices, cut down the differential between the incomes of collectivized peasants and the incomes of urban workers, and relax controls over the private sector. Analysis of *Socialist Upsurge in China's Countryside* shows that this tug-of-war over the optimum speed of the process of collectivization had profound implications, and marked an important stage on the slippery slope to irreconcilable conflict.

3. *Response to the condemnation of Stalinism.* Khrushchev's condemnation of Stalinism shattered Communist orthodoxy and loosened the disciplinary bonds which had hitherto limited open controversy in the Communist world. The fact that China was apparently not consulted before Khrushchev's speech further reduced the prestige of the Soviet Union in China's eyes, and perhaps gave the Chinese an added sense of freedom to create their own road to socialism. Mao's speech of 27 February 1957, 'On the Correct Handling of Contradictions Among the People' represented Mao's response, and even in the revised and qualified version which is the only one available to us, it is a document of great significance.[2] It

articles 'The High Tide of Socialism in the Chinese Countryside', in Ch'en and Tarling, *Studies in the Social History of China and Southeast Asia* (Cambridge: Cambridge University Press, 1970), p. 85; and 'Mao Tse-tung's Strategy for the Collectivization of Chinese Agriculture: An Important Phase in the Development of Maoism', I. de Kadt and G. P. Williams, *Sociology and Development* (London: Tavistock Press, forthcoming).

[1] See Roderick MacFarquhar, *The Hundred Flowers Campaign and the Chinese Intellectuals* (New York: Praeger, 1960), *passim*.

[2] This document is probably the most significant of Mao's writings since the foundation of the CPR, but it has never been fully analysed. Stuart Schram, *Political Thought of Mao Tse-tung* (Harmondsworth: Penguin, 1969) treats it well but briefly. Franz Schurman, *Ideology and Organization in Communist China* (Berkeley, California: University of California Press, 1968) mentions it only in the supplementary chapter of the revised edition. A. Cohen, *The Communism of Mao Tse-tung* (Chicago: University of Chicago Press, 1964) devotes a chapter to comparing it line by line with previous Marxist writings, to demonstrate Mao's lack of originality – a process which only demonstrates the author's own narrow idea of what originality consists of. A full analysis of the document and of the ever-changing exegesis to which it has been subjected in changing circumstances in China is badly needed.

attempts first to redefine in terms of Marxist contradictions the relations among interest groups and opinion groups in the socialist state, as well as the relations between the people and the government of a socialist state. Having argued that, with socialization complete and only vestiges of the former exploiting classes remaining, contradictions in Chinese society were now mainly of a non-antagonistic kind, beneath which there lay an identity of interest, Mao then went on to explain why these superficial contradictions still persisted and were still troublesome. His answer was that the system was bureaucratic and over-centralized, so that the linkages which hold together this identity of interest were obscured because command had replaced education.

The policy which he advocated to short-circuit bureaucracy and to expose the identity of interest – particularly in the relations between investment in industry and increased production in agriculture (the worker/peasant alliance) – was to put the peasant majority in a position as far as possible to create industry for themselves and in close relation to their own immediate needs.[1] It was at this point that Maoist political ideas and Maoist economic ideas fused into what was to become the rationale of the Great Leap Forward.

This economic decentralization which Mao proposed was faced, however, with an alternative and rival form of decentralization, the conflict with which was to assume importance in later years. Mao sought decentralization to the local communities. His rivals (whom we will not at this point attempt to identify) thought more in terms of decentralization from the economic ministries to the large enterprises and from the central government to the provinces, in the manner which was then under discussion in the Soviet Union.[2] There was

[1] Li Ch'eng-jui, *Chung-hua jen-min Kung-ho-kuo nung-yeh-shui shih-kao* (*Draft History of the Agricultural Taxes of the CPR*), (Peking: Ts'ai-cheng ch'u-pan she, 1959), *passim*. This vital book is explicitly a gloss with respect to land tax policy on Mao's 'Correct Handling' ending with Mao's insistence that land tax must be held at 1957 levels in spite of rising rural incomes, to enable the villagers to create industry for themselves. This, combined with the adjustments made in response to Mao's 'Ten Great Relationships' speech to improve rural incomes in comparison with urban incomes, was meant to provide the basis for local investment in the Great Leap Forward.

[2] For a brief analysis of the trends of reform policy in the U.S.S.R. since the death of Stalin, see Alex Nove, *The Soviet Economy*, 3rd ed. (London: Allen and Unwin, 1968), pp. 261–83.

no evidence at that time of deep conflict; perhaps neither side clearly distinguished the two types of decentralization. Already, however, in Mao's discussion of the political context of socialist economic growth, and against the background of the gap between the growth rates of industry and agriculture and a new awareness of China's population problem, especially as it affected employment, the Chinese were beginning to be faced with some of the policy choices which, as we have argued briefly in the introduction to this chapter, were common to many of the underdeveloped countries and which were to become sharper as the years went on.

Disagreement over the continued existence and the nature of the class struggle in China as of 1957 also developed. Many of the criticisms made of the regime in the Rectification Campaign of 1957 directly or indirectly deplored the continued categorization of people into antagonistic classes and assumed, at least implicitly, a national unity which transcended class as class still existed at that time. It is impossible to interpret Mao's 'On the Correct Handling of Contradictions Among the People' in any other way except that Mao then believed the same; but he hedged his belief with qualifications which made it possible, later and in changed circumstances, to interpret his speech in a different sense. A conflict existed here, potentially at least, the poles of which were on the one hand insistence that class struggle must continue, and on the other a view closely akin to Khrushchev's idea of a socialist state of the whole people. Between late 1956 and June 1957, the latter interpretation appears to have been winning, and with Mao's approval. The radical criticisms made during the Rectification Campaign brought the experiment to an end in the Anti-Rightist Campaign of the same year, but the political issues exposed were closely related to choices in economic policy, and this relationship was to work itself out in 1958.

4. *The Great Leap Forward and the communes.* Consideration of the Second Five-Year Plan took place against a background which included not only the problems and the opportunities arising from the repudiation of Stalinism, but the vigorous condemnation in the Rectification Campaign of bureaucracy, overcentralization, hierarchy and blind imitation (sometimes ludicrous in degree) of the Soviet Union. These criticisms were often associated with criticism of Mao personally, as head of the Party and the State, and it must

have been very galling to him to be held responsible for precisely these four evils which he had spent so much of his political life in opposing.

Economically, experience of a centrally planned economy since 1953 had revealed new problems. First, it could offer no solution to the problems of unemployment and under-employment in the countryside. Second, satisfaction with the dramatic success of the growth of heavy industry was tempered by the realization that, in the absence of an equally rapid development of agriculture and light industry, many of the new plants were working at less than full capacity. It was clear that the rate of growth during the First Five-Year Plan could not be maintained, far less improved upon, unless larger surpluses could be won from agriculture; and the attempt in 1954 to increase this surplus by raising procurement norms had produced a sharply disincentive effect on agricultural production,[1] so that it was clear that no substantial increase in procurement would be possible unless agricultural production was sharply increased.

We know now that Mao had made his position clear in his speech on the 'Ten Great Relationships', the text of which only became available during the Cultural Revolution. He argued that the best means of developing heavy industry was to increase investment in light industry and agriculture, and thus provide the stimulus of a growing market for the products of heavy industry.[2] He also argued for a system sufficiently decentralized to permit the exercise of economic initiative in the localities.[3] The speech, like most of Mao's policy pronouncements, was moderate and guarded. We have no reason to suppose that it was highly controversial at the time, though it certainly suggested, in its implications, an alternative line of development to that represented by the stress on heavy industry as the engine of development, which was then still dominant throughout the under-developed world. Between late 1956 and 1957,

[1] Mao Tse-tung, 'On the Ten Great Relationships', in J. Ch'en (ed.), *Mao* (Englewood Cliffs, N.J.: Prentice-Hall, 1969), p. 73.

[2] *Ibid.* p. 68.

[3] *Ibid.* pp. 74–6. For a brief analysis of the economic implications of the 'Ten Great Relationships', see my article 'The Chinese Model: Some Characteristics of Maoist Policies for Social Change and Economic Growth', in A. Nove and D. M. Nuti (eds.), *Socialist Economics* (Harmondsworth: Penguin Books, 1972), pp. 497–501.

however, various policy documents which adumbrated the Second Five-Year Plan seemed to suggest that while Mao's ideas may have been acceptable, their implications were not universally appreciated. While many steps were taken at this time such as a new stress on medium and small-scale enterprise,[1] which one must assume, on the basis of the 'Ten Great Relationships', would have had Mao's approval, the main thrust of the new economic proposals was not in the Maoist direction of a dynamic balance between agriculture, consumer goods industry and heavy industry. On the contrary, it was in the negative direction of attempting to restore a balance by slowing down the rate of investment.

Meanwhile, a critical debate had taken place on the population problem, in which the Malthusian pessimism of 'some comrades' (unspecified) was overwhelmed by arguments that locally based, labour-intensive and intermediate-technology light industries could provide employment for any likely increases in the Chinese population.[2] The Maoist argument on the possibilities of local small-scale industry went on to insist that such industry was no mere uneconomic sop to the existence of unemployment, but, on the contrary, provided the quickest means of accumulating capital for the creation of modern industry.[3] The chief aim of the Great Leap Forward was thus defined in this debate.

The strategy of the Leap, schematically presented, was as follows:

1. The massive use of state funds to set up a modern basic industrial complex in every provincial capital.[4]

[1] Not, however, to any great effect. See Carl Riskin's article in the *China Quarterly*, No. 46, cited above.

[2] On the population debate of early 1958, see the article by Sun Yeh-fang in *Jen-min jih-pao* (*People's Daily*), 17 February 1958; 'Refutation of Wu Ching-chiao's Slanders Against the Chinese People on the Population Issue', in *Ts'ai-cheng yen-chiu* (*Financial Research*), February 1958; 'It is good to have a large population', in *Chi-hua ching-chi* (*Planned Economy*), No. 6, 9 June 1958; 'Criticism and appraisal of the new theory of population', in *Ching-chi yen-chiu*, No. 2, February 1958. For Mao's optimistic view in 1955 see *Chung-kuo nung-ts'un ti she-hui-chu-i kao-ch'ao*, p. 647.

[3] On this argument, see *Cheng-chih hsüeh-hsi* (*Political Study*), No. 6, 13 June 1958, 'Several Views on the Technological Revolution'.

[4] The campaign to establish bases of heavy industry in each provincial capital can most easily be followed through NCNA English Language Service news releases during the first half of 1958. The editors of NCNA (English Service) seem to have been more systematic in reporting this aspect of policy than the editors of the Chinese national press itself.

2. The retooling of the modern industrialized sector to provide products, blueprints, design skills and training for direct assistance to agriculture and small-scale local industry.[1]

3. The mobilization of local savings[2] and surplus labour through the co-operatives for irrigation and flood control, more intensive tillage, the development of local supplies of consumer goods, the repair and manufacture of tools, the local processing of agricultural crops, and finally the development, in response to demands thus created, of local sources of power, raw material supplies, miniaturized chemical fertilizer production, and the production (where China's widely scattered near-surface resources of coal and iron ore permitted) of iron and steel.

It is hardly necessary now to dwell on the haste and confusion which was evident in the implementation of these policies; the dislocation and scarcities which resulted; the collapse of national planning; and the over-stretching of the labour force which resulted. The full history of the Great Leap Forward, however, has never been written, and we must guard against sweeping conclusions unwarranted by evidence. We have no reason to suppose that there was irreconcilable opposition in China to the ideas on which the Great Leap was based. Opposition grew as the Great Leap proceeded, but it must be remembered that the movement had rapidly changed into something very different from the original conception. The abdication of national planning was not intended, though planning was now supposed to respond to grass-roots growth and exercise a co-ordinating, rather than a commanding role. The massive and wasteful use of bank credit, with the inflationary pressures which this was bound to create, was in direct opposition to the original principle that local development could be based primarily on local

[1] NCNA English releases for the first half of 1958 again provide the best summary account of the re-tooling of modern industry to serve agriculture and local industry, and the new effort made to design small-scale installations for power-generation, oil refining, metallurgy and the local manufacture of chemical fertilizers. For such designs, see especially NCNA for May 1958.

[2] For further pointers to the sources of funds for the Great Leap, see *Ta kung pao* 6 April 1958; NCNA, 12 February, shows the large investment by the PLA; *Ta kung pao*, 28 January 1958, for the drastic decentralization of the distribution of bank loans; *Hsüeh-hsi* (*Study*), 9 May 1958, on the possibilities of capital accumulation in the co-operatives. The last is an elaboration of Mao's prefatory note in *Chung-kuo nung-ts'un ti she-hui chu-i kao-ch'ao*, p. 335.

savings. The lengthening of the working day to an intolerable degree was in direct contradiction to the explicit emphasis originally placed upon the more rational use of labour as oppposed to long hours of work. The commandism, which this and many other aspects of the Leap showed to have become dominant, was totally opposed to the original idea that the new possibilities offered to the local communities would open up new perspectives which would inspire the population voluntarily to undertake development for themselves. The dangerous and finally tragic neglect of agriculture was an ironical end to a movement which had begun with the rapid development of agricultural production as its focus. Finally, the haste with which the campaign was carried on may have had some relation to certain of Mao's own ideas: his belief that the 'Socialist Upsurge' method of development would initiate a rapidly accelerating process of diversification of growth; his belief in uninterrupted revolution (keep people going by continuously setting new problems); and his belief (probably shared by every government which ever produced a national plan for economic growth) that planning should not only calculate probabilities but create aspirations. Such well known aspects of his thought made the cadres more likely to err in the direction of haste than of caution.

The period of progressive retreat from the Great Leap policies was a time of confusion and uncertainty in the central administration of China, in which opinions gradually hardened as the weather worsened and nature launched a war of attrition against China's overstretched rural labour force. The first public criticisms made of the Leap went no further than attempts to bring it under control and remove the worst excesses. The points made did not reflect upon the theory of the movement as opposed to its implementation. Warnings were issued that day-to-day agricultural production must have priority over all else, and limits were put on the diversion of labour to other purposes. Construction projects which would not make a quick and substantial contribution to production were deplored. Calls were issued for better and more balanced local planning, and effective national supervision. Worry was also expressed, with reason as events proved, that exaggerated hopes were leading to exaggerated claims. Nor was the creation of the commune organization as the institutional framework for autonomous local development attacked at this stage, although reservations were expressed indirectly as to the viability of public mess-halls and the possible disincentive effects of the free supply system.

Even the criticisms made at the Lushan Plenum should not be accepted too readily as condemnation of the strategy involved in the Great Leap and the communes. The fact that P'eng Te-huai could so easily be isolated and forced out on this issue does not suggest the existence, at this stage, of widely supported and irreconcilable opposition to the Maoist strategy of social change and economic growth. Nevertheless, in September 1959, Liu Shao-ch'i, in summing up and dismissing the reservations which 'some comrades' held, showed that already it was being said that mass movements in economic construction were ineffective, that the short-term gains of leaping forward would inevitably result in chaos, and that 'a leap-forward rate of advance goes against objective economic laws'.[1] These opinions, which Liu Shao-ch'i condemned but may well have shared, certainly implied presuppositions about economics quite at variance with those of Mao, and were to provide the premises for the alternative which was to develop in the early 1960s.

4. *1959–65*. We are now considering the period with which most of the accusations made in the Cultural Revolution are concerned, and it is as well to emphasize again that, in this section, we have excluded these accusations from consideration and based our brief résumé of policy changes on the public documents of the time. We will continue to do so for the present, in order to deal with the Cultural Revolution perspective in a later section.

During the period of successive bad harvests, 1959–61, there was an attitude of *sauve qui peut*, in which considerations of long-term policy and socialist principle gave way to tolerance of immediate short-term measures to minimize hunger and distress. Villages and individuals, and to some extent industrial enterprises, were left to find their own salvation. The larger scale and more impersonal commune organization was replaced in day-to-day agriculture, and as the unit of income distribution, by the face-to-face village group: the production team. Private agricultural production on a large scale

[1] 'The Victory of Marxist–Leninism in China', *Collected Works of Liu Shao-ch'i, 1958–67* (Hong Kong: Union Research Institute, 1968-9, 3 vols.).

136

was permitted; even private land reclamation was allowed. In some places family-scale farming re-emerged. Small-scale industry and local construction were often suspended so that the whole rural labour force could be deployed in defence against flood or drought.

It would be incautious to assume that these policies represented in any sense a positive alternative to the Maoist strategy. They were essentially an enforced accommodation to critical circumstances in which control of events had slipped from the Party's grasp. However, some of the broader conditions of the period tended to favour the perpetuation of a relaxation of control and of collectivism as well as a withdrawal from positive involvement in, and encouragement of, local development. Those most hostile to the Maoist strategy had freedom in the disorientation of the times to express themselves. This was the period of *The Dismissal of Hai Jui*, of the *Evening Chats*, and the other literary expressions of the 'blooming and contending' period of 1960 and 1962.[1] The implementation of a variety of reforms in the Soviet Union and East Europe, along with theoretical writings which attempted to show that these reforms were consistent with Marxism–Leninism, provided, in an elaborated form, an alternative which could be linked to the similar but abortive institutional changes in China in 1957 in the direction of decentralization to the provinces and of autonomy for large enterprises.

These potentially divisive factors did not operate immediately or visibly. Indeed, 1962 ended with apparently restored agreement on a new revolutionary drive, aimed primarily at the re-collectivization of agriculture in order to mobilize its resources for the 'four transformations'. The slogans of the 10th Plenum of the 8th Central Committee[2] were however highly ambiguous: 'Agriculture the foundation, industry the leading factor' could be interpreted either to mean renewed priority for heavy industry on the foundation of agricultural procurement, or, alternatively could mean priority for agricultural development with heavy industry geared to serve and

---

[1] See Merle Goldman, 'The Unique Blooming and Contending of 1959–60', *The China Quarterly*, No. 37 (January–March, 1969), pp. 57–84; also J. Gray and P. Cavendish, *Chinese Communism in Crisis* (London: Pall Mall, 1969), pp. 69ff.

[2] See Union Research Institute (ed.), *Documents of the Central Committee of the CCP 1956–69* (Hong Kong: Union Research Institute, 1971), I, 185ff.

respond to the demands of agriculture. 'Class struggle must continue under the socialist state' could mean much or little; it could imply no more than bringing to an end the 'spontaneous capitalist development' which had taken place in the countryside in the years of crisis, or it could mean, as it came to mean in the Cultural Revolution, an attack on all those vested interests in administration, economic planning, education and health which were obstacles to policies which gave priority to the economic transformation of the countryside on Great Leap Forward lines.

In the public documents of the period September 1962 to September 1965, from the 10th Plenum to Lin Piao's speech 'Long Live the Victory of the People's War', we find little evidence of the tug-of-war which the revelations of the Cultural Revolution paint so vividly for this period. Judged by what was done rather than what may have been said or written within the Party, the 10th Plenum marked the resurgence of Maoist influence, though in a chastened and cautious form. The effects were obvious immediately. Teng T'o delivered his last *Evening Chat* and its theme was that discretion is the better part of valour.[1] In theoretical political writings, there was an abrupt change. In late 1961 it had still been possible for a Chinese political theorist, taking as his justification Mao's 1957 speech on contradictions, to write explicitly that the democratic process must allow freedom not only for the expression of differences of opinion but of differences of interest.[2] From September 1962 onwards, the stress was on discipline instead of freedom. In economic writing, concentration on the theory of prices and value, which Sun Yeh-fang's writings and speeches[3] had touched off, gave way to a politically loaded debate on whether or not labour inputs in construction should be reckoned as capital investment. Not only was socialist organization re-asserted through

---

[1] *FE/2177*; *Jen-min jih-pao*, 21 May 1966 ' *Ch'ien hsien*. Tool of Capitalist Restoration'.
[2] Yang Ch'i, 'Handle Earnestly the views of the Minority', *Shih-shih shou-ts'e*, 22 (21 November 1961).
[3] For the writings of Sun Yeh-fang, see *T'ung-chi kung-tso* (*Statistical Work*), 'Starting from the Value of Total Output'; *Ching-chi yen-chiu*, No. 5, 1956, 'Put Planning and Statistics on the Basis of the Law of Value'; *Ching-chi yen-chiu*, No. 9, 1959, 'On Value'. For left-wing attacks on Sun's 'Libermanist' ideas, see Meng Kuei and Hsiao Lin, 'On Sun Yeh-fang's reactionary political stand and economic Programme' in *Red Flag*, No. 10, 1966; Yuan En-chen *et al.*, 'Resolutely Counter-attack against Sun Yeh-fang for his Attack on the Party', *Union Research Service*, No. 44, p. 269.

the Socialist Education Movement and the Four Clean-ups (*Ssu ch'ing*) but a ground swell of Great Leap ideas – abolition of the private sector, for example, and the restoration of the brigade or even the commune as the unit of income distribution – began. It was firmly checked, but in language which condemned these ideas only as untimely rather than wrong. In *Hung ch'i* in 1964, T'ao Chu spelled out emphatically the aims and the advantages of the commune system.[1] In the same year, personnel of the PLA, in which Lin Piao had tuned the pulpits to the service of Mao's personal prestige, moved into a variety of civilian posts. If there existed by this time in the Chinese Communist Party an alternative to the Maoist strategy of social change and economic development, it was high time to defend it if it was not to go by default.

THE CULTURAL REVOLUTION PERSPECTIVE

We have now looked at the general development of policy in the light of public statements made at the time. These statements minimize internal disagreements as surely as the accusations of the Cultural Revolution maximize them. We will now bring in the Cultural Revolution materials and re-work our description, this time, however, by the analysis of the various issues rather than as a narrative.

The issues involved covered every aspect of Chinese life. One issue, though not necessarily in itself the most important or logically prior, can shed the widest light on the rest. This is the problem of agricultural mechanization.

One of the questions which, as we have seen, is inevitably raised concerning agricultural mechanization in labour surplus conditions, is whether the use of labour-saving machinery has any relevance at all. It is not entirely irrelevant. It must be remembered that the surplus of labour is seasonal and can exist along with a chronic labour shortage in the busy seasons of agriculture. Anything which saves labour at planting, transplanting or harvest time, can increase yields per acre. The availability of motive power can enable tasks to be

---

[1] T'ao Chu, 'The People's Communes are Marching Ahead', *Hung ch'i*, 26 February 1964. T'ao Chu's uncompromising 1958-type defence of the Communes indicates, better than any other document of the time, the revival of Maoist hopes.

done which may be beyond the capacity of human muscles, and this is of particular importance where agriculture depends so much on dams and ditches, or on terracing of slopes, as in China. This motive power can be used for other purposes: for short-haul transport, pumping, processing of crops, generating electricity, and a variety of ancillary occupations.

Mechanization need not take the form of the immediate acquisition of a large tractor. The gradual process of mechanization of Western farming in response to changing factor prices is familiar enough and may be the most economically appropriate process in China, with its low level of savings, its locally varying factor proportions and the certainty that these factor proportions will change as development proceeds. A gradualist process of this kind has substantial advantages. It can be paid for out of local savings, with the gains from each stage paying for the next stage. It involves a gradual education in the use of new tools in step with the increasing sophistication of successively acquired machines. Finally, if this gradualist process is in the hands of the local community, the acquisition of labour-saving devices need not increase the surplus of labour, but can be phased in response to the increasing demand for labour which the increased productivity of the machines themselves can and should create. Finally, by contributing to the possibility of local processing of crops and by the engineering experience which it involves, a degree of mechanization of agriculture can contribute to the natural foundations of the industrialization of the countryside – the local processing of crops and the repair and manufacture of farm tools.

All of these points are contained in the 'Opinions on Agricultural Mechanization' adopted, at Mao's urging, at a meeting held in Chengtu in March 1958:

The Conference unanimously approves of Chairman Mao's instruction concerning the farm tool renovation movement. The [said] movement, which has the participation of the broad peasantry, is the seed-bed of technological revolution and a great revolutionary movement.

The whole country should extensively and actively popularise the [farm tool renovation] campaign. While popularising this, the various localities should pay attention to their particular conditions and should never do things in the same way. To achieve agricultural mechanization mainly depends on the efforts of the agricultural co-operatives. Only by doing this can agricultural mechanization be managed with greater, faster, better, cheaper results. The renovation of farm tools, whether mechanized (including motive power machines and machine drawn tools for farming), semi-mechanized (the so-called new animal-power farm tools) or pre-liminary renovation of old-fashioned farm tools (the so-called improved farm tools) are all useful in raising the productivity of agricultural labour. We should not merely wait for the agricultural machines and neglect the popularization of the new animal-power farm tools and the improved farm tools. In the main, small agricultural machines should be developed, supplemented by an appropriate quantity of large and medium sized ones...The manufacture of agricultural machines (including machine-drawn tools, new animal power farm tools and improved farm tools)... should generally be carried out mainly by industry in each locality. Agri-cultural machinery repairing and fitting stations should be set up in certain counties and townships...

Every province, district and county must set up a farm-tool research institute, call together scientists, technicians, experienced blacksmiths and carpenters, and collect all kinds of comparatively advanced farm tools from the whole province, district and county for comparison, experi-ment and improvement, to trial manufacture new types of farm tools.

All common agricultural machines and small tractors should be bought and employed by the co-operatives themselves. As regards medium-sized tractors, they may be owned and operated by a co-operative, owned by the state and jointly operated by the state and a co-operative...

Farm tool renovation has its various aspects, including irrigation and drainage in water conservancy, farmwork in the fields, rural transport, preliminary processing of fodder and agricultural by-products, and the renovation of tools for the prevention and cure of diseases and insect pests.[1]

This document, the existence of which was only revealed during the Cultural Revolution, apparently marked an important phase in

[1] See the following sources: 'Thoroughly Purge the Towering Crimes of China's Khrushchev and his Gang in Undermining Agricultural Mechanization', *Nung-yeh chi-hsieh chi-shu* (*Agricultural Machine Technology*), 8 August 1967. Translated in *Union Research Service*, No. 49, p. 50; 'Resolutely Criticize and Repudiate China's Khrushchev for his Crimes in Undermining the Cause of Agricultural Mechanization' by the East-Is-Red Commune of the Chinese Academy of Agriculture Mechanization, in *Agricultural Machine Technology*, 23 May 1967, translated in *URS*, No. 48, p. 290; 'Let the Brilliance of Mao Tse-tung's Thought for Ever Shine on the Road to Agricultural Mechanization', by the Take-Over Committee of the Heilungchiang Provisional Department of Agri-cultural Machinery, in *Agricultural Machine Technology*, 8 July 1967, translated in *URS*,

a history of disagreements over agricultural mechanization which began in 1950 and came to its final crisis in February 1966 – though it is hard to understand how it was possible for Liu Shao-ch'i effectively to suppress it for eight years.

In 1950, it seems to have been generally accepted that the mechanization of agriculture could not take place until China was industrialized and until there had been a considerable rise in the prosperity of the agricultural sector. Liu Shao-ch'i stated this view emphatically in June 1950, making of agricultural mechanization a pre-condition for successful collectivization.[1] Po I-po, on the other hand, appears to have been primarily concerned with the economics of mechanized agriculture. In 1956, he emphasized that mechanization would increase the problem of surplus labour in the rural areas.[2] In 1957 he is said to have written a lengthy paper which is quoted as making the point that mechanization would do little to increase per unit area output. This seems to have been produced during a controversy in which Po I-po himself, on the one hand, and K'ang Sheng on the other, organized rival research efforts on the subject.[3] Many other quotations show that a substantial number of leaders of the administration shared these opinions. Liu Shao-ch'i, in a self-criticism in 1955, while claiming that he had had a change of heart over the possibility of achieving rapid collectivization through the mutual aid teams, is not recorded as having alluded in this context to his former opinion that collectivization was impossible before the means for full mechanization

No. 48, p. 296; 'A History of the Struggle between the Two Roads on the Agricultural Mechanization Front', by the Mass Criticism Group of the Administrative Bureau of Agricultural Mechanisation, 8th Ministry of Machine Building, in *Agricultural Machine Technology*, No. 9, 1968, translated in *URS*, No. 53, p. 51.

[1] In introducing the Agrarian Reform Law of June 1950, Liu Shao-ch'i said: 'Only when conditions are mature for the extensive application of mechanized farming, for the organization of collective farms and for the Socialist reform of the rural areas, will the need for a rich peasant economy cease.' Union Research Institute, *Collected Works of Liu Shao-ch'i*, II, 226. Most of the speeches of Liu which are quoted against him on this point in Cultural Revolution documents were public speeches from 1949 to 1951, and could be interpreted simply as part of the attempt at that time to re-assure China's richer peasants and her business men that New Democracy would last long enough for them to pursue profit in security.

[2] 'A History of the Struggle between the Two Roads on the Agricultural Mechanization Front', *URS*, No. 53, p. 51.

[3] *Ibid*; also 'Thoroughly Purge the Towering Crimes, etc.', *URS*, No. 49, p. 50.

were available.[1] It seems probable therefore that, as late as early 1957, there was a strong body of opinion in the Central Committee which held that mechanization was neither possible nor desirable at that stage, and probably therefore did not entertain high hopes of the successful creation and operation of collectivized farming in the absence of mechanization.

K'ang Sheng, however, acting on Mao's behalf, had visited the Soviet Union in 1953–54 to investigate the mechanization of Soviet agriculture, and had returned disillusioned with the Soviet tractor stations on the grounds that they were mere tax collecting stations which 'held the peasants to ransom and were divorced from the people'. In 1956, he organized an investigation into the relations between mechanization and surplus labour; the role of mechanization in increasing output; the problems of integrating mechanization with existing farming methods; and the possibility of mechanization out of local resources. The results, it is said, 'refuted with actual facts the pessimistic view on which opposition to the mechanization of agriculture was based'.[2] It seems likely that Mao's 'Opinions Concerning Agricultural Mechanization', as accepted by the Chengtu Conference in 1958, were based on K'ang Sheng's studies.

In the Great Leap Forward the policies represented by the Chengtu Opinions were, in any case, applied. The tractor stations were broken up and the tractors distributed to the communes. Local committees of technicians, skilled workers and peasants were set up to experiment in the improvement of tools and in small-scale semi-mechanization as a part – perhaps the central part – of the drive to develop local industry. But this policy was reversed with the general dismantling of the communes and the institutions of the Great Leap.

From 1962, the arguments were renewed, although in a new context since the partial industrialization of China had provided a greater, though still very inadequate, capacity to provide machines. Liu Shao-ch'i seems to have taken the lead in promoting a policy of selective mechanization. He chose a number of *hsien*, sometimes reported as 100, sometimes as 130, in which a drive for full mechanization was to take place, organized through tractor stations which

[1] *Ibid.* p. 50.   [2] *Ibid.*

143

would work for profit: the profits being used for the extension of mechanization to a similar batch of *hsien* after 10 years.[1] With 2,000 *hsien* in China, it was a long perspective. Standardization and rationalization were to be assured by vesting all production and operation of farm machinery in a monopolistic state corporation. Such a direction of development was totally opposed to Maoist ideas, for reasons which are apparent in the Chengtu Opinions and which have been analysed elsewhere.[2] In rejecting Mao's road to mechanization, his opponents were rejecting the whole of his economic strategy. Indeed, they were rejecting more than this. Mao's economic strategy was a particular application of more general ideas concerning social change, its motivation and its preconditions.

Can one then, at this stage, see emerging in China a clear alternative to the Maoist model of development? Were there 'two roads'?

First, it is clear that there had already been two roads during the First Five-year Plan. There had been, on the one hand, the orthodox road, giving the greatest possible priority to modern heavy industry as the main engine of growth. This was a variant of the Soviet road. On the other hand, there was the alternative, represented in China by Mao's ideas as expressed in *Socialist Upsurge in China's Countryside*, 'On the Ten Great Relationships' and 'On the Correct Handling of Contradictions among the People', which reversed this concept of the multiplier and sought to put the development of heavy industry in the context of, and responding to, the attempt to increase and diversify production in agriculture; to mobilize local savings and labour; to diversify the rural economy in order to provide local complementarities; to increase rural incomes, savings and purchasing power, and thus to generate a demand for the products of heavy industry, which would provide what was needed to create intermediate technologies appropriate to local factor proportions. The state's resources were thus to be employed essentially in a form of inducement investment.[3]

[1] See 'Let the Brilliance of Mao Tse-tung's Thought Shine on the Road to Agricultural Mechanization', *URS*, No. 48, p. 296.

[2] J. Gray, 'The Economics of Maoism', *Bulletin of the Atomic Scientists*, 1969, reprinted in H. Bernstein (ed.), *Underdevelopment and Development* (Harmondsworth: Penguin Books, 1973), p. 254.

[3] Ishikawa Shigeru, *Economic Development in Asian Perspective* (Tokyo: Kinokuniya Bookstore, 1967), especially p. 145.

By 1962, the situation had changed. The whole of the Chinese Party appears to have accepted that priority must be given to the development of agriculture, but there were still fundamental differences as to what this meant. Clearly these differences involved profound clashes of principle; but there is insufficient evidence to demonstrate that a positive, fully elaborated alternative to Maoist policies, expressed in specific measures and specific investment priorities, existed. The re-assertion of Maoist ideas immediately after the years of crisis at the 10th Plenum of the 8th Central Committee, may have prevented the appearance of such an alternative. The potential alternative was expressed mainly in negative ways. The only major positive proposal known is Liu Shao-ch'i's 1964 proposal for the reorganization of Chinese industry into a series of monopolistic trusts, including a trust for the production and operation of agricultural machinery.[1] The arguments by which Liu Shao-ch'i defended this proposal provide a starting point for the consideration of what its wider implications might have been, had Liu and his supporters been able to overcome Mao's personal prestige.

These trusts were to have monopolistic control of the manufacture and distribution of their products throughout China; many small-scale enterprises had already, by 1962, been either abolished or absorbed in state enterprises. The index of efficiency of the operations of the trusts was to be profit. In 1962, the tractor stations, restored after the Great Leap Forward, had already been told that they must show a profit within two years or be abolished. The trusts were to operate autonomously, free from day-to-day direction by the central ministries, and free from interference by local authorities, the implication being that they should handle their own investment, for the purpose of maximising profit.

We have seen that the greatest obstacle to successful community development in many Asian countries is the inhibiting effects of inequality. In China, a large and flourishing private sector in agriculture through which some individual peasants could gain individual profits (profits to which the improvements made by the co-operative efforts of the others would indirectly but quite sub-

---

[1] 'The reactionary Nature of China's Khruschchev in Energetically Promoting Trusts', *Agricultural Machine Technology*, August 1967, translated in *URS*, vol. 49, p. 30.

stantially contribute), would have created precisely the kind of situation in which, elsewhere, the poor majority have decided that it is not worth their while to contribute their labour to community development. The evidence is that Liu Shao-ch'i was willing to tolerate such a flourishing private sector.

A strategy based on widespread rural development by the mobilization of local resources, savings and labour depends, as we have seen on the provision of appropriate political leadership at the grass-roots level. There is evidence to suggest that Liu Shao-ch'i and others in the administration, preoccupied perhaps with what they regarded as the larger issues in national policy-making, paid little more than lip-service to the idea of cadre participation in labour, and thus diverged sharply from the Maoist idea of proper grass-roots leadership.[1]

Policies appropriate to localized development demand also a form of education which stresses mass literacy as opposed to a high level of education for a selected few, education which fully and systematically and very simply inculcates the modernizing ideology of which Maoism, whatever else it is, is a variant. There is no evidence that Liu Shao-ch'i or any of his associates actually opposed this programme of mass education, but there is certainly evidence, as discussed elsewhere in this volume, that Liu Shao-ch'i favoured the maintenance of a separate educational stream through schools of special quality, where full-time formal education would be given to a high level to the intelligent minority.[2] The dangers of this for the Maoist programme are obvious. Nothing could be more

[1] In a talk at a reception of 'responsible personnel' of the China Democratic National Construction Association and the All-China Federation of Industry and Commerce in 1960, Liu is quoted as having said: 'If Party members and cadres can take part in labour, *do a little bit of sweeping and cleaning* [italics added], then the masses will change their impression, and the relations between them and the masses will be improved accordingly.' See 'Forty Instances of the Reactionary Statements of the Top party Person in Authority Taking the Capitalist Road in Undermining the Socialist Revolution in the Countryside', *Rural Youth* (Shanghai, Red Guard Paper), No. 9, 10 May 1967, translated in *URS*, No. 48, p. 74. In other statements ascribed to Liu in this document and others, he uses careerist arguments to encourage youth to go to the countryside and participate in labour, urging them to make this small sacrifice now for their own future, using the proverb: 'Don't drop the melon while picking up the sesame seed.'

[2] See 'Emergence of Liu Shao-ch'i's "Dual Education" on Two Occasions', in *The Steel August 1st Combat Flag and Educational Reform Bugle Combined Issue* (Red Guard Paper), No. 1, December 1967. Translated in *URS*, No. 50, p. 249.

calculated nullify the effects of an egalitarian education system designed in the first place to serve the local communities than the preservation of a special category of pupils destined for high administrative or technical office from the beginning of their school careers.

There are also indications that Liu Shao-ch'i diverged from the Maoist model on matters of health policy.[1]

At the roots of these differences of approach lay more profound differences concerned with the evaluation of human motives. These different views of human nature are not unique to China. They obtrude in every political discussion everywhere, whether in seminar or pub, and, as applied to the motivation of work and effort they have given rise to a large sociological literature in recent times. To the Maoists the first condition of securing 'more, better, quicker, cheaper results' was to replace personal material incentives with incentives which would operate to create a responsible work force of the kind upon which all modern industrial societies depend for their efficiency.

There is ample evidence that Liu Shao-ch'i took a less liberal view of the possibilities of human nature in this respect. He favoured piece rates. He constantly encouraged careerist attitudes to public service which were already far too powerful traditionally in China. He was prepared to manipulate the price mechanism by raising the price of industrial goods to the peasant to increase the marketed surplus, in direct opposition to Mao's insistence in the 'Ten Great Relationships' that the differential between the prices of industrial products and agricultural products should be kept as narrow as possible to encourage peasants to buy.[2]

[1] For several documents accusing 'the big renegade traitor and scab Liu Shao-ch'i and his agents' of attempts to abolish or to bring under state control the attempts made by communes to create their own medical services, see *URS*, vol. 54, pp, 66ff. No specific accusations are made against Liu personally on questions of health policy. On Chinese health services since the Cultural Revolution, see Mark Selden, in Schurmann and Riskin (eds.), *New Perspectives on China* (New York: Pantheon, forthcoming).

[2] J. Chen, *Mao*, pp. 68–9. Mao's insistence on price policies favouring peasant accumulation can be contrasted with the apparent willingness of Liu Shao-ch'i – at least in the crisis of 1959–61, but perhaps at no other time – to manipulate prices against the rural sector: 'The peasants hold us at bay on the problem of foodgrain. We can also hold them at bay by controlling things like cloth, salt, kerosene, matches, farm chemicals, chemical fertilizers, agricultural tools, electric batteries, etc....From now on we must sell our

The point of crisis in these debates came on 23 February 1966, when the Hupeh Provincial Committee submitted to the Central Committee their Proposal on the Gradual Implementation of Agricultural Mechanization. A detailed account of what then happened was published during the Cultural Revolution.[1] This account cannot be checked from non-Maoist sources but, in view of the previous history of this issue, it seems plausible. In response to the Hupeh Committee's document (which seems to have been an updating of the Chengtu Opinions), an unnamed 'top Party person', on 26 February, once more brought forward Liu Shao-ch'i's scheme for an agricultural machinery trust. On 11 March, Liu Shao-ch'i wrote to Mao suggesting that the Hupeh proposal should not be generally circulated for the moment and proposed only that representatives of one of the ministries should be sent to Hupeh to conduct experiments. Mao replied promptly on 12 March, demanding that all central bureaux and all provincial, regional and municipal Party committees should send representatives to Hupeh to study the problem together and that each committee draw up its own draft plan in the light of their findings. Mao insisted once more that mechanization must be based on local self-reliance: 'A 'part of the right of machine-building should be fought for on behalf of the localities. It is wrong to choke them to death by centralizing everything.' It was at this point that Mao condemned Soviet agricultural policy as 'mistaken right from the beginning' and 'draining the pond to catch the fish'. Mao's criticism of 12 March was not circulated to the lower levels of the Party; instead a 1958 document written by Liu Shao-ch'i on technical revolution was distributed. The struggle ended with the full acceptance of Mao's policy by the 11th Plenum of the 8th Central Committee in August, at the meeting which launched the Cultural Revolution.

industrial goods to the peasants at higher prices...on the basis of "high price for high price".' Speech at the Report Meeting of the Office of Finance and Trade of the State Council, October 1960, reported in 'Forty Instances' cited above, p. 146, n. 1.

[1] 'Making a Last Stand for Self-destruction', by the East-is-Red Commune of the Chinese Institute of Agricultural Machinery, translated in URS, No. 49, p. 34.

THE 'LIUIST MODEL' AND ITS IMPLICATIONS

So far as the documents permit us to judge, the problem of agricultural mechanization is the only problem for which the Liuist wing of the Party seems to have offered a specific and elaborated alternative solution to the Maoist model. The lack of precise information on other policy questions makes it difficult to construct an overall 'Liuist' alternative: the so-called 'capitalist road'. Most of the documents of the Cultural Revolution described capitalist tendencies rather than capitalist policies, because, as we have suggested earlier, it was in terms of social trends rather than specific policies that the Maoists analysed the situation.

We are left, therefore, to try to build, for the guidance of further thought and research, a notional 'capitalist road' from the existing scraps of information on actual policies, and from the implications of the tendencies which the left wing of the Party described during the Cultural Revolution. Having erected this castle-in-the-air hypothesis, we can then submit it to such confirmation or criticism as the documents provide or may in future provide.

Analysed in this way, we can assume that the putative policies of the 'capitalist roaders' may have included the following:

1. The rate of investment would have been reduced to restore balance and to minimize economic and political tensions.
2. An increased private sector would have been permitted in the rural economy; collective responsibilities would have been limited, and family responsibilities possibly increased.
3. The management of industry would have been delegated to autonomous firms.
4. A profit motive would have been introduced into industry by paying incentive bonuses to management and workers, combined with increasing autonomy in management and investment.
5. The differential between worker and peasant incomes would have been increased, because incentive bonuses paid to workers would have tended to keep their wages more closely in line with the rising productivity of their labour.
6. A very considerable casual work force, earning low wages and without security of tenure or pension rights, would have been tolerated.

7. Agricultural mechanization would have been undertaken by the state on a profit basis.
8. Small-scale local industry would have been discouraged.
9. The role of the commune would have been minimized.
10. Control of the use of state resources by the local communities would have been sharply checked.
11. Planning would have become 'genetic' rather than 'teleological' – that is, it would become primarily a projection of trends and probabilities, and would not seek to create new aspirations and increased efforts.
12. Development, even local development, would be financed through state taxation rather than out of community funds.
13. Cadres' participation in labour would cease to be encouraged.
14. Political education of experts and intellectuals would have become nominal.
15. An elitist element would have been accepted in education, the locally financed production-oriented schools discouraged, formal academic standards maintained throughout the education system, and work-study minimized.
16. A freer and more critical role would have been permitted to artists and writers, those formerly accused of 'rightism' would have been rehabilitated, and intellectuals, managers and technicians given greater prestige and greater freedom.

On all of these points, we can put forward, provisionally, two types of evidence: first, that the public record of debate before the Cultural Revolution is such as to suggest – muted though it was – that these were possibilities which enjoyed some support in Party counsels; second, that all of them figure, however, vaguely or obscurely, in Cultural Revolution accusations.

It may well be, however, that too keen a search for such specific policy alternatives will lead us into complex explanations which only obscure some simpler, broader truth. Perhaps the essence of the Liuist strategy and of its implications can best be grasped in dynamic perspective, as it manifested itself in the course of the Socialist Education Movement of 1962–5, the prelude to the Cultural Revolution.

We have comparatively full documentation regarding this movement, including Mao's original directive of May 1963, the directives of September 1963 and September 1964, drawn up respectively under the influence of Teng Hsiao-p'ing and of Liu Shao-ch'i, and Mao's rebuttal to these in a new directive of January 1965.[1] The original aim of the movement was simple: to restore the system of collective farming which had been all but shattered in the three bad years of 1959–61. What was really at issue?

Scrutiny of the directives and of commentary on them does not suggest that at this time there was any dispute about the necessity of restoring collectivism. If anything, it would appear that at this time, and in this context, Liu Shao-ch'i, was prepared to be less tolerant than Mao towards rural private enterprise. The significant differences in these documents concern the methods to be used rather than the aim to be attained.

The attempt to restore the collectives revealed how far many of them had sunk, not just into a tacit return to private enterprise, but into an appalling mess of mis-allocation of resources, embezzlement of funds, collusion with the village elite, and even theft, terrorization and rape. The further the movement was pressed, the worse the situation appeared to be. Wang Kuang-mei's description of the situation in the 'Peach Garden Brigade' has a ring of truth: 'The 20-odd principal cadres of the brigade and its constituent production teams are linked together by their common "four unclean" interests...The "four uncleans" exist universally among the cadres.'[2]

Such a situation was obviously very difficult to handle merely by administrative action. Teng's solution to the problem, produced perhaps before the full seriousness of the situation was apparent, combined leniency towards petty offenders with firm and formal legal action against the more serious offenders. Liu, responding to his wife's experience in T'ao-yuan and elsewhere, adopted the more severe methods which she had believed necessary. Work teams, often incognito, worked in secrecy to establish contacts within the village. On

---

[1] For these Socialist Education Movement directives, see *Documents of the CCP Central Committee*, pp. 735–835. For a systematic analysis of these documents, and an account of the movement, see R. Baum, 'Revolution and Reaction in Rural China: the "Struggle between Two Roads" during the Socialist Education Movement (1962–1966) and the Great Proletarian Cultural Revolution (1966–1968)', unpublished doctoral dissertation, University of California, Berkeley, 1970.

[2] Quoted in R. Baum, *ibid.*, p. 114.

the basis of information thus obtained, they then launched a ruthless attack on all offenders, using struggle meetings and (according to some reports) physical brutality to extort confessions.[1] Liu's revision of Teng's instructions expressed this hard line.

Where corruption was widespread, covered up by collusion, and condoned out of fear by the village community, it is difficult to condemn such a proceeding as excessive from a moral point of view. But from the point of view of effectiveness, it was a method of dubious value in such a situation, especially when some of the 'crimes' involved – illegal concessions to private production and private trade – were popular in certain sections of the village. In any case, such proceedings, though they may terrify while they last, cannot in themselves provide a permanent improvement in the morality of the village leadership.[2]

Mao Tse-tung's conclusion was that the only effective method lay in mobilizing the masses, especially the 60–70% of the village comprising the poor and lower-middle peasants. The Socialist Education Movement (and the 'Big Four Clean-Ups', into which it was ultimately transformed) was, in essence, he said, a question of class struggle. One can only agree with Mao that the sole lasting guarantee against a corrupt and tyrannical administration is to put real power in the hands of the citizens who are being robbed and bullied. The relevance of class struggle is a little less obvious. Mao's own explanation was as follows:

The crux of the present movement is to purge the capitalist roaders in authority within the Party...

Some of their supporters come from below and some from above. Those

[1] *Ibid.*, pp. 152–3.

[2] Liu Shao-ch'i's diagnosis of the rural situation and its seriousness is well documented in the 'Forty Instances' (cited above, p. 146, n. 1). 'The enemies are mixed up with the basic-level cadres, and the struggle is extremely violent. When you go down there you may not be able to strike down the four categories and the cadres who have made mistakes. They have the upper hand at the start, because they are organized and prepared, and they have systematic ways of dealing with the work-teams...our Party members and cadres have not yet learned the way to struggle against the double-faced administration of landlords, capitalists and degenerate elements...We have not won any victory in the past year; we have lost the battle...investigation meetings cannot unearth problems...work teams should carry out some work in secret.' These excerpts from speeches made to various work conferences in August 1964 show clearly that the problem was collusion among the cadres and between cadres and part (how large a part?) of the village population.

from below are...landlords, rich peasants, counter-revolutionaries, and other depraved elements...Those from above are people opposing socialism in the communes, *ch'ü*, counties, districts, even provinces and departments of the Central Government...Some...shield their own relatives, friends or old colleagues who are engaged in capitalist activities...[1]

The implications of this are clear: the situation (which Mao insists exists also in the towns) is the consequence of collusion between those elements who have an interest in restoring capitalism and Party members in authority at all levels, and it includes the shielding of members of lower rank by those of higher rank. Thus, in Mao's view it is essentially not an administrative problem, but one of political power.

After this preamble, Mao goes on to insist that the poor majority in the village must be mobilized, a truly effective association of poor and lower-middle peasants formed, a competent leadership nucleus created for them, and the power given to the community itself and not to higher administrative levels to supervise and reform the 'four categories' (landlords, rich peasants, counter-revolutionaries, and depraved elements).

He then repeats his familiar instructions on the theme of seizing power: 'make use of contradictions, win the majority, oppose the minority and crush individuals separately'. For this purpose, a distinction must be made between the small minority of serious offenders, and those who have committed petty misdemeanours and less serious political deviations. Where so many are guilty (and perhaps few wholly innocent) great tolerance must be exercised. A long-term solution in which new and better habits are inculcated by effective popular supervision will be more effective than attempts to punish all offenders.

Throughout Mao's specific instructions as to methods, the insistence that the masses must have the power of decision is repeated.

Concealed land, when voluntarily admitted by the owner, may be exempted from taxes and state requisitioning and purchase for about five years, *after discussion by the masses*.

Whether those landlords, etc. who have worked honestly and done no evil for the past ten years should have their labels taken off...*shall be decided by the masses*.

---

[1] See *Documents of the CCP Central Committee*, pp. 825–6.

Whether it will be more advantageous for a production brigade to contain about 30 households *should be decided by the masses...None of this must be decided by the higher level.*

The cadres must receive supervision both from above and below *but mainly from the masses.*

In addition, cadres, when elected, would not generally be allowed to serve for more than four years, and the electors would have the right of recall.

It is clear that for Mao the cure for corruption, collusion, and the decay of collectivism is to put power in the hands of the poor majority of the village. It then becomes clear what was meant in the charge against Liu Shao-ch'i that his methods in the Socialist Education Movement were 'left in form but right in essence' – his root-and-branch policies concealed a bureaucrat's approach, and were essentially anti-democratic. Similarly, Teng Hsiao-p'ing's insistence on passing the offenders on to the higher levels to be dealt with there instead of by the village population themselves was, in Mao's eyes, undemocratic, though Teng's fault was less than Liu's.

In 1965, the People's Liberation Army, which had been playing an increasingly large role in Chinese society, especially since the beginning of 1964, intervened also in the Socialist Education Movement. What is the explanation of the apparent paradox that Mao Tse-tung, having condemned Liu's heavy-handed administrative actions, should now invoke the army – which would seem, at first sight, to be the most heavy-handed administrative action possible? This paradox, if paradox it is, is a persistent one. Every new intensification of Maoist mass-line methods has been accompanied in a greater or lesser degree by the exertion of armed force. The paradox easily resolves itself if we look at the history and characteristics of the Chinese army.

A guerrilla army, in so far as it represents genuine popular grievances or aspirations, must be in a very real sense the 'vanguard' of the political movement it represents. The dependence of a guerrilla army on the support of the population forces it to be not only a fighting but a preaching organization. Moreover, the dependence of guerrilla armies on the local population leads them naturally to become involved in economic operations, and we have seen that this function had been particularly developed in the case of the Chinese Communist armies in Yenan days.

The post-war PLA was no longer a guerrilla army, but it had retained some guerrilla characteristics. Although the Red Army had grown to a standing army of a million by 1946, it was still very much a political vanguard, representing a revolutionary form of nationalism, recruited largely from those who had suffered most bitterly at the hands of the Japanese and who had repudiated the society which had failed to defend them. The system of recruitment thereafter, through which the most politically reliable of able-bodied youth (of demographic necessity mostly peasant youth) were privileged to be summoned to the colours, tended to perpetuate the PLA's tradition as the vanguard of revolution. It remained, as it had been, a sort of twentieth-century Chinese New Model Army – made up of men who 'know what they fight for, and love what they know', bringing together under discipline and in an atmosphere of constant political discussion, young peasants from half-a-million scattered villages, a formidable political force. It has remained closely linked with the civilian population through the militia who are again chosen for their political reliability.

As the spearhead of revolutionary consciousness, the PLA assumes naturally a leading role in socialist construction, in which it has from time to time played a very large part; and as in other poor countries its administrative experience, its effective chain of command, and its technical and medical skills make it an important economic force.

This PLA tradition has of course not gone unchallenged. P'eng Te-huai and to a lesser extent Lo Jui-ch'ing took a more conventional view of the PLA's responsibilities, but under Lin Piao the old traditions were vigorously and self-consciously revived.

It is one particular stream of this military tradition, however, which most closely concerns the present argument. We have seen the importance in Mao's eyes of the act of the seizure of power as a part of, and not simply as the result of, political (and where relevant economic) radicalization. It remains to be added that this is in principle a violent seizure of power. However, if the army itself were to seize power, then the effects of a popular seizure of power would not follow. Therefore the role of the army has not been to act politically, but to hold the ring for popular political action. The tradition began not with the CCP but outside it, when in 1926-7 the Nationalist armies tolerated the Hunan peasant rising, though with misgivings. (A map of the rising shows how dependent the Hunan peasants were on Nationalist forces.) Throughout the various phases of land reform from Kiangsi onwards, this technique was used to a greater or lesser extent by the CCP, culminating in late 1949 when, after peasant excesses in land reform in Honan had forced the administration to stop the campaign, it was redesigned in such a way as to ensure the creation side by side of both a village militia and a new representative village government to control the campaign, with the PLA in the wings holding off landlords and Kuomintang irregulars until the peasant community was sufficiently organized and sufficiently competent to carry through its own revolution.

The role of the army in the Socialist Education Campaign was thus, on the precedents, compatible with a new 'seizure of power', this time by the newly reconstituted Poor and Lower Middle Peasant Associations; not only compatible, but predictable; and it was predictable that at the same time Mao should issue instructions that the weapons of the militia should be got into suitable hands.[1]

In both its rise and fall in the subsequent Cultural Revolution, the army's role was as before. It was brought in to hold the ring for the left; it was ousted after eighteen months of re-iteration that its role was that of long stop, and that army personnel should not do for the people what the people should be learning to do for themselves.

The intervention of the PLA in the Socialist Education Movement, therefore, tends to strengthen and not to weaken the conclusion that Mao repudiated administrative action and sought a re-assertion of majority control. Thus, in the protracted struggle of the Socialist Education Movement, in which there was ample room for policy disagreements of a familiar, indeed almost predictable, kind over collectivism versus rural private enterprise, such potential controversies were overshadowed by the question of the means by which collectivism should be re-asserted. The division was concerned with whether this should be done by administrative fiat from above, or by popular effort from below.

[1] *Documents of the CCP Central Committee*, p. 831.

Perhaps we have penetrated here to the essential conflict beneath the controversies over policy: the conflict as to whether socialism should be based on popular power, or on paternalistic administration. To Mao, the first opens up ever wider perspectives of many-sided development in the interests of the majority; the second, through the accretion of power, privilege and profit at the top, leads to authoritarian tendencies which, in their extreme expression, he stigmatized in 1963 as 'fascist'.

2

LEVELS OF ECONOMIC
DECISION-MAKING

Marianne Bastid

A preliminary question should perhaps be asked: is there such a thing in China as an 'economic' decision? A reading of the Chinese press during the last few years, especially the criticism of 'economism', tempts one to answer that any decision is first of all 'political'. In other words, in Chinese terms, there are no 'economic' decisions. Strictly speaking, that conclusion should bring this chapter to a brief end.

Nevertheless, this assumption may deserve some further enquiry. Even if it is based on theoretical grounds, the emphasis put by the Chinese authorities on politics, and on the political nature of every human action, is also linked to a specific aim so far as economic activities are concerned. This aim is to ensure that certain policies are not rejected in the name of assumed 'objective' laws of economics – for example, that the running of small rural industries is not opposed merely because in many cases it yields no sizeable financial profit in the short term.

How then can the line be drawn between politics and economics? Although any decision can rightly be said to be political, it is also true that there is hardly any decision which is either absolutely devoid of any tie with, or any effect upon, economic matters. In most cases, it is equally appropriate to speak of a political decision with economic implications, or an economic decision with political implications.

Western theory tends to define economic goals in terms of a sheer increase in production, consumption and profit-making. Is this also the Chinese notion of economics? Without straying into a lengthy discussion of the Chinese idea of politics, it suffices to say that such a purely materialistic approach to economics is precisely what the

159

Cultural Revolution denounced under the label of 'economism'. The revolutionaries called for a 'political economy': that is, for the shaping of production and consumption according to the needs and interests of the national community as a whole. They argued that non-material factors should be taken into account, and material ones should be considered within a broader social view of the needs of the collective. The 'profitability' of an enterprise should not be evaluated simply in terms of immediate gross increase in output or technical efficiency in a narrow sense, since attributes such as conscious mass-participation in economic development, large-scale diffusion of skills, the bridging of inequalities or the provision of a humane environment for the life of the people were even more important criteria. Such a 'political economy' is not totally un-economic, if by economic one means taking into account material gain or increases in production, but it does not hold that type of material achievements as ends *per se*.

For the sake of clarity and conciseness, this chapter will focus on decisions which involve production directly and immediately, including the means of production and the distribution or consumption of the products, as well as the financing of production, leaving it open to discussion whether or not these are 'economic' decisions. Because of a total lack of relevant materials, I am unable to say anything about these questions within the military administration, and intend to deal, therefore, only with the situation within the civilian administration.

Even within such restricted limits, we find that decisions fall into different categories. On the one hand there are those decisions which define objectives, on the other hand those decisions which deal only with concrete measures for the achievement of aims which have already been determined. In Chinese documents, the first type of decision comes under the headings of *chiao-tao, chih-tao, chih-shih, lu-hsien* or *fang-chen*, which, although somewhat different in meaning, all refer to general policy; the second type of decision is called instead *cheng-ts'e*, that is, specific policy, or policies, or operation. Of course, the boundary between the two is often very much blurred. The concrete measures for implementing a general policy may in fact result in a shift or distortion of the general policy itself. In a commune near Peking, for instance, because of the priority given to profit-making, the majority of manpower was exclusively engaged in side-line activities. After this so-called 'Liuist' policy had been criticized in 1970, all side-line activities were dropped; as a result the income of the commune decreased and the progress of agricultural production was adversely affected, since there was a lack of capital to buy fertilizers and farming implements, and the new directive of 'grain as the core, overall development' was not really implemented.[1] But even with such reservations, it is useful to bear in mind the distinction between general policy and operation.

The purpose of this chapter is primarily to analyze the distribution and working of economic decision-making power from 1969 to 1972, as accurately as scanty information allows. It is not to give a full-fledged interpretation or theoretical analysis of Chinese economic development, even if a few explanations are suggested. This kind of investigation had not yet been made and seems necessary before further elaboration, a task which I gladly leave to the social scientists and economists.

PAST EXPERIMENTS

In order to appraise current trends, it is necessary first to take a brief look back to the situation before the Cultural Revolution. Since 1949, various experiments in the centralization and decentralization of decision-making had been tried,[2] with none of them ever being either applied or reversed indiscriminately. Consequently, the situation in 1965 was by no means uniform. Indeed, its main feature appeared to be the coexistence of residues from various conflicting systems, each in its own way a practical application of the Marxist-Leninist principle of democratic centralism.

For the Chinese Communists, democratic centralism is not an undifferentiated notion; it is made up of two contradictory components, centralism, and democracy.[3] Centralism is a unification of

---

[1] *Jen-min jih-pao* (*JMJP*) (*People's Daily*) (Peking), 12 March 1972, p. 1. Similar example in a Shansi commune, *JMJP*, 27 August 1972, p. 2.

[2] For a careful analysis of those experiences, see F. Schurmann, *Ideology and Organization in Communist China* (Berkeley: University of California Press, 1968), pp. 86–90, 173–86, 188–308 and 322–64.

[3] See Mao Tse-tung, 'On the Correct Handling of Contradictions among the People', *Selected Readings* (Peking: Foreign Languages Press, 1967), pp. 354–5.

opinion enforced by the centre, while democracy relates to the expression of a multiplicity of opinions at the grass-roots level.[1] So far as decision-making is concerned, centralism implies a system where both general and specific policy impulses come from the centre. Democracy implies a system where policy impulses originate from a level below the centre. Consequently, democratic centralism may cover a wide range of combinations. There may be variations in the amount or type of specific policies which remain in the hands of the centre, as well as in the hierarchical position of those lower levels which are given decision-making power on specific policies; there may also be variations in the type and scope of specific policies which are left in the hands of each particular lower level. Moreover, the concept of democratic centralism allows a further division of competence, not only according to the object of decision but also in the decision-making method or process itself: initiative and participation may be allowed in varying degrees to different lower levels, even when the formal decision-making power is retained by a higher level.

Since 1949, there has never been an attempt to advocate an exclusive emphasis on democracy at the expense of centralism. It has always been a question of combination in a unity of true opposites. This has chiefly been achieved through varying degrees of decentralization. Decentralization, in practice, is seen as having two general forms: either decision-making power is transferred all the way down to the production units themselves, or it is only transferred down to some lower level of regional administration. There are, furthermore, two types of administrative structure and function: the branch principle and the committee principle. According to the branch (*pu-men*) principle, all administration is divided into parallel branches, each performing a function in one sector and being vertically commanded from the centre. According to the committee principle, administration is dominated by committees made up of members from different branches. If the committee includes representatives of branch agencies of the central government, then the lines of command flow in part horizontally. If it amounts in fact to control by a regional government or Party committee, then the local agency may lose its branch-type function.

---

[1] *Joint Publications Research Service* (*JPRS*) 52029, 21 December 1970, *Translations on Communist China* No. 128, 'Talks and Writings of Chairman Mao', p. 4.

In the early years of the First Five-Year Plan, stress was put on branch-type administration and centralization. This scheme, which was strongly influenced by Stalinist concepts, then seemed the most suitable for the speedy development of a still weak and restricted industrial base, as well as for the socialist transformation of the traditional production sectors, especially in view of the shortage of capital and of trained and politically reliable personnel, which made it risky to entrust too much responsibility to the lower levels.

From 1956 on, however, government became increasingly characterized by a process of decentralization which gave power to the provincial Party committees; by the growth of inter-branch coordinating agencies; and by the development of Party-dominated regional governments. Economic control tended to become concentrated in the hands of the Party. The Great Leap Forward marked the high point of the system of government by committees, during which central ministries found their operations obstructed by regional influences.

The new organizational approach in the 1956–9 period came at a time when the collectivization of agriculture, the transformation of most industrial and commercial enterprises into joint State-private ventures and the creation of numerous new enterprises had increased enormously the tasks of the central government, beyond indeed its actual ability to administer these enterprises and coordinate their activities in detail. The scheme was, presumably, partly a belated recognition that highly centralized control was impossible and that, in practice, local authorities had already taken over some of the functions supposedly reserved for the centre. On the other hand, Party organization had by then extended wide and deep enough to appear able to act as the local agent of authority. These facts probably accounted, at least partially, for a decision that was nonetheless primarily inspired by a wish to accelerate industrial and social revolution, namely the decision to shift the direction of China's development strategy. The new development strategy, which was closely linked with changes in the economic power structure, put its emphasis on the rapid increase of a wide range of small-scale rural industries, instead of on large-scale, urban-concentrated, heavy industrial concerns, on labour-intensive rather than on capital-intensive enterprises, and on the integration and subordination of production to political and social remoulding of the country at large.

The serious economic crisis which ensued during the 'bad years' of 1959–61 led to a retrenchment of these policies, with a view to increasing food production at almost any cost, and to bringing under control the excessive local autonomy which had been conducive to waste and disruption. In March 1960, the Central Government announced the decision to put 'agriculture in the first place'. This was in fact a change in the whole approach to development strategy which led, in turn, to more flexibility and diversity in organization, since agriculture is far too dependent on natural conditions to be governed in a uniform way as easily as industry. After 1961, stress was placed once again on branch administration, but not to the degree it had been in 1950–4. The Ministries of Finance and Trade, and of Industry, as well as the People's Bank were strengthened, but coordinating committees continued to play an important role both at the centre and in the regions. In early 1961, an attempt was made to grant broad decision-making autonomy to the production units themselves.[1] This lessened the power of provincial government, thus reversing the practice of the Great Leap. Beginning in 1962, however, provincial government seemed to have regained some of its lost powers.

THE SITUATION IN 1965

In the 1965 context so far as economic affairs were concerned, the 'Centre' consisted of the Party Central Committee, the State Council and the State Planning Commission. Strictly speaking these three agencies taken together made up the 'Centre'. Besides these, among the 90 ministries and special agencies subordinated to the State Council, some 50 were 'economic'. In a certain sense these ministries, because they are branch agencies, cannot be considered as part of the central organs. Therefore, the most important decisions could not be taken at their level, these decisions belonging either to the Central Committee or to the State Council or to the State Planning Commission. In practice, however, the Centre in the

[1] See F. Schurmann, 'China's "New Economic Policy" – Transition or Beginning', *The China Quarterly*, No. 17 (January–March 1964), pp. 80–91. .

limited sense defined above, often entrusted some of its powers to the various ministries. Moreover, the latter were frequently required to make decisions which applied to the whole country. In this respect, these decisions were of the same nature as those taken by the 'Centre' narrowly defined, and the various ministries can therefore be considered as belonging to the 'Centre' as broadly defined.

Apart from the 'Centre', the main other levels of decision-making were, geographically speaking, the provincial, municipal and local organs of power, and, looked at from a branch point of view, the enterprises – that is, the economic units in the production and distribution sphere. Using these criteria, the people's communes were in a special position, since they were both local agencies of State power and economic units in the production sphere.

In 1965, therefore, the situation was confused. Conflicting tendencies appeared: some toward centralization; some toward a decentralization to the level of regional committees; and some toward a decentralization to the level of production units. The prevailing features were: strong centralization of key industries,[1] decision-making power given to or taken by provincial Party committees in a significant but limited sector of economic life (mainly light industry) and a wide degree of management autonomy left to the communes and to the Party committees of industrial production units.

This system broke down with the Cultural Revolution attacks on economic ministries, on provincial Party committees and on factory management in late 1966 and early 1967.

---

[1] The 'trusts' for which Po I-po was heavily criticized during the Cultural Revolution. See *JMJP*, 26 April 1970, p. 4, an article by the State Planning Commission; *Hsing-tao jih-pao* (Hong Kong), 24 August 1969, a summary of an article published in China in *Ching-chi p'i-p'an* (*Economic Critic*).

METHODOLOGICAL PROBLEMS

In the general reconstruction of institutions and government channels of command since 1969, what has now happened to economic decision-making power? A first question to be asked is whether the spheres of central and non-central decision-making have or have not been redefined. We must then try to ascertain the actual distribution of authority and power among the various agencies at different levels. Finally, we shall then consider the decision-making process itself, together with the problem of conflicting decisions and the unification of economic policy.

The sources for this study are mainly the Chinese press, together with some oral explanations which were given to me during a visit to China in October–November 1971. One major difficulty in interpreting this material is the exact meaning of the term *kuo-chia* (State). I have noted in conversations that the Chinese are now using it almost indifferently for any authority which is above their own level. In the mouth of a commune or factory leader, *kuo-chia* may refer to the county (*hsien*), as well as to the province or to the Centre in Peking; it can refer to administrative as well as government or Party institutions. Within the extent of their knowledge, cadres are willing to specify which agency they have in mind when they talk about 'planned by the State' or 'decided by the State' but, in many cases, especially in all the printed material, the concrete meaning of *kuo-chia* is rather obscure. A similar imprecision surrounds another commonly used expression, *shang-chi* (upper level).

The method used here is entirely inductive. I have started by selecting examples of economic decisions which could be found in the Chinese press. In fact, such examples tend to be rare and often appear in reports which have nothing to do with economics. The reader may well find the sampling odd, but this is not my fault; it is merely a function of the way the Chinese press is composed. After analyzing the particulars of these various extracts, I then tried to find the logical links between them and to put them together like the pieces of a jig-saw puzzle to see what kind of shape emerged. This result remains a very sketchy shape, with many holes. It might perhaps be argued that such an intellectual reconstruction superimposes a hierarchy of premises about decision-making on to a hierarchy of administrative units. This cannot be denied. The problem is one of sources. Available sources present all their information on economic decisions within a very strong administrative framework. It might be that Chinese economic decisions are in fact made in quite a different way, or that the really important ones are decided by the most advanced mathematical methods or by a rationalization of budgetary choices,[1] rather than by mass-line discussion. Who knows! The fact remains that, since the Cultural Revolution, the policies of self-reliance and self-sufficiency have strengthened the economic role of administrative units, and this has been felt to be so by the local people. It seems legitimate, therefore, to draw up a schematic picture based on the hierarchy of administrative units, even if its value is relative and it later has to be revised.

THE PRESENT DEFINITION OF THE SPHERE OF CENTRAL DECISION-MAKING

It appears that, as a consequence of the Cultural Revolution, spheres of decision-making have been redefined to a certain extent as compared with 1965. It is hard, however, to tell how much this is the outcome of an overall plan, or how much it is simply due to more or less transient practical necessities which have arisen in the context of administrative readjustment. In any case there are, as we shall see, some noticeable differences already between the situation in late 1972 and what documentary evidence shows for late 1969 and early 1970.

As in 1965, some decisions are central decisions, or are taken by the Centre; others are taken outside the Centre, at other levels. Before going into further detail, we should try to make clear what 'Centre' and 'other levels of decision' mean today. On the whole, it appears that the definitions given above, for the 1965 context, still apply. On the one hand, however, the 'centrality' of the Centre has been enhanced by constant references to Chairman Mao as the authority behind central directives, while, on the other hand, the extension of the Centre has been reduced by a serious drop in the

---

[1] See for instance the propagation of the experiment analysis method in factories for choosing production methods. *JMJP*, 11 November 1972, p. 1.

number of ministries and special agencies subordinated to the State Council.[1] Some ministries or agencies have been amalgamated – for instance, the former Trade Ministry and Grain Ministry now form a single entity. Others have simply disappeared. The effect of this drop in the number of formal organizations is further heightened by an apparently sharp reduction in the number of administrative staff.[2] Even if the zeal and activity of the civil servants have greatly increased, those simple facts tend to indicate that their tasks and responsibilities are not quite the same as before. For levels below the centre, there are both public statements and other evidence to show that there has been a decrease in the number of staff staying permanently at their desks. But there is no evidence that the number of economic agencies and the total number of cadres or people in charge of economic affairs is any smaller than it was.

Central decision-making is still primarily concerned with the unified State plan, which determines production, investment and distribution targets, and also fixes the price of basic products. At this level, however, the tasks of State planning seem increasingly now to involve a qualitative rather than a simple quantitative approach. Central decisions are at once political, economic and social in character. They are not essentially technical decisions, although they must take into account the objective requirements of technology. As regards their political content, the main decisions concerning the economy are prepared inside the Party and result in resolutions or directives which then guide the work of State agencies.

In 1965, technical and economic requirements used to be incorporated into political decisions not only through consultations with central economic and technical agencies, but also through the participation of enterprises and local organs in central decision-

---

[1] Only 32 are known to be active, as compared with 90 before the Cultural Revolution. Among them, 22 can be called 'economic', as compared to nearly 50 in 1965. See *Chung-kung yen-chiu (Research on Chinese Communism))* (Taipei), v, No. 11 (November 1971), 40–8.

[2] The number of agencies has dropped by about two-thirds (from 90 to 32) but their staff by five-sixths (from 60,000 to 10,000), according to what Chou En-lai told Edgar Snow in early 1971. See Edgar Snow, *The Long Revolution* (New York: Random House, 1972), p. 14. No precise data are available which would enable us to state definitely that the reduction of personnel by five-sixths is uniform among the ministries but, even if the staff of the economic ministries has been cut less drastically than that of some other organs, various sources suggest that the reduction was substantial.

making. Production units or local organs used to prepare draft plans, which were then forwarded upwards in the bureaucratic hierarchy. All these drafts were synthesized and adjusted by the Centre for congruency and the final yearly plan, which was sent down to every unit and had a binding character, was the outcome of this synthesis and harmonization.

In the present situation it seems that the Centre fixes quantitative targets mainly for the provincial level but not below it. The province then has responsibility for assessing the situation further down.[1] On the other hand, the practice of having a preliminary outline, including directive figures, first sent down by the upper level for discussion has been resumed.[2] We thus find a reinforcement of central leadership which, through the preliminary plan outline, may, from the very start, channel the economic development of each province, together with a kind of quota system, very similar to the administrative techniques prevailing under the Empire for national procurements of finance and grain, as well as of scholars. In the nineteenth century, for instance, the central government would set the amount of grain and money which each province should forward to the throne, as well as the number of graduates for each provincial examination, while the task of actually managing and organizing levies or examinations was left with the local authorities. The idea was then – and presumably is still now – one of administrative efficiency, and of political balance and unity in a very large and variegated country with relatively difficult communications.

The planning process works in the same way at lower levels between the province and its immediately subordinate units, for instance the county, or between those units and their subordinates, the communes.[3] However, even if units below the provincial level do not receive their quantitative norms directly from the Centre, they are certainly guided in the elaboration of their plans by directives

[1] *JMJP*, 10 August 1972, p. 3, reports how Kirin province fixed the grain production of a county at 400,000 tons.

[2] *JMJP*, 24 August 1972, p. 4, for examples in agriculture; *JMJP*, 19 October 1972, p. 2, for examples in industry. The practice of the preliminary plan outline had been dropped by 1965; see C. Bettelheim, *La Construction du Socialisme en Chine* (Paris: Maspéro, 1968), p. 20.

[3] *JMJP*, 24 August 1972, p. 4; *JMJP*, 16 October 1972, p. 2; *JMJP*, 19 October 1972, p. 2; *Kuang-ming jih-pao* (*KMJP*), (*Kuang-ming Daily*) (Peking) 8 August 1972, p. 1.

given by the Centre. Those directives are on the whole of a general and qualitative character. They consist of the general line (*tsung lu-hsien*), relating to methods or style of operation; of guidelines (*fang-chen*), and of specific policies (*cheng-ts'e*). The respective contents of these different types of directives given by the Centre are well illustrated by the following quotation from an article written by the State Planning Commission:[1]

In accordance with the general line (*tsung lu-hsien*) of 'building socialism by going all out and aiming high to achieve greater, faster, better and more economical results', and in conformity with the overall guidelines (*tsung fang-chen*) of developing the national economy 'with agriculture as the foundation and industry as the leading factor', we must strengthen the support of agriculture by industry. We must carry out the guideline (*fang-chen*) of taking steel as the key link in industry, and correctly handle the relationship between metallurgy and other industries, and between basic and processing industries. We must handle correctly the relationship between industrial production and capital construction for industry and, in accordance with the needs and possibilities, and the principle of unity of subjective initiative and objective possibility, we must concentrate forces to fight a decisive campaign, build and produce simultaneously, create productive capacity at the fastest possible rate, and avoid dispersion of strength and too long a front. It is imperative to handle correctly the relationship between metallurgy and mining in the iron and steel industry, to strengthen the construction of mines and to guard against 'cooking without rice' and other things. Only by fully and consistently adhering to the guidelines (*fang-chen*) and specific policies (*cheng-ts'e*) of the Party in economic construction can the greatest economy be attained and the greatest waste be avoided on the whole industrial front and in the whole country.[2]

The qualitative directives laid down by the Centre do not in themselves give the lower levels adequate guidance in making all their choices. Some choices must be made according to criteria of

[1] *Hung-ch'i (Red Flag)* (Peking), No. 7, 1 February 1971, p. 47.

[2] It is worth noticing that this text makes a further distinction between 'overall guidelines' (*tsung fang-chen*) and guidelines (*fang-chen*). The difference seems to lie mainly in the scope: orientation for the whole economy versus guidelines for industry only. The difference between *fang-chen* and *cheng-ts'e* involves a time factor: specific policies might change more than once, although the guidelines remain the same. With the same guideline of 'taking steel as the key link in industry', specific policy might provide for building small factories. and later on for expanding large plants.

compatibility, or on the basis of global economic advantages, which may be the outcome of a combination of decisions taken at various levels or in various units. Compatibility of decisions, or global economic advantages, can be evaluated only at a higher level.

Before the Cultural Revolution, the Centre used to prepare provisional balances in terms of commodities, values and manpower. The recommendation of certain proportions as the most advisable – for instance between agriculture, light and heavy industry, or between income, consumption and accumulation – became an increasingly important aspect of planning. Such proportions were called balance ratios. There is much evidence that quantitative central directives of this type exist at present.[1] Moreover, warning phrases in the press, such as 'Look at the overall situation', or 'Handle correctly the relations between metallurgy and other industries, between basic and processing industries, between industrial production and industrial construction', certainly refer to the importance of abiding by these balance ratios. However, the further one goes down the power hierarchy, the less compulsory those ratios fixed by the Centre appear to be and the more they act merely as points of reference.[2] Besides, with the practice of 'adapting to local conditions' and the reaction against excessive uniformity or equalization in implementing economic policy in the basic production units, ratios may be infringed at the team level while the prescribed proportions are in fact being maintained when one looks at the overall statistics of a county or even a commune.[3]

On the other hand, among the quantitative decisions which are the prerogative of the central authorities, those concerning prices do

[1] Allusions to these balance ratios are found in the editorial of *JMJP*, 16 April 1972, p. 1; in an article on the role of the bank, *JMJP*, 13 April 1972, p. 4; in an article on planning at the county level, *JMJP*, 17 April 1972, p. 3; in the article by Ku Chien-wei, *JMJP*, 8 June 1972, p. 2; and the one by Chung Li-cheng, *JMJP*, 22 June 1972, pp. 1 and 3. See also the reference to a ratio for administrative expenditure in an article about Wutai county in Shansi province, *JMJP*, 22 March 1972, p. 2.

[2] In the above example (*JMJP*, 22 March 1972, p. 2), the county did not respect the set ratio. It spent less for administration and used the money for other purposes. In various communes which I visited in 1971, leading cadres mentioned that the accumulation fund (*kung-chi-chin*) received a higher proportion of the commune's income than provided for by the set ratio.

[3] *KMJP*, 9 August 1972, p. 1; *JMJP*, 24 August 1972, p. 4; *JMJP*, 16 October 1972, p. 2; *JMJP*, 6 November 1972, p. 3; *JMJP*, 11 November 1972, p. 2.

indeed have a compulsory character at all levels.[1] The Committee on National Prices has been maintained and, as before the Cultural Revolution, fixes only part of the prices, the others being determined at regional or local level. However, although it is impossible to be precise about this, there are reasons to believe that somewhat fewer prices are now centrally determined. With the call for industrialization on a provincial basis, it seems that deals for this purpose inside each province do not have to follow centrally determined prices so far as energy or construction materials, like steel, are concerned. The same would appear to apply to the products of the new local industries when they are for regional consumption. To the extent that this is true, the realm of decision-making by lower levels has thus been enlarged.

THE DISTRIBUTION OF COMPETENCE AMONG THE VARIOUS LEVELS OUTSIDE THE CENTRE

Decisions taken outside the Centre concern concrete measures for the implementation of policies decided at the top level, on which they in turn also depend. They include planning at provincial scale or lower and everyday economic management.

In order to reach a better understanding of the competences of each level, as well as their interconnections, let us look more closely, from the bottom up, at the range of decisions which appear to fall within the power of various economic agents.

Starting from the individual, one notices that, except for an eventual percentage of compulsory savings,[2] he decides himself how to use whatever wages he receives. Free disposal does not apply, however, either to private bank deposits – this question will be investigated further together with the role of the banking system – or to landed property. Sale of landed property may in fact take place only in the case of the very few people who keep a private house in a city, and it needs the approval of the local authorities.[3] For rural homes and private plots, the individual enjoys only private

---

[1] For instance, the price at which grain is bought by the State.

[2] Compulsory savings are by no means a general rule, and their rate varies greatly. They may apply to wages in cash as well as in kind, thus supplying the grain reserves of each family in the collective granary.

[3] Usually the street organization (*chieh-tao*) or the town-district (*ch'ü*).

possession; he cannot sell. There is evidence that, during the Cultural Revolution, private possession was further restricted in some areas even to the extent of abolishing the private plots, but this trend now seems to have been reversed. The numerous new houses, for instance, which the traveller notices in the countryside, are being built either by individuals, who are encouraged to do so, or by the collective – the team or brigade – and even in this case they are laid out as private individual houses, and their possession is left to a single family. The total area of the private plots is still governed by the very restrictive rules which prevailed in 1965,[1] but cadres do not seem shy about mentioning the plots and the improvement they bring to the families' standard of living.

While the decision to build one's house must be approved by the team, the use of the private plot lies entirely within the family's power, though the upper levels may encourage one or another form of utilization.[2] The output of the plot may be sold either on the market[3] or to the State commercial organization, with the authorities exerting strong pressure in favour of the latter course. The whole proceeds of the sale remain in the owner's hands and at his disposal. The same applies, with some reservations, to the output of family industry.[4] Some emphasis has been put since 1971 on encouraging 'family enterprises' (*chia-t'ing ching-ying*), such as home handicrafts, pigs, beekeeping and poultry raising, the gathering of medicinal herbs and even hunting for game.[5] This was first merely

[1] According to these rules, the total area of the private plots in a given team should not exceed 5% of the land under cultivation. It is impossible for an outsider to check whether the rule is really obeyed. He can only trust what the cadres tell him.

[2] For instance, a brigade in Honan province, after planting trees on all vacant land, extended the task to the private plots by giving seedlings and ownership of the trees to the peasants: *JMJP*, 24 March 1972, p. 3.

[3] These are rural markets which are, as a rule, open only to commune members, and where prices are locally fixed according to supply and demand, under control by the local authorities. See the article by Hung Chiao in *JMJP*, 3 September 1972, pp. 1–2.

[4] But some part of the profit appears to be deducted by the team or the brigade, especially if they have taken the responsibility either of providing the raw materials or of collecting and selling the goods. *JMJP*, 18 March 1972, p. 3, mentions a team which bought a buffalo and a small boat with the money earned by a mat-weaving private home industry which it had organized.

[5] *JMJP*, 19 January 1972, p. 4; *JMJP*, 18 March 1972, p. 3; *JMJP*, 21 March 1972, p. 3; *JMJP*, 24 March 1972, p. 3; *JMJP*, 17 April 1972, p. 3; *JMJP*, 12 June 1972, p. 3; *JMJP*, 7 August 1972, p. 3; *JMJP*, 27 August 1972, p. 2.

one aspect of the call to develop side-line activities in addition to agriculture; it then received slightly more stress in 1972, probably as a way to alleviate the consequences of bad crops on the peasant's income that year. Such private enterprises must be 'legitimate' (*cheng-tang*); they should not divert the peasants from collective work as their main business; they may be run with the manpower available in the family only; and their output should preferably be sold to the State.[1] But provided these rules are complied with, there should be no limitation in quantity to that kind of activity, which in some cases might represent a fair amount of the peasants' incomes.[2] To be sure, in the towns, private enterprise has suffered a deadly blow through the Cultural Revolution, most of the remaining State-private joint ventures (*kung-ssu ho-ying*) having been assigned to collective ownership.[3] The small businesses, like making shoes out of rags, which were conducted more or less illicitly in some places, mostly by housewives, have been absorbed into workshops and factories under the neighbourhood authorities (*chieh-tao* or *ch'ü*).[4] The opportunity and encouragement that peasants are given to engage in some kind of trade, even though hedged about by rules, seem nevertheless to enlarge significantly the sphere of individual economic decision-making for those who still form the majority of the population.

The distribution of decision-making powers among the team,

[1] *JMJP*, 18 March 1972, p. 3. The example given in this report of a rich peasant in Kiangsu province who dropped all agricultural work to devote himself to the making of mats with the help of three hired girls, and who sold the mats on the market with due attention to prices, may date back to the early 1960s; the context hints that the case happened some time ago, and it should not therefore be given too much significance. But the principles which are laid out for this business are important, especially because they put no restriction on quantity. The same trend appears in an article of *JMJP*, 21 March 1972, p. 3, which criticizes some Szechwan cadres for the 'mistake' of limiting private pig-raising by peasants; also in articles on Anhwei and Hunan counties, *JMJP*, 17 April 1972, p. 3.

[2] *JMJP*, 18 March 1972, p. 3. On the basis of the sale price indicated for the mats at the beginning of the article, a poor peasant family could get 348 *yuan* for its 600 mats woven in a year, an amount which is almost twice what a commune member draws from collective work in a fairly prosperous commune.

[3] See for instance *Hung ch'i*, No. 2, 27 January 1969, pp. 26–9. According to foreign travellers to Sinkiang, some farms there were still on a State–private basis during the summer of 1972. This might be a privilege of minority areas, since the private owners were reported to be Uighurs or Kazakhs.

[4] *Hsing-tao jih-pao* (Hong Kong), 15 August 1970, p. 5.

brigade, commune, county and provincial levels conforms first to a geographical principle. In its negative aspect, it seems that if a project concerns more than one province, the final decision cannot be made at the provincial level; if it concerns several counties in the same province, it cannot be decided at the county level, and so on.[1] This is no different from the situation prevailing before the Cultural Revolution, except that the final decision is now usually left to the level immediately above, rather than to a still higher one.[2] Such a development is an outcome of administrative simplification, but it is also linked to the downward transfer of financial burdens, by which the central government has shifted a large part of basic civilian investment responsibilities to the lower levels[3] on the principle of 'He who pays the piper calls the tune'. In the case of simple deals or contracts between units at the same level, the units concerned have full decision-making power within the limits of their own rules of management, and provided the deal does not infringe the State plan; otherwise, the next higher level must intervene. For instance, a recent article on the Ta-lien Steelworks[4] shows that the factory not only has the right to conclude contracts, but also to

[1] This hierarchy of responsibility is quite striking in the case of projects involving water conservancy, electrification, railroads and roads. See a New China News Agency (NCNA) report from Chengchow, 21 December 1969, as printed in *Survey of China Mainland Press* (*SCMP*) (Hong Kong: U.S. Consulate General), No. 4566, 30 December 1969, p. 11; *JMJP*, 5 August 1971, as translated in *SCMP*, No. 4959, August 1971, p. 108; *JMJP*, 13 August 1971, as translated in *SCMP*, No. 4963, August 1971, p. 153; *JMJP*, 12 May 1971, as translated in *Current Background* (*CB*) (Hong Kong: U.S. Consulate General), No. 935, 29 June 1971, pp. 1–12.

[2] This remark is drawn from direct enquiry and press reports on actual behaviour.

[3] Besides general emphasis on 'relying on one's own strength', much stress is put on the need for brigades, communes and counties to take most of the material burden of electrification, road, railway or industry building in their own area. *JMJP*, 22 March 1972, p. 1; *JPRS*, No. 54557, *Translations on People's Republic of China*, No. 166, 24 November 1971, p. 7, translating *Ching-chi tao-pao* (Hong Kong), 25 October 1971, p. 22; *Hsing-tao jih-pao*, 7 October 1971, p. 4; *JMJP*, 12 May 1971, as translated in *CB* No. 935, 29 June 1971, p. 12; NCNA, report from Chengchow, 23 November 1969, as printed in *SCMP*, No. 4547, 1 December 1969, p. 19; NCNA report from Shihchia-chuang, 2 December 1969, as printed in *SCMP*, No. 4553, 9 December 1969, pp. 13–14; NCNA report from Tsinan, 5 December 1969, as printed in *SCMP*, No. 4555, 11 December 1969, pp. 12–13; NCNA report from Foochow, 7 December 1969, as printed in *SCMP*, No. 4556, 12 December 1969, pp. 14–15; NCNA report from Shihchia-chuang, 15 December 1969, as printed in *SCMP*, No. 4562, 22 December 1969, pp. 14–15; and NCNA report from Chengchow, 21 December 1969 as printed in *SCMP*, No. 4566, 30 December 1969, p. 11.

[4] *JMJP*, 5 February 1972, p. 1.

lay down its own conditions for them and to fulfil them or not. On the other hand, a factory might be blamed for buying food from a brigade with resources which the plan had not specifically allotted for this use.[1] Elsewhere, we see direct transactions between production teams, in which the brigade level interferes only when something occurs with which the prevailing rules do not deal, such as that the seller wishes to refund part of the price to the buyer because he discovers that he had charged too much.[2]

The geographical principle of the distribution of decision-making power does not mean, however, that any level below the Centre has full power over the decisions which concern exclusively its own territory. Nor does the rule that he who provides the money makes the decision have any absolute value. The power of each level of authority within its own geographical area is obviously limited, if only by the unitarian State structure, and the hierarchic system of territorial administration. As the slogan 'Look at the overall situation' reminds us, nothing can be considered as strictly local. Even the smallest matter has, in the end, a bearing on the general state of affairs, and cannot therefore be left wholly to local autonomy, but must be brought under more centralized control. However, although the legal framework has not yet been officially changed,[3] in practice, the role and interplay of jurisdictions seem to have changed in some respects. Roughly speaking, it can be said that more power appears to have been assumed at the brigade level, at the county (*hsien*) level, and at the provincial level or at their hierarchical equivalents. These relationships, however, are still in flux and the emphasis may shift from one level to another.

This changing emphasis is particularly striking in the rural areas as it affects the production team. During and after the Cultural Revolution, the production team has generally kept the responsibility for counting work-points and allocating income to its members. Some local attempts, in 1968 and 1969, to shift that responsibility to the brigade have later been condemned as a 'left adventurist

---

[1] From a small poster seen by the author in a village of Kiangsi province.
[2] *JMJP*, 21 November 1969, as translated in *SCMP*, No. 4548, 2 December 1969, pp. 6-7.
[3] The available drafts of a revised Constitution (see *Chung-kung yen-chiu*, 10 December 1970, pp. 23-9) include some new arrangements as regards local authorities, but the 1956 Constitution is still theoretically in force.

line'.[1] The campaign to emulate the famous Tachai brigade has stressed political work and the importance of an agricultural infrastructure but has not included (except in the mind of some local zealots) the specific practice of work-points accounting at the brigade level. Moreover, in view of the small population of Tachai (nearer in size to a production team than to the average brigade), it is questionable whether its experience in accounting could become a valid model without a modification of the work-points system itself and a preliminary levelling of the production capacity of all the teams forming each brigade. Brigade leaders may have had such a preliminary levelling in mind when some tried imposing a kind of authoritarian uniformity (p'ing-tiao) on the activities of the teams under them, requiring all teams to sow an equal surface with wheat, to engage in the same side-line activities, or to contribute the same number of workers for irrigation projects.[2]

From 1967 on, the brigade authorities seemed generally to maintain closer control than before over the decisions made by the teams.[3] They could, in fact, repeal any measure taken by the team concerning work-point accounting, remuneration, or the proportion between the team's reserve fund and the amount allocated to team members, and they could enforce other rules and criteria. Such interventions, which were always carried out in the name of true fulfilment of Party policies, and not at the request of the teams, seemed fairly frequent.[4] Even the sowing plan in some places appeared to be decided by the brigade, which thus had a say in the work organization of the team.[5] But since the middle of 1972, several articles in

---

[1] Article broadcast by Heilungkiang Radio on 30 October 1971, quoted in *The China Quarterly*, No. 49 (January–March 1972), 'Quarterly Chronicle', p. 186. See also the article by the Party committee of Nan-hsien in Hunan province, *JMJP*, 20 June 1972, p. 4.

[2] *JMJP*, 24 August 1972, p. 4; *JMJP*, 17 October 1972, p. 1.

[3] In some places, this appears in the landscape itself: all brigade members, who formerly used to live in scattered hamlets, have been resettled together in newly built houses forming one single village.

[4] See for instance *JMJP*, 18 March 1972, p. 3, on a Liaoning brigade and on a Kweichow brigade; *JMJP*, 6 March 1972, p. 3, on a Hopei brigade and on a Chekiang brigade; *JMJP*, 12 June 1972, p. 3 on a Shantung brigade; *JMJP*, 15 November 1969, as translated in *SCMP*, No. 4546, 28 November 1969, p. 11, on another Chekiang brigade.

[5] This shows up in the article by the Party secretary of Liu-chuang brigade in *JMJP*, 12 March 1972, p. 2; also *JMJP*, 17 April 1972, p. 3, in the article by the county committee of Tao-hsien.

the Chinese press have insisted on the necessity of respecting the teams' 'autonomy' (*tzu-chu-ch'üan*).[1] The competence of the team as stated in actual news reports from the countryside and in a somewhat theoretical article signed by Lung Lin which appeared in the *People's Daily* on 16 October 1972, includes the day-to-day management of production and the allocation of income to the team members. The team also has the right to decide on the sowing plan according to local conditions, and to devise its own measures for increasing production (whether it will open new land or rather concentrate on improving the *per mu* yield). The team may adapt, and even reject, at its own convenience the advanced experiences which are being propagated by the upper levels such as the application of 'models' like the Tachai model, as well as the mere introduction of new seeds. Material or manpower resources outside regular plan requirements cannot be drawn from the team by the upper levels without its agreement. All these rights, however, are subject to the preliminary condition that procurements required according to the State plan must be fulfilled and Party policies must be applied. For instance, a team would not be allowed to manage production by allotting the cultivation of collective fields to individual families. It is stressed moreover that respect for the autonomy of the team does not mean that the team acts as it pleases. The brigade and the commune may always change the arrangements made by the team, provided they do it through discussion and negotiation with the team and not in an authoritarian, compulsory way. Besides, it is the brigade and commune alone which assign the duties of each team for the fulfilment of the grain quotas and other tasks designated by the State plan, and which check the faithful completion of the team's work, even though they are denied the right to extract additional procurements or to increase the original targets.

These recent clarifications on the competence of the team seem mainly designed to foster more zeal for work and more productivity on the part of team members,[2] through a careful and flexible adaptation of policy implementation to the particular situation and needs

---

[1] *JMJP*, 24 August 1972, p. 4; *JMJP*, 31 August 1972, p. 2; *JMJP*, 16 October 1972, p. 2; *JMJP*, 17 October 1972, p. 1; *JMJP*, 6 November 1972, p. 3; *KMJP*, 9 August 1972, p. 1.

[2] Such are at least the declarations of intentions. See *JMJP*, 24 August 1972, p. 4; *JMJP*, 16 October 1972, p. 2; *JMJP*, 17 October 1972, p. 1.

of each unit. Although the rights of the team are in some ways guaranteed, the economic system at the team level, and consequently the economic decision-making powers of the team are not really enlarged as compared to the situation just before the Cultural Revolution. Significantly enough, the team is allowed to keep its own workshops, or small processing industries, where low cost or lack of other supplies make it convenient, but it is not encouraged to start new projects on its own.[1]

It is at the brigade level that the enlargement of the economic system is much more obvious. Besides a closer supervision over the team's work and the assignment of quotas, the brigade is now taking over the organization of collective side-line activities, which previously were the responsibility mostly of the teams, and it is the brigade which decides how to sell their production.[2] It is also the brigade level which has benefited from the decentralization measures in the school and commercial systems. The economic implications of school management include maintenance of the buildings, payment of at least part of the teachers' salary and the right to fix school fees and to dispose of the students' manpower in the busy farming season. Commercial administration (*shang-yeh ching-ying*) by the brigade involves power over the personnel and control over the correctness of ordinary operations, but no financial power.[3] Though it leaves little room for economic decision-making, this system paves the way for the closer economic cohesion of the brigade, and the role of the brigade is further enhanced through the campaign for the development of an agricultural infrastructure and of small industries. A large part of the various land-reclamation projects, and of the building of hydro-electric power stations and granaries, is undertaken at the level of the brigade, and on its initiative.[4]

[1] *JMJP*, 31 August 1972, p. 2; *KMJP*, 9 August 1972, p. 1.

[2] *JMJP*, 18 September 1969, p. 4, on a Hopei brigade whose members insist that they 'have the right' (*yu ch'üan*) to make the arrangements as they please; *JMJP*, 18 March 1972, p. 3, on a Kiangsu brigade; *JMJP*, 24 March 1972, p. 3, on a Honan brigade.

[3] *JMJP*, 5 February 1969, p. 5; *KMJP*, 19 January 1969, p. 1; *Nan-fang jih-pao* (*Southern Daily*) (Canton), 19 January 1969, p. 2; *ibid.*, 29 January 1969, p. 3.

[4] See for instance NCNA report from Chengchow, 1 December 1969, as printed in *SCMP*, No. 4552, 8 December 1969, pp. 16–18; NCNA report from Nanking, 22 November 1969, as printed in *SCMP*, No. 4547, 1 November 1969, p. 16; NCNA report from Foochow, 7 December 1969, as printed in *SCMP*, No. 4556, 12 December

Although the scale of such projects is rather small, they are numerous. In Chin-ch'eng county (Shansi province), 1,779 out of the 1,915 industrial units – that is more than 92% – are administered at the brigade level.[1]

For some time, brigades in some places have commandeered from the teams, without compensation, the capital and manpower necessary for such projects. These practices have now been disavowed but the brigade, nevertheless, keeps the right and duty to seek the cooperation of the teams on the basis of voluntary agreement and mutual benefit, even if it is requested to draw the majority of the capital from the output of its own enterprises.[2]

The strengthening of the brigade level does not mean that the commune level of administration is just a form deprived of substance, but the importance of the commune level is more that of a transmission gear.[3] It gets individuality of its own mainly when either its area or its population is small. Thus, the percentage of commune-managed industrial units versus county and brigade-managed ones is 14.4% in Kwangtung province while it is only 4.2% in Chin-ch'eng county in the southern part of Shansi province, where the average area of communes is larger.[4] Otherwise, the duties of the commune level remain that of assigning production quotas to the brigades, of checking or control, and also of conveying directives from above. Although the commune does not make them itself, all important decisions, especially financial ones, taken by the brigades must be approved by the commune.[5] The carrying out of central policies may also be a matter of decision-making for the commune level. We find, for instance, that in accordance with

1969, pp. 14-15; *JMJP*, 30 July 1969, p. 5; *JMJP*, 11 May 1971, p. 3; *JMJP*, 18 March 1972, p. 3; *JMJP*, 10 August 1972, p. 3; *JMJP*, 24 August 1972, p. 4.
[1] *Ching-chi tao-pao* (Hong Kong), 13 September 1971, p. 16, as translated in *JPRS*, No. 54557, 24 November 1971, *Translations on People's Republic of China*, No. 166, p. 3.
[2] *JMJP*, 24 August 1972, p. 4; *JMJP*, 16 October 1972, p. 2.
[3] Note the interesting remark made to Jan Myrdal by the Chairman of Liu-lin Revolutionary Committee that in the last few years the commune has not carried out any big project as a commune. J. Myrdal, *China: The Revolution Continued* (New York: Vintage Books, 1972), p. 12.
[4] *Ching-chi tao-pao*, 13 September 1971, p. 16, and *Chung-kuo hsin-wen* (*China News*) (Peking), 6 September 1971, p. 1, as translated in *JPRS*, No. 54557, 24 November 1971, *Translations on People's Republic of China*, No. 166, pp. 3 and 8. In the Shanghai suburbs, where commune area is small, most factories belong to the commune level.
[5] J. Myrdal, *China: The Revolution Continued*, p. 12.

Chairman Mao's directive that men and women should receive equal salary for equal work, the Party committee of a Shensi commune issued 'its decision' for the implementation of 'equal work, equal salary'; the committee then saw that the decision was effectively carried out by the brigades.[1] On the whole, at the present stage, the role played by the commune level appears to be more administrative and political than economic.

Since the Cultural Revolution, the authority and responsibilities of the county (*hsien*) level are going through a revival which reminds one of the administrative pattern in imperial times, though its basis is different. This *hsien* revival is linked to the economic choice of stressing development through small and medium-scale enterprises since, while most *hsien* could not afford very large scale undertakings, they offer an adequate geographical and administrative setting for tapping the resources necessary for more modest projects.

Beside starting factories, county initiatives embrace water-control, electrification, road and even small railway building.[2] Apparently, the same applies also to cities under the provincial government and to the districts (*ch'ü*) under special municipalities.[3] In addition to its responsibility for investments, the county draws up the plans, determines the source of raw materials and the disposal of production and keeps the main share of the profit. Of course, all these decisions are not made by the county with full autonomy; conformity with

[1] *JMJP*, 6 March 1972, p. 3. The same thing occurred in a Shantung commune where the Party secretary decided that the rule 'equal work, equal salary' would apply only to certain types of work: *JMJP*, 17 October 1972, p. 1.

[2] *Ching-chi tao pao*, 13 September 1971, p. 16; *ibid.*, 25 October 1971, p. 22; *Chung-kuo hsin-wen*, 6 September 1971, p. 1; *JMJP*, 19 September 1971, p. 2, as translated in *JPRS*, No. 54557, *Translations on People's Republic of China*, No. 166, 24 November 1971, pp. 2–8; *JMJP*, 12 May 1971, as translated in *CB*, No. 935, 29 June 1971, pp. 1–11; NCNA report from Chengchow, 23 November 1969, as printed in *SCMP*, No. 4547, 1 December 1969, p. 19; NCNA report from Kwangchow, 27 November 1969, as printed in *SCMP*, No. 4550, 4 December 1969, p. 21; NCNA report from Shihchiachuang, 2 December 1969, as printed in *SCMP*, No. 4553, 9 December 1969, p. 13; NCNA report from Shihchiachuang, 15 December 1969, as printed in *SCMP*, No. 4562, 22 December 1969, pp. 14–15; NCNA report from Tsinan, 13 August 1971, as printed in *SCMP*, No. 4962, August 1971, p. 121; *Hsing-tao jih-pao*, 7 October 1971, p. 4, on Mei-hsien in Kwangtung; *JMJP*, 22 March 1972, p. 1, on Wu-t'ai county in Shansi province; *JMJP*, 25 March 1972, p. 1, on T'ai-an country in Shantung province; *JMJP*, 19 June 1972, p. 1, on Hsin-hui county in Kwangtung.

[3] NCNA report from Changchun, 26 October 1970, as translated in *SCMP*, No. 4772, 4 November 1970, pp. 135–6; *JMJP*, 6 August 1972, p. 2.

national or provincial guidelines and approval by the upper levels on important issues are also required. The part played by the county as an entrepreneur, however, increases its role in the planning process. After receiving general assignments from the province, the county allots specific tasks to the communes; it is in a position to direct their production towards definite targets, according to its particular neeeds,[1] and to generalize experiments.[2] The county's role in the economic field is somewhat similar, at a higher level, to that played by the brigade, namely to create and maintain coherence and integration.[3]

The special district, or administrative district (*chuan-ch'ü*), seems to have little economic role, except for coordinating activities in areas populated by national minorities.[4]

It is more difficult to evaluate how the decision-making power of the provincial authorities now compares to the pre-Cultural Revolution situation. It has been stated many times since 1966, both in the Chinese and in the foreign press, that in the 'Liuist' era the provinces used to disregard central directives and formed 'independent kingdoms'.[5] By reshaping the provincial committees, the Cultural Revolution was thus an attempt to curb unruly satraps. But, at the same time, foreign commentators generally agree that a high degree of provincial autonomy has been both an objective of the Centre and a result of the Cultural Revolution.[6]

Looking into the scarce and scattered available information on the

---

[1] For example, in Shun-i near Peking, it is the county which decides that the communes must resume the side-line activities which had been dropped in 1970: *JMJP*, 12 March 1972, p. 1. Also *JMJP*, 11 August 1972, p. 3, on Cho-tzu county, *JMJP*, 11 November 1972, p. 2, on An-hsiang county.

[2] *JMJP*, 5 August 1971, p. 2, on the building of granaries; *JMJP*, 18 August 1972, p. 4, on Ching-yang county; *JMJP*, 17 October 1972, p. 1, on Yung-ch'eng county.

[3] *JMJP*, 6 June 1972, p. 3, on Chung-shan county; *JMJP*, 19 June 1972, p. 1, on Hsin-hui county; *JMJP*, 14 July 1972, on a Kweichow county; *JMJP*, 26 August 1972, p. 4, on a Chekiang county; *JMJP*, 17 October 1972, p. 1, on a Shantung county.

[4] Cf. a symposium on finance and trade work convened by Hainan administrative district: Hainan broadcast in mandarin, 3.00 GMT, 12 March 1971. Also *JMJP*, 26 March 1972, p. 1, on Hunan.

[5] For instance *JMJP*, 8 June 1972, p. 2.

[6] *China News Analysis* (Hongkong), No. 809, 24 July 1970; also Edgar Snow's interview with Chou En-lai as quoted in E. Snow, *The Long Revolution*, pp. 13–14. However, J. Domes, 'Some Results of the Cultural Revolution in China', *Asian Survey*, XI, No. 9 (September 1971), 932–40, stresses provincial independence only as an unlooked for and threatening result.

actual functioning of the provincial apparatus, and listening to what the county level cadres have to say about its working, it appears that provincial authorities now have more strictly legal power at their disposal than in 1965. As far as education, planning, buying and selling, and most job assignments are concerned, the province is the highest authority for all lower levels. The increased provincial jurisdiction over planning is especially important. Evidence of this is provided not only by the different lengths of provincial plans, but also by their different slogans.[1] Even the hurried traveller will notice that in Kiangsi his guides put emphasis on industrial development, while in Shansi they stress the achievements in building the agricultural infrastructure.

As is true for the *hsien* level, the extension of the provincial sphere of economic competence is linked with the campaign for the development of local industry.[2] The Centre, however, has not only given the provinces an increased right to start factories and organize the industrial network in their area; it has also provided them with more means to achieve it. Many factories which were managed by the Centre (*kuo-ying*) have been transferred to local, in fact provincial, management (*ti-fang kuo-ying*). According to a well-informed source, in 1965 the centrally managed enterprises totalled 70–80% of national industrial production.[3] Among them, except for the largest steelworks and their associated mines, the oil industry and the units working for national defence, other industries are now managed by the province where they are located.[4] This does not mean that the Centre waives all power and control over such factories; but in addition to financial responsibility for their management, the province gets a share of the benefits and, together with responsibility for supplying them with raw materials, the province acquires a say in the objectives and use of their output. Although no reliable data

[1] 'Preparing for a New Leap Forward', *South China Morning Post* (Hong Kong), 26 October 1969, p. 10; *China News Analysis*, No. 786, pp. 4–5; *ibid.*, No. 799, pp. 6–7.

[2] See for instance *KMJP*, 16 August 1971, p. 1, on Honan province; NCNA report from Tsinan, 5 December 1969, as printed in *SCMP*, No. 4555, 11 December 1969, pp. 12–13, on Shantung province; *Peking Review* (Peking), 11 September 1970, No. 37, p. 20, on Shanghai municipality.

[3] C. Bettelheim, *La Construction du Socialisme en Chine*, p. 26.

[4] *Hsing-tao jih-pao*, 3 May 1970, p. 4. I also had an opportunity in October 1971, to check on the spot that the management of the big Canton paper mill and other former *kuo-ying* factories had really been transferred to the province.

are available about the percentage of national production which now comes under provincial rule, it is probably fair to assume that from 20–30% in 1965, the proportion has gone up to over 50%.

Generally speaking, the increased jurisdiction of local authorities has meant a tighter control over factory management.[1] Unfortunately very little has been published in the Chinese press concerning decision-making in the factories, which involves different problems from those in the agricultural sector. The factory committees seem to have lost the free hand over production and transactions involving fixed capital which, in some cases, they had succeeded in gaining for themselves before the Cultural Revolution.[2] Otherwise, neither the type of decisions which belong to the industrial enterprise (technical improvements, organization of manpower) nor the levels at which they are made (team, workshop, factory committee) seem to have undergone any formal modification. Planning apparently entails the same extensive negotiations and hard bargaining between the factory leadership and the higher authorities as before.[3] The change, where it has occurred, is more in the decision-making process itself, and is part of a general phenomenon.

THE DECISION-MAKING PROCESS

Although the decision-making process is not something peculiar to the economic sphere, it needs to be briefly analyzed in order to clarify the problems relating to conflicts between decisions and to unification of economic policy.

From the team level up, any individual decision-making is harshly condemned (especially if it has any financial implication).[4] The individual may make a proposal, and is encouraged to do so, but the

[1] From comments made to the author by factory cadres in various places, in October and November 1971.

[2] See the account by Barry M. Richman, *Industrial Society in Communist China*, pp. 789–98. For a criticism of this tendency, presumably inspired by Sun Yeh-fang's theories: 'Class Struggle in the Field of Socialist Construction and Economics', *Hung ch'i*, 1970, No. 2, translated in *Chinese Economic Studies*, IV, No. 4, 275ff.

[3] *JMJP*, 19 October 1972, p. 2, on the Ta-yeh mines.

[4] See the criticism of a young worker who bought a few tools which he needed (*JMJP*, 24 October 1970, as translated in *SCMP*, No. 4774, 6 November 1970, p. 239), and of a brigade head who ordered a cement pipe (NCNA report from Tsinan, 23 November 1969, as printed in *SCMP*, No. 4547, 1 December 1969, pp. 13–14).

decision should be taken collectively. The organs which are formally entitled to make decisions are the revolutionary and Party committees corresponding to each level. Within the prevailing hierarchic framework of command, it would, however, be idealistic to pretend that the weight given to proposals does not depend partly on the respective position of the individuals who make them. Even if the head of the revolutionary committee has consulted people under him and listened to their opinions with modesty, the very fact that he sponsors one proposal rather than another appears to be a powerful factor in the endorsement of that proposal.[1] Moreover, the Chinese press is actually full of accounts of 'good' Party secretaries who go out on inspection and make decisions, apparently by themselves.

Consultation with the masses is, of course, recommended, but depends entirely on the committees. The masses may only suggest or criticize; the adoption or repeal of decisions belongs exclusively to the committees themselves. This seems to be the result of a recent evolution. In 1969, statements to the effect that 'the poor peasants of such and such brigade or county have decided to start such and such work' were frequently found in the press. These have been replaced since early 1971 by phrases like: 'the Party (or revolutionary) committee has decided to start such and such work'. The framework for mass consultation is increasingly on-the-spot investigation, or more informal gatherings such as classes for the study of Mao's thought, rather than by using mass organizations like the Poor Peasants' Associations, which were revived just before and during the Cultural Revolution. The Poor Peasants' Associations may now convene only if called together by the Party committee, according to what rural leaders said in late 1971. Such meetings are thus

---

[1] 'Learn economic work from all competent people', *JMJP*, 30 May 1972, p. 3. This article recounts how, after consulting a vice-chairman who had been away when the production plan was being decided on, the chairman calls a meeting in order to reverse the decision already taken by the committee, and to adopt the proposal made by the vice-chairman. It also shows that when a production expense has to be approved, it is first submitted to the chairman, who either decides himself and then reports to the revolutionary committee, or passes it on to the revolutionary committee with the grounds for his own opinion, which has a good chance of being approved. Also *JMJP*, 19 October 1972, p. 2: a cadre who wishes to oppose a technical decision taken by the factory Party committee is warned by his fellows to be cautious, because the decision has been taken according to the Party secretary's opinion.

entirely in the hands of the decision-makers, who confess that they are not very frequent.

Other mass organizations, such as the Women's Associations, the Youth League or the Trade Unions, are, according to the very words of their responsible cadres, channels through which decisions are carried out rather than formulated. Moreover the standing committees, which in fact do the bulk of the work, are, since late 1969, mainly composed of cadres, since most 'representatives of the masses' have been sent back to productive labour.[1] The 'representatives of the masses' on the revolutionary committees were usually chosen from among those who had shown themselves to be the most ardent activists during the 1966–8 political struggle and, under such circumstances, activism was in many cases the same thing as ultra-leftism. Sending back to production the 'representatives of the masses', who incidentally had frequent clashes with their colleagues on the committees and made work difficult,[2] was one aspect of a wide political drive against ultra-leftism, of which Ch'en Po-ta and Lin Piao have been the illustrious victims at the top.[3]

While they recognize that there is no institutional change in the interplay between lower and upper level, local people in China insist that this interplay is 'more real' than before, when only lip service was paid to it. I am personally inclined to believe them, since the simplification of bureaucracy and the mortification of cadres during the Cultural Revolution certainly helps such interplay; on the other hand, the prudence and relativity of the above statement cannot be disguised.

The rivalry between Party committee and government or executive committee (now named revolutionary committee) at the same level is surely far less acute than ever it was before the Cultural

[1] *JMJP*, 22 November 1969, as translated in *SCMP*, No. 4551, 5 December 1969, pp. 6–9; *JMJP*, 24 November 1969, as translated in *SCMP*, No. 4552, 8 December 1969, p. 12; *JMJP*, 10 December 1969, as translated in *SCMP*, No. 4561, 19 December 1969, pp. 1–7.

[2] *KMJP*, 11 September 1972, p. 1, shows the recent improvement of these relations through adequate measures.

[3] This whole interpretation comes from an authorized Chinese source, whose name I cannot quote. But the situation was certainly not the same everywhere: see for instance the account by the Party secretary of Huang tu kang commune near Peking in A.Z.M. Obaidullah Khan, 'Class Struggle in Yellow Sandhill Commune', *The China Quarterly*, No. 51 (July–September 1972), pp. 543–6.

Revolution, since the identification between the Party committee and the leaders of the revolutionary committee is almost complete.[1] The Party secretary and deputy secretaries always hold the equivalent positions in the revolutionary committee,[2] and Party committee members form the majority on the standing committee of the revolutionary committee, whose other members include a number of ordinary Party members. The division of competence between the Party and revolutionary committees is between direction and general policy on the one hand, and concrete measures of implementation or professional work on the other. For instance, on financial matters at the county level, the Party committee would formulate the rules by which funds can be drawn from the county treasury, requiring written application and receipt, strict specification of allowances and justification of expenses. But the responsibility for organizing the actual distribution and disposal of funds, and the issuing of receipts, lies on the revolutionary committee.[3] The distinction between direction and concrete measures applies also when two levels are involved in a decision. Let us take the example of a mine managed by the county in Kiangsu province. This mine needed a direct access road to facilitate the clearing of the ore. The decision to build a road was taken by the county Party committee, but the actual layout of the road (whether a straight line across the fields, or a longer and more complicated itinerary away from cultivated land in the hills) was chosen by the revolutionary committee of the mine and then approved by the county Party committee.[4]

More complex are the relations between the branch agencies (*pu-men*) and the political organs at the same level. They concern only the county level and above, because the small groups for the management of commerce and the like at the commune level and below are rather commissions inside the revolutionary committee itself. Available information shows that the branch agencies are

---

[1] These remarks on the composition of Party and revolutionary committees are drawn from the figures given to the author in various places in China.

[2] This fact (which is one meaning of the slogan *i-yuan-hua ling-tao*) probably accounts, on the contrary, for the present increased tension between individual and collective leadership mentioned above, since it concentrates the leading function in one person only, while before the Cultural Revolution the head of the Party organization held only a subordinate position in the corresponding People's Committee, and vice-versa. [3] *JMJP*, 11 August 1972, p. 3. [4] *JMJP*, 13 November 1972, p. 2.

subordinated to a revolutionary committee at the same level, and that their own Party organization is led by the Party committee at the same level. For instance, the Shanghai Metallurgy Industry Bureau is subordinated to the Shanghai Revolutionary Committee and the Party committee of the Shanghai Metallurgy Industry Bureau is led by the Shanghai Party Committee. It is through the Shanghai Revolutionary Committee, not from a Peking ministry, that the Bureau receives assignments, though it is in direct touch with the Peking ministries for contracts.[1] The Bureau's decisions may always be recalled by the Shanghai Revolutionary Committee but, at this level of a huge and complex administration, it is likely that the Bureau has very largely a free hand in its professional field. The growing economic decision-making power of levels below the Centre probably means, especially at the provincial level, and even in large districts, an increasing importance of their branch agencies,[2] while the influence of central branch agencies is shrinking.

Does this mean that technicians are gaining ground on politicians? A rehabilitation of pure technicians has certainly been noticeable[3] lately, but the trend is rather that the staff of the specialized bureaus, as well as of the political committees, is mainly composed of political cadres who have acquired high technical capacities. In most agencies and units, real power belongs to that single techno-political body inside which the influence of the Party committee, identified with the revolutionary standing committee is constantly growing. This constitutes once again, as during the Great Leap Forward, a high tide of government by committees, as opposed to branch-type administration, but the composition of the committees is far more specialized than it used to be. This question relates to the general problem of conflicts of decision and the unification of economic policy which is discussed below.

---

[1] From information given by cadres in a Shanghai factory.

[2] NCNA, Peking, 11 November 1971, as translated in *JPRS*, No. 54739, 17 December 1971, *Translations on People's Republic of China*, No. 170, p. 36; NCNA, Tientsin, 21 August 1971, as translated in *SCMP*, No. 4967, 2 September 1971, p. 100; *JMJP*, 8 June 1972, p. 2; *JMJP*, 14 July 1972, p. 1.

[3] *JMJP*, 21 March 1972, p. 1; *JMJP*, 28 March 1972, p. 3. These very revealing articles mention technicians as vice-chairmen of the revolutionary committee in important units. *JMJP*, 19 October 1972, p. 2, recommends that cadres with a long professional experience should be taken into the factories' leadership and form the core of the factory management.

CONFLICTS AND THE UNIFICATION OF DECISIONS

In theory, according to the principles of unified Party leadership (*tang t'ung-i ling-tao*) and even of democratic centralism, which instead of being brushed aside are vigorously asserted again, no level under the Central Committee has absolute decision-making power on any matter. The upper level also plays the role of arbiter in conflicts between two lower level units. Then, at least in theory, the hierarchical and centralized organization of the government and the Party makes it easy to solve any conflict which may arise, and to control the unification of economic policy.

In practice, this hierarchical authority does exert itself and interferes with decisions already made in a regular way by lower levels,[1] but we have no sufficient data to state how often, in what way, and whether this intervention is really efficient. Even if the brigade leaders have rectified the work-point account in a team after the summer harvest, so that men and women get equal shares for equal work, is it sure that the men in the team do not find a way to recoup themselves when making accounts for other work? In China, we usually never know when things are going wrong; it is only when they have been successfully rectified that we happen to learn that in the past they have been wrong for some time. All we can say at the moment is that from 1969 until the end of 1972, there is no precise evidence that, in the economic field, things have been or are really getting out of central control. The calls to abide by the State plan and Party policies may be interpreted as warnings rather than anything else and they are quite understandable in the process of building a new system of economic development in such a huge country.

On the other hand, one can also speculate at length about the circumstances which led to the fall of Lin Piao, and about the power of regional commanders who may be building the economy of their province without regard for the national State plan, keeping all resources within the province and trying to get the lion's share of

---

[1] *JMJP*, 27 March 1972, p. 2, gives the example of the district committee intervening to cancel arrangements made by one of its agencies. *JMJP*, 5 August 1972, p. 1, mentions the interference of the county authorities which rectify the allocations of income made by the team. For a similar intervention by a commune Party secretary, see *JMJP*, 11 November 1972, p. 2.

centrally allocated funds. That such tendencies do exist cannot be denied. As the *People's Daily* reported on 8 June 1972:

A few units and comrades have yet failed to view the relationship between the part and the whole correctly in the current work of capital construction. Disregarding the State plan, they have gone after quantity, scale and comprehensiveness, engaging in construction projects outside the plan as they please, thereby stretching the capital construction battle front, causing long delays in completing State construction projects and affecting the development of the national economy. A few units have been engaged in high-standard but non-productive construction projects, under all sorts of pretexts and resorting to all sorts of means.

The problem is to determine the extent of deviations in time, space and material resources involved, and also the level at which they occur. The extent of deviations would probably be easier to assess if Chinese politics were not in a constant flux which transforms the main current into deviations and vice-versa. There is no stable yardstick. Although the slogans of economic policy have remained the same since 1969, their various points have been differently emphasized by the central leadership in the course of the last three years, as is evident from the press. Consequently, present deviations may sometimes be simply hangovers of past orthodoxy. For instance, in 1969, it would have been considered as a deviation for a brigade not to develop its own economy at all costs, while now it is considered as a deviation to disregard the protests of the teams when called upon to contribute their resources for the brigade's economy.

What are the reasons for such shifts? We do not know the true explanation and may only suggest hypotheses on a very thin basis of evidence, as long as the Chinese archives are not made available, and perhaps even then. Thus, economic reasons, ideological reasons and the political struggle among the leaders probably account together to a varying degree for the recent changing trends in economic policy and organization. To sum up briefly, the sophisticated and complex administrative apparatus which existed in 1965 provided for a regular economic development, but a slow and routine one. Its working and requirements were so complicated that they made it difficult to take into consideration all the potentialities of the land, or even the industrial base, and to achieve the proper utilization of available manpower. Planning was made from above by experts, from the top of a pyramid of reports and control figures, but with too little actual contact with reality. Although flexibility was indeed greater in the industrial sector than during the First Five-Year Plan and gave good results, still 'latent forces' remained to be brought into play. Rural development may well have appeared to be more victimized by the system, not only because the burden of bureaucratic and technocratic vexations would be more onerous for a population generally less accustomed to red tape than the urban industrial cadres, but also because the countryside had to wait for the relatively slow growth of urban industry before it could hope to benefit from industrialization. To stimulate economic zeal, ideological and material incentives were used together, but ideology was too much a part of the bureaucratic apparatus, while material incentives were perhaps too small and regarded with too much suspicious scepticism by the population in view of past experience, to produce any far-reaching or decisive effect on workers' productivity.

For such drawbacks, the economic system of 1969 provided a range of radical remedies. Administration was simplified and, at the higher levels, reduced. This was not, as during the Great Leap Forward, because the higher levels did not have enough personnel or expertise to administer and coordinate; just the reverse. It was designed to fight excessive bureaucracy and technocracy. But, as during the Great Leap, administrative simplification was complemented by encouraging the initiative of the masses and lower levels, and it was linked to a shift in development strategy. The development strategy of 1969 bore similarities to that of the Great Leap: it also relied heavily on the mass line; on the mobilization of the whole population and of all available resources; on efforts to improve agricultural infrastructure; and on industrialization through small-scale labour-intensive rural enterprises. But there are also differences. New industries are primarily those which support agriculture. The industrial network is much more clearly laid out, with a hierarchy of responsibility from the province down to the brigade, according to the scale of the projects. Management of economic operations is concentrated at the brigade level (small scale projects in both industry and agriculture), the county level (medium-scale projects in both agriculture and industry) and the provincial level (large scale projects); the alternate administrative levels – commune or special district – mostly supervise the operations of the level immediately below them. It might be said that lessons have been learned from the experience of the Great Leap; but it is also true that there were more resources and skills available in 1969 than ten years before. One more difference is that the drive to increase production is not at present integrated into a remoulding of the political and social structure as sweeping as the creation of the people's communes.

In addition to its economic designs, the system of 1969 had political advantages. It short-circuited the higher bureaucracy among which the followers of Liu, Teng and P'eng were relatively numerous. By giving a larger say in regional development to local people, it could give satisfactions to provincial military leaders whose will and power had been shown to be so important in the turmoil of the Cultural Revolution. The system embodied also a much more vigorous revolutionary ideology than the economic organization of 1965. For 'commandism' and bureaucratic practices, it attempted to substitute the mass line. It paved the way for the smoothing out of antagonisms and differences between the countryside and the cities, between agriculture and industry, and between mental and manual labour. It belied the thesis of the convergence of all industrial 'modern' societies, according to which redness and expertise stand in an antagonistic contradiction, expertise will win out in the end, and large centralized technocratic bureaucracies, organizations and industrial systems will necessarily prevail. In terms of the division of labour, of the social structure, of the patterns of interests and values, and ultimately of the pattern of national integration, one can say that in 1969 China experimented with a new model of development, one which had been sketched out during the Great Leap, but was now far more precise and reasoned.

By late 1970 and during 1971, however, set-backs in these programmes became noticeable and these were accentuated in 1972.[1] Less emphasis has since been put on the creativity of the masses,

---

[1] For local accounts of the evolution since 1969 see for the rural sector: *JMJP*, 10 August 1972, p. 3; *JMJP*, 24 August 1972, p. 4; *JMJP*, 26 August 1972, p. 4; *JMJP*, 17 October 1972, p. 1; *KMJP*, 9 August 1972, p. 1, and for the industrial sector: *JMJP*, 6 August 1972, p. 2; *JMJP*, 19 October 1972, p. 2; *JMJP*, 13 November 1972, p. 2.

or on mass representation and participation, with more emphasis on technical experience, on the responsibility of the cadres and on their function as leaders. Rather than focus on mass mobilization, on the increase in the number of production units, on self-sufficiency or the manufacturing of complete machines, the development of local rural industry at the district level and below has come to focus on the reduction of industrial manpower, on the full use of existing equipment and on manufacturing separate or spare parts as well as on repair services. The rehabilitation of technically experienced older cadres is partly a reaction against the ultra-leftist tendencies of the young activists who were brought on the stage by the Cultural Revolution and presumably supported by the Ch'en Po-ta and Lin Piao faction. The whole range of recent trends in the economic sphere should be seen less as a sheer settlement of political accounts than as an attempt to ensure production, and prevent a deterioration after the 'flying leap' of 1969–70, especially since, after a few years of over-capitalization, the peasants' productivity proved to decline sharply. The relative failure of the harvest in 1972 added pressure for further adjustments in the same direction.

Nevertheless, from the available evidence, it appears that the recent adjustments have not modified the ambiguous interplay of competence between administrative levels. This system is characterized by a 'deconcentration' rather than a decentralization of decisions. The present motto of 'two initiatives are better than only one' differs somewhat in emphasis from Chairman Mao's own statement of April 1956 in 'On the Ten Great Relations', in which he advocated more power for local government, though noting that this was limited by the constitution to making rules and regulations as distinguished from legislative power (*li-fa ch'üan*).[1] In many cases, 'initiative' is almost too strong a translation for the Chinese term, *chi-chi-hsing*, which does not convey the idea of starting something completely new, or of invention, but means only acting positively and with enthusiasm. In practice, local initiative is allowed to operate only within the framework of a directive or plan received from above, with no encroachment, at least in the early stage, on the set pattern for the allocation of funds and resources and without

[1] This text is available in *Chung-kung yen-chiu*, No. 38, 10 February 1970, pp. 116–24. On local power, see p. 121.

prejudice to the regular procurements already assigned to the unit concerned. Quite frequently, for instance, a production team or brigade will start improving or building its hydraulic network, but such an undertaking is no more than following the central call for developing an agricultural infrastructure. Moreover, either funds and resources have been allocated for this purpose by a higher level (commune or county), or the unit relies upon itself, mainly by a massive input of manpower. In the latter case, it does not appear that the financial investment can exceed the amount which the unit is normally allowed to assign for production expenses without approval by a higher level.

The trend towards the transfer of responsibility down to lower levels has recently been described by Western literature in terms of local 'autonomy', although at present the Chinese media never use the Chinese equivalent of this phrase, *ti-fang tzu-chih* or *tzu-chih*, and have also almost dropped (except in stressing national independence) an expression less reminiscent of Kuomintang political concepts, *tu-li tzu-chu*, which can be rendered as being independent and one's own master. What remains is only *tzu-chu ch'üan*, the right to self-determination, which is essentially a prerogative of the team, as we have seen above. But even if it is legitimate to try to appraise the current changes in the Chinese power structure in terms of autonomy, it should be pointed out that autonomy does not necessarily imply going against central directives, but may only mean, in effect, applying central directives according to local conditions. No doubt it is merely in this latter sense that Peking sees the present encouragement to local initiative. Methods of operation or specific policies, but not general policies, may be left to decision-makers outside of the Centre. Those decision-makers who are favoured as a result are not the basic production units (teams or factories), but intermediate levels (brigade, county and province). Besides, lower levels appear to enjoy greater independence in production decisions than in investment decisions. In most cases, either major expenses must be approved by a higher level, or they necessitate a loan or subvention which enables the higher level to intervene. This mechanism is fairly clear below the provincial level,[1] but we lack adequate information to tell how it works between the central

[1] *JMJP*, 8 June 1972, p. 2.

government and the provincial level. Does the Centre keep effective power over regional investments?

The Centre certainly does not allocate all provincial inputs and plan production, nor does it control distribution of all provincial current output, but only a share. Which one? There is no way to ascertain this at the moment. Besides, the situation may vary from one province to another and from one year to another. In any case, by retaining the largest steelworks and the oil industry under its direct authority, the Centre has means to control provincial industry from these crucial squares in the input-output table.

It should be pointed out that, besides the strengthening of hierarchical administrative control, the commercial and banking systems are very important factors for maintaining balance and unity in the economic sphere. For business matters, commercial agencies are subordinated to a level higher than the one where they operate; if they operate in a commune, they do not obey the commune level but the county level, and so on. By proposing contracts, the commercial system is able to exercise influence on the economic choices of production units, and to co-ordinate their development.[1] They are also instrumental in fixing local prices in accordance with the general economic balance. Though even more obscure, the role of the bank system, which remains completely in the hands of the Centre, might be the most important, especially in a period when basic investments are again placed to the fore. Withdrawal of funds is subjected to the rules established by the People's Bank; accounts can be temporarily frozen if general conditions call for this; the bank has jurisdiction over loans, and may even change the priorities decided on by her debtors.[2] However, information, and especially quantitative data, are so scarce that it is impossible to assert whether trade and banking organizations have overwhelming power in an economy which remains partly non-monetary.

[1] *JMJP*, 19 January 1972, p. 4, shows the role of commercial organization in stimulating side-line activities in a Kwangsi county. The same appears for an Anhwei county in *JMJP*, 17 April 1972, p. 3. On the coordinating role of the commercial organization and its task to enforce directives for the production plan, see also the article by Shang Yeh-wen in *JMJP*, 18 July 1972, p. 3, and that by Hung Ch'iao in *JMJP*, 3 September 1972, pp. 1–2.

[2] *JMJP*, 6 November 1970, p. 4, shows such an example in Chengtu, in Szechwan province; *JMJP*, 14 July 1972, p. 1, shows the action of the bank in a Kweichow county. Other information above comes from direct enquiry.

CONCLUSION

The present situation is characterized by an increased dichotomy between impulse and decision-making. To put it schematically, in 1965, both the impulse and decision-making itself used to be the prerogative of the same body. Now, although a given body has no right to decide a given matter with full sovereignty, it may give the impulse for a decision to be made by the unit which enjoys the decision-making power in that field. This has been made possible through a number of administrative techniques, some of them very old, like the quota system which simplifies the upward and downward transmission of orders and requests; like the simplification of the bureaucracy;[1] and like the utilization of the county not only in administrative terms but also in the economic organization.

Although, from a legalistic point of view, the devolution of nothing more than the right of impulse seems a very thin institutional change, it may in fact be even more important than full formal decision-making power on limited matters, because the impulse also amounts to a pledge that a consensus can exist to carry out the decision once the competent authorities have laid it down. If the revolutionary committee of a brigade asks for permission to build a dyke, it is most likely prepared to mobilize the members of all its teams, and to spare the necessary resources to do the work. If such a proposal is allowed to originate only from the upper level which also has the decision-making power, it may often happen that the brigade concerned will be slow or reluctant to carry out the project, because it seems to be untimely or inadequate. The problem is how to foster entrepreneurship for the economic take-off within a socialist framework. An extension of the decision-making power of the basic production units may damage planning. On the other hand, if those units have full power on some matters and no say at all on others, they will probably concentrate their efforts on those areas which are entirely in their hands and be passive as regards others. Commune members will prefer to build new houses for themselves rather than start a glass factory which is imposed on them by the county. But if they have an opportunity to make their voice heard as to what kind of industry, preferably a fertilizer factory, they wish first, they might

---

[1] The slogan for this, *ching ping chien cheng*, is a quotation from Ssu-ma Ch'ien.

spend less on house-building, for which they are their own masters, in order to save for industrial investment, although formal decision-making in this field does not really belong to them.

The real efficiency of the present system, however, relies on the potential of energy and enthusiasm which was liberated when the Cultural Revolution overthrew barriers and taboos, on the willingness of local people and leaders to voice their opinion and contribute a selfless effort. If this energy and enthusiasm scatter into more projects than the available material resources permit, if they rush recklessly ahead or if they are discouraged by political feuds and instability, then the Chinese economy will face again the same delays and bottlenecks which impeded its rapid spurt in 1965.

3

RURAL INDUSTRY
AND THE INTERNAL TRANSFER
OF TECHNOLOGY

Jon Sigurdson

Linkages between agriculture and rural industry, and between rural industry and urban-based modern industry, are clearly important factors in the social and economic development of China. The nature of these linkages may assure both an integrated social and economic development, and a more solid basis for planning from the bottom up, as opposed to central planning. This chapter will discuss the recent development of rural industry, which is at the centre of the linkages, and its impact on industrialization in China. It will analyse the nature of the transfer of industrial technology from the cities and discuss also the role of leadership in the transfer, since this is important in an environment where prices and other market mechanisms cannot be used to initiate and control development and is also likely to be important in order to achieve a desired distribution of industrial activities. The question of regional balance is also touched upon in the light of the Chinese leadership's apparent awareness that rural industrialization should be used to lessen economic and social inequalities.

The Chinese approach to linking rural industry with agriculture requires certain inputs – particularly technology, and to a lesser degree skilled manpower – from the modern industrial sector. The creation of demand in rural areas for appropriate technologies, and the development of such technologies, are important aspects of the present stage of development in China. However, the question of the development of appropriate technologies is only briefly discussed here, as sufficient data are not yet available. The existence of linkages also appears to be a prerequisite for the creation of large industrial networks of 'subcontractors', and the character of these networks is discussed at some length, since they seem to be an important feature of industrialization in China.

In conclusion, an attempt is made to deal with recent Chinese discussions on the relative importance of steel and electronics to Chinese development strategy. Electronic technology is, no doubt, widely used within the defence sector and also for a number of civilian purposes, but the Chinese appear to wish to postpone any large-scale introduction of electronic technology in order not to disturb the present stage of economic and social development.

The frame of reference used for discussing rural industry in this chapter evolved from visits to two rural counties in China in December 1971, and from the study of Chinese press and broadcast materials. All my information – both from personal discussion about policy and from news items – seems to confirm that the Chinese are attempting to develop the rural areas in an integrated way and that, in this development, rural industries play a number of very important roles.

RURAL INDUSTRY

The objectives of rural industry* may differ from one area of the country to another. They depend, among other things, on the closeness of big industrial cities and the relative economic development of the surrounding area which defines their market. However, the primary objective is always to serve agriculture.[1] This objective can be broken down into the following three components. First, rural industry has to produce iron, farm machines, machine tools, chemical fertilizer, building material, etc. Second, farm and other machines have to be repaired, and many of the necessary spare parts

---

* Rural industry is defined in this context as any local industrial unit run by county, commune or brigade. The enterprises may be collectively owned, jointly owned by State and collective units, or wholly owned by the State but under local management. Rural industry includes units attached to middle schools, hospitals and health clinics. Here, rural industry within a county (*hsien*) is usually discussed because of the importance attached to this level of industry in news reports from China. For certain purposes it may, however, be appropriate to consider the region which, on the average, consists of 10 counties. Production technology in rural industry ranges from the very primitive to modern up-to-date process technology, depending on product, size and stage of development.

[1] See for example 'County-run Industry on Shanghai Outskirts', New China News Agency (NCNA), 11 May 1972, p. 4, *Hsinhua Weekly* (London), Issue 171.

are manufactured by rural enterprises. Third, farm and side-line produce has to be processed. In fulfilling primary objectives in areas close to big industrial cities, rural industries are often required to make use of scrap and waste from big factories. Among the secondary objectives, the manufacture of products needed by modern industry appears to be the most important, and, in a number of places, rural industry also produces export items.

Rural industry exercises a primary influence on agriculture, and provides a basis for future mechanization. It has been stated that China should be able to achieve basic mechanization of her agriculture by 1980.[1] The paradox of the mechanization of agriculture, however, is that a relatively abundant and fast growing factor – labour – is replaced by machinery, when the availability of farm workers is not diminishing and may even be increasing. There are, however, important economic reasons for the mechanization of Chinese agriculture. First, the timing of many agricultural tasks requires machinery in order to achieve optimal results, and the large-scale introduction of land-saving innovations such as multiple cropping and close planting require more manpower per unit of land, so that certain tasks must be mechanized. Second, it is often economically rational to replace human and animal power by machine power. Labour-saving innovations such as the use of herbicides for weeding can be profitable, as can be seen from the following comment:

Weeding generally takes up about one-third of total farm labour. Since manual and mechanized weeding can no longer meet the requirements of improved farming techniques and mechanization, the use of herbicides has become the most economic and effective method. The Huangshih commune of Milo county, Hunan, found that the weeding effect of herbicides applied by a single labourer in one day equalled that of one day's manual weeding by 30 labourers and the cost of herbicides was less than 1 *yuan* per *mou* [approximately $6 per hectare].[2]

There are also very important non-economic motives for agricultural mechanization: it creates the basis for more advanced forms

[1] Information given by a cadre in the Shanghai Municipality Farming Bureau in December 1971.
[2] NCNA in Chinese, 10 June 1972, *BBC Summary of World Broadcasts* (*SWB*), *Part 3* (*The Far East*) FE/W678.

of social organization in the Chinese countryside. Since it is not possible to continue to demand sacrifices from the rural population while the urban population lives in relative comfort and affluence, agriculture must be mechanized.

The problem is that, once a certain degree of mechanization is allowed, it may be difficult to set limits to further mechanization. However, the mechanization of agriculture and related activities in China is not only dependent on local purchasing power, but is also made dependent on the capability of a given locality to produce almost all the necessary farm machinery and most of the machines needed to make that machinery. This necessitates the local formation of industrial skills and industrial capability, which takes place alongside the mechanization of agriculture, and thus creates a basis for future labour absorption when less manpower is needed in agriculture. Consequently, the mechanization of agriculture in China should not be seen in isolation but as part of the overall development strategy.

Why though does China seek to develop local industries which tend to be on a small scale and relatively backward, instead of modern large-scale plants in order to mechanize agriculture and modernize the countryside? There are several reasons for this. First, industrial production, if based mainly on large units which require a great deal of capital equipment and transport, could grow only slowly because of the heavy demands their development would make on the engineering industry and on the railways, both of which are needed to develop other branches of the economy. Second, modern large-scale industrial plants do not create much employment and they are usually urban-based. An emphasis on modern plants would therefore severely disturb the present distribution of the population. Third, new technology and new machines have to be adapted to and introduced into areas where people have an essentially conservative mentality. The local character of a small-scale, rural, industry may often shorten the time needed to make the necessary adaptations. This is particularly true for farm machinery accessories which must be adapted to local soil, climatic and other conditions.

LINKAGES BETWEEN AGRICULTURE, RURAL AND
MODERN INDUSTRY

As a basis for further discussion, it may be helpful at this point to look briefly at the linkages between agriculture, rural industry and modern industry.[1] Modern industry, which in terms of employment is relatively small, is characterized by a relatively high degree of mechanization and further expansion of this sector would not create sufficient employment to absorb the manpower coming of working age. Agriculture, on the other hand, provides much of China's exports, which are exchanged for industrial commodities needed by the modern sector. It requires industrial inputs to raise yields, but the low degree of mechanization in agriculture and relatively low productivity initially prevent the substantial accumulation of capital which is required for the mechanization of agriculture.

In the first stage of changing the relations between modern industry and agriculture, rural industry is introduced as a transmission belt for knowledge. Initially, the linkage with modern industry is mainly a one-way relationship, in which rural industry is provided with much of the necessary technology, capital-embodied as well as non-embodied. The linkage between agriculture and rural industry is characterized by a mutual relationship where rural industry is responsible for much of the technical skill formation in the agricultural sector and also supplies increasing amounts of agricultural inputs. Agriculture, in its turn, supplies raw materials and capital. Important factors in the further development of linkages are the level of market demand and the availability of appropriate technologies. The price mechanism is of little importance, and the initiatives of local leadership at different levels explain much of the new activity. (See the diagrams in Fig. 1.)

In the second stage, rural industry and agriculture become partly integrated, with agriculture supplying industry with increasing amounts of raw materials for light industry, and rural industry

[1] Similar linkages in Chinese society have been discussed with reference to the public health system in a paper by Susan Rifkin and Raphael Kaplinsky: 'Health Strategy and Development Planning: Lessons from the People's Republic of China', *Journal of Development Studies*, January 1973. An important aspect of the new public health system in China appears to be the emphasis on the effective demand from the rural sector which corresponds to the effective demand for technology in agriculture.

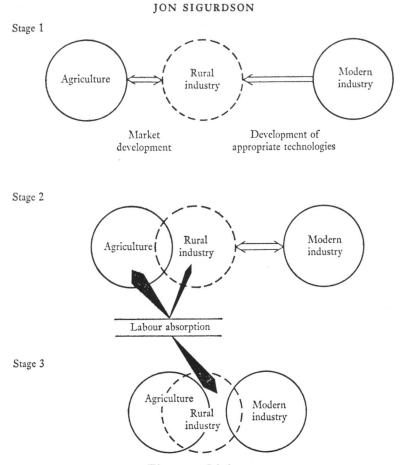

Figure 1: Linkages

processing much of the rural farm produce. The increase in purchasing power arising from the increased productivity in agriculture
makes it possible to finance more machinery. Labour absorption, at
this stage, will still mainly take place within agriculture or related
activities, but will also be increasing in the sector of rural industry.
Rural industry reaches a certain degree of sophistication and differentiation, and can supply modern industry with some products.
Thus, in this second stage, the linkage between the two sectors
develops into a mutual relationship.

In the third stage of the sequence, rural industry and modern industry become more or less integrated. Some production is shifted from the modern sector to the rural industry sector. Quality standards and standardization within the rural industrial sector improve considerably, thus permitting a considerable expansion of the subcontracting system. Rural industry and related services become, at this stage, increasingly important for labour absorption, and a fairly substantial transfer of employment from agriculture to rural industry can take place as agriculture is mechanized. As an example of this phase, it is interesting to note that Ts'unhua county in Hopei province, where agriculture is only partially mechanized, has an industrial employment – if all activities are added together – of between 10 and 15% of the labour force of the county.[1]

Thus, it can be seen that rural industrialization, based on local resources of skilled manpower and capital, is going to provide the basis for the mechanization of agriculture, which will, in turn, make it possible for peasants to engage in new tasks (e.g. multiple cropping) and raise agricultural yields. With higher yields, more industrial crops can be grown and this, in turn, will give local light industry more raw materials. In the process, labour is absorbed into rural industry and purchasing power is also increased, thus creating a local market for light and other industrial products.

Basically, rural industry should use locally available raw materials, produce locally, and distribute locally. This implies that arranging plans, allocating raw materials and organizing factory production must be based on local decisions. But as soon as secondary objectives (such as the manufacture of products for modern industry) are emphasized, local planning is increasingly coordinated with more centralized plans, which often means those of the next higher administrative level. In meeting the primary objective of serving agriculture, a symbiotic interaction develops between the rural industrial sector and the surrounding agricultural sector. In the third stage of development, when secondary objectives begin to come into the picture, a similar symbiotic interaction is developed between the rural industrial sector and that of modern industry. These interrelations

[1] See 'Rural Industry – A Traveller's View', by Jon Sigurdson, *The China Quarterly*, No. 51 (April–June 1972), pp. 315-32.

are very important for both the social and economic development of China.

Rural industry in China is being developed gradually and is closely coordinated with agricultural development so as to cause no disruption to the local economy. In many localities all over China, a problem-finding and a problem-solving capacity will gradually be built up. This will make it possible to specify local resource availability and demand more accurately. The countryside can thus put forward demands on the basis of increased purchasing power and knowledge. The differences between the countryside and the cities may then diminish, this being an important social goal. Many developing countries are today faced with the problem that they cannot provide enough employment opportunities for people reaching working age. It appears that the rapid development of the rural areas has laid the foundation for solving this problem in China. During the first stage of this development, however, employment is not created primarily in industrial production, but in repair and maintenance, in production of industrial raw materials, in transportation and in other services and in an increasingly diversified agriculture. At the same time, industrial structures are created outside the big cities. With simultaneous expansion of national and local enterprises, the former can increasingly draw on the manufacturing potential of a large number of small enterprises.

It is clear that, by definition, industry must be highly differentiated in order to achieve its primary objective of serving agriculture. The high degree of differentiation desired in practice is also clear from Chinese reports on industrial systems in those counties which have been publicized as models where, in one case, over 900 different items were said to have been produced in well over a hundred enterprises.[1]

The objectives of rural industry will of course be more or less comprehensive according to local conditions. The availability of raw material is particularly crucial. Thus, coal, which is used as raw material for the production of chemical fertilizer and for making coke needed in the production of iron, is not locally available all over China. Similarly, iron ore deposits, even if widely scattered, are not available everywhere. Wherever possible however, every county is

[1] 'Ts'unhua county in Hopei province', NCNA, 17 September 1971, *SWB*, FE/W641.

expected to set up the so-called 'five small industries' system, consisting of plants for the production of iron and steel, chemical fertilizer, cement, machinery and energy-production units in the form of coal pits or small hydro-electric plants. This system is designed to meet the first component of the primary objective: that of producing industrial inputs for agriculture. Such plants are usually run by the counties themselves, but sometimes communes are assigned the responsibility for running smaller plants.

A three-level repair network with units at county, commune and brigade level is the physical manifestation of the second component of the primary objective, i.e. repair and maintenance of agricultural machinery. This network is almost always combined with the manufacture of farm tools and farm machinery. Between the three levels of the network there is a fairly clear division of labour: brigades are responsible for minor repairs; commune stations carry out medium-scale repairs; and major repairs are, in principle, handled by the county station. At brigade level, the repair and manufacturing station may have only a few employees and a few simple machines, such as a forging hammer and a grinding machine. Commune stations may have from a score to a hundred employees, and often have lathes as well as cutting and shaping machines, while county level stations tend to be relatively well equiped with machines, and engage in the manufacture of different equipment and machinery, including simple machine tools, as well as repairs. The repair and manufacturing networks are developed gradually and it must be remembered that they are far from complete even in counties publicized as models.

The third component of rural industry's primary objective is the processing of farm and side-line produce. To do this, shops for oil pressing, flour milling, cotton ginning and sugar refining are established. Further processing, such as fruit canning and textile manufacture, may also be included, but the extent of these activities is, to a considerable extent, dependent on the availability of local raw materials and the purchasing power of the locality.

So far as the production of chemical fertilizer and iron for making farm tools and machinery is concerned, this is, in most counties, usually subsidized through the profits made on light industrial products. Those communes and brigades which are well off can afford to spend more money on consumer goods and these are priced to give considerable profits, so that the well-to-do communes and brigades are indirectly supporting the poorer brigades which benefit equally from the fertilizer and iron produced.

Local industrial development has, in certain industrial sectors, already been of considerable importance. In January 1972, for instance, the Chinese press reported that 60% of chemical fertilizer production comes from small and medium enterprises,[1] most of which were run by counties. Total fertilizer production in 1971 was approximately 17 million tons, so that local enterprises must have produced about 10 million tons.[2] Similarly, 20% of the total pig-iron production of about 20 million tons comes from small iron and steel plants,[3] so that approximately 4 million tons of pig iron is produced in some 1,000 small plants all over the country. Small fertilizer and pig-iron plants came into existence in the late 1950s, and there seems to have been a continuous development of technology ever since directed towards making them appropriate to their particular environment. The limit may indeed have been reached in terms of geographical distribution, leaving further development to be in terms of size. As for farm machinery, which is mostly produced in local plants, this has increased approximately 100% from 1965 to 1970,[4] but there is no information available to transform this percentage into concrete figures. It is equally difficult to find out how much development there has been in the rural light industry sector, and how far the repair and manufacture networks[5] have been ex-

[1] 'New Leap in China's National Economy', *Peking Review*, No. 2, 1973, p. 8.
[2] In Edgar Snow's last interview with Chou En-lai, he was given the figure of 14 million tons for the total chemical fertilizer production in 1970: Edgar Snow, *The Long Revolution*, p. 155. Official data released at the beginning of 1972 said that fertilizer production increased by 20% in 1971.
[3] 'The iron ore and pig iron turned out by local small and medium-sized iron and steel enterprises throughout the country this year accounted for one-fourth and one-fifth of national output respectively.' NCNA in English, 27 July 1971, *SWB*, FE/W642.
[4] 'Advance along Chairman Mao's line in agricultural mechanization', *Jen-min jih-pao* (*People's Daily*), 17 September 1971, *SWB*, FE 3793.
[5] Tangshan region, Hopei, which has a population of 6.5 million, reported that 'the rapid development of local industries has brought about an enlarged farm-tool repair and maintenance network serving counties, communes and production brigades in the region – a network which now comprises 24 county-level farm machinery repair and manufacturing plants, 440 commune-level farm machinery repair and manufacturing stations, and 2,000 production brigade-level farm machinery repair and assembly points' (NCNA, 5 June 1972, *SWB*, FE/W677).

panded, but there can be no doubt that rural industrialization has reached a considerable level of development, even if there are marked geographical differences.

THE ROLE OF LEADERSHIP

The introduction and acceptance of new and appropriate technologies often seems to require a special type of leadership, even though some mechanisms can be devised to encourage their automatic acceptance. The rapid development of local industry in rural areas is necessary for the further development of agriculture, but is also a consequence of the favourable development of agricultural production in recent years. Improved seeds and their popularization through agricultural scientific networks have, together with increased irrigation and more fertilizers, considerably increased yields per acre in many areas. This has two important consequences. First, the increased grain yields have made it possible to expand the acreage available for industrial crops, thus supplying industry with more raw materials. Second, through increased agricultural production, purchasing power and the potential for savings and investments have increased. The peasants can thus buy more agricultural inputs such as machinery and agrochemicals, which in turn will further increase the productivity of agriculture and decrease labour intensity.

The initial development of agricultural production would appear to be an important prerequisite for starting rural industries. In China, however, such development has not been evenly spread. For example, it has been reported from Hengtung county in Hunan that, since the leadership paid attention to concentrating on progressive units only, and disregarded giving specific assistance to backward communes and brigades, the 13 comparatively backward communes in the county did not undergo a major transformation, although production developed greatly on the remaining 26 communes. The county then sent about 1,250 cadres to stay at 843 production teams in 101 brigades in the relatively backward communes. The people sent included political and administrative as well as technical personnel. As a result, so it was reported, the backward communes and brigades were quickly transformed. The strengthening of leadership in these areas resulted in an increase of total grain production in the county of 29.8% in 1970, as compared with 1969. According to the same report, improvement in the leadership of backward brigades was carried out on a wide geographical basis. Since the beginning of 1971, it was said that leading cadres of counties, districts and communes in the Hengtung region have led about 6,000 office cadres to stay at a total of 1,453 rather backward brigades, which constituted one-third of the total brigades in the region. They gave education in ideology and political line for basic-level cadres and commune members and these units were said to have improved remarkably in only a short period, with grain output increasing by 15 to 30% above the figure for 1970.[1] Leadership improvement can, in fact, deal with a number of different aspects, such as willingness to try new seeds, the popularization of new seeds, accounting systems and willingness to make investments which will pay off later on, as well as the more strictly political matters generally referred to in press reports.

Conscious decisions to foster technologies appropriate to rural areas take a vast amount of political will on the part of government and Party leaders, partly because of the strong urban bias which has apparently been a serious problem even in China. Furthermore, the type of technological development chosen will play a large part in determining the nature of the society which emerges in China. This point is relevant to Mao's letter to Lin Piao dated 7 May 1966, which says, among other things:[2]

While the main task of the peasants in the communes is agriculture... they should at the same time study military affairs, politics and culture. Where conditions permit, they should collectively run small plants... Where conditions permit those working in commerce, in the service trades and Party and government organizations should do the same.

This directive has usually been interpreted as an indication of Mao's fascination with the problem of the creation of a 'new man' in China. However, it may be appropriate to look at these instructions as a tool, one among many, to create more relevant knowledge and

[1] Improvement of backward communes and brigades in a Hunan region, Hunan Radio, 27 March 1972, *SWB*, FE/3953.
[2] *Current Background* (Hong Kong: U.S. Consulate General), No. 891, 8 October 1969, p. 56.

attitudes for a development strategy which, to a considerable extent, must be based on local inter-disciplinary planning.

Attempts to delegate planning authority to local communities have, in many countries, produced unsatisfactory results. This has partly been due to lack of technical skills or resources, or both, but the failure is basically a political one. It appears that an important consequence of the Cultural Revolution in China is that skills and resources are quickly developed in the countryside to permit local overall planning. While broad strategies and policies must be centrally determined, wide authority has been delegated to the localities to plan for themselves. But to make the decentralized approach work the central planners – at all levels – must have a full understanding of the relevance of local developments. Similarly, diversification in the countryside means that more and more people are moving into new activities and consequently peasants need the knowledge and attitudes appropriate to their new tasks. At the same time, urban-based industry is increasingly drawn into interaction with rural industry. If these relations are to develop favourably, the people in all sectors must have a thorough understanding and knowledge about each others' conditions and activities which can only be obtained through a combination of study and experience. Thus, Mao's directive of 7 May 1966 may be seen primarily as a measure designed to foster attitudes and create knowledge which are interfunctional in character and appropriate for the present stage of development in China. The necessity to know all sides of multisector planning applies, of course, still more to officials at all levels. This might partly explain the emphasis which in recent years has been given to the May Seventh cadre training schools.

Such a need for a better understanding of the requirements of the countryside had, of course, been recognized long before the Cultural Revolution. In September 1960, for instance, an editorial in the *Pei-ching jih-pao* (*Peking Daily*) made the point by saying:[1]

The organization of the flow of cadres between cities and the countryside, first of all the organization of a number of urban cadres to go to the countryside by turns to give aid and support to technical transformation of agriculture, is a new kind of development for the revolutionary tradi-

[1] 6 September 1960, translated in *SCMP*, No. 2354. Emphasis added.

tion of the Party. . . .*As a result* of the selection of cadres for dispatch to the countryside the *different aid-giving units are able to understand the needs of agriculture better*, and are therefore able to give better aid and support to agriculture in all kinds of work.

REGIONAL BALANCE IN RURAL INDUSTRIALIZATION

The previous discussion has suggested that the question of leadership is of great importance in initiating economic and industrial development. But leadership in isolation is not sufficient to check regional differences. The importance of local initiative is much stressed in economic planning in China at the moment and this may favour the development of areas which are already well developed, particularly in the initial stages of local development. There are, to be sure, means at the disposal of the upper levels (meaning region, province or nation) to guide the distribution of industrial activity and thus the distribution of income. Nevertheless the question of regional balance and regional variations needs to be discussed.

The rural areas in China have benefited greatly from the creation of networks for different purposes. The machine-building network in Hopei which, it is proposed, should be organized as in Fig. 2, can be taken as an example.[1] The province has two different networks, one for the production of complex products like diesel engines, tractors and trucks for use in rural areas, and one for the repairing and building of farm machinery and other products which are almost exclusively used within counties. The two networks interlock at the county level, as can be seen from Fig. 2.

Most services are organized in the form of networks, with increasing specialization towards the top of the hierarchy. Almost all services in rural areas – public health, education, agricultural extension networks, machinery repair networks – were in the initial stages of development subsidized by higher levels through the allocation of skilled manpower, transfer of equipment, etc. However, it should be noted that the building of these networks is far from complete. All the services mentioned above influence, directly or indirectly, the productivity of the units which benefit from them. Through increased productivity, the members of the units will get

[1] Hopei Radio, 27 September 1972, *SWB*, FE/W695.

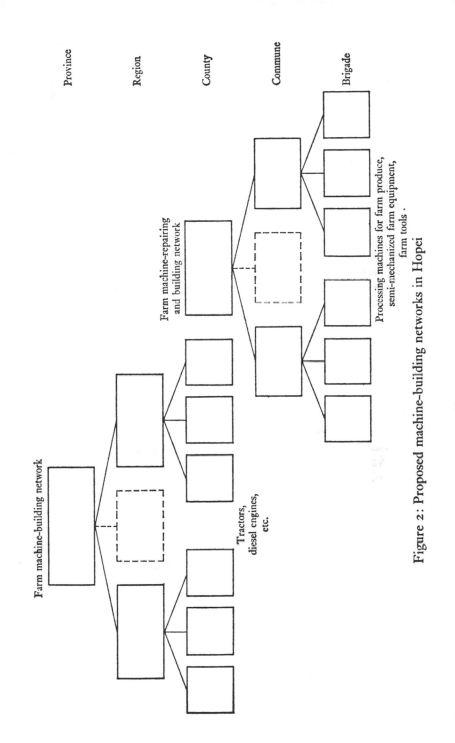

Province

Region

County

Commune

Brigade

Farm machine-building network

Farm machine-repairing and building network

Tractors, diesel engines, etc.

Processing machines for farm produce, semi-mechanized farm equipment, farm tools .

Figure 2: Proposed machine-building networks in Hopei

higher incomes which will enable them to buy more consumer goods which are priced to give a surplus at higher levels.

The upper levels (region, province or nation) will also continue to control admission to institutions of higher learning and are also likely to control the allocation of highly skilled manpower. As more and more sophisticated skills are needed for local industrialization (by counties or communes), the centre will be able, within certain limits, to use the admission of students and the allocation of skilled personnel as a means to guide local development.

The distribution of skilled manpower and equipment may also be a means by which the centre coordinates central and local planning. A county industrial system is never likely to manufacture special alloy steels or specialized bearings, but such products will be needed in the future. These, and other similar items, are likely to be manufactured only by some of the national enterprises at the top of the industrial hierarchy. As specialized equipment is increasingly demanded by local industry, the localities will become increasingly dependent on the centre for the allocation of certain critical equipment.

The operation of the rural industrial system has to be seen as a whole, and some plants may have to be run at a loss. That this possibility is envisaged can be seen from the following statement: 'The development of iron and steel, chemical fertilizer and farm machinery industries needs a lot of investment and produces little profit. For a short time, they may even run at a loss.'[1] The control of investment funds is thus an important means of controlling the geographical distribution of industrial activities. Investment in new local process plants, such as iron plants or chemical fertilizer plants, and the expansion of such plants, is usually of a magnitude beyond the capacity of the local level. Similarly, the distribution of electricity and the provision of feeder lines from main networks can become another way of forcing coordination between local and central planning. Despite this possibility of subsidization, however, the general policy is that local industry be built on a sound technical and economic basis. This is suggested by the following: 'As for those small industries which failed to follow the correct orientation

[1] Development of agriculture and industry in a Hunan region, Hunan Radio, 22 July 1972, *SWB*, FE/W684.

and whose raw materials, fuel and electric power were not definitely available, they were not allowed to continue their building.'[1] But the effect of widely differing conditions for starting local industry on the level of investment and planning is shown clearly in the following quotation from Hunan:

Some counties have developed agriculture comparatively rapidly and have surpluses and ample raw materials, so more industry is run there; where that is not the case, not so much industry is run. Some counties have a rather weak industrial foundation and so the region builds more factories there. Some counties have industries run by the centre or the province, so the region runs none at all or not many factories there.[2]

THE COORDINATION NETWORKS

In an article on automated manufacturing techniques in developing economies, Jack Baranson points out that the 'ability of the Japanese to substitute human skills for machine capabilities or deficiencies in raw materials was already evident at the turn of the century. Second-hand textile machinery was imported by Japan from England, cheaper short-staple cotton was used in combination with additional workers to mend broken threads, and repairmen were hired to keep older equipment going.'[3]

This approach has much in common with Chinese policy towards the development of rural industry. Local industrialization is, apart from the process industries, to a considerable extent based on worn-out machines or obsolete equipment handed down from large urban-based industries.[4] In rural industries these machines are repaired, adapted and carefully maintained. While raw materials of top quality are supplied to the big national industries, the local industries usually have to use second or third grades. The iron content of iron ore used in county-run iron and steel plants may be lower than 40% (as compared with 60% in the big national plants).

[1] *Hung ch'i* (*Red Flag*) (Peking), No. 10, 1972, article by Yü Chung-yuan on relations between agriculture and industry, *SWB*, FE/4127.

[2] Hunan Radio, 22 July 1972, *SWB*, FE/W684.

[3] 'Automated manufacturing techniques in developing countries', Jack Baranson, *Finance and Development*, VIII, No. 4 (December 1971), 10–17.

[4] Factories' links with rural communes, NCNA in English, 20 November 1972, *SWB*, FE/W701.

To make this approach work, China has had to develop high levels of conversion and management skills, for less-automated equipment places a very heavy burden upon supervisory and operator skills. With inferior equipment, industrial workers have to do more in adjusting tolerances, feeding the raw materials and controlling the quality and reliability of finished parts. To achieve this in rural areas, it has been vital to start industrial training from the ground up by producing mainly small and medium farm machinery at the outset.

This approach also involves much adaptation and rethinking. When advanced techniques that embody precision and uniformity are used in labour-intensive units, heavier demands are placed upon machine operators to read blueprints, set up tools and in other ways substitute human skills for machine accuracy. China is today developing a high level of machine labour skills and factory discipline in previously non-industrialized areas, and a pool of experienced engineering and technical skills necessary to convert production techniques to local equipment and materials is gradually being developed. The use of old machines is, initially, both the justification for this approach and the necessary training ground. The effects of small industrial units on the modern industrial sector can be illustrated by the development of the production of bearings.[1] China still lacks both the capacity to manufacture bearings, as well as capacity to manufacture machines to make bearings. Thus, while the country has the technology to manufacture any bearing needed, this is often only possible in very limited quantities. Similarly, the Chinese machine industry can produce most of the machines needed for mass production of different types of bearings, but this capacity is likely to be limited for the most specialized machines.

The commitment to self-reliance means that the Chinese planners will emphasize the further development of production technology as well as production capacity and production equipment for bearings. It appears in this context that the small local machine enterprises can be used for import substitution of machines as well as products. As the national enterprises are not likely to be able to meet the requirements from all those sectors using bearings, the production of bearings within certain quality and size ranges can

---

[1] This capability is also evident in other fields like the manufacture of small electric motors, generators and diesel engines.

gradually be transferred to small local plants. Consequently, the national enterprises are enabled to get free capacity in terms of workshops, machinery and manpower, and can allocate more resources to the manufacture of bearings which would otherwise have been imported.

A similar development is affecting the machine tools industry where the manufacture of relatively simple machine tools is gradually transferred to small plants. Consequently, the well-established larger plants have some free capacity and can concentrate resources on the manufacture of more specialized machines which, among other uses, are needed for the manufacture of bearings.

China now has many small bearing plants run by regions, counties and communes.[1] These enterprises are usually fairly small, with between fifty and a few hundred workers. The production of bearings in such plants is usually only one of the activities in multipurpose repair and manufacturing enterprises. Such production has in many places started with the repair of bearings, the necessary replacement parts being supplied from elsewhere or gradually manufactured within the unit. Available information indicates that a number of these enterprises will eventually develop into small specialized bearings factories, producing a rather limited number of varieties.

Most of these enterprises have been established since 1966 and particularly during the past two or three years. They are the outcome of a policy which was initiated in 1958–60 to meet the local demand for relatively simple bearings needed for agricultural machinery and for carts used for long-distance transportation etc. However, very few of the enterprises set up in 1958 stayed in operation. There are two main reasons for this. First, there was no effective demand for low-grade bearings until the recent development of local industry. Second, the necessary cumulative skills, equipment and capital for setting up small bearing factories were not available until recently.

When setting up a new plant, technology is usually transferred from other small bearing plants as well as from provincial or national bearings plants. A relatively large number of workers usually go to

[1] Kuanghan county, Szechwan, *SWB*, FE/W641; Hopei region, *SWB*, FE/W642; Payinkuoleng Mongol Autonomous Chou, Sinkiang, *SWB*, FE/W669; information given to the author when visiting bearing plants in December 1971.

study in other plants for periods from a few weeks to six months or more. Very little of the equipment in small plants is new, and specialized old machines are taken over from provincial or national bearing plants.

Production of bearings in small enterprises is often started within existing farm machinery repair and manufacturing plants. With the policy of the three-level repair and manufacturing network being implemented and the networks being expanded, two trends are emerging which are changing conditions for the local manufacture of bearings. First, more and more bearings are needed for horse-drawn carts, agricultural machinery and simple machine tools which are locally manufactured, within the three-level network. Second, the fairly experienced, county-run, repair stations have free capacity available when many of their repair responsibilities are transferred downwards to the commune and brigade stations. The county repair and manufacturing stations can then move into the production of industrial commodities, and one of these products has tended to be bearings.

Small bearings factories may be able to take over the production of a considerable proportion of the intermediate size ranges where quality requirements are not so stringent. Some small enterprises are already able to manufacture bearings used for simple machine tools, electric motors and, probably, many of the bearings used for farm machinery. There are already places where small plants have started to manufacture bearings for motor vehicles. If quality can be improved and quantity increased in the small plants, this will mean that large national enterprises can concentrate more of their resources on high quality bearings.

The transfer of used equipment from the large to the small enterprises may also mean that large enterprises will be able to modernize earlier than would otherwise have been the case. The transfer of old machines is facilitated by the fact that wages and social overheads are considerably lower in local industry in the countryside as compared with those in urban-based industry. The average wages in county-run enterprises are likely to be 35 % lower than in an urban-based national enterprise. It should also be noted that the transfer of used equipment may be part of a plan to achieve a long-term division of labour between big and small enterprises.

Another area in which rural industries are playing an increasingly important role is where a large number of enterprises are coordinated for specific industrial projects. Thus, in industrially developed areas, rural industry is enabled to participate in up-to-date, high-precision levels of industrial production. In areas with a relatively weak industrial foundation this type of coordination enables rural industry to raise its technical level. As a consequence, many small enterprises are quickly drawn into close relations with other units of a network and in this process conversion and management skills are developed.

Our earlier discussion of the role of leadership, of regional balance and of the concept of the coordination network, implies two kinds of technology transfer. One is the horizontal transfer of technology between enterprises at county level or below, and the other is the vertical transfer of technology from provincial enterprises downwards. Both these transfers are illustrated in Fig. 3. However, it should be noted that these categories of transfer cannot achieve a regionally balanced development at the provincial level, with the inescapable consequence that provinces with a weak industrial foundation will stay weak.

The way in which the creation of provincial coordination networks for the manufacture of motor vehicles and other heavy and complex products involves a horizontal transfer of relatively complex technology between enterprises high up in the industrial hierarchy is also illustrated in the figure. Industrial centres such as Shanghai, Peking and Tientsin and the cities in the north-east have played an important role in this transfer of technology. Once a coordination network for the manufacture of vehicles has been set up the province can draw upon this knowledge pool for a number of purposes.

The coordination technique is mainly used for comprehensive production and the motor vehicle industry is a good example of this. Hitherto, most provinces have not been able to manufacture motor vehicles because complete sets of equipment and advanced techniques were required throughout the production process. Today, more than 20 provinces and municipalities can produce cars and trucks. One of the important factors in the rapid development of the motor vehicle industry in China has been the extended use of coordination between large numbers of plants. On the basis of the experience in mass coordination when the Great Leap Forward

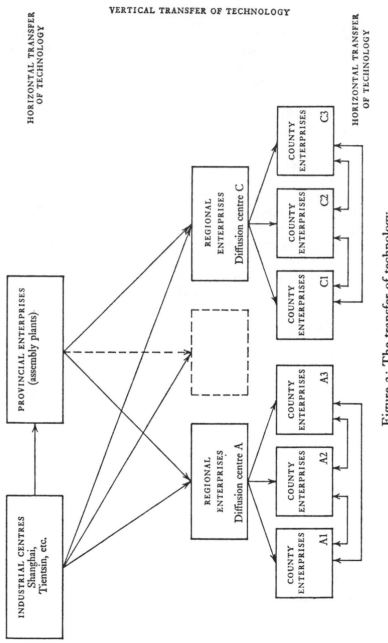

VERTICAL TRANSFER OF TECHNOLOGY

HORIZONTAL TRANSFER OF TECHNOLOGY

HORIZONTAL TRANSFER OF TECHNOLOGY

INDUSTRIAL CENTRES
Shanghai,
Tientsin, etc.

PROVINCIAL ENTERPRISES
(assembly plants)

REGIONAL ENTERPRISES
Diffusion centre A

REGIONAL ENTERPRISES
Diffusion centre C

COUNTY ENTERPRISES A1

COUNTY ENTERPRISES A2

COUNTY ENTERPRISES A3

COUNTY ENTERPRISES C1

COUNTY ENTERPRISES C2

COUNTY ENTERPRISES C3

Figure 3: The transfer of technology

began in 1958, automobile repair shops, machine building factories and other small and large plants form a coordinating network within a province or within a large municipality.[1]

The production of vehicle parts is usually undertaken in multipurpose subcontracting units. This makes it possible to achieve great flexibility in the use of manpower and equipment. The manufacture of different parts is assigned to the unit which is best qualified and equipped for the task. Thus the use of coordination usually makes possible the substitution of labour for capital. There are other important reasons for choosing the coordination approach in manufacturing vehicles. If comprehensive vehicle plants were built with modern automatic machines, it is possible that demand might be inadequate in relation to the high initial output of modern technology plants. The coordination approach enables a gradual development of vehicle design and a gradual development of productive equipment and of the necessary raw material supply system. Coordination enables a fairly flexible interaction of the production factors. Thus, it becomes easier to strike an appropriate – and changing – balance between the use of capital and labour when making decisions regarding equipment, manpower and raw material.

A further reason for the coordination approach is the elimination of the risk that knowledge is monopolized within comprehensive industrial units. It appears that the attack on 'economism' during the Cultural Revolution was partly to eliminate workers' exclusive commitment to their own enterprise, resulting from the operation of extensive bonus systems related to the economic performance of their own enterprise. This relation between wages and short-term economic performance must have made workers and management less willing to accept the cooperation concept and engage in assistance to less developed units.

Although coordination networks for the vehicle industry are the most prominent and complex of all such networks, the coordination approach is not limited to that industry alone. Similar networks have also been created for small walking tractors with 10 or 12 Hp engines. In this case, it is not provinces and municipalities, but cities and regions, which are the units involved. In recent years, many cities

[1] 'Local automobile industry expands rapidly', *China Reconstructs* (Peking), October 1970.

all over China have started production of walking tractors based on a coordination network of several enterprises. Around the big industrial cities there is also a growing number of such coordination networks, mainly based on enterprises within the county, set up for the manufacture of combustion engines or complete walking tractors.

For further industrialization, it is essential that quality standards be set and standardization encouraged, so that local industrial systems can eventually fit into the centrally controlled industrial structure. The local distribution of industrial products within a geographically small area is likely to make feedback mechanisms work efficiently to improve the quality of poor products. Thus, coordination networks are important for drawing a number of small enterprises into working relations with quality and standardization-conscious enterprises. It also appears that the centre encourages the development of strict standards through placing orders with county-run and commune-run enterprises for products at prices which enable the local enterprises to make a profit.

APPROPRIATE TECHNOLOGIES

The continued development of rural industry in China appears to depend on two interrelated factors: the development of local demand for industrial products, and of technology appropriate to the local resources.

With regard to the latter, rural industry is involved in two main currents of technical knowledge. First, rural industry provides the surrounding agricultural area with a variety of knowledge. Agricultural workers from teams and brigades are trained in local industries, e.g. to repair pumps, electric motors and other necessary equipment for the irrigation networks. In addition, other people are trained to repair farm tools and farm machinery and in the techniques involved in use of fertilizer. Further, most of the rural industries send repair and instruction teams to assist in relevant tasks within the agricultural units. Thus, the rural industrial system serves as an important training ground for local technicians.

The second current is that from cities to the rural industries. This transfer takes place in a number of ways. Some knowledge is capital-embodied: for example, much of the technology in small plants producing chemical fertilizer, iron and steel etc. Other knowledge is distributed through books and other printed material. Because of widespread unfamiliarity with industrial technology and lack of ability to interpret printed technical descriptions, it has, however, been necessary in China to rely extensively on personal contacts to transmit technical knowledge. In this case technical knowledge may be carried by two categories of persons. Technicians, engineers and managers from advanced plants travel to the sites of small rural plants to assist in all stages from planning to production and distribution. At the same time people from the localities are sent for shorter or longer training periods to advanced industrial units and are given posts of responsibility for technical or managerial matters when they return.

Rural industry is based almost exclusively on local resources of manpower and capital, although equipment from the cities is a prerequisite for initiating much of its development. In this context it should be stressed that the chief feature of rural industries in China is not their smallness of scale but their local character. Local character requires that they be based on technologies which make optimal use of locally available natural resources, manpower and equipment. Rural industries are, of course, in addition often small, particularly in their initial stages of development. This is a reflection of the limited local supply of capital, as well as of the limited local market for the products manufactured. As markets develop, so do the industries and the technologies utilized so that a plant may go through successive stages of changing production technologies, as long as the resource base permits this.

The following measures have been important in fostering the development of technologies which are appropriate for the economic development in rural areas in China:[1]

1. The development of 'entirely' new technologies in research and design institutes. The design of chemical fertilizer plants seems to exemplify this.

2. The use of old designs and processes and second-hand machinery which were developed for factor proportions which resemble

---

[1] These categories correspond to those mentioned by Sarah Jackson in *Economically appropriate technologies for developing countries: a survey*, Overseas Development Council, 1971.

those in rural areas. Second-hand may not primarily mean old worn-out machinery, but rather equipment which has become obsolete and is uneconomic in the economic factor climate of the cities. It may still have years of life under economically favourable conditions in the countryside.

3. The adjustment of factor prices to reflect the relative scarcities in rural areas so that local industries generate innovations appropriate to their factor endowment. The pricing of equipment and machinery 'imported' into a county appears to have been calculated in order to achieve a substantial shift to the use of labour instead of capital both in making and using equipment.

The industrial technology which has been developed outside China or in the urban-based industrial sectors in China, is usually not appropriate for use in small-scale industries in the Chinese countryside. Therefore upper-level (regional, provincial, national) research and design institutes have been assigned the task of making designs which are appropriate for local small-scale production.

Most local fertilizer production comes from relatively small synthetic ammonia plants usually run by counties. A new type of work process was introduced in 1958. The first plants using the new process were set up in the late fifties and had an annual production capacity of 800 tons of synthetic ammonia. The annual production capacity in new plants is now usually 3,000 to 5,000 tons of synthetic ammonia. High-quality coke was originally required for the production of synthetic ammonia, but the process was gradually changed to use high-quality anthracite. Additional changes now make it possible to use relatively poor-quality coal. Lignite and poor-quality anthracite which could previously not be used are now mined in all the southern provinces in China. After processing, the materials are used in many places for local production of synthetic ammonia.[1]

This development has meant a thoroughgoing adaptation of the design and production process to suit the market demand of counties which on the average have 300,000 people and a cultivated area of around 60,000 hectares. It has also meant adaptation of the process to raw materials which are locally available. Without this latter

[1] 'China expands small nitrogen fertilizer industry', *Hsinhua Weekly* (London), 9 May 1972, pp. 20–1.

development the costs of transporting coal would in many places have made it impossible to set up local small-scale fertilizer plants. But it should be noted that both lines of development have only gradually come about.

The design of a small blast furnace may still be partly indigenous but the production technology is modern, in order to maintain necessary quality standards. Equipment allocated from central sources is based on standard blast furnace sizes of 8, 13, 28, 50, 100 and 120 m³. The smallest of these gives an annual production of approximately 2,000 tons of pig iron.[1] It should be noted that it is only in the blast furnace that a modern up-to-date process is used. The casting of ingots, production of coke and internal transportation are all done with indigenous labour-intensive methods.

More than half of China's 2,000 counties now have their own small cement plants. These are in very different stages of development in terms both of technology and size. The biggest ones produce around 50,000 tons of cement per year and often use twin vertical kilns. The small ones may not produce more than a few hundred tons per year, but are then usually in their initial stage of development. The very small plants use simple concrete pitches for the sintering process. Costs and quality are usually related to the size of the plant and, above a certain capacity range, the vertical kiln is usually introduced. Recently, the further development of the pitch design has been emphasized; this would replace the vertical kiln, even for relatively large small-scale plants. The new design comes from Liaoning province in the north-east and is based on a horizontal brick design. It is claimed that it requires less steel and other critical material and can be built more quickly. It appears now to be widely popularized.[2]

The present stage of production technology for small plants has been reached through a gradual process. Central research and design institutes are likely to have played an important role in the initial stages but local plants are now an important source for improvements and incremental innovations. The smallest sizes may eventually not be used for new process plants as raw material, equipment and

[1] Information given when visiting Ts'unhua county in December 1971.

[2] *'Small Cement' Technical Material – Circular Kiln* (Peking: Chinese Construction Industry Publishing House, March 1972).

market development can be controlled in order to fit the larger plants already from the beginning.

The development of process plants, like those for chemical fertilizer and iron, is centrally supervised to enable continuous and widespread improvements. This makes it possible to compare the performance of alternative innovations and adaptations in order to choose still better designs for new plants.

Innovations in productive equipment used in rural enterprises producing or repairing machinery are left almost completely to the localities, to enable them to make best possible use of their combination of capital, manpower and raw material. The manufacture and use of indigenous machines are encouraged wherever the capacity of modern – expensive – machines would not be fully utilized. Machinery and equipment used in agriculture is still a main area of rural innovations, and it has often been stressed that mass campaigns to improve farm tools and to develop semi-mechanical and improved farm tools, could greatly improve labour efficiency.

The development of appropriate technology for rural industries takes place continuously as the rural industry systems become more and more differentiated. There is an important progressive element in this, in that, as the market develops and the underemployment slack is reduced, the appropriate technologies will adapt to greater scale and capital intensity requirements.

The trial manufacture of new equipment, small or large, is usually commissioned to several units. A regional or provincial industrial bureau is usually the coordinating body for major equipment, but the trial manufacture for minor equipment may be commissioned by the county industrial bureau to units within the county.

As the size and sophistication of local industry develop, so does local capacity for finding its own solutions. Thus, when development becomes partially self-sustaining, and the locality becomes increasingly able to analyse its requirements for further economic and social development, the symbiotic relation between urban-based industry and rural industry becomes important. Industrial organization which permits the effective use of small-scale industries in cooperation with modern industrial complexes seems to have been developed in many areas in China. But to function effectively the small rural industries have not only to be able to convert techniques

226

to meet standards of the modern industrial sector, they must also be able to coordinate their activities effectively and schedule production within the larger industrial complex. These conversion and management skills are effectively developed in rural areas as the local industrial systems become more and more differentiated.

THE SIGNIFICANCE OF
'ELECTRONICS VERSUS STEEL'

During the past two years there has been much discussion within China about the relative importance of the steel industry as opposed to electronic technology.[1] This has sometimes been interpreted as a discussion between the military and civilian sectors, with the military advocating more electronics, for advanced weaponry. This is likely to be part of the explanation, but should not obscure other considerations which may be more basic to the whole development strategy of China. The electronics versus steel 'controversy' can also be seen as an educational theme which is used to educate planners at different levels about the priorities for further development. Important areas for the use of electronic technology are data processing and automation, and it could be argued that prematurely introducing advanced electronic technology into these areas would adversely influence China's development strategy.

Electronic technology, for instance, is extensively used for information processing and all large companies and all planning agencies in industrialized countries make extensive use of electronic technology for planning purposes. Electronic data processing is today a necessity for the centralized operations of large companies. But China, on the contrary, is today stressing the dispersal of industrial activities. Small and medium plants are becoming increasingly important and an inter-functional approach in planning is being stressed at all levels. For this purpose there are positive disadvantages in using electronic data processing since it favours large plants (or plants under centralized control) and requires highly standardized

[1] See for example 'People's Daily on relative importance of electronic industry', Peking Radio, 12 August 1971, SWB, FE/3766; Kuang-ming jih-pao, 13 December 1971, 'Line struggle in industry – A criticism of Liu Shao-ch'i's and other political swindlers' theory of "electronics as the core"', SCMP, No. 5045, 3 January 1972.

procedures. Such techniques would run directly counter to programmes for mobilizing local resources of raw materials, manpower and savings, and would leave little leeway for local initiative.

Rural industrialization requires a large number of machine tools for the manufacture of machinery needed for the mechanization of agriculture. Machine tools can be highly automated and integrated into groups of machines in line-production by the use of electronic technology which, in turn, reduces the need for skilled manpower. Such tools have high capacity but are not generally suitable for simple, small-scale production. Rural areas, with their nascent industries, would certainly not yet be ripe, either in terms of scale or level of sophistication, for the application of electronic technology.

Emphasis on electronic technology would, at present, among other things, mean technology for specialized, automated, high-capacity plants which would, of course, be urban-based. Machinery produced in long series could then be supplied to the countryside, but there would be few possibilities for local adaptations. As a consequence, many rural areas would be left out, either because they lacked the financial means for buying machinery or because the machinery was not suited to their conditions. The other alternative in producing machinery for the countryside has been to make relatively low-grade iron and steel available to almost all counties throughout China and let them all gradually develop their own machinery-manufacturing capability based on local skill formation and closely adapted to local land characteristics and the financial resources available in that area. This approach in supplying the countryside with machinery requires less electronic technology, but more ingenuity in developing local steel production, from the mining of minerals to the manufacture of rolled steel.

If one looks at the characteristics of the local machine building industry where most of the machine tools are being used, it can be seen that the machine tool operator controls the output of his machine. The quality of work is determined jointly by the capabilities of the machinist and of the equipment. Unless a supervisor does the job himself, there is no way to avoid the limit imposed by the expertise of individual machine operators; unless, that is, production is automated. These characteristics contrast sharply with those in the production of iron or chemical fertilizer, where most work is done by teams and the presence of a small number of knowledgeable personnel permits the operation of facilities by a work force consisting largely of unskilled labour.

Further, with demand for most individual products relatively small and subject to change, China is seldom able to support the type of specialized, single-product enterprises which could reduce the need for employee skills by utilizing automatic equipment designed for one product. Thus, machinery production in China requires a large labour force, with a degree of training and experience perhaps superior to that of the average machine-building worker in industrialized countries, where machine-building is becoming increasingly automated. Production of machinery requires not only a high degree of technical skills, but also broad dispersion of these skills among the work force. This explains the gradual approach being used in building up the three-level system for repair and manufacturing, from the repair and manufacture of small simple farm machinery to the manufacture of relatively complicated machine tools, like cutting and shaping machines. The high level of technical skills and their wide dispersion already achieved explains the capability of many counties to manufacture electric motors, ball bearings and diesel engines.

Heavy emphasis on the development of electronic technology would, at present, be likely to damage the development of more balanced socio-economic relations between cities and countryside and minimize the present growing complementarity of the two sectors. Electronic technology introduced now – before extensive skill formation has taken place all over the countryside – would be likely to increase greatly the difference in productivity between modern industry and rural industry, since electronic technology would, at present, be used mainly in urban-based, and relatively large plants. In addition to this, emphasis on electronic technology would be likely to reduce the availability of those planning resources needed for the transfer of technology to rural areas and the development of a local steel industry. Thus, the decision to emphasize steel instead of electronics may also have been influenced by a desire to start extensive development of electronic technology at a later stage when the necessary development costs can be spread more thinly on a wide economic base.

However, reports about the Chinese electronics industry show that the planners are well aware of the potential value of electronic technology for future industrial development, although they appear to be arguing that electronics should not be used indiscriminately without due consideration to long-term as well as short-term socio-economic consequences. The Chinese consider that the social and technical revolutions are complementary. The social revolution is an integral part of China's development strategy, in which the social and economic development of the countryside – the creation of employment, economic growth, etc. – play an important role. While these attitudes are mainly directed towards China's internal development, they do also provide support for a foreign policy aimed at the Third World which seeks to show that China is solving problems which are common to many other Third World countries.

CONCLUDING REMARKS

The development of rural industry in China is not related only to the modernization of agriculture but also to China's overall development strategy. The development of rural industry can be evaluated by a number of different criteria such as capital accumulation, the creation of employment, or income distribution, but sufficient data are not available for any full evaluation and I will only try to suggest here some of the consequences of the present policy.

It is too early to draw any definite conclusions about the effects of present policy on capital accumulation. However, it is likely that considerable amounts of capital are mobilized through reduced consumption and through extra labour which, in the initial stages, is almost completely unassisted by modern machines. Local leadership may well amount to introducing the Chinese equivalent of the 'Green Revolution' and mobilizing people to make the necessary contributions for a local fertilizer plant, a local repair station or new farm machines. If this is the case, the local character of rural industry may be credited with success in achieving local capital accumulation. Furthermore, the local character of rural industry is likely to reduce the demand for capital in the national transport system and to mean that less expansion will take place in cities, thus reducing the demand for urban housing, schools, transportation, sewage systems and other urban utilities. It is also likely to be of considerable importance that the upper levels (region, province, or nation) have at their disposal large networks of small, adaptable plants. The development of new products, new processes or new management techniques can then be assigned to small local plants without disturbing the planned targets of the national enterprises. Finally, technologies which are developed in rural industries are likely to be relatively independent in terms of maintenance and complementary support.

So far as income distribution is concerned, available information indicates that unevenness of distribution within a region is considered adversely to affect overall development, and consequently, much attention is paid to the relatively backward communes and brigades in order to initiate a self-sustaining development. The resulting diversification of agriculture makes it possible to give meaningful employment throughout the year to commune members with varying physical strength and skills. Diversification also creates conditions for a more nearly optimal use of farm land, since land can be used for a number of purposes and not only for growing grain.

In the long run, a considerable proportion of the manpower in the countryside may be employed in the rural industrial sector, particularly when many local enterprises are fully drawn into interaction with the urban-based industrial sector. In this context, it should be remembered that China eagerly wants to develop her vast rural market, since this is a prerequisite for the full development of her industrial potential. The national programme for agricultural development over the period 1956–67 clearly states, 'the countryside with its more than 500 million population, provides our industry with the biggest domestic market in the world'.[1] As one takes a longer term perspective, so the size of this market becomes increasingly important for China, since it will enable her to spread the development expenditure for new costly technology over a wide economic base.

The development of rural areas, based on local industries and services, is likely to create new relations between cities and countryside. The present differences may virtually disappear; an even income distribution will emphasize the importance of local decisions;

[1] *1956 tao 1967 nien ch'üan-kuo nung-yeh fa-chan kang-yao* (*The National Programme for Agricultural Development 1956–67*) (Peking: Jen-min ch'u-pan-she, 1957), p. 2.

and a new pattern of urbanization may be the outcome. Thus, in China, economic and social objectives in planning are closely interrelated. Finally, one must note also the military objectives of the development of rural industrial systems.[1] Some Chinese leaders may have seen a choice between a defence strategy based on conventional hardware and a strategy using the strength of a vast inland area to repel an attack. The first alternative would heavily tax Chinese capital and skill resources, and this may well have given support to those among the leadership who wanted to emphasize the development of rural industry.

[1] It appears from the motives and facts presented in this paper that rural industry has been rapidly developed mainly on economic and social grounds. However, it should not be overlooked that this development in the countryside has important consequences for national defence. It has often been pointed out by the Chinese that the many small synthetic ammonia plants through only minor changes can be converted to producing explosives. Counties with a differentiated industrial system also claim that they can manufacture hand weapons and other equipment needed for defence, such as simple electronic communications equipment. Moreover, the capability of local industrial systems to provide many or most of the inputs required by agriculture of course reduces the vulnerability of the country in case urban-based industries and/or the national transportation system should be destroyed by an enemy.

4

LABOUR ORGANIZATION AND INCENTIVES IN INDUSTRY, BEFORE AND AFTER THE CULTURAL REVOLUTION

Christopher Howe

In the first part of this paper I shall sketch the system of labour organization and reward that was evolving in the mid-1960s, and describe briefly the merits and problems inherent in it. In the second part I shall go on to describe the way in which the development of the Cultural Revolution, between summer 1966 and late 1968, was related to and impinged upon this system. Finally, in the last part of the paper, an attempt will be made to see how the system has emerged from the traumatic events of 1966–8 and, more specifically, to see whether there have been any fundamental changes as a result of the Cultural Revolution or whether the current trend towards 'normalization' can reasonably be described as leading towards a system 'Liuist' in substance, although not of course in name.

THE PRE-CULTURAL REVOLUTION SITUATION

The organization of industrial labour may be considered under two heads. First, there is the apparatus responsible for controlling labour movements between enterprises, areas and sectors. Second, there is the apparatus of control within the enterprise itself. These two levels may be called the macro and micro levels respectively, and we shall begin by considering the nature of organization at the macro level.

In a market economy, workers are normally free to move between enterprises, areas, etc. and their choice of enterprise will tend to be guided by the net material benefits (mainly wage benefits) available at different places. This tendency will, of course, be limited by the availability of openings, and by factors such as custom and habit. This type of worker freedom is also found in most socialist economies, although in such economies workers with special skills are often subject to direct allocation.

From an early date, the Chinese used some direct controls over worker movement, but it was not until the late 1950s that a system of labour control covering the whole workforce was finally developed. The main rationale for this system was that, without it, the control of migration to the cities was impossible. The development of employment controls in the early 1960s was such as to provide a nice balance between centralized control and local flexibility. For although all local labour plans, i.e. plans at the level of city or province, were subject to aggregate national-level targets, these national targets did allow for some flexibility. Moreover, at the very lowest level, the involvement of street-level organizations in employment work ensured that the inefficiencies of excessive centralization were avoided.[1]

I mentioned above that the drive to control migration to the cities was an important factor in the imposition of direct labour control. Had it been possible to make a sharp division between the rural and urban sectors for purposes of labour administration, the workings of these controls would have been relatively simple, but in China, as in other economies where the agricultural sector is large and subject to seasonal influences, and the industrial sector small and subject to cyclical influences, such a division cannot be made. In such economies, rational manpower utilization calls for a system that combines a steady build-up of a permanent skilled core of workers with the means to make temporary transfers of less skilled labour, which can move in response to variations in the level of activity in the agricultural and industrial sectors. An outstanding example of such a system that has persisted even after relatively high levels of industrialization have been reached is that of Japan.

In China, the reality of this problem was recognized in the late 1950s,[2] and various devices were developed to handle it. For example, there were collective contracts which provided a framework for agreements between collective farms (later communes) and

[1] This is discussed in Christopher Howe, *Employment and Economic Growth in Urban China, 1949–1957* (Cambridge: Cambridge University Press, 1971), chs. 7 and 8.
[2] Cheng K'ang-ning, 'Summarize the experience of 1956; reform labour and wage work', *Chi-hua ching-chi (Planned Economy)*, 1957, No. 8, pp. 9–13.

factories for the supply of temporary labour mainly for construction work. Similarly, it has been possible for individuals in the cities to make individual contracts to work on a temporary basis in the industrial sector. Thirdly, special arrangements have been made for workers to engage in regular rotation between the agricultural and non-agricultural sectors.[1] These arrangements are particularly prominent in industries based on agriculture located in urban peripheries, e.g. sugar refining, construction, and various branches of light industry dependent on agricultural raw materials.

It is not clear exactly how many workers were covered by systems of this sort. In 1958, temporary workers accounted for 12,000,000 of the workforce, and the number probably grew in the 1960s to the point where it accounted for some 30% to 40% of the total non-agricultural work force.[2]

Turning now to the micro level, evidence on the nature of labour organization within enterprises in the 1960s is not easy to acquire, but some trends are clear. During the Great Leap Forward, there had been widespread abandonment of formal accounting and planning practices, together with a decline in the effectiveness of the Soviet-style responsibility system and a general decline in the importance of formal structure. After 1961, these trends were reversed. 'Every enterprise', said the *People's Daily*, 'should set up and perfect a system of responsibility for administrative leadership at factory, workshop and group levels.'[3] How far this went it is hard to say, but Red Guard materials were later to describe these developments as the spawning of the '10,000 rules' of Liuist bureaucracy.

---

[1] 'The Head of the planning bureau of the Ministry of Labour, Wang Chieh, confesses his views on the conversion of apprentices to temporary workers during the Third Five Year Plan', *Lao-tung chan-pao* (*Labour Battle Weekly*) (*RG*), 3 February 1968. 'The labour system of industrial and farming work in rotation is actively tried out all over China', New China News Agency (Peking), 27 December 1965. Red Guard pamphlets (RG), are available in the RG series of microfilms issued by the Center for Chinese Research Materials, Washington D.C.

[2] *Black materials on Liu Shao-ch'i and the system of temporary and contract labour* (in Chinese) (Canton, 1968) (RG). See also Wang Chieh's confession cited above.

[3] Ma Wen-kuei, 'Basic principles governing the administration of socialist industrial enterprises, *Jen-min jih-pao* (hereafter *JMJP*) (*People's Daily*), 3 June 1964, *Survey of the China Mainland Press* (hereafter *SCMP*) (Hong Kong: U.S. Consulate General), No. 3245, 1964. 'Work in accordance with established rules', *JMJP*, 22 May 1962 in *SCMP*, No. 2755, 1962.

At the same time as enterprise organization was being made more hierarchical and disciplined, there were also reports of a revival of the system of Workers' Congresses, which might have been expected to provide some degree of increased worker participation in industrial organization.[1] These congresses were a development from the Workers' Representative Congresses of the 1950s. According to a report in *Hung ch'i*, they had the right to hear and discuss work reports by the enterprise director, as well as to examine and discuss production, financial, technical and wage plans.[2] Although, however, it was stated that the work of these congresses should be 'centred on production', in fact it seems probable that their main function was to act as a platform for the expression of worker demands for improved welfare facilities and material rewards. There is little evidence of meaningful participation in enterprise level planning decisions.

The last feature of enterprise organization worthy of note for our purposes is the consolidation, in the 1960s, of the leading role of the Party committee in the enterprise. This consolidation continued a trend in enterprise organization that dated from 1956 and marked the Chinese industrial enterprises as a distinctly different type of organization from the Soviet enterprise, in which it had always been official policy to minimize the power of the Party committee and to maximize the authority and responsibility of the enterprise managers. It may well have been true that the rehabilitation of persons with skills in 1960–2 involved some diminishing of Party authority but, in relation to the situation during the early part of the First Five-Year Plan, the consolidation of the Party is unmistakable. One remarkable confirmation of this is the fact that, according to one report, the Party secretary became the highest paid member of the enterprise's staff.[3] The only significant change in this situation came in 1965, when the PLA began to take an interest in economic organization.

The nature of worker organization is an important factor in

[1] 'Give full play to the role of Workers' Representative Congresses', *JMJP*, 11 October 1961 in *SCMP*, No. 2604, 1961.

[2] Li Chun-chih, 'On the system of Workers' Congresses in state operated enterprises', *Hung Ch'i (Red Flag)*, No. 2, 1962, pp. 33–7.

[3] 'The treatment of workers and staff in a Wusih tyre factory', *Yuan-tung kuan-ch'a (Far East Perspective)* (Hong Kong), 16 June 1963.

determining morale, attitudes to the acquisition of skills and productivity. A more obvious determinant of these, however, is the wage system. The most important point to note with regard to the wage system in the mid-1960s is that its significance had been greatly diminished by the development of direct controls over labour movement between enterprises and areas. Although wages could still be used to encourage workers to acquire skills or accept responsibilities, under a system of direct labour allocation their function of inducing worker movement to desired industries, sectors or areas, was not strictly necessary. It is true that direct allocation would be hard to operate if workers were required to move in ways diametrically opposed to those indicated by the wage system, but in the early days of direct allocation, there was not much likelihood of this.

Apart from questions relating to the structure of wages, the most notable feature of the mid-1960s is the fact that between 1957 and 1966, there appears to have been no increase in real average wages of workers or staff in the non-agricultural sector. This is shown in Table 1 below. It will be seen that, whereas real average wages grew at 6.0% per annum between 1952 and 1957, between 1957 and 1963 the rate fell to minus 0.8%; allowing for some rise during the 1963 wage reform, this implies that real wages were static between 1957 and 1966.

The relationship between the demotion of wage structure in favour of direct controls and this standstill in average real wages was close; one of the reasons for abandoning the use of wage structures as the primary control was precisely that experience showed that the continual adjustment of wages to get the structure right led to successive rises in the average level – rises that were inefficient because they encouraged the flow of labour from the rural sector where income rises were limited by the growth of productivity. Thus the wage standstill between 1958 and 1971 must be regarded as a real success, since it conformed to the policy intentions expressed in the late 1950s, particularly in the 'rational low wages policy' and related developments of 1957–8. Seen in a comparative perspective, this success was remarkable, for there are many contemporary developing economies which have tried unsuccessfully to stabilize real and money wages in order to stimulate employment, control inflation and bring about a more equitable and efficient distribution

Table 1. *Growth rates of real and money wages of all workers and staff and industrial workers and staff, selected periods, 1949/50–1972 (per cent per annum)*

	Money wages		Real wages	
	All workers and staff	Industrial workers and staff	All workers and staff	Industrial workers and staff
1949/50–1952	17.5	14.5	21.2	17.0
1952–1957	7.4	5.7	6.0	4.0
1957–1963	−0.8	n.a.	−2.1	n.a.
1963–1972	1.9	n.a.	1.9	n.a.
1952–1972	2.4	n.a.	1.9	n.a.

SOURCES: Wage data 1949–72 from *Ten Great Years* (Peking: Foreign Languages Press, 1960), p. 216; New China News Agency despatch, in *Survey of the China Mainland Press*, No. 3269, 1964; 'Living Standards in China improve', *Peking Review*, 30 September 1971. 1972 data from visitors' reports, personal and published – for example, 'China: a new tranquillity', *Newsweek*, 19 June 1972. Price data from *Ten Great Years* p. 174, and *Ta-kung pao* (*Impartial Daily*) (Hong Kong), quoting New China News Agency, 3 December 1964.

of income between those engaged in the industrial and agricultural sectors.

The decline of wages as an incentive instrument in the 1960s increased the necessity for the development of alternative devices to stimulate work effort, such as emulation campaigns. In the 1950s, emulation work had followed the Soviet pattern in which workers strive to become 'labour heroes'. In this, emphasis is placed on the importance of increasing the *intensity* of work effort in order to fulfil the targets of the enterprise plan, and the beneficiaries of these exercises are mainly individuals – model and advanced production workers. A feature of this type of emulation work is that the benefits always include material gain in cash or kind.[1] In the 1960s, emulation continued in China and indeed increased in scale, but the campaign criteria switched from plan fulfilment to emphasis on shop-floor level technical innovation and also on political performance. In

[1] For example, 'Temporary regulations concerning the question of premiums for socialist emulation' in *Chung-yang ts'ai-cheng fa-kuei hui-pien, 1956* (*1956 Compendium of Central Government Finance Laws and Regulations*) (Peking: Law Publishing House, 1958), p. 179.

addition, the winners were frequently collective units, e.g. shops or factories, rather than individuals. Despite these changes, the links between emulation and material benefit remained, and in view of the standstill in real average wages, probably increased in importance, if not in amount.[1]

The problems of the pre-1966 system

The system of labour control and incentives which has been described above offers at least partial solutions to many of the problems that bedevilled the Chinese economy in the 1950s, and still trouble many developing economies today. It provides means to control rural-urban migration directly, while, at the same time, controlling the increasing divergence of urban and rural incomes which creates an incentive to evade direct control; it also provides means for organizing the utilization of the labour force in a way that minimizes open unemployment and provides, through the temporary/contract system, links between the industrial and non-industrial labour forces. On the incentive side, the use of emulation campaigns offers a partial substitute for incentive systems that rely overwhelmingly on expensive systems of wage differentiation. Nevertheless, this system of controls and incentives was not stable, and did indeed contain some serious deficiencies. The pressures created by these deficiencies emerged during the Cultural Revolution, and in some ways contributed to its outbreak.

One of the most important problems in the system related to the question of temporary workers. Although temporary workers with grievances had existed in the 1950s, their presence then had not been socially explosive. One important reason for this was that the rapid growth of the industrial sector in the 1950s had enabled it to absorb temporary workers at a steady pace. Thus, for many, the temporary sector was merely a transit point, and for those who simply participated in temporary work when it suited them, the wages, in less regulated days, were often high. In the 1960s, however, the sharp decline in industrial growth limited the capacity of the economy to absorb temporary labour. At the same time the planners became

---

[1] This is based on discussions and observations by the author in China and documentary material such as, 'Bring to enterprises the PLA's excellent style of work', *Nan-fang jih-pao (Southern Daily)* (Canton), 21 July 1964 in *SCMP*, No. 3291, 1964.

increasingly aware of the value of the relative flexibility and cheapness of temporary workers and encouraged enterprises to hire on a temporary rather than a permanent basis wherever possible.[1] Thus, a system which probably lessened rural-urban differentials was found, nonetheless, to be creating new *intra-urban* differentials. Intra-urban differentials had, of course, existed before, but the temporary/contract system made them more legitimate, more formal, and apparently more permanent.

Let us now consider the problems related to micro organization and incentives. We shall consider these together here, because it is the incentive aspect of organization which interests us: we are concerned, in other words, with the way in which the nature of a worker's participation in enterprise activity affected his performance and the productivity of his enterprise.

The most important problem in the incentive system was that it was proving difficult to incorporate in it the degree of flexibility necessary to handle variations in the relevant technical and economic factors.[2] Empirical studies of incentive systems have brought out the point that, although all such systems are concerned with the overriding goals of productivity and stability, the routes to these goals, and therefore the type of incentives most appropriate to them, may vary considerably. Thus, in sectors where technology is modern; capital per worker large; raw materials supplies assured; and accurate coordination essential (sector I), the incentive system must encourage a disciplined, predictable work performance. But in sectors where these conditions do not hold (sector II), creativity and the ability to cooperate in handling unexpected problems are more important than discipline and predictability. Putting it crudely, it may be argued that, in China, the system appropriate to sector I required a differential wage system and hierarchical organization, while the system appropriate to sector II required internal controls and the development, through education and propaganda, of a sense

[1] Opinions vary about precisely how rapidly industry has grown in the 1960s. An authoritative recent estimate is Robert Michael Field, 'Chinese industrial development: 1949–70', in *People's Republic of China: An Economic Assessment* (Joint Economic Committee Congress of the United States, Washington: U.S. Government Printing Office, 1972), pp. 61–85.

[2] For example, 'Turning to work shifts and groups; turning to the worker masses for the purpose of serving production', *JMJP*, 24 September 1965, *SCMP*, No. 3555, 1965.

of participation in, and identification with, the successes of the enterprise. In the period before 1966, the revival of bonuses, 'the 10,000 rules', and the continued, though muted, use of complex wage and salary grading systems made it appear that the overall incentive system was still not satisfying the requirements of sector II.

The other strain in the incentive system arose from the imposed freeze on real, average wages. For although, as argued above, this proved to be an effective and significant achievement, it is not surprising that it had some side effects. One of these was the revival of bonus and welfare payments. Such payments had been discouraged and abolished in the late 1950s, but in the 1960s they were revived, and levels of payment were reported which were far above those allowed in the last published regulations.[1] Whether this revival simply brought benefit levels back to the pre-1958 level, or whether the income in benefits was so large as to constitute an unplanned increase in the average wage level, we cannot know. I would incline to the view that the average increase in such benefits simply served to offset other factors that were depressing average wages. Irrespective of this, however, since bonus/welfare payments were only made to permanent workers, they increased the differential against the temporary workforce. Thus, in sum, it is clear, first, that pressures for an increase in the average level of remuneration were strong by 1965;[2] second, that the bonus-welfare system was a possible loophole in wage control and a source of inequality between both enterprises and sectors; and third, that dissatisfaction arising from these sources must have had some depressing effects on morale and productivity.

LABOUR ORGANIZATION AND INCENTIVES
DURING THE CULTURAL REVOLUTION

This part of the paper will deal with three topics. First, I shall discuss what might be called Cultural Revolution 'policy' towards labour organization and incentives. This involves abstracting from Cultural

---

[1] *Notice on opposition to Economism*, in *SCMP*, No. 4129, 1968; 'Some problems concerning bonus work in commerce enterprises', *Ta-kung pao* (*Impartial Daily*) (Hong Kong), 1 January 1962.

[2] 'Political work in Unions', *Kung-jen jih-pao* (*Workers' Daily*) (Peking), 7 April 1965 in *SCMP*, No. 3454, 1965.

Revolution materials both what appear to be the views of the leadership of the Cultural Revolution, and the grass-roots views as expressed in local pamphlets and newspapers. Second, the discussion will move on to examine the sort of changes that actually took place in labour matters between summer 1966 and the end of 1968. In conclusion, I shall look at the rationality of both 'policy' and events in this period.

Cultural Revolution 'policy'

In considering 'policy', apart from certain specific directives, the major source of our knowledge is the polemics of the debate between what were termed the Liuist and Maoist views. How accurately these portray Liu's own views or those of his supporters is fortunately not relevant to this enquiry, since all I am concerned with is what deductions can be made about positive policies between 1966 and 1968 from accounts of the 'negative examples' of the Liuists. The historical authenticity of these examples does not affect their value for this purpose.

In the case of macro-level labour controls, Cultural Revolution policy favoured the maintenance of a system of external controls on labour direction and hiring by industrial enterprises or bureaucratic units. We deduce this, not only from contemporary directives, but also from the attacks on Liu Shao-ch'i, Li Li-san and others who were said to have advocated a 'free labour market'. According to these attacks, Liu had been impressed by Soviet Libermanism in the late 1950s, and had planned to introduce into China a system within which enterprises were largely freed from central control, and allowed to pursue their self-interest (profit maximization) in relatively free factor and product markets.[1] This system involved allowing enterprises to hire and fire, and freed individuals from the restrictions of the system of direct labour allocation.[2] This was, in

[1] 'See the counter-revolutionary history of Liu Shao-ch'i', *T'i-yü chan-pao (Physical Education Struggle Paper) (RG)*, 27 April 1967; 'The fallacy advocated by the top ambitionist in economic work refuted', *Kuang-ming jih-pao*, 22 April 1967, in *SCMP*, No. 3928, 1967; 'Material incentive is the reaction to bringing proletarian politics to the fore', *Kuang-ming jih-pao*, 10 March 1970, in *SCMP*, No. 70–1, 1970.

[2] 'Liu Shao-ch'i', in *Biographies of counter-revolutionary revisionists* (in Chinese) (Canton, 1968); 'See how Liu Shao-ch'i encouraged a "free labour market" and implemented a capitalist system', *Lao-tung chan-pao*, 3 February 1968. According to the latter, the 'freedom' of the reformed labour market was to apply to all categories of workers and

fact, a practical policy in China, since it could be initiated simply by legalizing existing small-scale illegal enterprises which did in fact hire and fire freely.

The other component of macro labour control policy was, of course, the abolition of the system of contract and temporary labour. The most remarkable statement of this policy was made at a confrontation between the Central Cultural Revolution leadership and the leadership of the Ministry of Labour and Trade Unions, who were responsible for the old system. At this confrontation Chiang Ch'ing described the contract system as 'equivalent [in its manner of treating workers] to capitalism', while activist contract workers made accusations of exploitation and denounced the injustice of the system. Apart from this, attacks on the contract labour system figured prominently in newspapers and broadsheets produced by Red Guards and activists of various kinds.[1]

At the micro level, Cultural Revolution policy was to reverse the trends towards hierarchical, authoritarian, non-participatory and bureaucratic styles of enterprise leadership, which were said to have been growing in the 1960s under powerful political patronage. This policy involved the abolition of formal grading systems and the creation of new, representative, centres of authority within enterprises in the shape of factory revolutionary committees.[2] The main reason for this reform was said to be the necessity of creating a network of intra-enterprise relationships within which the potential technical creativity of the workforce could be released. The failure of the old, and the success of the new styles of management were measured by the number of technical innovations originating from the shop floor.[3]

The 'Liuist' economic system, with its 'free labour market', had important implications for wage and incentive work; for if labour was

staff. It is interesting to note that freedom of job choice was a demand of graduates in the 1957 Hundred Flowers Campaign.

[1] *The record of a conversation held between the small group leading the Cultural Revolution and representatives of the National Alliance of Red Revolutionary Workers* (in Chinese) (RG) (Canton, 1967).

[2] The principles of the new style of leadership were enshrined in the Anshan Steel Constitution, 'Anshan Steel Constitution', *Kuang-ming jih-pao*, 21 March 1970, in *SCMP*, No. 70-10, 1970.

[3] 'The struggle between the two roads in factory management', *Kung-jen tsao-fan pao* (*Workers' Rebellion Paper*) (RG), 28 November 1968.

free to move and enterprises free to hire, the role of wages as an allocator of labour resources would have to be reactivated. The Liuist approach to wages was thus equated in Cultural Revolution attacks with an active approach to wage structure, and a willingness to let the average level of wages rise.[1] The Maoist view, on the other hand, was supposedly a continuation of pre-Liberation policies which were 'basically egalitarian...work being done by effort and courage, absolutely not relying on material incentives'. In terms of wage forms, the Cultural Revolution view was that 'frills' such as bonus, premium and welfare systems should be abolished.

One important aspect of this dispute over wages was the contrast in attitudes to the rural–urban income differential. These differences followed quite logically from differences regarding the value of wage policy and the policy towards the average wage level. The Cultural Revolution view was that the rural–urban differential should be minimized, if not eliminated. (This view was a confirmation of the kind of policy dominant since 1957.) The Liuist view, on the other hand, reputedly favoured keeping a significant differential. 'The workers' life,' Liu was quoted as saying, 'is hard. The workers have an eight-hour day, working intensively in bad conditions, and their life expectancy is shorter than that of the peasants.'[2]

The Cultural Revolution view on all these matters was thus very much a continuation of the 'rational low wage' policy of 1957, although in demanding total abolition of supplementary payments and the old system of special wage grades for staff (and possibly even for workers), this policy was being pushed beyond its old limits.

The last important aspect of Cultural Revolution labour policy was its attitude to the question of the Trade Unions. In a word, the policy was one of violent hostility, on the grounds that the Trade Unions were upholders of all the worst features of the pre-1966 labour control and incentive systems. As defenders of the privileged permanent workers, Trade Unions supported the Ministry of Labour's policy of expanding the contract labour system, and of preserving the benefits of collective welfare amenities and the labour

---

[1] 'Why were high wages not reduced?', *Shuang-ch'en yüeh* (*Frosty Morning Moon*) (RG), 10 January 1968.
[2] 'The true face of Liu Shao-ch'i in the 1957 anti-rightist struggle', *Tung-fanghung pao* (*East is Red Daily*) (RG), 4 January 1967.

insurance law for the permanent workers. The Trade Unions were also viewed with distrust as being part of the power structure in the unreformed industrial enterprise.[1]

What happened between 1966 and 1968

It is very difficult to make generalizations about the implementation of labour policies and laws during 1966–8: our information is too partial and too fragmentary. The media and other contemporary documents naturally report the extraordinary, and we are perhaps overly impressed by this. But how does one correct a bias whose size is unknown? On the whole, the safest guides in these matters are probably *People's Daily* editorials and directives, since these would presumably not concern themselves with phenomena that were trivial, localized or otherwise unimportant.

In the previous section, we saw that an important part of Cultural Revolution 'policy' was the maintenance of the system of labour allocation. There is evidence, however, that controls over labour movement were very weak in this period.[2] Control over migration, for example, was undermined by official encouragement of Red Guard movements and other disorders. In addition to this, the abolition of the Ministry of Labour, the loss of power by the traditional holders of enterprise authority, and the anarchic implications of slogans such as 'each man liberate himself', all led naturally to a widespread breakdown of discipline, of which one manifestation was illegal labour mobility of various kinds.[3]

The second pillar of Cultural Revolution macro labour policy – the abolition of contract or temporary worker status – seems also to have been frustrated. For example, one local directive stated that 'temporary employees may not be turned into permanent workers. Those who reside in villages may not move into the cities and towns to tout for a job...In employment [work] contracts must follow

[1] 'Is he a leader of the working class or a traitor?', *Hsi-tsang jih-pao* (*Tibet Daily*), 7 October 1967; 'Thoroughly criticise and repudiate China's Khrushchev's counter revolutionary line in the workers' movement based on "three kinds of Trade Union and one syndicalism"', *JMJP*, 27 May 1968 in *SCMP*, No. 4214, 1968.

[2] *JMJP*, 12 January 1967; 'Mobilize rural labour which has flowed into the cities to return to the countryside', *Wen-hui pao* (*Cultural Contact Daily*) (Shanghai), 3 May 1968 in *SCMP*, No. 4184, 1968.

[3] Refusal 'to accept assignments' is reported in, 'Educate young workers more intensively in discipline', *JMJP*, 21 August 1969, in *SCMP*, No. 4486, 1969.

strictly the regulations of the Party Central Committee.'[1] This directive fits in with the conservative line of the national directives on labour matters, and with reports which have stated that Chou En-lai was pilloried in wall posters for his refusal to abolish the contract system.[2]

At the level of the enterprise, meanwhile, the attack on the Party and Unions culminated in the establishment of factory-level revolutionary committees. Membership of these committees was drawn from the ranks of workers as well as Maoist sympathizers among the staff and old leadership. The committees were reportedly the supreme authority within enterprises, and their initial tasks were the simplification of staff structures and the reform of technical and disciplinary rule systems. The scope of reorganization is indicated by the example of one factory where it was reported that the number of staff specialists and planning officials had been reduced from nineteen to four, while the total number of staff not directly involved in production fell from 2,500 to 300.[3]

The planned reform of the wage system was, as noted, not too radical by past standards. The elimination of premiums, bonuses and supplementary payment systems, for example, had started before 1966. The proposed abolition of official grading systems, however, was new. How far all this went is not entirely clear. It appears that, although there were some reports of the persistence of bonus payments, the old system of performance-related payments did go. But the fate of the principle of assigning people to specific occupations and paying them according to standardized tables is less certain.

[1] 'Regulations issued by the Hopei workers' assembly', Anhwei Radio, 16 January 1968, quoted in *China News Analysis* (Hong Kong), No. 695, February 1968. The Central Committee's *Notice against economism* is in *SCMP*, No. 4129, 1968.

[2] The role of Chou En-lai in this matter is suggested by hostile wall posters reported in Colina MacDougal, 'Second class workers', *Far Eastern Economic Review* (Hong Kong), LX, No. 19, 9 May 1968). It was also reported that attempts were made to keep temporary workers off the factory revolutionary committees: 'The present contract worker system is a great poisonous weed contrary to Mao Tse-tung's thought', *Lao-tung chan-pao*, 3 February 1968.

[3] Good accounts of the development of the committees appear in issues of *Shin Chūgoku Nenkan* (*New China Year Book*) (Tokyo: Chūgoku Kenkyū Sho 1966–); 'Tientsin industrial workers win new victories in revolution and production', *NCNA*, 7 September 1968. An interesting retrospective account of the nature of rule simplification is, 'Grasp ideas, systems and techniques', *JMJP*, 8 October 1971. 'China's chief steel centre makes remarkable progress in revolution and production', NCNA, 22 September 1968.

The reform of the enterprise power structure with its principle of interchangeability (i.e. workers to manage, managers to do physical work etc.), logically renders the grade system for staff meaningless. However, the directives against 'economism' do repeatedly insist that wage 'anomalies' and the established system shall not be tampered with unless Central Committee and State Council authority has been obtained. It seems likely, therefore, that, even at the moments of greatest upheaval and stress, the basic wage system for workers (as distinct from the supplementary systems) remained intact. Curiously, this result would seem to be the net effect of conflicting pressures on the system. On the one hand, the pre-Cultural Revolution authorities within enterprises wanted to change wage payments to gain support from the workers; on the other, the radicals wanted to abolish grading and premiums in a way that would destroy the utility of wage systems for many years (as had happened in 1958). Thus the conservative defence of the existing system and existing levels of money payments can be seen as a response to these conflicting pressures. In political terms, the excesses on the one side could be used to control the demands of the other.[1]

The 'policies' and events of 1966–8 in retrospect

The words and actions of the Cultural Revolution can be shown to make considerable sense in terms of the problems of economic development, as they can be observed in China and many other countries since the Second World War. The efforts to control labour force movement and migration, to lessen economically inefficient and socially dangerous income inequalities, to lower bureaucratic costs within enterprises, to control the level of industrial wages, to encourage skill, creativity, and flexibility, all add up in principle to a rational programme. But did they do so in fact in the Cultural Revolution? I think that, in some ways, they did not. The reasons are as follows:

(1) The attempt to maintain macro level employment control while, at the same time, abolishing the Ministry of Labour at the

---

[1] See article 5 of 'Urgent Notice', *JMJP*, 12 January 1967. Evidence of illegal wage payments is found in 'Revolutionary elements unite under the great red banner of Mao Tse-tung's thought to set about the total defeat of the capitalist, counter-revolutionary line', *JMJP*, 14 January 1967. See also 'Shanghai Revolutionary rebels achieve great victories in striking economism hard blows', *JMJP*, 17 January 1967.

centre, was bound to run into some difficulties. However ideologically corrupt the Minister of Labour and his senior staff may have been, the Ministry had been responsible for the development of labour control, and it made no sense to dissipate its experience in this area.[1]

(2) There was a profound contradiction between means and ends in the basic Cultural Revolution policy. For while the ends included effectual abolition of the status, privileges, security and material advantages of the permanent industrial workforce, the means to effect this capitalized precisely on the aspirations of the less privileged temporary (and even rural) workers to achieve these things. Thus the only possible outcomes were, either that the old system went and the less privileged found themselves the victors of an empty fortress, or that the system stayed basically the same. Either way, there was bound to be continued frustration.[2]

(3) The desire to restructure intra-enterprise relationships and rely on internal incentives to induce creative work performance, while rational in some sectors, was quite inappropriate in others. What was needed was a more balanced incentive policy, not a violent swerve in one direction.

DEVELOPMENTS SINCE 1969

The most important developments between 1969 and the end of 1972 have been the revival of bureaucratic and technical rule systems in enterprises together with important shifts in wage policy. The situation with regard to macro employment control is less clear, but as far as can be discerned at present, the fundamentals of the temporary worker and labour allocation systems remain unchanged.

The first indication of the new trends in enterprise organization was the drive to re-establish labour discipline. The effects of the Cultural Revolution on discipline were obviously bad. It is true that awareness of the discipline problem was continuous, but in periods

[1] There is still no trace of the Ministry or its disgraced chief, Ma Wen-jui. See 'Restructuring of bureaucracy nearly complete', *Current Scene*, x. 7 (1972), 12–16.

[2] A striking illustration of the importance of lack of welfare privileges to the contract workers is, 'Rise up and rebel temporary and contract workers!', *Shou-tu hung-wei-ping (Capital City Red Guards)* (RG), 13 September 1966.

when intra-worker factionalism was rife, when the '10,000 rules' were condemned and when individuals were encouraged to effect their personal, spiritual liberation from the 'slave mentality', the breakdown in order must have been substantial. Apparently these problems were particularly serious in the case of younger workers who, said the *People's Daily*, 'have shown signs of non-observance of labour discipline and of extreme democratisation'.[1]

Closely related to the re-establishment of discipline has been the revival of technical and accounting rules as guides to enterprise activity. 'It is necessary,' wrote the *People's Daily*, 'to draw a line of distinction between healthy and rational laws and regulations and "surveillance, strangulation and oppression", and between socialist business accounting and "placing profits in command".'[2]

All this is very reminiscent of the articles published during 1961–2 which were referred to in the first part of this paper. This rebirth of rule systems has naturally been accompanied by the re-emergence of the rule makers. We saw earlier that, during the Cultural Revolution, the factory revolutionary committees were charged with the tasks of overhauling the enterprise rules and simplifying the complex bureaucratic systems which were responsible for them. In model enterprises, drastic reductions in specialized staff were reported and the policy of encouraging task rotation between workers, managerial and technical staff must have reduced specialization in administration, even in enterprises where reorganization was not as Draconian as in model enterprises.

The revival of bureaucracy has taken longer than the revival of discipline and attention to rules but, by late 1972, it appeared to be well under way. An illustration of what is involved is found in the recent activities of the Swatow Municipal Party Committee. In late 1971, this committee undertook an investigation into the utilization of skilled staff in State-owned factories and found, not surprisingly, that many skilled administrators were not doing jobs for which their training fitted them. At a meeting of local industrial leadership personnel, the costs of such misallocation of specialized

---

[1] 'Intensify disciplinary education and raise young workers' revolutionary consciousness', *JMJP*, 24 September 1969, in *SCMP*, No. 4510, 1969; 'Strengthen discipline; seize even greater victories', *JMJP*, 21 July 1969.

[2] *JMJP*, 4 February 1972.

staff were emphasized, for, it was explained, 'it takes time to know the situation in an enterprise and to become familiar with production and work. If cadres are transferred frequently, their activism will be affected and their professional specialities cannot be brought into full play...This actually means denying practical experience and shows that the poison of the reactionary fallacy that "politics can squeeze out everything else", preached by swindlers like Liu Shao-ch'i, has not been washed away.' As a result of this investigation and meeting, experienced industrial administrators were sought out, rehabilitated and, 'together with the masses, they have worked out and established various management systems'.[1]

How common campaigns of this kind have been we cannot be sure, but in enterprises where such campaigns have been completed, the net result seems to have been an organization far closer to the pre-1966 than to the Cultural Revolution situation. For, whereas we cited earlier an instance of reform during the Cultural Revolution which involved a reduction of staff from 2,500 to 300 and of specialist administrators from nineteen to four, one recent case of re-organization reported that the newly reconstituted and overhauled administrative structure reduced the proportion of personnel not directly engaged in production by only 5%, as compared with the pre-Cultural Revolution position.[2]

The re-emergence of specialist administrators has inevitably led to some decline in the importance of the revolutionary committees – for part of the case for these committees was precisely that they should eliminate wasteful and ineffective functional departments by taking over their work directly.

The other development relevant to the functions and authority of the revolutionary committees has been the strengthening of Party leadership. It is clear from numerous press articles that economic life at all levels is being returned to the guidance of Party committees. Initially, Party control has been strengthened at municipal and provincial levels, but once this has been accomplished, the drive for control at enterprise level takes place.[3]

[1] 'Employment of industrial cadres in Swatow', Kwangtung Radio, 12 November 1972, *BBC Summary of World Broadcasts, Part III, The Far East* (hereafter *SWB*), FE/4145.
[2] 'With the line as the key link manage a socialist enterprise conscientiously', *JMJP*, in *SCMP*, 72-31, 1972.
[3] 'Strengthen Party leadership, grasp production management', *JMJP*, 13 December

There were moments during the Cultural Revolution when the wage system of the non-agricultural labour force seemed likely to lose all of its essential features. Had this happened, it would have been one solution to the problem of the urban–rural differential in so far as this differential consists of systemic differences rather than differences in average levels of consumption. However, as argued earlier, official directives consistently held to a conservative policy on wage issues, and insisted that the authority of the State Council and other central authorities remained paramount in wage matters. Two changes which did take place were (i) the abolition of individual bonuses (which according to some sources were immediately consolidated into a common bonus, unrelated to individual or collective work performance); and (ii) the development of task switching ('three in one combinations'), which made irrelevant the formal wage systems within which wages were related to carefully defined occupations.

During 1971 and 1972, important changes have been taking place in wage matters. One significant step has been a wage reform that has reportedly raised average wages by 10%.[1] This marks the end of a nine-year pay freeze and, perhaps, a turning point comparable in importance to 1957. Reports suggest that the reform – like that of 1963 – concentrated on workers with long seniority in the lower paid grades. This reform may prove to be the beginning of a series of reforms. Although in the first instance it appears to have been egalitarian (raising the wages of the lower paid), the revival of the hierarchy of grade systems and the new emphasis on technical criteria do lay the basis for renewed efforts to rationalize the wage structure. In the case of grade systems, it is clear that, in addition to workers' and technicians' grading scales, administrative personnel are now on a national, twenty-four grade system.[2] This compares

1971; 'Strengthen Party leadership over economic departments in a practical way', *JMJP*, 7 December 1971. This point is also confirmed by most recent visitors to China.

[1] These points are based mainly on discussions with recent visitors. One published reference to the reform is, 'China: a new tranquillity', *Newsweek*, 19 June 1972. The pre-1971 freeze is described in *Chūgoku Sōkan 1971 (1971 China Compendium)* (Tokyo: Ajia Chōsakai, 1971), pp. 437–8.

[2] Mitch Meisner, 'The Shenyang transformer factory – a profile', *The China Quarterly*, No. 52 (October–December 1972), p. 731. This interesting report goes further than any other published article in describing the revival of Soviet-type planning in China.

with a thirty grade system in the 1950s, which was reduced by unspecified degrees in 1958, 1960 and 1963.[1]

With regard to wage determination criteria, visitors' reports, and a *People's Daily* editorial published in November 1972, confirm that political criteria are out, and that even the ambiguous 'work attitude' criterion, so frequently referred to in the 1960s, is now only occasionally mentioned.[2]

The future of bonus and supplementary wage systems may also be bright, since, obviously group bonuses unrelated to performance will be increasingly hard to justify, and there is already evidence that individual payments are being resumed. At present, however, the most striking fact about supplementary payments is that recent reports of total welfare expenditures by factories suggest levels of expenditure far higher than anything ever reported before. For example, an authoritative article in *Hung ch'i* quoted – with approval – a case where welfare expenditures amounted to 36% of annual wage expenditure.[3] This figure may be compared with the 20% level, which in 1958 was regarded as far too high.

These striking changes in wage policy are being related in China to the decline of important political figures and the loss of influence of their followers. For example, cadre briefings on the fall of Lin Piao are reported to state that the long wage freeze of the 1960s was Lin's personal policy and opposed by Chairman Mao; as for Liu Shao-ch'i, it now appears that, while talking about 'work points in command' and 'material incentives', he actually 'emphasized egalitarianism in a wild attempt to deprive the workers of rewards commensurate with their work and negate the principle of "equal pay for equal work".'[4]

We turn lastly to the question of the nature of employment control. It was argued earlier that both the fundamental principle

[1] The details of the Chinese wage system are discussed in more depth in Christopher Howe, *Wage Patterns and Wage Policy in Modern China 1919–1972* (Cambridge: Cambridge University Press, 1973).

[2] Mitch Meisner, *The China Quarterly*, No. 52; 'China drops its political bonus scheme', *The Sunday Times*, 12 November 1972; 'The essential distinction between two systems of distribution', *Hung ch'i*, No. 7, 1972, in *Selections from China Mainland Magazines*, 72–7.

[3] 'The essential distinction between two systems of distribution', cited above (n. 2).

[4] 'Importance of proper remuneration for labour', Peking Radio, 4 September 1972, *SWB*, FE/4090.

that workers should be allocated to their employment by external agencies, and the policy of making a distinction between temporary and permanent workers, were maintained during 1966–8; although, in practice, there was undoubtedly much illegal labour mobility in these years, due to the effects of the disappearance of the Ministry of Labour, and to the general dislocation of the period. I do not know of any recent detailed accounts of the nature of employment planning since 1969, but what is known seems to confirm that (a) the principle of external control is maintained for all levels of manpower; (b) in the case of graduates and the highly skilled, this control is centralized; and, (c) in the case of new entrants and temporaries, many workers have been recruited in recent years as a result of local, unsupervised, contracts between communes and factories. Control of this last type of hiring is now being recentralized. Initially this takes place at local levels, but ultimately local levels (municipalities and provinces) will be working within a centralized planning framework of the type established in 1961.[1] In the recent past the abolition of the Ministry of Labour must have been a crucial factor in loss of centralized control. But this has not necessarily been a mortal blow to control at lower levels since, even if local labour bureaux have disappeared, their staffs and functions could be absorbed by local planning agencies.

The main reason for thinking that the system of labour control will be recentralized is that there is growing evidence that enterprise targets are again becoming complex and technical, that plans are being made for monthly, quarterly and annual periods, and that these developments are part of a process in which central planning is gradually being extended to cover a substantial portion of the modern sector of the industrial economy.[2] It seems highly probable that the renewed bureaucratization at enterprise level is being

[1] 'Labour problems in Kwangsi County', Kwangsi Radio, 25 October 1972, *SWB*, FE/4130.

[2] '*Heilungkiang Daily* on importance of fulfilling State Plans', Heilungkiang Radio, 4 October 1972, *SWB*, FE/4115; see also Mitch Meisner, *The China Quarterly*, No. 52 (October–December 1972). It is interesting to note that even reports of local initiative in the semi-handicraft consumer goods sector emphasize the planning rather than spontaneity aspects of new enterprise. For example, 'The local people, under unified state planning, set up some 300 enterprises to convert local bamboo, timber, palm leaves, leather, hides, clay and wild plants into 2,300 kinds of consumer goods', see 'More and better consumer goods', *China Reconstructs*, February 1972, pp. 46–9.

paralleled by a similar tendency at the centre, and that excessive decentralization of planning power will soon be labelled as another Liu-Lin deviation to be corrected as quickly as possible.

CONCLUSION

This review of recent changes leaves one with the basic question: has the Cultural Revolution really changed anything? Are we back to the pre-1966 situation? Was the Cultural Revolution itself no more than a particularly acute phase in a partially comprehended bureaucratic-incentive cycle? Probably not. One reason for thinking this is that the course of economic and political change in China must surely reflect some learning processes. It seems inconceivable that the release of severe tensions in China, which revealed so starkly the implications of certain institutional arrangements and policy lines, will not continue to have repercussions for the future. A second, more specific factor is the institutional changes which have taken place, in particular the disappearance of the Trade Unions and the Ministry of Labour, and the continuance of the revolutionary committees in enterprises.

In the immediate future, perhaps the most important reflections of the Cultural Revolution will be in wage and incentive policy. One aspect of this is the evidence that there is now recognition of the fact that incentive forms and organization must relate to the scale and modernity of enterprises within which they are to be applied. 'Particularly in large enterprises,' states one article, 'it is imperative to guard against the tendency to stress unduly management by the masses, while ignoring management by specialized personnel.'[1] If this principle is given the recognition it deserves and its implications worked out in detail, a barrier of great significance will have been passed on the road to a rational organization and incentive policy.

Beyond the confines of the industrial sector, a second point of awareness will probably be recognition of the importance of controlling the size of differentials within urban areas. Awareness of the urban–rural differential was one of the most important determinants of economic policy between 1957 and 1965, and I think it likely that

[1] 'Management problems in North East General Pharmaceutical Factory', Peking Radio, 24 October 1972, *SWB*, FE/4135.

the fear of the consequences of sharp intra-urban differentials will be a significant factor in the next decade. It will not, I think, lead to the disappearance of the temporary worker phenomenon, but will result in care being taken that inequalities between temporary and permanent workers, whether in terms of the level and predictability of income or of non-cash benefits, do not become excessive.

Institutional change now appears to be far less important than had been commonly assumed in 1971-2. The Trade Unions have been revived and their duties appear to be similar to those of the pre-Cultural Revolution period. Indeed, it is clear that, in many cities, staff of the central Trade Union administration were working in their offices long before the re-establishment of the Unions was formally announced in April 1973. The Ministry of Labour has not been revived as such, but its functions have been transferred to the State Planning Commission. At the local level, the Labour Bureaux continue under their old name, and presumably their duties remain the same. We have no recent examples of labour legislation but we know that such legislation continues to govern other economic work and one may therefore presume that administrative rules of different types continue to control the processes of labour control and planning.

Despite the impressive continuity of pre- and post-Cultural Revolution bureaucratic organization, the ideals of the Cultural Revolution are bound to remain a potent, corrective or disruptive force for some time to come. One proof of this is the difficulties that have been encountered in reversing Cultural Revolution trends in the past year or so. A report on a Shensi textile mill, for instance, said that:

When the mill wanted to strengthen enterprise management further and to set up and strengthen rational regulations and systems, some said, 'This is in fact like someone wearing a new pair of shoes but following the old road. Government, restriction and suppression have been restored once more.' When the mill unfolded socialist labour emulation and prepared to give appropriate material rewards to those who had a good attitude to labour and had recorded outstanding achievements in accordance with socialist principles, some people commented that it was 'championship mentality and putting bonuses in command'. When the mill encouraged the workers to improve their technical knowledge for the Revolution, some people said; 'This is putting technology first'. All these muddle-headed ideas in the minds of the cadres and masses proved how deeply the evil influence of the counter-revolutionary Revisionist line put forward by swindlers like Liu Shao-ch'i had affected them, and that the evil influence was far from having been purged.[1]

To some extent this passage reflects the sheer confusion of the situation: a point emphasized by a later passage in the same article. 'Many declared that they would differentiate clearly between the Red and the black lines. They would do their utmost if the line was Red, and would repudiate it if it was black. However, they just could not distinguish clearly the Red line from the black.'

But even when the lines become clearer, some Cultural Revolutionary concepts and attitudes are likely to persist as a real force in enterprise life; and as long as the revolutionary committees survive, there will be an institutional channel for their expression.

[1] 'Criticisms of revisionism in a Shensi textile mill', Shensi Radio, 6 November 1972, *SWB*, FE/4141.

5

CHINA'S EDUCATIONAL REVOLUTION

John Gardner and Wilt Idema

INTRODUCTION

Chinese Education 1949–66

In 1949, the new leadership announced that from then on China's educational system would serve the workers and peasants and would be geared to the needs of production and construction. What this meant in effect was that, as part and parcel of the Soviet developmental model adopted by the Chinese at that time, the existing system was modified and expanded in accordance with Soviet ideas. The very important private sector was nationalized, and Party control established throughout; the works of Sun Yat-sen and Chiang Kai-shek were replaced with the Marxist classics and textbooks were rewritten to conform to the new orthodoxy. Courses were reorganized in favour of concentrating on economically 'useful' subjects, and there was considerable expansion of technical education, particularly at the tertiary level, in order to produce the experts who would be needed for the heavy industry which was going to be the backbone of China's modernization. The influence of the Soviet Union was strengthened further by the widespread borrowing of Soviet teaching materials. In quantitative terms change was extensive; for example, the number of primary school students rose from 26 million in 1949 to 64 million in 1957, and university students increased from 117,000 to 441,000 in the same period.[1]

But the pattern of development was very uneven in certain respects. Educational provision, particularly at the tertiary level, remained unduly concentrated in the big cities, and the rural areas did not benefit from expansion to anything like the same degree.

[1] Two useful books on education before the Cultural Revolution are: R. F. Price, *Education in Communist China* (London: Routledge and Kegan Paul, 1970); and S. E. Fraser, *Education in Communist China, An Anthology of Commentary and Documents* (London: Pall Mall Press, 1971).

This became a matter of increasing concern to certain Chinese leaders, most notably Mao himself, who tried to redress the balance during the Great Leap Forward. The Leap was fundamentally an attempt to break away from, or at least modify, China's reliance on Soviet developmental strategy, and education was seen as a major issue in this. In 1958 and 1959, an ambitious attempt was made to provide educational opportunity in the rural areas by the creation of 'half-work half-study' schools in the communes. Essentially the idea was that these schools would be cheap to run and would give peasants an education suited to the needs of rural development. Students would study on a part-time basis and thus would not deprive their locality of their precious labour power. For a variety of reasons, this 'educational revolution' made little impact, and in the lean years which followed the Leap most of them were closed down.[1]

In the early 1960s, economic difficulties, exacerbated by the withdrawal of Soviet assistance, forced China to pursue policies of consolidation rather than expansion. This was very noticeable in education where, at all levels, the emphasis was placed on quality rather than quantity, and academic criteria were applied to the virtual exclusion of all others. The system became highly elitist and it was actually more difficult in many areas for children of peasants and workers to receive an education at any level in the early 1960s than it had been in the late 1950s. Although, by 1963, the improved economic situation resulted in further attempts to establish schools run on 'half-work half-study' principles, this led to only minor improvements and, in 1965, according to the *People's Daily*, '30 million school-aged children were not in school, most of them being rural children'.[2]

The Cultural Revolution

The Cultural Revolution witnessed a major attack on the system prevailing up to 1966, an attack often involving students themselves, particularly in middle schools and universities. Between 1966 and

---

[1] The most detailed study of half-work half-study schools remains R. D. Barendson, *Half-Work, Half-Study Schools in Communist China* (Washington, D.C.: Office of Education, 1964).

[2] *Jen-min jih-pao* (*JMJP*) (Peking), 18 May 1965, *Survey of the China Mainland Press* (*SCMP*) (Hong Kong: U.S. Consulate General), No. 3475, p. 14.

1968, numerous criticisms appeared at all levels, condemning most aspects of the 'old' system and laying down the principles to be applied in reforming it. The basic charges were as follows.

First, not enough people were being educated, and there were great imbalances of a social and geographic nature. The heavy concentration of schools in urban areas discriminated against children in the countryside, and the application of rigorous academic criteria for admission favoured to a disproportionate extent children from relatively well-to-do and prosperous families.

Second, the nature of much formal education was held to be irrelevant to China's real needs. Although the more obviously 'useless' subjects had been greatly reduced in importance after 1949, even such 'useful' ones as the sciences were often taught with an over-emphasis on theoretical abstraction divorced from the problem of practical application. At the higher levels especially, even practical training was found to be faulty in that it often consisted of mastering techniques of limited social value; this situation is exemplified by the attention paid in medical schools to such topics as neuro-surgery while issues of general public health were ignored.

Third, the system was costly. Courses were long, especially at university level, and consequently expensive. Too many people were being educated to an unnecessarily high level, acquiring skills for which there was only limited demand, hence the return on investment was viewed as inadequate. It was also argued that much money was being wasted on such frivolities as expensive buildings and equipment. As most of the educational budget was contributed by the great mass of the population, who derived little personal advantage from education, the situation was seen to be fundamentally unjust.

Finally, education was condemned for failing to produce the correct attitudes in those receiving it. Political education was either ignored or had become an empty ritual which failed to inculcate a spirit of idealism among the young. Far from wishing to 'serve the people', many students became elitist, contemptuous of the masses and ignorant of their needs. They saw education as a means to improving their own status and salary rather than as a way of preparing themselves for community service. Urban in both origins and outlook, there were few school or university graduates who relished the thought of applying their skills in the villages, where the need was greatest.[1]

Although many rural schools continued to function throughout the Cultural Revolution, formal education virtually ceased in the urban areas. Teaching stopped in 1966, and years of intensive debate took place, involving students, teachers, workers, technicians, peasants, soldiers and, of course, cadres. As the political situation gradually stabilized much experimentation took place. In some areas reform attempts began to be implemented in 1967, but in other areas schools and universities did not reopen until as late as 1970. Nevertheless a clearly definable educational strategy is once more apparent.

The principles and practices of this strategy are by no means new. For the most part they embrace familiar ideas advanced by Mao Tse-tung over the past forty years, some of which were applied to education in Yenan, and others during the Great Leap Forward. Indeed, in some respects, they are by no means exclusively 'Maoist', echoing as they do policies and views advanced by Chinese of varying political persuasions in the 1920s and 1930s.[2] What is new, however, is the extent to which these ideas are being put into effect. Chinese education is now being structured to harmonize fully with the specific 'Maoist' developmental strategies discussed elsewhere in

---

[1] Despite the fact that the Chinese analysis of the defects of their educational system up to 1966 shows a remarkable likeness to Gunnar Myrdal's criticisms of contemporary educational systems in south-east Asia, we should not forget that up to 1966 Chinese education was much more integrated with total social and economic development than was the case elsewhere. The problem was, of course, that those in charge of the system had become unable or unwilling to progress still further. See Gunnar Myrdal, *Asian Drama* (London, Allen Lane, The Penguin Press, 1968), especially Part 7, *passim*. A detailed 'Maoist' critique of Chinese education is to be found in 'Chronology of Seventeen Years of Two-Road Struggle in Education', *Chiao-yü ko-ming (Educational Revolution)*, No. 4, 1967, *Joint Publications Research Service* (Washington, D.C.), No. 43204. Western accounts include: Marianne Bastid, 'Economic Necessity and Political Ideals in Educational Reform During the Cultural Revolution', *The China Quarterly*, No 42 (April–June 1970), pp. 16–48; John Gardner, 'Educated Youth and Urban–Rural Inequalities 1958–1966', J. W. Lewis (ed.), *The City in Communist China* (Stanford: Stanford University Press, 1971), pp. 235–86.

[2] It may be interesting, for example, to compare the present educational experiments with those conducted during the twenties and thirties by people like T'ao Hsing-chih. On the criticism that the modern school system was unsuited to the realities of the Chinese countryside see Liao T'ao-ch'u, 'Rural Education in Transition: A Study of Old-fashioned Chinese Schools in Shantung and Szechuan', *The Yenching Journal of Social Sciences* (Peking), IV.2 (1949), 19–67, where the continued existence of the traditional type of school is explained by that very factor.

this volume. That is to say, the educational system is now seen as the instrument for the abolition of the 'three major differences' between town and country, worker and peasant, and mental and manual labour. There is an attempt to universalize education, at least at primary school level, and a policy of positive discrimination has been adopted to ensure that those who are most deprived get their share. Vocational rather than narrowly academic education is emphasized, and the reforms constitute an attempt to conduct modern, technically orientated education in a society which, basically, remains non-mechanized. The system tries to be 'proletarian' both by stressing ideological education to produce students who will serve the masses, and by giving the masses themselves greater responsibility in the management of educational institutions. It aims to destroy existing values, attitudes and expectations regarding education, which see it as a means of joining the elite; and to replace them with a concept of education as a universally available prerequisite for useful participation in a modernizing economy.

The primary orientation of the new system is towards the rural areas. Mao by no means rejects the role of large urban-industrial complexes, but he clearly questions the centrality accorded them by many economic planners. Even in the cities, Chinese education now stresses the importance of labour-intensive production rather than capital-intensive development. But it is the reservoir of latent manpower and talent in the countryside on which Mao pins his hopes, and here he shows a willingness to face an issue all too often ignored. For, as one authority has observed, 'the need to relate the school system to rural development is perhaps the most important and difficult single educational reform facing developing countries'. What such societies need are schools which will serve as a 'useful introduction rather than a perpetual deterrent to rural life'.[1]

In this chapter we shall focus essentially on the formal educational institutions: those which cater primarily for the young. This is not to deny the importance of other educational forms. It is noticeable, for instance, that adult education has increased in importance since the Cultural Revolution, with the growth of more spare-time education, correspondence courses and short-term training classes, etc.

[1] Richard Jolly, 'Manpower and Education', Dudley Seers and Leonard Joy (eds.), *Development in a Divided World* (Harmondsworth: Penguin, 1971), pp. 215–16.

Indeed, the evidence suggests that the Chinese are moving towards the institutionalization of 'life-time' education whereby people can be given additional training as and when they need it, regardless of age. Nevertheless, for the time being, the schools and universities will continue to play the leading part in training the nation, and we shall confine our discussion to them. Similarly, we shall not consider the 'May 7th Cadre Schools', for, despite their name, these have a specialized and limited function.

THE REORGANIZATION OF PRIMARY AND
SECONDARY EDUCATION

Criticism of rural education started in autumn 1968, when the state schools were compared unfavourably with the 'half-work half-study' schools run by the production brigades. In May 1969, a 'Draft Programme for Primary and Secondary Education in the Chinese Countryside' was published in the *People's Daily*. This suggested that in the rural areas education should be popularized on the basis of a '5–2–2 system' (five years' primary, two junior-middle school, and two senior-middle school); the curriculum was to be reformed; and all schools were to be placed under local management. Since that time, there has been much experimentation and numerous 'models' have been publicized. Initially, considerable attention was paid to matters of finance, organization and curricular reform. More recently, the emphasis has been placed on the priority to be given to universalizing primary education, on the need to lower the drop-out rate, and on improving the professional competence of teachers. Great regional variations with regard to the implementation of reforms still seem to exist.

Popularization

Since the Cultural Revolution began, countless articles have fulminated against the restricted educational opportunities available to many children prior to 1966, and most regions are now attempting to provide universal primary education within the next four or five years as well as to expand secondary education as far as possible. Although no national statistics have been published to date, many localities are already claiming considerable success. Thus one commune in Wu-ch'i *hsien* (Shensi) claims to have increased the number of schools there from 26 to 57 'within a short space of time', and one production brigade has raised the number of its children in school from 60 to 150. In the whole *hsien* 96% of poor and lower-middle peasant children are now in primary school. P'ing-lu *hsien* (Shensi) reports that 90% of the relevant age group are in primary school, and that 87% of primary school graduates can now attend junior-middle school, the number of middle schools having increased from 4 to 71. A commune in Shantung claims that only 6 of its 929 children are not in primary school; these are physically handicapped and teachers visit them at home. In general, the expansion of junior-middle school education is particularly striking. Changsha municipality claims to have doubled the number of middle school students since 1966, and Kwangtung province has reported an increase of 250%.[1]

In our opinion there is no real reason to doubt such claims, especially when it is borne in mind that these are examples of the 'best' areas. However, the matter of initial enrolments is not, in itself, of any great significance: many of the poorest developing countries can boast impressive statistics in this area. The real issue is the question of 'drop-outs'. The problem in many states is not that children never enter school; it is that they do not stay in school long enough to gain any tangible benefit. For example, in Ghana it was once calculated that it took 26 school years to produce one primary graduate.[2] Similarly, in the early 1950s, over one-third of the children who enrolled in the first grade of primary school in Chile, Costa Rica and Peru dropped out before reaching the second grade, and under one quarter completed the full six years.[3]

Such a situation is clearly harmful in terms of the wastage of human talent involved, for most educators would agree that a child who receives less than three or four years of primary education will have acquired virtually no socially valuable skills; he is unlikely to have achieved even basic literacy. But the position is not simply one

[1] *Kuang-ming jih-pao (KMJP)* (Peking), 20 October 1971, *SCMP*, No. 5007, pp. 155–6; *KMJP*, 13 November 1971, *SCMP*, No. 5022, pp. 131–4; *JMJP*, 20 November 1971, *SCMP*, No. 5026, p. 190; *JMJP*, 1 June 1971, *Current Background (CB)* (Hong Kong: U.S. Consulate General), No. 945, p. 1.
[2] Adam Curle, *Educational Problems of Developing Countries* (New York: Praeger, 1969), p. 48.   [3] Jolly, 'Manpower', p. 208.

of no gain, it is one of positive loss. For it costs as much to give a child his years of wasted education as it does to teach another child who goes on to complete his course.

In the Cultural Revolution this problem was referred to frequently as one of the evils associated with the 'Liuist' line. Apart from the mass closures of 'half-work half-study' schools in the early 1960s, and the dismissal of students who were unable to meet rigidly academic criteria, there were many attacks on the failure of schools to operate flexibly. Schools were concentrated heavily in areas of high population density; the cities had more than their fair share; and even in the countryside they were based mainly in rural townships and the largest villages. Consequently children in remote and sparsely populated areas had to travel considerable distances to attend, and middle school education was frequently only within the reach of those able and willing to be boarders. Moreover, school timetables often failed to take account of local conditions. Many children were away from home for most of the daylight hours and could not contribute to agricultural work. Terms and holidays often took no account of the agricultural cycle, so that children were in school during the busiest seasons, yet were on holiday when there was no work for them to do. Financial matters were also a problem, as the largest state subsidies tended to go to the big schools in towns and sizeable villages, while remote and poor regions had to rely on their own resources if they wished to have educational facilities for their children.

Chinese educational policy is now designed to ameliorate these problems. It is now the practice to take schools to the children rather than vice-versa, even though this means the proliferation of many small schools, particularly in the rural areas. A good example of this is P'ing-lu *hsien* where 'mountain peaks rise on top of one another, the land is criss-crossed with gullies and valleys, and the inhabitants are scattered all over the landscape. Of the 1,171 natural villages, some 666 are hamlets with less than 15 households each.' Schools now operate in all villages having about 10 children, and visiting teachers are provided for isolated households. There are 203 production brigades in the *hsien*, each having an average of 2.5 primary schools, and there is a junior-middle school for every three production brigades. Hence 'the children of poor and lower-middle peasants can go to school without leaving the villages or the brigade'.[1] In parts of Inner Mongolia, teachers visit isolated students on horseback. Schools also operate at different times to suit the needs of the 'consumers'. Some are half-day, others work an alternate-day system. Some operate morning, afternoon and evening classes. Holidays are fixed in accordance with the agricultural needs of the locality.

A crucial question has been that of finance. The provision of universal education at the primary level alone is a major source of expenditure in any society, but it can be particularly onerous in developing countries where the percentage of the population in the school age group tends to be much higher than in the developed world. The Chinese response, therefore, has been to try to provide education relatively cheaply. Although very little in the way of hard financial data has been published, it is evident from many accounts that the official line is one of frugality. It is emphasized that the state's role in financing education is strictly limited, and the 'mentality of looking upwards and stretching out hands for help' has been roundly criticized. The state advocates that labour power should be substituted for capital expenditure whenever this can be done. There are warnings against 'ostentation'; schools need not be 'custom-built', and disused brickyards, old temples and caves have been mentioned as suitable sites which can easily be made habitable by the voluntary labour of the local community, whose members are also encouraged to make school furniture and equipment. The produce of the small farms and workshops run by the schools, which often serve as local agricultural experimentation stations, are also expected to make some contribution to the cost of education.

It might be argued that this emphasis on self-reliance (and the concomitant decentralized control of schools discussed below) is socially divisive and fundamentally unjust. Certainly the experience of many countries suggests that when 'welfare' matters are left to the local community appalling imbalances can occur; prosperous districts are able to provide excellent facilities while poor ones go to the wall. This is well illustrated by the dichotomy between decaying city centres and affluent suburbs which characterizes so much of urban America. But China's leaders appear to be well aware of the

---

[1] *KMJP*, 13 November 1971, *SCMP*, No. 5002, pp. 131-4.

dangers inherent in the situation, and state expenditure is directed to alleviate inequalities.

Thus, although localities which establish and maintain schools without calling on the state for manpower and money are held up as models for emulation, it is also pointed out that the state will help where necessary. Aid to relatively affluent districts has been discontinued or greatly reduced, but it has been re-allocated to the poorer and more remote rural areas. In fact, state expenditure on education in some areas at least (and possibly nationally) is rising considerably. In 1972, for example, Fukien province reported that it was 16% greater than in 1971. In addition to discriminating positively on a geographic basis, the state also discriminates in favour of primary education. In the words of a work forum in Chekiang province, 'manpower and financial and material resources allocated for the educational front by the state, should be first devoted to ensuring the universalization of five-year primary education'. Secondary education should be developed if local conditions permit, but the localities have been reminded of the need to make educational work 'more compatible with objective realities'. What this means in effect is that the state has no intention of stepping in when communities run into financial difficulties because of over-expanding secondary education. The absolute priority given to primary education is well attested by a recent report on P'ing-shun *hsien* (Shensi). Here 95% of children in the relevant age group were enrolled in primary school and 73% of them were actually completing the course. Despite this considerable achievement the *hsien* authorities were criticized for their 'blind optimism' in going on to popularize junior-middle schools at this stage. It would appear that the 'universalization of primary education' means exactly that.[1]

This is not to claim that the Chinese reforms are geared to produce absolute equality of educational opportunity in the near future. In a country with the regional diversity of China such a goal would be positively Utopian, and this is officially recognized. It is evident from many reports that urban areas continue to provide lengthier courses of primary and middle schooling than the rural districts. But the gap is far narrower than it has ever been, and the cities now pay proportionally more for the better amenities they enjoy.

[1] *JMJP*, 26 March 1972, *SCMP*, No. 7215, p. 149.

School organization

To implement the policy of rapid expansion the central leadership has given considerable attention in recent years to the need to involve as many people as possible in the educational process. Since the Cultural Revolution, China has not possessed a Ministry of Education, but it has been reported that the Central Committee has established a group to oversee the ideological aspects of education, while the State Council has one to oversee general administration. Education departments are active components of revolutionary committees at provincial, *hsien* and municipal level. Scattered reports indicate that their functions include organizing courses to raise the political and professional level of teachers, and assisting in the compilation of new teaching materials and in the standardization of experimental textbooks produced within their locality.

More important than the mere existence of functional departments, however, is the fact that virtually all officials are exhorted to play a part in educational work. Since 1970 especially, the leadership has mounted a campaign to overcome indifference towards educational matters on the part of those who emerged in positions of responsibility when the revolutionary committees were established, and senior Party cadres in particular have been urged to strengthen their leadership over educational reform. Those who regarded educational matters as of secondary importance have been rebuked, and they have been reminded that 'if education does not follow the pace of economic development, the speed of economic development will be slowed down'. A national conference on educational work was held in April 1971, and since then considerable attention has been given to the holding of frequent educational conferences from provincial level downwards, to the sending down of officials to 'squat at a point' to solve educational problems, to the despatch of propaganda teams to the grass-roots, and to the building up of Party units in the schools.

However, the emphasis on such official involvement does not constitute a return to the system prevailing before 1966 when even the rural *min-pan* schools were firmly controlled by *hsien* education bureaus. It is difficult to assess just how far decentralization goes in practice, but in theory at least the role of such officials is to assist the masses at the basic levels to establish and run schools, and not to control them.

Although the pattern is a varied one (indeed rigid adherence to a national standard is criticized as a 'Liuist' deviation) certain generalizations may be made about the ways in which schools are organized. In the rural areas the most common system is for production brigades to run their own primary schools, although sometimes this may be done by production teams. Middle schools are usually run by the communes. Poor and lower-middle peasants are represented on the management committees of these schools which have among their functions the hiring and firing of teachers (no longer a *hsien* prerogative), the selection of students and the right to recommend suitable students for further education, the determining of course content to meet local conditions and needs, and the provision of appropriate teaching materials. Representatives may also participate in teaching, as can other members of the community. In the initial period of reform it was also emphasized that they should supervise the ideological transformation of the teachers.

In the urban areas it was often reported in 1969 that factories should run middle schools. However, recent visitors have found that this is rarely the case, and schools at all levels are most commonly run by neighbourhood organizations. Children are supposed to attend the school managed by their own street committee so as to improve the contact between school and parents, and to integrate school training and family education.

The curriculum

One of the most significant changes to have taken place in Chinese education is the shortening of school courses. It is difficult to identify a 'norm' in a system which encourages flexibility and diversity, but the most common arrangement appears to be for primary education to be completed in five years, while junior and senior-middle school each require two years. Wherever conditions permit, the junior-middle school classes are to be attached to primary schools. Such a shortening allows all children to finish a complete basic education before they have reached an age at which they can contribute their full-grown labour power at the production front. Although this reform now means that a senior-middle school graduate may have received three years less education than he would have done before 1966, it is claimed that this does not imply a lowering of standards, but merely the elimination from the syllabus of material deemed to be 'irrelevant'. This means that course content is pruned of 'unnecessary' theory, and that all subjects are taught with the needs of production in mind at all times; as far as possible the system encourages the inculcation of knowledge of immediate applicability. In general, the primary school syllabus now consists of courses in politics and language, arithmetic, revolutionary literature and art, military training and physical education, and productive labour. Middle schools provide education in Mao Tsetung Thought (which includes modern Chinese history, contemporary Chinese history, and the history of the struggle between the 'two lines' in the Party); basic knowledge of agriculture and/or industry (including such relevant subjects as mathematics, physics, chemistry, and economic geography); revolutionary literature and art (including language); military training and physical education; and productive labour.[1]

These alterations have resulted in the rewriting of much of the teaching material previously used in schools. Although visitors to China have reported that some of this material emanates from provincial and *hsien* level, and that more centralization is now taking place, there would appear to be far greater diversity than before. A particularly interesting development has been the official encouragement given to the grass-roots to produce teaching material relevant to local needs. Although it might be argued that this is unnecessary as far as subjects like literature and mathematics are concerned, it is clearly a sensible policy for the more practically oriented courses. Obviously a course of 'basic knowledge of agriculture' suitable for a wheat-producing commune in Shensi will be of little value to a tea-producing one in Fukien, hence the emphasis on producing material which deals with specific matters affecting the area in which it is used.

The role of political education has been strengthened. The insistence that education must produce specific attitudinal changes

[1] See, for example, the 'Draft Programme for Primary and Middle Schools in the Chinese Countryside', *JMJP*, 12 May 1969, New China News Agency (NCNA), English, 13 May 1969, *SCMP*, No. 4415, pp. 9–15.

means that political material is now used in virtually all courses. Sometimes this would seem to operate to the detriment of academic standards as, for example, in the case of those schools which claim to have produced new foreign language courses based almost entirely on the writings of Chairman Mao. It is difficult to believe that such courses are able to implement the principle of 'teaching in a living manner'. But other examples indicate that, from the Chinese point of view, political points can be made in a way which does not conflict with the 'objective' needs of a given subject. For example, one mathematics class was set a problem based on the story of a worker in the 'old society'. When this man was young his family were poor and starved. Consequently they were forced to borrow grain from a 'wolfish landlord' who charged interest at a usurious rate. Pupils were provided with the relevant figures and asked to calculate the amount of grain which the family had to repay. Such an example not only taught them to work out compound interest, but also gave them the official line on the behaviour of landlords. In similar manner a lesson in modern Chinese history might consist of inviting poor peasants into the classroom to talk of their sufferings before 1949, and to contrast that life with the prosperity they enjoyed in the People's Republic. On such occasions peasants display the old rags they used to wear and the meagre goods which were all they possessed; sometimes students are given meals of the kind the peasants ate in famine years.[1]

By the use of such techniques those who have no personal experience of life before 'liberation' are given an excellent appreciation of the worst features of the 'old society'. But political education is not designed merely to show how bad things were, it is intended to ensure that such conditions can never arise again. Essentially, the educational process is seen as a means of producing attitudinal change as much as, if not more than, inculcating specific skills and techniques. To be true 'revolutionary successors' students must be socialized with the acceptance of a code of behaviour which takes 'struggle' as the norm, whether it be directed against 'incorrect' ideas, hostile social forces, or Nature itself. It is stressed that the young have within themselves the creative power to solve the manifold problems of Chinese society, if only they will strive

[1] *Peking Review*, No. 10, 1969, p. 17.

for the communal good instead of for short-term and selfish ambition. They must overcome the traditional temptation to see study as the path to officialdom, and must be prepared to engage in manual labour. They must be taught not only to tolerate the idea of spending their lives in the villages, but also to desire it actively.

Political education, therefore, embraces everything that contributes to an understanding of the problems of China (admittedly as defined by the present Party line) and is intended to arouse a willingness to strive to alleviate them (again, by moving in a direction specified by the present Party line). To a considerable degree these problems are seen in economic terms and so the relationship of education to production is stressed heavily. Apart from emphasizing that students of all ages should engage in labour on principle for the good of their revolutionary souls, courses involve, wherever possible, considerable practical work.[1] Ideally this involves a two-way process. Schools are expected to run their small farms and factories, while local communes and factories are expected to assist in organizing the curriculum and providing specialized training in production matters. Initially, this emphasis on productive labour appears to have been taken too far in some areas, but since the autumn of 1971 a number of articles have stressed the need to strike a proper balance and see to it that the teaching of basic knowledge is not neglected.[2]

The teachers

Few would quarrel with Mao's much-quoted statement that the 'question of educational reform is mainly a question of teachers'. The changes discussed above can only hope to be successful if there are sufficient teachers to staff the greatly expanded school system, and if they are willing to work wholeheartedly to put such changes

[1] In assessing the role of practical education in China it is essential to appreciate the 'cultural' context. A Western child is in daily contact with a great variety of modern, mechanized and electrical appliances; he learns about their operation and develops a feeling for possibilities of application, more or less unconsciously. A Chinese child, particularly if he lives in the countryside, has few opportunities of this kind. When this ignorance is compounded by an educational system which has always stressed the importance of 'book knowledge' and rote-learning, the difficulties it presents to a society wishing to modernize are readily apparent. Hence the Chinese preoccupation with inculcating practical skills and encouraging the young to engage in 'scientific experiment' is by no means an 'unbalanced' approach.

[2] See, for example, Nanking Radio, 15 April 1972, BBC, *Summary of World Broadcasts, Part III, Far East (SWB)*, FE/3970.

into effect. It was the failure to tackle these problems which undoubtedly contributed to the demise of the 'half-work half-study' schools set up in and after 1958. In the Cultural Revolution teachers at all levels were attacked for their unwillingness or inability to implement 'Maoist' policies, and in the cities at least many pedagogues were subjected to unprecedented unpleasantness, often at the hands of their own students.

Yet whatever their shortcomings before 1966, most of the teachers appear to be back at their jobs. It is simply impossible for the leadership to dispense with the services of such skilled manpower, and in recent years it has bent over backwards to give encouragement to those teachers whose experiences made them feel that 'there is no future in teaching' and 'it is a disaster to be a teacher'. But this is not to say that teachers have regained their old status. On the contrary, many of their perquisites have disappeared. They are no longer government officials and white collar workers. Instead they are treated as members of the units in which they function and are paid accordingly. Primary school teachers, for example, are members of production brigades and are paid in work points. While they may still be rather better off than the peasants, scattered evidence from some areas suggests that the difference in living standards is not as wide as it was before 1966.

Furthermore, they have been required to accept 'remoulding'. Many of them have undergone criticism and manual labour in the course of the last six years and this will continue, though in less extreme form. Political education for teachers means that they must join their students in learning from the masses. They must engage in productive labour and receive ideological instruction from their political betters. They are also expected to accept criticism and suggestions from their students, but this should not be taken to imply that pupils are permitted to act in the way they did in the Cultural Revolution. A major problem in Chinese schools has been the survival of the traditional attitude that the teacher was the fount of all wisdom, whose smallest utterances were to be parroted uncritically, and the insistence that students speak up is in large measure designed to do nothing more radical than produce the element of discussion one would find in Western schools. Indeed, it is now emphasized that criticisms should be 'positive' and helpful, and made in a polite manner. Thus a recent article on Changchun No. 29 Middle School noted with approval how the leadership there 'came to understand that discipline is the guarantee for the implementation of line, [and that] proletarian courtesy and discipline are a direct reflection of socialist morality and mental outlook'. This school in fact has 'formulated regulations and specific requirements concerning courtesy and discipline', whereby 'good conduct' is commended and those who violate discipline are criticized.[1]

The 'professionals' of pre-Cultural Revolution vintage have suffered a further set-back in that they are no longer the sole purveyors of knowledge, for there has been a massive increase in the number of teaching personnel in the past few years. As schools were opened tens of thousands of new teachers were called into being, and some areas have claimed that as many as one-third of the teaching staff in primary and middle school are recent recruits.[2] Many of these were people of obviously low cultural level, poor and lower-middle peasants and workers selected by their production brigades and factories for service in local schools. Another source of supply was demobilized army men and serving soldiers 'transferred to civilian posts'. More important in terms of quality and possibly in sheer number were the 'educated youths'. These were young people who had received their education in the cities before 1966, millions of whom were sent to 'put down roots' in the villages. During the Cultural Revolution, many of them pulled up their roots to return to the towns, but in 1968 strict measures were imposed to send them back, together with countless others whose education was deemed to have been summarily 'completed' when the Cultural Revolution closed the schools. Many of these youths had completed at least junior-middle school, and a number had spent at least some time in tertiary-level institutions. Yet even these people lacked training in teaching methods, and their own educational experiences were not necessarily relevant to the sort of course being taught from 1969 onwards.[3]

---

[1] Changchun Radio, 4 May 1972, *SWB*, FE/3985.

[2] *KMJP*, 31 October 1971, *SCMP*, No. 5013, p. 248; *Hung ch'i* (*Red Flag*) (Peking), No. 6, 1971, *Selections from China Mainland Magazines* (*SCMM*) (Hong Kong: U.S. Consulate General), No. 707, p. 4.

[3] For details of educated youth in the countryside see John Gardner, 'Educated Youth', pp. 268–76.

The leadership has, therefore, made determined efforts to provide some training for most teachers, though no one could pretend that the training given would be regarded as adequate by the standards of 'developed' countries. Under the general direction of the Party and revolutionary committees, provincial-level normal colleges and *hsien* and municipal normal schools have embarked on a series of 'crash' training programmes in the past few years. Where possible, unqualified or under-qualified teachers leave their schools and undergo a full-time course lasting anything between three months and a year. Training college instructors go to specific localities and put on short intensive courses during the busy farming seasons when the schools are on holiday. Some visit classrooms and give 'on the spot' instruction. A number of colleges have set up 'tutoring stations', detaching a few instructors to establish small branch colleges which each serve a group of communes or a city district. But it is admitted that the lack of trained staff in normal schools is a major hurdle, and that many unqualified teachers cannot be given much in the way of personal instruction. Therefore, much use is made of correspondence courses.

Experienced 'professional' teachers also have a part to play. The senior staff of a middle school, for example, are sometimes asked to supervise the teachers in the primary schools of their locality. Teachers at the same level are expected to use the system of 'teaching and learning from one another' whereby colleagues teaching the same subject at different schools meet regularly and pool their knowledge.

In quantitative terms the results claimed are impressive. Between July 1969 and July 1971 Kwangtung Normal College put on 31 courses to train middle school teachers. These were run at *hsien* and municipal level, and 8,000 teachers attended. In addition, mobile teams visited 91 communes and taught 10,000 teachers 'on active duty'. The normal school of Ch'ao-an *hsien* claims to have trained more than 2,000 teachers in the same period.[1]

Qualitatively, of course, such hastily trained teachers cannot be expected to match the standards of the old 'professionals', but two

[1] For reports on teacher training programmes, see: *JMJP*, 1 June 1971, *CB*, No. 945, pp. 1–10; *KMJP*, 13 October 1971, *SCMP*, No. 5005, pp. 74–7; *JMJP*, 20 November 1971, *SCMP*, No. 5026, pp. 190–4, 198–200.

points are worth stressing. First, the Chinese do not claim that such training as has been given in recent years is all that is to be required in the future. There is no reason to suppose that it is more than a short-term programme to supplement more orthodox schemes and not to replace them. Second, scattered pieces of evidence suggest that the new teachers, especially those who were peasants and workers, are generally being used in courses related to production and politics, for which they may well be better equipped than old teachers, and most of them are working at the primary level. While their relatively high level of 'political consciousness' enables them to play a supervisory role vis-à-vis their more 'bourgeois' colleagues, it is the latter who teach the more academic courses like mathematics and language, particularly in the middle schools.

Schools also utilize the services of part-time staff on an extensive basis. Sometimes, middle-school students will do some teaching in primary schools or will give instruction to children who, for whatever reason, are unable to be given a school place. Work units may send personnel to schools for a few hours' teaching a week, and some operate exchange schemes whereby regular teachers and workers change places for a few months – a system supposed to raise the workers' love of learning and the teachers' love of labour. Part-timers are most commonly brought in to teach politics and vocational subjects.

Thus China's teachers are far from being a homogeneous occupational group. The state's policy in recent years has been to enlist the services of as many people as possible in order to get the educational revolution off the ground. No doubt many teachers will fail to rise to the occasion; some will continue to despise manual labour and involvement in production and some will be hopelessly incompetent. Some students will be bored by the meanderings of aged and inarticulate peasants. But this will not necessarily be the normal pattern. China may well have found a method of providing a reasonable level of educational attainment for virtually all children in the relevant age group. If she does, she will have made more progress than most, if not all, those countries we term 'developing'.

The case of Nan-an hsien

The experience of many educational 'models' has been publicized in recent years. Some, like the Peking No. 31 Middle School, have a tradition of academic achievement going back to 1949 and before.[1] Others, like that of the Yü-ch'ang production brigade, of Chao-yuan *hsien*, Heilungkiang, were established as part of the 'educational revolution' of 1958.[2] Most interesting, however, are examples of institutions and areas which have changed dramatically as a direct result of the Cultural Revolution. In this context it is worth examining in some detail the effects of these changes on one Chinese county, Nan-an in Fukien, bearing in mind that this is offered as an example of the new system at its best.[3]

Before the Cultural Revolution, this county possessed 310 primary schools, 17 junior-middle schools and 7 senior-middle schools. Forty of its 247 production brigades did not have a single primary school, and 7 of the 24 communes lacked middle schools. By 1971, however, the situation had changed radically. There were then 621 primary schools, 259 junior-middle and 59 senior-middle schools. In addition to these, spare-time education had been developed extensively through the establishment of 1,350 evening primary schools, 258 evening middle schools, and the provision of special classes for boys and girls engaged in herding and tea-picking respectively. The county had also established 113 intermediate technical schools to provide training in accountancy, medical and health service work, electrical engineering, farm mechanics, etc. Political evening schools for adults, and nursery education were also popularised. Nan-an, with a total population of 850,000, could claim 18,000 full-time students and 80,000 part-time, so that 95% of its school-age children were receiving some kind of education.

All new schools were financed locally without outside help, many of them running their own farms and conducting agricultural experiments. The teachers needed were recruited from among poor and lower-middle peasants, demobilized PLA men, and 'educated youth who have laboured for over two years in the countryside and behaved themselves well'.

[1] See, for example, *KMJP*, 29 July 1970, *SCMP*, No. 4176, pp. 88–92.
[2] *Hung ch'i*, No. 6, 1971, *SCMM*, No. 707, pp. 59–66.   [3] *Ibid.*, pp. 40–9.

It is claimed that this educational revolution has had widespread effects in many spheres. Apart from raising the political conscious-ness of the masses and striking a telling blow at the bourgeoisie, it has eradicated 'feudal' customs, especially those connected with marriage, and reduced illiteracy. Most importantly, perhaps, it has trained a group of 'backbone elements' to work as rural accountants and technical innovators in the communes. Schools have experi-mented with different seed strains, and have produced the new '920' insecticide, bacterial fertilizer and carbohydrate fodder. The 30% rise in grain output claimed for 1970 is partly attributed to the educational revolution.

THE TERTIARY SECTOR

Advanced scientific research, organized in the Academy of Sciences, appears to be the sole area in which sweeping changes have not taken place. It is true that scientific journals ceased publication during the Cultural Revolution, and the Academy did receive some criticism, but there have been no accounts of radical reforms therein. In view of the general lack of attention paid to this area, and also the reports of notable scientific advances in the period under dis-cussion, it seems that China's top scientists have been permitted to get on with their work relatively free from interference. In part this no doubt reflects the extraordinary difficulty, faced by all modern societies, in assessing the worth of scientific research at the highest levels, especially when it may have a bearing on national defence. But it may also indicate that such work had been brought into line with the 'Maoist' developmental strategy before the Cultural Revolution began, most notably in the campaign for 'the three great revolutionary movements' of class struggle, struggle for production, and scientific experiment.[1]

However, in the other institutions of the tertiary sector, the Cultural Revolution ushered in a lengthy period of turmoil and change. Although the 'Workers and PLA Mao Tsetung Thought Propaganda Teams' entered the universities in August 1968, it was

[1] See M. R. Meisner, 'From Theory to Practice, Science and Revolution, the "Three Great Revolutionary Movements" in China 1965–1966', S. K. Chin and F. H. H. King (eds.), *Selected Seminar Papers on Contemporary China* (Hong Kong, 1971), p. 85.

not until summer 1970 that Tsinghua and Peking took in their first full batch of first-year students and became the national models for university reform. Between 1968 and 1970 the old students were summarily graduated and sent to the countryside, experimental classes were organized to develop a new curriculum and new teaching materials, the teaching staff was 'remoulded' and a new enrolment system set up. At the same time the universities conducted many short-term training classes in factories and communes, gathering materials for their own curricular reform and assisting in the many political, economic, technological and educational reforms taking place elsewhere. By the summer of 1972, almost all universities had reopened, though some were still in the stage of conducting their own experimental classes. Few of them, however, have as yet taken in their full quota of students, and it is not yet possible to predict what the results of a full intake will be on the reforms discussed below.

Organization

We have found very little information on the organization of tertiary education *per se*. The Ministry of Higher Education has disappeared and lines of command between the centre, the provinces and municipalities themselves are by no means clear. The system is obviously more decentralized than before, and there has been some expansion at this level too. Many new colleges have been established, though some of them are obviously tertiary-level institutions in name only, as for example, the various factory-run 'colleges' which are often doing little more than provide spare-time education for workers. Initially, such workers' colleges, and particularly the one run by the Shanghai No. 1 Machine Tools Factory which was praised by Mao himself, were given considerable publicity as an alternative to the regular institutions. Their limitations quickly became apparent, however, and the propaganda for them has now been toned down considerably.

The established universities remain the centre of the tertiary system and all have undergone reform. The original teaching staff and cadres have generally retained their jobs and salaries, but many of them have been forced to remould themselves through long periods of manual labour and contact with the masses. Where possible, they were assigned to factories and institutions having something to do with their own speciality, so that their sojourn with the masses would serve also as a professional refresher course. At this level it would appear that there has been no extensive recruitment of new staff, although peasants and workers do 'mount the rostrum' on a part-time basis to teach both politics and industrial and agricultural techniques.

The actual management of universities, however, is no longer left to professional educators alone. During the Cultural Revolution, the original leadership for university reform was provided by the 'Mao Tsetung Thought Propaganda Teams', which went on to the campuses in 1968 to restore order and to establish revolutionary committees to administer these institutions. Members of the committees were selected from among students, revolutionary staff, cadres and from the propaganda teams themselves. At first the revolutionary committees appear to have been dominated by the teams, and in the sense that many team members were skilled labourers and technicians, 'proletarian control' of higher education appears to have been literally true for a brief spell when much experimentation took place. Gradually, however, the teams' influence was reduced and other groups became more important. In particular one should note the reconstruction of university Party committees which was completed in most areas by the summer of 1970, and the publication of official injunctions at that time that 'working class leadership in everything does not mean monopolizing everything', a reference to the need to let academic specialists have a greater say in the running of their institutions. This is not to suggest that the role of the workers is now negligible; many of them are still in evidence in important positions as recent visitors have testified, and some have become members of university Party committees. But it would certainly appear that a more balanced pattern of university administration is now emerging.

The students

Since the universities re-opened (which in the case of some departments was not until 1971 or 1972) it has been official policy to admit students from those groups which previously had little chance of progressing so far or, if they actually gained admission, were likely to do badly because of the 'bourgeois' academic standards applied. The traditional entrance examinations have been abolished, and applicants are selected on the basis of various other criteria. It is stressed that students should in the main be selected from the ranks of poor and lower-middle peasants, workers, the PLA, and basic-level cadres. In addition to the approved class and/or occupational background, students require a history of activism, manifested in studying and propagating Mao Tsetung Thought, participating in the three great revolutionary movements, and integrating with the workers and peasants. In general this means that they will already have worked for their living. It is suggested that the ideal age for entry is at about 20, after 2 or 3 years of practical experience in agriculture or industrial production. Although it is expected that most students will have completed at least junior-middle school, 'mature' students are encouraged provided that they have lengthy practical experience to substitute for formal schooling.[1] Initially, it appears that there was a tendency to play down the importance of students having an adequate level of education before admission, but reports published in 1972 indicate that this is now being corrected.[2]

At present policies are being applied to ensure that university education is more readily available to areas and groups which were previously somewhat deprived. Thus universities are enjoined to pay particular attention to the more remote and mountainous areas, and to the national minorities. More places are to be given to girls, especially at 'medical, normal, and literature and art colleges', and some localities have been criticized for their 'feudal' view that it was not worth sending girls to university because 'a daughter who has been given away in marriage is like spilt water, and the girls will belong to other people when they are trained'. Of the first batch of students admitted to Tsinghua University 20% were girls, and at Peking it was 30%.[3] The new system undoubtedly discriminates

---

[1] The break with traditional admissions procedures appears to have raised expectations which cannot always be fulfilled. *Shensi Daily* found it necessary to inform its readers that it is still impossible to satisfy the desires of all workers, peasants and soldiers who wish to go to university, and that it is quite normal for the applications of some comrades not to be approved. Sian Radio, 9 April 1972, *SWB*, FE/3963.

[2] See, for example, Nanning Radio, 5 September 1972, *SWB*, FE/4088.

[3] Caroline Benn, *Times Educational Supplement*, 19 November 1971.

against students of 'bad' family background, but it is still permissible to admit a few of them provided they have 'consistently drawn a line between themselves and their families'.

The selection process itself is described as one of 'voluntary application, recommendation by the masses, approval by the leadership, and re-examination by the universities concerned'.[1] In practice there appears to be a direct link between universities and production units, with the latter vetting the applications of all those members who wish to enter higher education. Theoretically at least the process follows the 'mass line' with discussion flowing up and down for a lengthy period before final agreement is reached. As always when the mass line is involved it is difficult to know just how influential grassroots opinion is. It seems likely, however, that while the support of one's unit may not guarantee admission to university, it is now probably impossible to get in without it. Once at university, students' living expenses are paid by the state and, in the case of worker-students with five years experience, wages will continue to be paid.

On completing the course students are expected to return to their original (and usually rural) units except for those who have posts assigned to them by 'the unified state plan'. We have found no information as to how much choice a graduate may be permitted as to the area or job to which he shall go, but in most instances there would appear to be little.

The curriculum

As at lower levels, courses have been shortened. Whereas previously university courses lasted four years, and sometimes much longer, it is now generally the case that technical and medical courses will last for three years, and arts courses for two. In technical courses the number of specializations has been reduced, and new ones have been developed which are geared to specific industrial needs at the present time. Courses aim to integrate classroom teaching, practical work and scientific research, and students and teachers must participate in all three. Universities run their own factories and farms, and maintain close relationships with particular work units, a system which is meant to benefit both, in that students can acquire valuable practical experience, while the factories and farms enjoy immediately

---

[1] *KMJP*, 16 March 1972, *SCMP*, No. 5102, p. 42.

281

the fruits of university research.[1] The level of training students receive appears to vary widely from university to university, being determined by such factors as the status of the institution, the professional level of its teaching staff, the technological level of the work units with which it cooperates, and, of course, the subject being studied.

Theoretical study was somewhat neglected when the first experimental classes were opened after the Cultural Revolution, but recently it has received rather more emphasis. Since spring 1972, it has been reported that in many universities students and teachers 'have gradually made a distinction between strengthening basic theoretical teaching and the divorce of theory from practice; between diligent study and scientific experiments for the revolution and the bourgeois drive for personal fame and gain; and between strict standards for students, including giving necessary examinations, and over-stress on good marks'.[2]

But the most important criterion by which courses are judged remains their ability to make an immediate contribution to the practical needs of China's developing economy. Where foreign knowledge can contribute to solving China's problems, its use is not to be shunned, and teachers who were afraid to draw on its results have been urged to do so. What is still condemned is the blind desire to keep up with 'world standards' when this involves an uncritical imitation of methods which are relevant only to the developed countries.

An excellent example of the way in which science courses are now geared to the practical is provided by the case of the Department of Biology at Amoy University.[3] Before the Cultural Revolution, this department allegedly wasted a great deal of money in its research programme. A 'station for scientific research on ducks' operated for more than ten years, and each year cost the state between 10,000 and 20,000 *yuan*, and consumed more than 20,000 catties of grain. All of this to keep 300 ducks. The purpose of the research is unstated but it would appear to have been of little importance. However, after the university's Mao Tsetung Thought Propaganda

[1] China's universities are now more involved with research than they were in the past, especially in terms of 'research and development'.
[2] NCNA, 11 April 1972, *SWB*, FE/3963.
[3] *KMJP*, 12 October 1971, *CB*, No. 945, pp. 31-4.

Team had led the teachers and students to remould their thinking, the latter went to the countryside to carry out scientific experiments together with the peasants. It is claimed that 'by making do with simple and crude things, repairing old equipment and utilizing waste materials and starting things with indigenous methods, they expended only the sum of six *yuan* for a set of indigenous equipment to conduct scientific experiments and produced "920" bacilli for destroying rice-stalk borers, and *ch'un-lei* antibiotic'.

The department also improved the content of its teaching of pedology. Previously the textbook used, which 'was 300 pages thick', had taught only how to recognize soils but not how to transform them. After teachers had spent time at an army farm in Tsinan famed for its 'advanced experience', however, the textbook was completely revised so that 'what is learned is put into application, thus enabling the students to grasp faster the methods for determining the salinity, acidity and fertility of the soils and extract *hu-min* acid from the soils for use as fertilizer'.

The emphasis on serving local needs as speedily, cheaply, and efficiently as possible has had interesting effects on the nature of medical education. Previously this generally involved at least six years of training, usually in urban centres. This has now been reduced to three years, and there has been considerable decentralization as medical schools have opened clinics and teaching posts in the countryside. Right from the start the student is brought into contact with patients, and learns to diagnose and treat the most common diseases, while learning the theoretical background in the process. Especially noteworthy is the insistence that traditional Chinese medicine be integrated with modern Western medicine. Acupuncture has been widely publicized for its use in anaesthetics, but much attention has also been given to the systematic use of indigenous drugs. Medical schools have also concentrated on running short-term courses to train 'barefoot doctors' as part of the very important campaign to improve rural public health.[1]

It should be emphasized that the training given to 'barefoot doctors' and other medical workers is not envisaged as being a

[1] For a description of the reform of medical education at Chungshan University in Canton, see S. G. McDowell, 'Educational Reform in China as a Readjusting Country', *Asian Survey*, XI. 3 (1971), 256–70.

'once and for all' matter. The idea, rather, is that medical education should be an ongoing process involving alternate spells of practical and academic experience. Thus a 'barefoot doctor' will return to the countryside, apply his new knowledge and attempt to impart as much of it as he can to members of the local community. After a few years he will return to university for further long-term or short-term training, and this process may be repeated several times during his working life. For in medical education, as elsewhere, the idea is not just to popularize relatively basic skills as quickly as possible but to build on them at a subsequent stage in the recipients' careers. If this practice continues to be applied it should do much to refute charges of the 'low level' of higher education in China.

Courses in the humanities are also organized on practical lines, following the injunction that students should take 'the whole of society as their workshop'. Thus colleges of economics have adapted their programme so as to produce people capable of managing the financial administration of a commune or production brigade. As part of their studies students are sent to communes to undertake surveys while participating in mass movements. Similarly, part of the Chinese literature course at Peking University consists of 'practice', whereby students participate in mass campaigns and use their literary skills by composing wall posters, and writing and performing political plays. The Chinese have not by any means, however, jettisoned entirely the culture of the pre-Cultural Revolution period. Recent publications of scholarly works include, for instance, some which were prepared before the Cultural Revolution began, and some older works have been reissued. Indeed the break with the recent past, as far as the humanities are concerned, appears to have been less drastic than the first onslaught of the Cultural Revolution would have led one to believe.

Similarly, the nature of ideological education has been somewhat modified in the last year or so. In the early phases of reform an excessive emphasis was placed on Mao Tsetung Thought and many teachers seemed to live by the principle 'when in doubt, quote from Mao'. This has now been toned down considerably. Politics still occupies a vitally important place in all curricula nevertheless, its functions being, first, to provide the poorly prepared student with the confidence and determination to persist in his studies, and, second, to ensure that he remains aware of the purpose of his education. The combination of ideological and practical education, with the constantly reiterated question 'Whom do you serve?' suggests that China's new graduates may well be better suited to life in the villages than were those of pre-Cultural Revolution vintage.

CONCLUSION

Chinese education is still, to some degree, in a state of flux. Many of the changes introduced immediately after the Cultural Revolution are being modified and, some would argue, watered down. Conversely, there are no doubt new experiments in progress to which no publicity has been given as yet. Perhaps the greatest difficulty one faces in evaluating any aspect of education is that of 'time lag'. It will obviously be many years before one can assess the effects of this attempt to break away from the 'traditional' system of training a small elite to a very high level while neglecting to provide 'basic' education for all. Hence our concluding remarks must of necessity be tentative.

Clearly, it is easy to find grounds for pessimism, and the official press itself refers not infrequently to errors and shortcomings. In some cases, especially where the role of workers and peasants has been particularly strong in educational institutions, the educational revolution may have meant little more than turning students into general labourers whose 'cultural level' must consequently be no higher than that of the masses themselves. Elsewhere, particularly in relatively wealthy rural areas and cities, for example in Kiangsu, old attitudes die hard, and the intellectuals have managed to stress formal academic study in contravention of official policy, though presumably not to the degree that obtained up to 1966. Some might argue that we shall soon witness a repeat of the situation that arose in the early 1960s when the radical educational measures introduced in 1958 were speedily dismembered, and one could point to recent statements on the need to pay more attention to academic matters as the first sign of this.

We believe, however, that there is every likelihood both that the present system will endure and that it will be reasonably successful. The 1958 reforms failed because they were implemented alongside a well-established set of educational institutions. Consequently, the new schools were judged by the old criteria and were found to be inferior. The lean years following the Leap provided an excellent excuse for their detractors to close them down. The present situation, however, is one in which the educational reforms constitute not an alternative or auxiliary system but the new orthodoxy, universally applied. Peking University no doubt still enjoys more prestige than an agricultural college in the Mongolian grasslands, but the gaps between the two are far less than they were. Moreover, the economy now flourishes, and thus there is less reason to justify a return to conservatism. Most important of all, however, is the fact that education is now subjected to an unprecedented degree of political control. From the central leadership downwards, educational reform has been the subject which has probably received more attention than any other in the past few years; the masses also have increased their influence at all levels in this area, and it is difficult to see them rejecting a system of mass education for their children in favour of an elitist one in which it is virtually guaranteed that they will do badly.

In the short term then we believe that the new system will continue without substantial modification. In the long term, we suggest that it will have a tremendous impact on Chinese society and its development. It is worth noting here that the 'conventional wisdom' concerning education, with its stress on the exclusive importance of an intellectual elite, has been subject to much well-informed criticism in the West in recent years, as applied both to developed and developing countries. Apart from calling into question many of the alleged social 'benefits' of conventional educational systems, many academics, economists, and industrialists now doubt the effectiveness of well-established educational forms in promoting economic growth.

In the most superficial form these doubts are reflected in the increasingly accepted idea that arts graduates are not necessarily equipped to occupy responsible positions in the post-industrial state, and that people with a scientific background are more suitable. But while there is now a general acceptance of the idea that economic development and industrial efficiency depend as much, and possibly more, on technological innovation as on capital accumulation, it is now being suggested that the role of university-educated scientists in this process may well have been exaggerated.

In this context a recent study of technological innovation in British industry is of particular interest. The authors point out that the belief that 'pure' or 'curiosity-oriented' scientific research generates a constant flow of ideas which are readily put to use in the economy cannot be accepted without qualification; 'the transition from "pure" knowledge to wealth is less simple and direct than is commonly supposed'. Similarly, the role of the gifted and highly trained individual, the 'boffin' beloved of popular mythology, is not necessarily of importance, for they note that 'innovation almost by definition is a corporate and collaborative effort' and that even when a contribution is primarily technical the person making it 'does not always hold high formal qualifications in science and technology'. Of special significance is the authors' statement that they 'have been struck by the frequent and real importance of people with the Higher National Certificate type of qualification'.[1]

Ironically the holders of this certificate are not even classed officially as 'qualified manpower' in Britain, but their training bears close resemblances to that now given to students at Chinese universities. The courses they undergo combine theory and practice, formal study being given in technical institutions and not universities. While the Higher National Certificate is not regarded as being the equivalent of a degree, its worth is well recognized by industry. Furthermore, it should be noted that future expansion of higher education in Britain is expected to take place increasingly within the framework of technical colleges and polytechnics.

If, then, this sort of education is seen to be relevant to the needs of an advanced economy, it is evidently even more so to one which still faces most of the problems of underdevelopment. We believe that the Chinese reforms constitute a rational attempt to cope with certain crucial issues which are either ignored or badly managed in most of the poorer countries and, some might suggest, in many of the rich ones too. First, there is the insistence that the educational system impart knowledge of practical value to those who receive it. We accept fully the criticism that the shortening of all courses and

[1] John Langrish and others, *Wealth from Knowledge* (London: Macmillan, 1972), *passim*.

the reduction of time spent in the classroom means that students at all levels will amass far less information than was the case before 1966. But we consider the absorption of facts of marginal relevance to be less important than the creation of positive attitudes towards specific issues. The purpose of education is to teach people to think, and the problem-oriented approach has much to commend it. The history of economic aid to developing countries over the past two decades is studded with dismal examples of highly trained 'experts' providing the most up-to-date scientific information with scant regard to its practical value in a particular context. For example, experts proved conclusively that yields of a certain crop could be increased dramatically if farmers scrupulously weeded the fields in the weeks following germination, and urged that this be done. No doubt this was excellent advice in conditions of labour surplus and land scarcity, but this particular case was one where land was plentiful and labour was short. The peasants very sensibly chose to increase the acreage and ignore the weeds, and consequently harvested a far larger crop than they would have done if they had behaved 'correctly'. This incident took place in Tanzania,[1] but it is typical of the situation which arises when specialists are not required to familiarize themselves with local conditions. The Chinese system of forcing the educated to 'learn from the masses' must ensure that such nonsense is not perpetrated to the same degree.

Secondly, there is the question of the dissemination of knowledge, a major problem in all societies, but particularly in poor ones. Peasants are often conservative because of 'the deadweight of tradition' and refuse, therefore, to support change. But in many instances their conservatism is perfectly rational, for they live at subsistence level and are naturally reluctant to depart from practices which they know will at least keep them alive, in favour of unknown techniques which they must take on trust. There is a world of difference between a system whereby peasants are asked to follow new methods which have proved successful in some distant research station, and one where scientific experiment is conducted by staff and students in their locality, and under their own eyes. When commmune members see their local agricultural college obtaining spectacular

[1] Leonard Joy, 'Strategy for Agricultural Development', Seers and Joy, *Development*, p. 178.

results by using new seed strains or fertilizers under the same climatic and soil conditions as their own, they too will innovate.

Besides, the present school system tries to ensure that the peasant masses throughout China will at least be able to read and write, and will have some basic training in the use of mechanized equipment and modern farming methods. The priority accorded to primary education, in particular, should provide a foundation for the popularization and acceptance of new and more sophisticated techniques in the future. At the same time political education should give the peasants an idea of the direction in which society is moving. In particular, they will be able to form expectations as to what could happen to their own local community over a certain period of time.

Finally, the social consequences of education merit attention. A fundamental problem affecting all societies is that of the 'marginals'. In developed countries the increasing sophistication of the post-industrial state has created a large pool of people who are fundamentally unemployable in that they are only equipped to carry out functions which can be handled more efficiently and cheaply by machines. This is now also true of many of the developing countries where the application of capital-intensive techniques has forced untold millions to eke out a miserable existence in shanty towns, with little hope of employment except petty crime. But in these societies the problem is also found at the top, in that they tend to produce a large number of people who have been educated to a high level, but in subjects for which there is little need. The cynical remark that the most successful growth industry in India has been higher education contains a great deal of truth, and the unemployed and underemployed university graduates found in such countries represent appalling waste in social as well as economic terms.

The Chinese response to this is to give a basic and useful education to everyone. A smaller number will then receive more specialized training which focuses on developing an independent capacity for solving problems. It envisages, moreoever, a continuous process of adult education which will train people for new situations and jobs, as the economy requires and allows. This system should contribute to the rapid modernization of society and might also be valued in terms of human dignity.

6

A REVOLUTION TO TOUCH MEN'S SOULS: THE FAMILY, INTERPERSONAL RELATIONS AND DAILY LIFE

Andrew J. Watson

INTRODUCTION

It is part of my thesis that the culture of the individual is dependent upon the culture of the group or class, and that the culture of the group or class is dependent upon the culture of the whole society...

...the class itself possesses a function, that of maintaining that part of the total culture of the society which pertains to that class.

...the reader must remind himself as the author has constantly to do, of how much is here embraced by the term *culture*. It includes *all* the characteristic activities and interests of a people.

...Culture can never be wholly conscious – there is always more to it than we are conscious of: and it cannot be planned because it is also the unconscious background of all our planning.

T. S. Eliot: *Notes towards the Definition of Culture.*

In examining the patterns of family life, interpersonal relations and daily activity of a society, we are looking at some of its most basic cultural features. These features not only reflect something of the fundamental nature of that society but, in many ways, they also act as the method of transmission of the culture from one generation to the next. The values and attitudes of upbringing and socialization are echoed in more general social structures and activities. Conversely, changes in social organization and class structure themselves stimulate new patterns for personal and family life.

Although there is a continuous process of development and of interaction between old and new, it is rare for even the most profound revolution to produce immediate and abrupt changes. Often a revolution marks the culmination of a long period during which change has already been taking place. Where it does take the form of the sudden appearance of new factors, social or material, then the responses to this new environment must grow out of existing norms and be influenced by the old patterns. While individuals can accomplish extensive changes of outlook within a short space of time, societies take longer.[1] It is a basic consideration of this paper that the effects of the Cultural Revolution on the family, interpersonal relations, and daily life in China should be seen as part of and in the context of the longer term changes that have been affecting Chinese society for most of this century. Although the movement centred on problems of political power and contemporary policy decisions, it was also another stage in the continuing conflict between old attitudes and new aims. This can be illustrated in many ways. From the start the Chinese declared that the Cultural Revolution was a major attack on ideas and habits lingering on from the old society. Close parallels were drawn between it and the other great debates that have taken place throughout recent Chinese history and the history of the Chinese Communist Party. There was a conscious comparison between the role of the Red Guards and the role of youth at the time of the May Fourth Movement. Many of its central themes, such as the relationship between leaders and led, the role of education, the importance of remoulding cultural and mental attitudes as a part of social development and the relationship between town and country, are problems that the Chinese had been tackling for most of the previous fifty years. Moreover, many of the answers proposed grew out of experiences in the Yenan period and in the period since 1949. The continuity of change is greater than the influence of one movement. In sweeping aside the 'four olds', Mao clearly intended the Cultural Revolution to give fresh impetus to this process and also to adjust existing trends.

Although it is difficult so soon after the movement, and with

[1] This is a fact which has been stressed by all revolutionary leaders. Lenin in '*Left-wing*' *Communism, An Infantile Disorder* said, 'The dictatorship of the proletariat is a persistent struggle – bloody and bloodless, violent and peaceful, military and economic, educational and administrative – against the forces and traditions of the old society. The force of habit of millions and tens of millions is a most terrible force' (Peking edition, 1965, p. 32). Mao also makes frequent similar comments: 'the influence of the bourgeoisie and of the intellectuals who come from the old society will remain in our country for a long time to come' (*On the Correct Handling of Contradictions Among the People*, quoted in *Quotations from Chairman Mao Tse-tung*, Peking: Foreign Languages Press, 1966, p. 18).

limited information, to judge what effect there has been at this level, the two main areas affected appear to have been superior-inferior relationships and the involvement of the individual in social and political activities. In the former I believe, although with some reservations, that the movement has resulted in a greater degree of equality and relaxation, while in the latter, there is more willingness to assume responsibility and take initiatives among certain social groups. Whether the influence of these developments will persist remains to be seen. Certainly, their direction is a continuation of processes that have been taking place over a long period. They represent objectives for which Mao has continuously worked and they also grow out of the impersonal forces of the new social and economic environment. While the Cultural Revolution had an impact on many other aspects of personal and daily life, there is little indication of how deeply such impact was felt and whether it has resulted in exceptional or long-lasting changes. The experience will long be remembered by both the protagonists and those on the sidelines but, until more time has elapsed and more evidence becomes available, worthwhile or accurate generalizations about the effect it has had on their daily lives cannot be made.

Before considering the precise areas of change more closely, it is necessary to examine some of the underlying factors. An essential feature of the debate over cultural change at this basic level in China has been the stress laid on the relationship between class and culture. Like Eliot in the quotation at the head of this chapter, Mao and other Marxist–Leninist thinkers conclude that the two are inextricably intertwined. While Eliot is distinctive in arguing that this is a positive reason for preserving a class society, Mao rejects both the class society and its culture. In his opinion, the culture of the new society should consist of the culture of the proletariat together with compatible elements from that of the peasants. Its growth depends on the conscious activity of a distinct elite group, the Party, and it takes place in an environment of struggle with the old. However, Mao steps beyond this when he internalizes the class struggle within the individual and argues that conscious action by the individual can bring about fundamental cultural change.[1] Hence,

[1] This aspect of Mao's view of the individual is discussed in Donald Munro, 'The Malleability of Man in Chinese Marxism', *The China Quarterly*, No. 48 (October–December 1971), pp. 601–40.

over the whole range of activity, each person is encouraged to consider his actions in the light of the set of values proposed by Mao and the Party. Does he go swimming on his day off because it is fun, because he wants to win the provincial games, or because he wants to temper himself for the struggle? Throughout the Cultural Revolution, the Chinese were asked to look deeply into the motivation for all their actions, however trivial, and to strive to match the new ideals. Even though the practical outcome often fell short of these ideals, actions were justified in terms of them. Thus the ideological position that basic cultural change derives from the shift in power from one class to another is reinforced at an individual level by the drive to reshape values and attitudes, a drive requiring the conscious and willing participation of the individual.

As argued above, the Cultural Revolution cannot be seen as the starting point for an entirely new process of change in the everyday life of the Chinese. Fundamental changes had already taken place during the previous fifty years and these are still being digested. The family has been transformed from an extended unit, male dominated and with strict generational hierarchy, into the independent nuclear family with more internal equality.[1] In part, this was due to the conscious action of specific groups such as the young and the educated. They demanded an end to footbinding and more women's rights, and they rejected the extremes of filial piety. In part transformation came as the result of other social developments. The new forms of urban, industrial employment, the extension of recreational activities, the development of formal education and so forth, all altered the functions of the family unit, giving more importance to the nuclear pair and more independence to the female. The movement for the emancipation of women, particularly since 1949, has opened up a whole new range of activity and outlook for half the population and forced the other half to adjust. Traditional

[1] The traditional family unit in South China is analysed in M. Freedman, *Chinese Lineage and Society: Fukien and Kwangtung* (New York: Athlone Press, 1966). For the process of change this century see C. K. Yang, *The Chinese Family in the Communist Revolution* (Cambridge, Mass.: M.I.T. Press, 1959). As Freedman points out, in practice the traditional Chinese family was small and did not comprise more than three generations. However, the underlying ethos coloured its arrangement and governed its expansion in times of wealth. The extent of change before 1949 was uneven. Remote rural areas had experienced minimal change compared to that undergone in the cities.

patterns of family and group loyalty have given way to new loyalties with more general and sometimes more impersonal foundations. The attitude of the individual to his family, interpersonal relations, and social activity is developing along new lines.[1] The authority of the head of the family is no longer sacrosanct. The individual looks outside his immediate circle for education, employment and the provision of many essential services. People are more concerned about developing interpersonal relations than just filling allotted roles and they are not so afraid of conflict. Attitudes towards various kinds of social achievement and involvement are also much more positive. Many of these changes began in the early years of this century, and they do not all owe their origin to the Communist Party. The communist revolution has intensified them and by its economic and social reforms added a new impetus. Moreover, by means of regular campaigns and continuous propaganda, the conscious attention of the individual has been focused on such aspects of life. Before the Cultural Revolution most students kept diaries, modelled on that of the hero-figure, Lei Feng, in which they idealized their daily life and its meaning. Usually the description surpassed reality and there was a large element of formalism involved. After all, the student's career depended in part on achieving a good political performance. However, there was also an atmosphere of commitment to the new morality, intense within educational institutions but extending to varying degrees throughout society.

Despite the far-reaching nature of many of these social and personal changes, traditional attitudes have often persisted and, in some cases, resisted attempts at eradication. It should not be surprising that, in a transitional society such as exists in China which is experiencing rapid social and economic development, it is possible

[1] It is difficult to produce any reliable measurement of the extent of such change. D. C. McClelland, 'Motivational Patterns in Southeast Asia with Special Reference to the Chinese Case', *Journal of Social Issues*, XXIX. 1 (1963), 6–19, argues, on the basis of statistical studies of the social attitudes shown in children's schoolbooks, that significant changes have taken place since 1949 in attitudes towards achievement, social involvement and interpersonal relations. By contrast, R. H. Solomon, 'Mao's Effort to Re-integrate the Chinese Polity' in Barnett (ed.), *Chinese Communist Politics in Action* (Seattle: University of Washington Press, 1969), pp. 271–364, suggests, on the basis of a very small sample of psychological tests, that many traditional attitudes linger on. It is probable that this divergence reflects the reality of the mixture of attitudes existing in China.

to detect an intermingling of the new and the old as well as the coexistence of many contradictory features. Collectivization, the increase in modern inputs and the rational use of labour have undermined the role of family and lineage in the countryside. In contrast, the 'Liuist' policies for retrenchment in the commune system have operated the other way and tended to re-emphasize the economic importance of the family unit. During the Cultural Revolution and since, there have even been references in the media to 'clan feuds' or 'clan attitudes' emerging in factional disputes and affecting policy implementation.[1] The tendency to remain loyal to one's own particular group has also continued to cause trouble. Revolutionary committees and even new Party committees formed since the Cultural Revolution have been publicly warned against this failing.[2] Many traditional forms of social politeness and custom continue to dictate social interaction. In 1929, Agnes Smedley recorded the following interview with an opium-dealing president of a local Chamber of Commerce:

I asked how much opium was smoked in that village in, say, one week. Dressed in his long blue fur-lined silk gown, he sat on the edge of his chair, his hands braced on his knees, and stared at me as a snake watches a bird. Recovering his composure, he graciously announced that it was an honour to meet a foreign lady who took an interest in Chinese affairs. My life must be bitter and I surely found the cold weather distressing. No, I replied, I liked the cold weather, but was interested in the opium traffic, of which I had so often read. Did I enjoy good health and did I like China? he asked. My health was excellent, I assured him. Had I seen the very old pagoda near the city? I had seen it, but was not interested in it as much as in opium. He smiled pleasantly and assured me that it had been an honour to make my acquaintance and he hoped I would call again, although he felt certain my important work would make that impossible.[3]

[1] See, for example, *Jen-min jih-pao* (*People's Daily*) (Peking), 30 January 1969, 28 January 1971, 14 September 1971, and the *B.B.C. Summary of World Broadcasts* (*SWB*) *Part III, The Far East*, FE/4057.

[2] The Party committee of Tung-feng Commune in Ts'eng-cheng County of Kwangtung had to overcome 'sectarian trends' and 'had problems in dealing with those who were acquaintances and those who were not. They would treat leniently their acquaintances and harshly those who were not.' Canton Radio 16 May 1972. *SWB*, FE/3993.

[3] A. Smedley, *Battle Hymn of China* (London: Gollancz Left Book Club, 1944), p. 34.

Perhaps on the topic of opium it is unlikely that any serious reply could have been expected. What is of interest here is not the subject but the behaviour of the merchant in dealing with such an alien approach. Although the cadres of today are not to be compared to the old opium dealer, they share with him a similar aversion for direct questions and a preference for the indirect response. There can be few foreigners who worked in China before the Cultural Revolution who have not experienced similar behaviour: a request on a sunny day to visit a particular place, for instance, met by a statement of the value of the foreigner's work and solicitude that the poor weather would make such a visit impossible.[1] Similarly, during a visit in 1971, I found that direct questioning on the nature of Red Guard organization and factional fighting at Tsinghua University was answered with much ideological discussion and the suggestion that time was running short although, when questions took another line, there appeared to be no need to hurry. There is thus a noticeable continuation of certain formal rules of politeness which are used as signals of agreement, disagreement, approval and so forth.

The foregoing discussion digresses in some ways from the central theme of this paper: the changes wrought by the Cultural Revolution. However, it serves to underline three basic points. First, the area of change we are dealing with is related to fundamental ideological beliefs held by the Chinese leaders. Secondly, the changes of the Cultural Revolution have to be seen in the context of the long-term processes of change within Chinese society. Finally, patterns of action and reaction persist despite the changing context. They form what Eliot refers to as 'the unconscious background of all our planning'.

THE BASE LINE OF CHANGE

In order to understand the impact of the Cultural Revolution, it is necessary to consider some of the key prevailing attitudes in China towards the daily life of the individual and his relationship to society, to examine some of the features of life before the movement began,

---

[1] Whatever the real reason for the refusal, the opportunity is given to withdraw the request, thus saving face and avoiding the need to invoke authority.

and to discuss the methods consciously being employed to promote change in this area.

One of the most fundamental aspects of Chinese attitudes is the strong tendency not to distinguish between the life of the individual and his role as a member of a group. Life is not seen as divided into areas where social and political factors are predominant and areas where the needs and interests of the individual are paramount. This was very true of traditional society, with its network of family, lineage and locality loyalties, coupled with fear of isolation from the group and deference to an authoritarian system of moral and social rules for correct conduct.[1] Mao's conclusion that all thoughts and actions are branded with the mark of a particular class and reflect distinct political stands, has re-emphasized the overriding importance of the group in the life of the individual and, in some ways, widened the areas of life in which social pressures are seen to operate. He does not conceive of a hierarchy of behaviour levels, some related to social and political pressures and some related to purely individual needs. Instead, there is a continuum of behaviour patterns in which any activity can be seen as a reflection of more general social and political values. In practice, the individual will act in a particular way for a wide variety of reasons and similar situations will provoke differing responses depending on who is present, perceived needs, anticipated results and so forth, and Mao recognizes this fact when he concedes that the particular environment of each individual should be considered.[2] However, by a variety of means, every Chinese is encouraged to select a course of action which most closely approximates to the politically ideal. Whatever the reason for his action, the question 'why?' will provoke a rationalization in terms of accepted ideology.

This tendency to conform to what is socially correct is not merely the product of external pressures on the individual. During the Cultural Revolution, when there was great freedom for the individual to choose his course of action, it was notable that people rapidly coalesced around large groups or factions which commanded strong loyalty, until it was discovered that central approval was given to an

---

[1] See the discussion in Yang, *The Chinese Family*; Freedman, *Lineage and Society*; and Solomon, 'The Chinese Polity'.

[2] See Munro, 'Malleability', pp. 617–18.

opposing group, when large numbers promptly changed sides.[1] Another aspect of this conformity was the formalism of the language and style of criticism used during the movement. It was thus possible for the mass organizations to be strongly influenced by central editorials and statements in the absence of any coercive pressures to comply. Each new editorial gave a fresh impetus to the movement. At a different level of behaviour, where central authority was less directly involved, there was much formalism in the use of quotations from Chairman Mao. For most of the period of the Cultural Revolution it was impossible to begin a meeting of any kind without reading several quotations in unison, and mechanistic application was taken further by the circulation of lists of specific questions with references to the quotations to be consulted for the answers.[2] This ritual of conformity did not prevent conflict or innovation, but it did impose a style of action and expression on all the participants. 'Waving the red flag to oppose the red flag' was the only course open to Mao's opponents. Thus, although those involved in factional disputes were sharply aware of the issues giving rise to the conflict,[3] on many occasions there was superficially little to distinguish between the arguments and the slogans of the two sides.

One of the most prominent features of life in China on the eve of the Cultural Revolution was the balance between modern and traditional attitudes. Developments since 1949 had placed new political and social pressures on individual and daily life. At the

[1] The process is illustrated in N. Hunter, *Shanghai Journal* (New York: Praeger, 1969). For example, support for the rebels by Peking during November 1966 led to a rapid change of sides in Shanghai (pp. 179–90).

[2] An example is the list entitled 'What to do when you have problems? A list of answers in *Quotations from Chairman Mao*' which originated in the Number One Secondary School of the Chinese People's Liberation Army University and was reprinted in Lo-ho City in Honan. The list has 100 questions covering a wide range. Some examples are:
'What do you do when you come across reactionary arguments and ideas? See pages 10, 14, 18.
'What do you do when you have insufficient confidence before study and work? See pages 78, 172, 222.
'What do you do when your opinions are not the same as those of your comrades? See pages 100, 216, 226, 241.
'What do you do after an argument with a comrade? See pages 132, 134.'
(The page numbers refer to the Chinese edition of the *Quotations*).

[3] This is not meant to imply that large numbers of people were not confused or that the conflicts were always over issues central to the Cultural Revolution.

same time, they had begun to release individuals from traditional constraints. The marriage law, giving freedom of choice of partner and of divorce, had removed what was often a particularly severe restriction on individual liberty. The stress on the vital role of youth had allowed young people to be more assertive about their needs and role within the family and society at large. The destruction of the old privilege groups and the spread of more egalitarian ideas had enabled far more people to develop their talents in education and work than was previously possible. However, not all these changes were fully realized. Documentary evidence shows that traditional marriage customs still had a strong hold in Fukien Province in 1962 and 1963.[1] During the Cultural Revolution, the young Red Guards found it necessary to criticize attempts by parents to restrict the activities of their children. Part of the rationale of the Cultural Revolution was, indeed, to prevent the growth of new privilege groups and the spread of 'two track systems'.

The interaction of modern and traditional ideas extended beyond the differences in constraints on the life of the individual. They provided alternatives for a wide variety of situations. Should a dead parent be cremated or buried in the traditional manner? How many children make an ideal family? Should the geomancer be consulted over the siting of the new house? How far and how quickly can local customs and superstitions be changed without arousing resentment? There was a conscious confrontation between the traditional and the modern which was often related to generational, regional and urban–rural differences. Such conflicts found expression in the media and in books directly discussing the problems involved. These writings covered such questions as marriage customs, the role of married women, methods of raising children, family planning, ghosts, superstitions, funeral customs and so forth.[2] Although the debate over such problems was often expressed in political terms, it is a debate common in other parts of the world where planned modernization is being undertaken. In practice, the choice of alternative patterns of behaviour depends on the position of the

[1] Captured Party documents from the commune of Lien-chiang, quoted in Freedman, *Lineage and Society*, pp. 185–6.
[2] An example is *P'o chiu su li hsin feng (Destroy Old Customs Establish New Styles)* (Tientsin: Jen-min ch'u-pan-she, 1965).

individual. The young urbanite can be expected to show the most modern behaviour and the old peasant woman in a remote village is most likely to retain a traditional outlook.[1]

A second major feature of life in China, with an important bearing on the daily activity of the individual, was the tendency towards a strongly hierarchical social organization. The period of consolidation after the Great Leap Forward had created stable lines of control and operation in most activities. Although the division of responsibilities was not always clearly defined,[2] the individual was generally confronted with a predictable power structure and knew the sort of behaviour that would achieve various goals. Moreover, there was little direct emphasis on the role of ideology in practical activity and decision-making.[3] In industry, the worker faced a detailed salary structure and welfare scheme. His trade union gave him further opportunity for advancement.[4] His rights and duties in the factory were clearly laid down. In the communes, there had been a retreat from strong collective control and a revival of some of the aspects of individual peasant operation.[5] The peasant devoted varying amounts of time to the collective economy and to his own undertakings and could plan his activities accordingly. However the collective remained the central feature of his life since it provided the greatest amount of his income and handled welfare, recreation, relations with authority, large-scale and modern agricultural inputs and so forth. Its role may well have been reinforced by the striking parallel between the

[1] The point considered here is not whether urban and rural attitudes represent good or bad political standpoints (it is clear that Mao considers the 'creative energy' of the peasants a positive force) but their relative position in the changing patterns of daily life.

[2] For example, B. Richman, *A Firsthand Study of Industrial Management in Communist China* (Berkeley: University of California Press, 1967) reports a variation in the degree of autonomy at enterprise level. He also notes that, although there was a demarcation between the tasks of technical management and party cadres, there were examples where one or the other had come to play a dominant role.

[3] F. Schurmann, *Ideology and Organization in Communist China* (2nd ed., Berkeley: University of California Press, 1968), p. 506 ff, sees the division between ideology and practice as one of the fundamental motives for the Cultural Revolution.

[4] P. F. Harper, 'Trade Union Cultivation of Workers for Leadership', in Lewis (ed.), *The City in Communist China* (Stanford: Stanford University Press, 1971), pp. 123–52.

[5] Instances of this were enumerated on a visit to a commune near Weinan, Shensi. See A. J. Watson, 'The Guiders and the Guided', *The China Quarterly*, No. 49, (January–March 1972), p. 141.

size of the communes and the traditional socio-economic networks.[1] In education, the path of advancement was very clearly defined and organized, with examination successes leading to a 'good' career. The various forms of 'irregular' schools that had grown up during the Great Leap period had given way to the formal structure. In these, as in other areas, individual activity followed relatively well organized paths. A further aspect of this social structure was the wide-ranging importance of the unit (tan-wei)[2] in the life of the ordinary person. In many ways it defined much of his social being. In cities, the unit issued work cards, a basic means of identification. It was the source of such things as ration coupons, travel permits, and other official documents. Library membership, for example, was obtained only through a reference from the unit. It also provided for recreation, welfare and health services. In the case of large-scale or new enterprises, the unit included dormitories, clinics, creches and schools. The result was an integrated community which centred most of its activities on itself. From political life to sport and recreation, the individual thought and acted in terms of his unit.

Apart from the effect of impersonal changes in the environment, such as new economic forces and technical development, a variety of methods have been employed since 1949 to influence and change daily life. The most formal of these have been changes in the legal structure. The marriage law is perhaps the clearest example of this, although laws and regulations concerning ownership, residence, movement and so forth must also be included. A major role has been played by the educational system, which is seen as an important tool for promoting the new life and morality. Not only does the content of education serve a didactic purpose, but the performance of the individual in matching the new standards is also a factor in assessing his fitness for advancement. Various propaganda media have been mobilized to encourage people to change their way of life. The themes of novels, stories, plays and films do not so much reflect reality as represent the direction in which it is hoped society will

[1] See the argument in G. William Skinner, 'Marketing and Social Structure in Rural China', Journal of Asian Studies, XXIV. 1 (November 1964), 3–43; XXIV. 2 (February 1965), 195–228; XXIV. 3 (May 1965), 363–99.

[2] The term was used generally to refer to the unit or institution which employed you or in which you functioned. It could thus be a school, factory, commune, bureaucratic unit and so forth.

move. This is true of a wide range of artistic and recreational entertainment. Folk songs in the local style, comic dialogues, short skits, school concerts, comic books, all relate the new ideas to everyday activity, often in the form of conflict with the old. Other propaganda, such as the exemplary lives of model individuals and newspaper editorials, is more direct in its approach. Social pressures are also exerted on individuals to conform. Clearly, someone who wishes to make his career in the Party, government, or other areas of responsibility must meet the standards of behaviour expected of someone in such a position. More generally, the system of study groups and the residential committees act as channels for the transmission of new ideas and measures of the individual's performance. Finally, there are the large campaigns, of which the Cultural Revolution is the greatest example. Some are essentially political in nature, others, such as the annual hygiene campaign, road safety campaigns, movements to economize and so on, have a more limited target. However, all of them have a bearing on the daily behaviour and activity of the individual.

The aims and motives of this conscious attempt to change the daily life of the Chinese are many and varied. The most basic are those which are older than the Communist Party in China and formed part of the motivation of people like Mao in turning towards communism. They centre on the rejection of the old as the source of China's weakness in comparison to other countries and as an impediment to the growth of a strong, united country with modern services, industry and agriculture. Although much of the old has already disappeared, the battle against tradition still continues. Associated with this rejection has been the drive to accept new values, many being adapted from Western origins, both communist and non-communist. Such things as female emancipation, a new status for youth, and a change in the nature of the family have been striven for both as targets in themselves and as elements of a more general social regeneration. Finally, there are the changes whose aim is the preservation and expansion of the leadership of Mao's thought and the Communist Party. These would include the acceptance of a new view of life based on struggle and contradiction, belief in the vanguard role of the Party and obedience to the code of conduct promoted by the Party in various rules and regulations.

In general terms, the attitudes, methods and aims discussed above have applied in China, before, during, and since the Cultural Revolution. The relative intensity of the different factors has varied considerably, depending on the immediate situation within the country and the actual policies of the leading group. However, the effect of the Cultural Revolution on the daily life of the individual must be seen within their context.

THE IMPACT OF THE CULTURAL REVOLUTION

During the Cultural Revolution, the personal life of most Chinese was affected to a greater or lesser extent depending on age, geographical location, social status, employment and inclination. The influence of the movement was particularly strong in cities, towns and the villages along important communication routes, as well as among young people. Even remote country areas probably experienced some repercussions, though daily life may not have been directly affected. At various times during the movement, daily routines, working conditions, living standards, recreational activity, social welfare, and the general environment were all disrupted or distorted and changed by events. The two most important causes were the fluctuations in the central political struggle and the intricacies of local factional disputes. The first of these led to variations in the overall emphasis, such as between revolution and production, or between rebellion and discipline, and also sometimes more directly to a clear statement of the next goal of the movement. Thus, for some periods the individual found himself in a situation where work discipline was relatively lax but political pressures on free-time activity were strong, interwoven with periods when extra efforts at production were required but he could withdraw slightly from political debate. Naturally, these pressures were felt in different strengths in different places and, to an extent, at different times. Moreover, there was always a constant interplay of many other local political factors. Local factional dispute produced tensions between various groups, often between groups within the same unit (*tan-wei*), strikes, transport blockages, market shortages and actual fighting. After the initial period, local economic and authority interests were also involved. In places where factional disputes were particularly severe, the local effects frequently overshadowed the influence of the centre.

The extensive freedom for criticism, the ease of geographical movement, the growth of the mass organizations with their own 'career structure', nation-wide information networks and identification with strictly local issues, all provided a new environment for individual behaviour. They radically altered the position of the individual with regard to previous social pressures and in respect of his relationship with authority. In some instances the result was a rejection of the existing norms and a swing towards more self-centred behaviour, such as the demands of 'economism', the call by rusticated youths to return to the cities, the possibilities for settling private debts, and the sheer enjoyment of the removal of discipline. However, such behaviour was not the aim of the movement and has continuously been criticized. Moreover, new pressures were exerted on the individual. The strongest of these was the need to avoid acting in any overt way which would make him a target of the movement. This included such things as the possession of objects or books that could be classified as bourgeois, practising religion, having a history of foreign connections, wearing extravagant or untypical clothes, having a fancy haircut, eating expensive food, wasting food and so forth. After the first few months of the Cultural Revolution, some of these outward manifestations became less important and they were outweighed by the political and factional struggle. However, everyone was continuously wary about such behaviour and it was only during 1971 and 1972, with the general relaxation associated with the campaign against Lin Piao and the extreme left, and the publication of authoritative articles in the media[1] that such things became less damning.

Since the Ninth Congress of the Party in April 1969, there has been a steady shift away from many of the attitudes and proposals of the Cultural Revolution, a process accelerated by the campaign to criticize Lin Piao. The reaffirmation of aspects of social organization that existed before the movement has brought with it many echoes of life as it was. The authority of the Party has been rebuilt and the importance of the military reduced. In many cases the

[1] 'Shih she-hui-chu-i ti fu-wu-hsing kung-tso yueh tso yueh hao', (Do better work in socialist service trades), *Hung ch'i* (*Red Flag*) (Peking), No. 4, 1972.

changes proposed by various groups during the Cultural Revolution have been rejected either in favour of the retention of the system they criticized or in favour of only slight modifications. The commune structure and method of remuneration remains the same and attempts to alter it have been opposed.[1] There has been increasing emphasis on the role of technical management and rules and regulations in factories. Attitudes arguing that rules are unnecessary and that politics can replace all else have been denounced. Although important developments in such things as education, management, and economic policy have come about, it is often a case of a new emphasis rather than whole-scale reconstruction. A good example is change in cultural areas. Classical history, ancient literature and arts have all been rehabilitated. The museums and temples have been reopened. While their position is very similar to what it was in 1965, there is a greater degree of emphasis on ideological interpretation and political role. The return of these and other features should not be taken to indicate that the Cultural Revolution has had no effect, but that the effect has been less sweeping than at one time seemed likely. What then have been the results of all this on the life of the individual? Has it been just another campaign in which the usual methods have been used more intensely and new manoeuvres introduced, or have there been more lasting effects? With no definitive information on which to base any conclusions, it is virtually impossible to produce answers with confidence. Possible areas of change may be estimated but how reliable and how far-reaching such estimates can be remains open to question. What follows must necessarily remain a subjective impression.

I have chosen to make behaviour in relation to authority and behaviour in relation to active social involvement the two central themes of this study for several reasons. First of all, they were at the core of many of the debates and criticisms voiced during the Cultural Revolution. The discussion of the role of the masses in policy formulation and decision making, the stress on the need to prevent the growth of a revisionist elite, the insistence on closer social ties between leaders and led, the criticism of arrogant leadership generating subservient 'docile tools', and the call for everyone to

---

[1] This topic has been examined at length in the Chinese media. A typical example is the article by Chihchou Regional CCP Committee broadcast by Hofei Radio, 28 June 1972, *SWB*, FE/4033.

participate in the debate over political lines were all factors tending to assert the importance of the low-ranking individual and encouraging him to become actively involved. Secondly, the actual events of the Cultural Revolution led to a radical, even if temporary, change in the relationship between ordinary people and all their former leaders. Large numbers of people were provoked to initiate social activities that they would not have previously contemplated. Young people attacked and threw from power the teachers and authorities within their schools and universities. They also took part in a wide range of debates and activities throughout society. Workers were able to ignore their managers, abolish factory rules and devote much of their time to events outside their units. Everyone was able to participate in the investigation, denunciation and removal of Party authorities at all levels.

A final reason for concentrating on these two themes is that they remain central to much of the outcome of the Cultural Revolution. The 'mass line' style of leadership still occupies a prominent position and is reflected in many of the organizational changes that have taken place. Revolutionary committees, cadre schools, educational reforms and changes in medical, financial and marketing services all indicate a continuing attempt to make the relationship between leaders and led more equal and to make leaders more concerned for their subordinates by extending services to areas previously neglected. However, the intention has not been entirely to destroy authority. The steady trend during 1971 and 1972 to reassert authority against disruptive indiscipline has placed a check on the extent to which ordinary individuals can assume the freedom to act as they please. The implied willingness of lower levels to criticize and argue against higher levels has been balanced by the reaffirmation that, nevertheless, orders have to be obeyed. Experience during a brief visit to China in April 1971 suggests, however, that, although the actual decision-making power has not been taken from people in leading positions, there is a relaxed and positive relationship between them and their inferiors. Ordinary people played a fairly important role in introducing their units and were not afraid of interrupting or correcting senior figures present. The former president of a language institute, once known as 'President Chang' and avoided if seen in the distance, had retained much of his authority but was now called 'old Chang' even by the junior staff.[1] Another result of the Cultural Revolution has been the increase in opportunity for some groups to participate in activities outside their own units. Workers and peasants have a role in education and other cultural spheres. Schoolchildren are involved in society and productive labour more directly. The extent to which any of them feel unworried by taking the initiative in social activity must depend on their vision of authority. Since there is greater pressure for more interplay between superiors and inferiors there is more likelihood of people being prepared to act positively.

Although the main thrust in the two themes considered has been towards more equality and more initiative, it is not to be expected that all Chinese would agree on the extent or quality of such changes. It is unlikely that they have all been equally affected, and for some the change has been in the reverse direction. Cadres who have been criticized, remoulded and re-employed and members of the masses who succeeded in following the correct line are likely, in the light of their new experience of each other, to agree that change along such lines has taken place. Members of groups that were finally suppressed and rebels who found their idealism unrealized may well have ended with a more cynical attitude. Others are still uncertain of their new position. Veteran cadres, for example, have often been exhorted to step forward and resume active work, but many remain hesitant. Teachers in a Shantung middle school were reported to be wary of teaching anything but politics and were afraid of 'committing the mistake of controlling, restricting and suppressing the students'.[2] The end result cannot be seen as a definitive change for all but as the uneven growth of new possibilities.

THE OUTCOME FOR THE INDIVIDUAL

Since it is impossible to generalize about the daily life of some 800 million individuals with sharply differing environments, economic pursuits, customs, dialects and so forth, it might be more helpful

[1] The difference between 1965 and 1971 in the relationship between the president and his staff at the Sian Foreign Languages Institute was very striking; see A. J. Watson, 'A unified China after the years of disorder', *The Times* (London), 14 May 1971, p. 16.
[2] Cited by Shantung Radio, 20 July 1972. *SWB*, FE/4053.

to look at the effects of the Cultural Revolution on some aspects of the life of particular groups. Here again, however, the dangers of over-generalization must constantly be borne in mind.

The group whose life was most affected by the Cultural Revolution were youths and young adults. A distinction must be made between those who participated in the Red Guard movement and are now finding roles in adult life and those young people who are entering schools and universities without having participated in the movement to the same extent. For many of the former, the Cultural Revolution has been one of the key turning points in their lives. Their role as the destroyers of the 'four olds' brought them into sharper conflict with authority and older generations than any other group of youths since the May Fourth Movement. Since Chinese tradition equates age with authority and wisdom, this generational conflict is likely to have been a source of great tension, both socially and within families. The initial reaction of veteran workers and older people generally was to resist the young heretics.[1] By the time the latter's views were being more widely accepted, they had moved far to the left and begun the long slide down the greasy pole of factionalism. When their place was taken over by the workers' propaganda teams in 1968, many of the older generation no doubt felt that their initial misgivings over the chaos (*luan*)[2] of rebellious youth were justified.

In their personal life, the youths were slow to realize the extent of the freedom they acquired in 1966. Initially, the prime object was to discover the correct line and follow it. Extreme demands were made on themselves and on others to live a life of political and moral purity. However, as time passed and authority crumbled, more and more of them began to explore life without the constraints of the Party and bureaucratic structure. A good number of the demands for the removal of rules and regulations and freedom from bureaucratic control were more self-centred than constructive in intent. In addition, the youths began to show their independence in small ways. Many took up smoking, and enough of them married to make

---

[1] Many were organized to resist by the Party branches, but in Sian there was a general antipathy towards the Red Guards for a long period. A similar reaction occurred in most areas, for example Shanghai; see Hunter, *Shanghai Journal, passim*.

[2] The status of *luan* as a negative feature of social relations in China is examined in Solomon, 'The Chinese Polity', pp. 312–13.

an impact on the rate of population growth.[1] Revolutionary liaison and 'long marches' were used as an excuse to visit famous historic and scenic spots. On the whole such lapses were not the general rule, but the growth of factions bred its own anarchy and indiscipline. Local loyalties became deeper and more important than the centre and 'the branch stream engulfed the main stream'. The subsequent restoration of discipline by outside authority contradicted the Red Guards' own view of their leading role. The divisions between the various student groups were overcome by 'heart to heart talks' under the supervision of teams of workers, and subsequently the students were sent to factories and the countryside to unite with the workers and peasants and to learn where they had gone wrong. Thus, although they could claim a major place as the stimulants of change, ultimately their role in the rebuilding of new structures has been minimal and subject to guidance from authority and older generations. Rejection of authority has been replaced by control by authority. After a period of intense praise and activity when little they could do was wrong or prevented, they have been disciplined and have had their power withdrawn. Since that time, much propaganda has been devoted to encouraging these youths to lose their arrogance and over-confidence and recognize their inexperience.[2] This has been reinforced by campaigns, such as that of the early part of 1972, calling for greater factory discipline and underlining the need for young workers to learn from veterans.

The end result of this process on the attitudes of the youths concerned has doubtless been very mixed. Those in the countryside who were less directly and continuously involved, and whose actual future prospects have not changed, may well feel that the movement has made a substantial contribution to local development. The growth and spread of modern inputs into agriculture and the extension of rural education and medical services since 1966 may be regarded as benefits deriving from the political outcome of the Cultural Revolution, to which their own small part in the Red Guard struggle contributed. Those in the towns who were swept

[1] According to a comment by Chou En-lai to Edgar Snow in 1970. E. Snow, *The Long Revolution* (London: Hutchinson, 1973), p. 45.

[2] Examples are the two stories describing the way veteran workers guide and educate the capable but brash youngsters assigned to their factory. *Chinese Literature* (Peking), No. 8, 1971, pp. 75–88.

along by their commitment to the Maoist vision and, despite the twists and turns, have remained committed, will also feel that their role in the movement was positive. Others have probably concluded that their involvement in political activity has been purposeless. Their idealism has not been realized and their vision of the great role they could play in their country's development has found itself translated into less glamorous work in the countryside. According to some accounts, it is motives like these that have prompted some youths to leave China for Hong Kong.[1] It is probable that this latter attitude has, to a greater or lesser extent, affected many of the former Red Guard activists. Although they have sharpened their critical faculties, the fact that they have since been subject to correction and discipline may well have made them reluctant to play an activist social role again, particularly as the immediate outcome in 1968 was a period of re-education in the countryside. However, for those who did not adopt an extreme position, events during 1971 and 1972 have served to mitigate such feelings. On the one hand, the campaign to blame many of the excesses and errors of the movement on the extreme left has given them the opportunity to repudiate their former behaviour by placing the guilt elsewhere and to re-evaluate their previous interpretation of events. On the other hand, recent propaganda on the role of urban youths in the countryside has laid stress not on their re-education but on their opportunity to lead and participate in political and cultural life and to find new purpose in agricultural mechanization. It is not to be expected that they will now feel any greater equality with the authority that has decided their fate or that they will feel greater freedom for participation in social activity. However, their disaffection can be alleviated and a more positive role found.

For new generations of youths, the aftermath of the Cultural Revolution has both reintroduced aspects that existed before and produced a number of important changes, particularly in terms of career outlook. The Young Pioneers have been replaced by Little Red Soldier and Red Guard units, though the roles are roughly similar, while the Communist Youth League has been restored. The ambitious student still has the problem of correctly balancing

[1] D. Raddock, 'Innocents in Limbo', *Far Eastern Economic Review* (Hong Kong), LXXVI. 18 (29 April 1972), pp. 18–20.

political and vocational performance. While it might be tempting to argue that the Cultural Revolution has shown youth a way to rebel against authority, there appears to be little in the reconstruction of the Party, education, and career disciplines which indicates a formal channel for the expression of such extensive criticism. The power to draw the line still remains with authority and the environment of the campaign is distinct from everyday activity. However, what is important is not that authority exists and has to be obeyed but the kind of relationship that the individual has with it. The fact that students and pupils now sit on revolutionary committees, contribute to teaching and examining, and can discuss and propose changes and plans for school activity may well contribute to their confidence and self-esteem. Even if they know that ultimate decisions are not theirs, they need no longer feel such 'docile tools'. Other important developments in the lives of the young have come from the reconstruction of the educational system. Schools are pedagogically less authoritarian, they have a greater ideological content and they give much more practical training. The emphasis on a closer relationship between the masses and the schools has brought about a larger degree of interaction between teachers, pupils, parents and the local community. The rapid extension of schooling in the countryside has offered education to many more children, even if such schools still cannot match the quality of those in the cities and towns. Perhaps the greatest change facing these youths as a whole is in terms of involvement in society. The constant practical work, and the two-year break between school and university for the few that continue into higher education, should lead to much more maturity in the young people's view of their society and their role in it.

The second group most affected by the Cultural Revolution have been the cadres. They can be divided into two groups, those who were cadres before the movement began and those who emerged during the course of events. Although many of the former must have anticipated the way the movement would run, with criticism, self-criticism, investigation, confession and rehabilitation, and, in the light of such anticipation, attempted to satisfy the minimum requirements to 'get over the pass' (*kuo kuan*), few can have expected events to go so far or to demand such painful self-searching. For large numbers of them, particularly those within the Party who were unused to being on the receiving end of the criticism, the anticipated routine really became meaningful. The experience itself, regardless of the final outcome, must have had a strong impact. Nevertheless, now the movement has ended and the great majority of them are still at their posts, the question remains whether their attitudes have been deeply changed or whether they have just made cynical adjustments. The Party secretary with high blood pressure, seeking refuge in a hospital during the early part of the movement when under severe criticism, who said that what was important was not what the misguided critics said but what was printed in the editorials – has he, after his severe criticism, rehabilitation through labour in a May Seventh school and re-appointment as secretary in another institution, really changed inside or does he feel his earlier analysis has been borne out? However, whether they have changed because of cynical opportunism or because they really have come to repent their former practices, the way of life of the cadres has altered significantly. Their former privileges have gone. Special housing, clothing, and food and better education for their children have all been curtailed or removed. Although their salaries remain, many of the trends which suggested the growth of a new class have for the moment been checked. The aim is to prevent their functions being used as the basis for special social status. Apart from the change of attitude that was expected to result from the Cultural Revolution, various other institutional innovations have reinforced developments in this direction.[1] The revolutionary committees enforce more direct contact with lower levels. Rotation systems for participation in labour and the May Seventh cadre schools provide a much more formal scheme for integrating mental and manual work than existed before 1966. So long as they do not degenerate into token activities, they should lead to a closer understanding of the lives of the ordinary people. Talking to Chinese cadres about their attitude to the May Seventh schools has given me the impression that for many of them the catharsis of the criticism, followed by the relatively relaxed environment of the school and the fact that few of them had lost their jobs, had resulted in a much more positive commitment to continuing to use their skills than might have been expected from the

[1] Not all the changes are entirely new. Participation in labour, for example, has long been a feature of managerial life.

early part of the movement.[1] Certainly, the regrowth of institutional and bureaucratic activity during 1971 and 1972 suggests that the Cultural Revolution did not impair their abilities. It remains to be seen whether former attitudes and behaviour will also reassert themselves.

The new cadres who emerged from the Cultural Revolution fall into two categories: those from the army and those from the masses. The former had stepped into the vacuum created by the widespread disruption of late 1966 and early 1967. Many of them were uncertain of their role and, being forced to make decisions by virtue of their position, they often came into conflict with Red Guard groups. Such conflict came to a head during 1967 with the call for a campaign within the army.[2] Although the call was immediately rescinded, some of the more persistent groups such as the Sheng-wu-lien Red Guard group in Hunan never dropped their attack.[3] However, in general the army was able to stand apart from the political debate. During the latter period of the Cultural Revolution, the presence of a man able to take decisions without facing criticism from one or other of the factions may well have prevented total institutional collapse. Certainly, the soldiers functioning in revolutionary committees and military control commissions represented the only unimpeachable source of authority. The campaign against Lin Piao has revealed that this fact has coloured their relationship with the civilian cadres on their committees. They have tended automatically to assume leadership over their colleagues and to take decisions without consultation or discussion.[4] Since late 1971, the importance of these army cadres has begun to decline. They are less evident in revolutionary and party committees at lower levels and it may be assumed that the associated campaign for collective leadership has reduced the extent to which they can act without reference to others.

[1] However, as discussed above (see p. 308), a significant number have remained reluctant to become involved in anything that might make them a target for criticism.

[2] *Hung chi'i*, No. 12 (1 August 1967), pp. 43–7.

[3] See their statement, 'Whither China', from the Red Guard newspaper *Kuang-yin hung-ch'i*, No. 5, 1968, translated in *Survey of the China Mainland Press* (*SCMP*) (Hong Kong: U.S. Consulate General), No. 4190. Although a certain amount of mystery surrounds the Sheng-wu-lien, the documents attributed to them may be taken as an extreme statement of Red Guard attacks on the army.

[4] During the last quarter of 1971 the Chinese media issued many reports on the role of army cadres in civilian units. Examples were given where efforts were made to reduce the importance of the soldiers. A typical report came from Shantung Radio on 13 November 1971, *SWB*, FE/3852.

Now that the factions have disappeared and the bureaucratic structures have been rebuilt, it is to be expected that the soldiers will give way to the returned veterans.

The members of mass organizations who were appointed as cadres in the Party and government have faced some extensive changes in their way of life. Even if, in many cases, their actual power is limited, their new functions have greatly affected their daily routines and relations with others. It has not been easy for them to match the requirements of their new role. From a very early stage in the formation of the revolutionary committees it was found necessary to remind them that they should not 'cut themselves off from the masses' and develop bureaucratic and authoritarian ways of working. The return of the veteran cadres has also put them at a disadvantage in that by comparison they lack many of the skills and much of the experience necessary for their work. By contrast the old cadres have retained much of their authority and can claim a longer revolutionary experience. In some cases this has led to disagreements between the two groups and division into separate cliques. Undoubtedly the fact that the new cadres had once been members of groups sharply opposing the veterans cannot have helped this situation. The debates of the Cultural Revolution are still faintly echoed in this way. During 1972 attempts have been made to ease this problem by suggesting that it grew from the extreme left policies now associated with Liu Piao.[1]

Industrial workers were another group that was deeply involved in the Cultural Revolution. Their 'rebel' organizations and activities rapidly equalled those of the young after the first few months. Whereas, however, the students were fired by idealism, the workers were debating immediate issues such as material incentives, management methods, the role of trade unions and so forth. In the end the changes in factory organization have not been so great or numerous as the debates indicated. The daily routine of work, political study and recreation is much the same as it always was. The adoption of military terminology in organization, with the work-force divided into companies (*lien*) and platoons (*p'ai*) is probably little more than a change of name. Such name changes have also affected other

---

[1] An official discussion of this problem can be found in *Hung ch'i*, No. 7 (1972), pp. 63–7. Translated in *SWB*, FE/4045.

institutions, including schools. The criterion of profitability for an undertaking has not been discarded. Technical management and rules and regulations are still found to be necessary. The strengthening of management during 1972 has been aimed at removing any remaining traces of indiscipline. Even material rewards which were so savagely denounced have reappeared in the form of 'appropriate rewards' though they do not appear to be as extensive as some of the bonus systems that operated before the Cultural Revolution.[1] Other developments have had a greater impact. The trade unions have disappeared and in their place are the workers' congresses.[2] The latter fulfil some of the old roles of the trade unions in that they are the factory organization run by and for the workers but they have a less orthodox power structure and do not offer such extensive opportunities for promotion and career advancement. Instead, the workers' congresses are the descendants of the mass organizations in the factories. Their chief functions are political work and liaison with management. They are the forum for the discussion of new policies proposed by the workers or by the management. They are also the body from which the mass representatives on the revolutionary committees are drawn. It is explicitly stated that they are mass organizations and not responsible bodies for decision making. In addition they organize cultural activities such as sport and literacy classes and can provide some educational facilities for the workers. The career training and promotional advantages that were associated with the trade unions have not disappeared but have been incorporated more directly into factory organization. Most factories run various kinds of combined management and worker committees for such things as design work, production planning, financial work, accounting and so forth. The workers participating are directly drawn into a wider area of career experience. This has been reinforced in larger factories by the institution of various on-job training schemes. Perhaps the most important development in factory life has been the institution of revolutionary committees with worker participation in decision making bodies. These committees are found at all levels in a factory from the overall

[1] See a report from Fukien dated 15 November 1972, *SWB*, FE/4150. Other reports around the same time made similar comments.

[2] Since this was written the trade unions have reappeared in modified form.

ruling body down to company level. Below that there are revolutionary leading groups which do not have such direct influence on decision-making but are more concerned with the daily running of the factory, dealing with such things as quality inspection, working hours, safety, equipment checks and so forth. Even if the extent of the workers' power at the upper levels is limited, they have the status of being represented and at shop floor level they have an important say in daily activity.

Perhaps the greatest change in the lives of the workers has come from their new roles in a wider social context. They have undoubtedly gained in social stature since their propaganda teams helped to solve the 'old, big, and difficult' problems left from the factional struggles of the Cultural Revolution. The praise they received for political rectitude at the time has confirmed their status as proletarian leaders. Moreover, they have continued to play a role in a variety of fields outside their factories. In education they participate in the revolutionary committees of all urban schools and universities; they are called upon to assist and advise in the running of school workshops; they give classes in politics and in their skills; and they are consulted before young workers are admitted to university. Whatever their real power in such matters, they must have gained a great deal of self-esteem. Moreover, it is not just a few workers who experience these activities. Arrangements are made for periods of rotation in outside posts. Eventually, large numbers of workers will have taken part. In other cultural spheres the changes have not been so great. Together with the peasants, the workers are still the chief subject matter for literature and for painting. However, the fact that more of them are having their works published may have added to their confidence in undertaking such activities. It is, after all, only since the Cultural Revolution that newspapers have published historical and philosophical writings attributed to workers. Like people in other walks of life, the workers have also gained their quota of barefoot doctors and representatives on the various governmental revolutionary committees. In sum, the widespread participation by the industrial workers in the Cultural Revolution has reaffirmed their political status, given them added responsibility and importance within the factories, and expanded their influence into social areas with which they previously had little contact.

Other groups have been less widely or directly affected by the events of the Cultural Revolution. Although the peasants did participate, it was on a much smaller scale. Suburban communes could be the scene of important incidents or struggles but the majority experienced far less immediate impact, a typical example being the disruption of a construction project because the local Red Guards denounced the brigade leaders and did not appoint anyone in their place.[1] One reason for this is the simple one that there were fewer bureaucratic, political, and educational centres in the countryside and thus less focus for the political struggle. Another is that many country areas had already experienced their Cultural Revolution in the form of the Socialist Education Movement.[2] In 1967, when centralized authority was at its weakest, the scope for rural malpractices was quite considerable, but there is no indication that the commune system broke down or that there was widespread failure in tax collection and the procurement of agricultural goods. By contrast, there have been reports that, during the later period and until the fall of Lin Piao, attempts were made to revise the commune towards the more centralized model of 1958.[3] Ultimately, however, there have been no basic changes in commune organization, apart from the institution of revolutionary committees with peasant representation. During 1972, the pre-existing framework was reaffirmed, together with confirmation that private plots, subsidiary family sidelines, and subsidiary commercial activity all have a role to play.[4] The real changes have not grown from any precise reorganization instituted by the

[1] Both effects were personally observed during 1966 in Sian. A fight at a commune on 16 December 1966 provoked a new factional division. The other incident was recounted by a relative of one of the peasants involved.

[2] An example is Hsiao-hsin ts'un Commune near Sian. See Watson, 'The Guiders and the Guided', p. 141. The Socialist Education Movement is analysed in R. Baum and F. C. Teiwes, *Ssu-ch'ing: The Socialist Education Movement of 1962–1966* (Berkeley: Center for Chinese Studies, University of California, 1968).

[3] A report from Anhwei stated, 'From 1968 during the first six months of 1969, some of the communes and production brigades in our region, under the influence of the erroneous line which was 'Left' in form but Right in essence... arbitrarily changed the ownership system and distribution policy for the rural people's communes at the present stage.' Anhwei Radio, 9 August 1972, *SWB*, FE/4067.

[4] Most comments on commune organization reaffirm the original structure. For a discussion of rural commercial activity see the broadcast by Fukien Radio, 14 June 1972, *SWB*, FE/4023, or by Anhwei Radio, 21 June 1972, *SWB*, FE/4026. There have been many discussions of the role of family subsidiary undertakings. A recent example came from Peking Radio, 12 August 1972, *SWB*, FE/4069.

Cultural Revolution but from the economic policies that have been implemented in recent years. The terms of trade between the agricultural and industrial sectors have been weighted in favour of the former. There is greater emphasis on industrial support for agriculture and the extension of small scale industries in the countryside than there was before the movement. Commercial enterprises have been ordered to extend the ways in which they can support agriculture and improve the living standards of the peasants. In addition the expansion of rural educational and medical services, chiefly financed and run by the peasants themselves, has added a new dimension for collective activity and loyalty. The communes continue to grow and there has been a slight re-emphasis on the collective and away from the individual, but the Cultural Revolution has in no way changed the aims and intended effect on peasant outlook or activity.

The position of women in society has not really changed as a result of their participation in the Cultural Revolution. Female emancipation did not become a major feature of debate except in the loose sense that traditional outlooks and beliefs were challenged by the attack on the 'four olds'. Even the fact that Mao allowed his handwriting to be used for the title of *Chung-kuo fu-nü* (*China's Women*) in August 1966 and the accompanying editorial stated that the paper would henceforward carry Mao's thoughts to all revolutionary women did not provoke any major wave of concern for women's problems. Certainly there were no mass organizations consisting specifically of women or which focused great attention on such issues. It may be that the prominent role played by Chiang Ch'ing encouraged women at lower levels to take leading parts in mass organizations and factions. They were as vociferous as their male comrades in expressing their criticisms. But this could also have occurred without Chiang's example. The fact that so many women did take part is less an expression of status newly gained than an illustration that past work for female emancipation is having some impact. However, the propaganda for Women's Day 1972 suggested that the struggle still goes on. The commentary in the *People's Daily* stated:

Leading cadres should abide by the principle of equal pay for equal work, criticize the exploiting classes' outmoded thinking of favouring men and belittling women, criticize the old customs and habits restricting women from participating in socialist revolution and socialist construction...[1]

New literary output has also dwelt on this theme. One story told how a construction leader was unwilling to allow women to join his construction team and was amazed by their power when they finally forced him to accept them.[2] Another told of an old carpenter who was unwilling to let his daughter be trained in his trade since he didn't consider it 'women's work'.[3] On the whole, the Cultural Revolution merely provided another setting for a social change that has been taking place over a long time and still has a long way to go.

THE OUTCOME FOR THE FAMILY

The cause of revolution in the family structure has been a major target for many modernizers in China since the late nineteenth century. The writings of K'ang Yu-wei on the subject have not been surpassed in their revolutionary proposals by anything the Nationalists or Communists have said or done.[4] Moreover, although the nature of the Chinese family is undergoing a fundamental change, the process owes as much to the new economic and social environment as to the will of those consciously promoting change. The horizons for family activity have been effectively reduced by encroachments upon its traditional functions by state and collective undertakings. It has lost its place as the main support for education, career advancement, health and welfare and extensive economic cooperation. Increasingly family life in China has become dominated by the relationship between husband and wife and by the more limited economic and social unit that they form. However, not all the traditional family virtues have been discarded or replaced. A study of family relations in China as reflected in literature came to the conclusion that in the period before the Cultural Revolution

[1] 19 March 1972. Translated in *SWB*, FE/3951. Other articles and editorials make similar cases.
[2] 'Half the Population', *Chinese Literature*, No. 7 (1971), pp. 62–8.
[3] 'A Slip of a Girl', *ibid.*, No. 8 (1972), pp. 74–84. Other examples can be found in issues Nos. 5, 6, and 9 (1971), and No. 3 (1972).
[4] See K'ang's *Ta-T'ung Shu* translated by Lawrence G. Thompson, *The One-World Philosophy of K'ang Yu-wei* (London: George Allen and Unwin, 1958), especially Part 6, 'Abolishing Family Boundaries and Becoming "Heaven's People"', pp. 169–209.

many of those virtues, including some denounced in the fiction of the May Fourth period, were being idealized, and that there was 'a consolidation of the family and a greater respect for the older generation'.[1] It is too early yet to analyse post-Cultural Revolution literary output for signs of change in this respect.

It has been argued that the Cultural Revolution was a major attack on Chinese kinship relations.[2] However, that analysis is based on the assumption that the structure and content of kinship in China are fundamental to all other social interaction. In other words, the way a Chinese child is brought up and the obligations and attitudes acquired towards family authority and other relatives forms a pattern which underlies all his social relationships. Thus a call to attack the government and party leaders also amounts to a call for revolution in kinship relations. While this view does permit some attractive generalizations, it tends to ignore the widespread changes in social and family life that have taken place over the past century. An opposite viewpoint has suggested that examining the contribution of family life to other social relationships is profitable, but the approach should not be taken as all-embracing; the family is not 'a model of society'.[3] Since neither the Party elite nor other social authority has disappeared, and since there has not been any drive to reform or change family organization and functions as a result of the Cultural Revolution, it may be concluded that the movement was not intended to bring about any major transformations, and whatever effects it may have had have grown out of other developments.

In the countryside, the denunciation of the 'Liuist' line, embracing such things as large private plots, free markets, extensive family commercial undertakings and family-based production quotas may have further reduced the family's economic importance. At the very least it has forced attention away from the private to the collec-

---

[1] Ai-Li S. Chin, 'Family Relations in Modern Chinese Fiction' in M. Freedman (ed.), *Family and Kinship in Chinese Society* (Stanford: Stanford University Press, 1970), pp. 87–120.

[2] Francis L. K. Hsü, 'Chinese Kinship and Chinese Behaviour' in Ho and Tsou (ed.), *China in Crisis*, 1, Book 2, Chicago (Chicago: University of Chicago Press, 1968), pp. 579–608.

[3] Freedman, *Family and Kinship*, 'Introduction', p. 6, 'A good deal has been said in the past, usually in a simple-minded way, about the Chinese family as a model of its society. That it certainly is not, but it would be profitable to explore the consequences for general social behaviour...of domestic training for social relationships.'

tive and, if the reports on the reduction in the size of private plots are any indication, slightly reduced the profitability of the former. But it is difficult to estimate how strong the effects have been. Certainly it might still be possible for the head of a large family to devote all his time to the family plots, as did the head of a family with twenty-two members on a commune visited in late 1966. Moreover, the trend against private undertakings has been balanced by the fact that income on the communes still depends on family labour power and subsidiary undertakings. In many ways this is an incentive to produce large families and maintain generational co-operation, since parents and married children pooling their labour and other inputs can increase total family income. At a more practical level, there have been no real transformations. Families still live in their own houses with possibly two or three related units sharing the same courtyard or living side by side. The women do most of the domestic work while the men work in the fields. Over the years such things have been changing, particularly for the younger generation. Young women now growing up in the communes have a very different attitude towards what they may say or do, and they are often found playing an active role in organization. While this process of change certainly has important implications for family life in the country-side, it does not owe its origin to the Cultural Revolution.

In the cities the family retains the social and economic functions it had in 1965 and none of the organizational changes have impinged directly upon it. However, some distinctions must be made between the roles of different members. Those who go out to work and to school operate in political and social environments quite distinct from the family. Those that remain at home are much more closely integrated into neighbourhood activity. The neighbourhood forms their chief source of contact with society outside the family. During the Cultural Revolution, local public security stations, street committees, and residential committees were all subjected to the same scrutiny that other Party and government organizations received. The consequent formation of residents' revolutionary committees and study groups has tended to involve home-based family members more directly in political activity than previously.[1] It has been argued

[1] The case is made at length by Janet Weitzner Salaff, 'Urban Communities after the Cultural Revolution', in Lewis, *The City in Communist China*, pp. 289–323.

that this will work against the 'tight family authority structure and the patterned relations of social deference and obligations between generations and sexes' and that the aims of the Cultural Revolution were 'to tightly integrate the family into the polity and to cut in on family relationship and solidarity.'[1] As emphasized previously, such aims are not peculiar to the Cultural Revolution, and developments in this direction have come from many of the changes in China this century. It is perhaps a little premature to argue that the movement has had any measurable effect in this way.

Another aspect of the Cultural Revolution which militated against the traditional family unity was the rebellion by youth. In many instances, parents attempted to prevent their children from taking part. In other cases, the children directly criticized those features of their family life that they felt to be wrong.[2] Sometimes youths criticized their parents spontaneously, on other occasions they were subject to external pressures. These trends may have been reinforced by the possibility of family members joining opposing factions. However, such inner tension probably did not encompass the great majority of families. Tsinghua University Red Guards reported that during the periods of bitterest factional fighting many students returned to their families as a way of avoiding involvement.[3] An indication that the parental role is still in some ways decisive, and that many young people are reluctant to leave home, is given by the fact that campaigns to persuade young people to go to rural areas to live and work have had to devote much propaganda to persuading parents to accept the move.

Our knowledge of the relationship between married or 'engaged' couples remains as limited as it was before the Cultural Revolution. Presumably couples still get married for reasons of love, status, parental pressure and so forth as they did in the past. It is unlikely that the marriage ceremony will always take place to the accompani-

[1] *Ibid.*, pp. 318-19.
[2] *Ibid.*, p. 321, quotes the following comment from Shanghai: 'Over thousands of years our family relations have been that the son obeys what his father says and the wife obeys what her husband says. Now we must rebel against this idea...We should make a complete change in this...It should no longer be a matter of who is supposed to speak and who is supposed to obey in a family...If a grandfather's words are not in line with Mao Tse-tung's thought, it is absolutely justified for his grandson to rebel against him.'
[3] Oral report during a visit in April 1971.

ment of quotations from and songs based on the works of Mao as they did in at least some instances during the movement. However, the stress on the independence of the young may prove yet another blow to the importance of parental will in the choice of spouse. In this as in other developments within the family, the Cultural Revolution has merely confirmed the direction of changes that were already taking place.

THE OUTCOME FOR SOCIAL INTERACTION

Undoubtedly the most powerful impact on interpersonal relations during the Cultural Revolution was the formation of factions. Not only did they provide entirely new centres of personal loyalty but they also produced extremely acute divisions between people who previously had worked amicably together. Since these divisions were reinforced by sharp verbal and physical confrontation, it is not surprising that it took several years for their strength to die out. The fact that many of the new leading groups at lower levels included members originally taken as representatives of particular mass organizations meant that initially conflicting group loyalties continued to have a subdued effect, and even now they may not have entirely disappeared.

The factions had a variety of origins, some growing from particular local incidents and others resulting from the manoeuvres by different political groups within the Party and government. Eventually they coalesced around popular leaders and local issues. Throughout the movement there was a tendency to identify each group with a particular leader. People joined for a variety of reasons. Although on the surface it was difficult to draw a clear political line between them, individuals felt that some groups were more politically correct than others. People also participated according to the unit within which they worked or studied, the district within which they lived and their age. Usually, at each of these levels, there existed several Red Guard groups divided into two camps. Motives for joining particular groups often depended on distinctly personal issues such as the status of employment, the trend in one's class or workshop, the way one felt about the people in the group and the people the group criticized. Eventually these sub-groupings united into loosely co-ordinated larger units called headquarters. Such units were highly unstable, and a succession of them could be formed and decline within a few months. The Shanghai Commune and the revolutionary committees became the descendants of these loose combinations.

The slow destruction of the mass organizations has removed their power as a political force and, although it is difficult to imagine that the enmities and friendships created do not still have some slight social effect, observation shows that many people who formerly supported different sides now happily work together. This was quite obvious during a visit to the Sian Foreign Languages Institute in 1971. Former opponents were working easily together and they affirmed that they, themselves, had been surprised at the speed with which factional differences had been overcome. Perhaps this has been expedited within many institutions by the transfer of cadres and personnel to new posts since the end of the Cultural Revolution.[1] During the initial period of the move to overcome factionalism, great publicity was given to personal reconciliation, particularly between the various leaders. This reflected the extent to which personal loyalties were involved. Later, individuals were blamed and punished for misleading the masses. Thus rank and file members got the opportunity to escape personal responsibility and to find a way to develop easier relations with former factional enemies. The one clear legacy that factionalism has left is in the regional variations throughout the country in the extent and type of new reforms. Until 1971, at least, different areas of the country had reached different stages in the implementation of new policies and in some cases the content varied. Workers' congresses, for example, were established in Canton, Hangchow, Nanking and Sian but were only just being organized in Shanghai. In addition the emphasis in Sian was initially on a city-wide congress rather than factory level.[2] At one time this regionalism or 'theory of many centres' posed a real threat to central authority, but it has now ceased to be a worry.

Associated with the factionalism and breakdown of normal social order during the Cultural Revolution, there was an increase in lawlessness, general criminal activity, and economic malpractices.

[1] This was noted on many occasions during my 1971 visit.
[2] Personal observation.

During late 1967 and most of 1968 campaigns were run to deal with the problem. A series of articles in the *People's Daily* by an author named Jen Li-hsin attacked the trend towards anarchy which led people to 'sabotage the socialist economic construction and jeopardize the safety of the state and the people's living. Or, they disregard law and order, do all sorts of evil and degenerate into criminals.'[1] Jen's general pronouncements were reflected in greater detail in the Red Guard press, which denounced economism and 'speculative, profiteering activities'.[2] Thereafter came reports of the arrest and imprisonment of various kinds of hooligans and criminals.[3] In August 1968, in Shanghai, a campaign was mounted against 'hooligans and teddy boys' who were 'engaging in fights and looting, insulting women in broad daylight, stealing and picking pockets, and carrying out gang warfare'.[4] Eventually order was restored by the use of workers' provost corps, which patrolled the streets like police, and severe punishments including public execution. The widespread occurrence of events such as the above indicates that the problem was one which was felt in every province and which resulted in most kinds of crime. However, since it was chiefly associated with the lack of normal social controls, the steady reconstruction since 1969 has been accompanied by a marked decline in such behaviour. Before the Cultural Revolution, honesty was a marked feature of the general tenor of life and received great stress in all forms of propaganda. It now appears to have regained its position.

A final point for consideration in this section is whether the Cultural Revolution has led to any changes in the individual's attitude towards making and keeping friends. It has been argued that, since 1949, the pressures of political life had led to a decline in deep personal friendship and a growth in a more generalized comradeship. Such things as unwillingness to expose your true feelings for fear

[1] Jen Li-hsin, (a pseudonym meaning 'Duty to establish the new'), 'Anarchism is the Political Bridge to Counter-Revolution', *Jen-min jih-pao*, 25 February 1968, translated in *SCMP*, No. 4130, pp. 1–3.

[2] For example, *Kuang-t'ieh tsung-ssu*, No. 28 (February 1968), translated in *SCMP*, No. 4129, pp. 1–4.

[3] For example, *Nan-fang jih-pao* (Canton), 19 March 1968, translated in *SCMP*, No. 4149, pp. 6–11.

[4] *Wen-hui pao* (Shanghai), 4 August 1968, translated in *SCMP*, No. 4251, pp. 5–10.

of laying yourself open to criticism, fear lest you should learn things about people you liked which would be dangerous when you had to criticize them, and a wariness about getting to know strangers until you were sure of their political status were quoted as examples of factors that militated against friendship.[1] However, such pressures do not really apply at lower social and intellectual levels. The ordinary worker or peasant is not closely involved in activities which would make political deviation either an acute threat to Party policy or a common occurrence. Lapses at such a level need not result in a great degree of punishment or social ostracism, except in cases of criminal activity. Personal security is not so greatly at risk in friendship, since the pressures of political life are much less. Moreover, there is a much less sophisticated degree of political awareness. In such circumstances, deep personal friendship including the sharing of intellectual and emotional experience is perfectly possible. An additional implication of the argument that friendship cannot be formed is that most Chinese either have something to hide or are hostile to much that goes on in the new society and dare not voice their true feelings. The less this applies to an individual, the less the pressures against forming friendships.

At higher social levels and among people with authority or with social aspirations, some pressures against deep friendship did indeed exist, particularly if one's career could be put in jeopardy by making politically suspect contacts or by the wrong word at the wrong time. Even so, this is not an entirely new feature of Chinese life. In traditional and republican China, the individual's choice of friends also influenced the course of his career. If the Red Guard publications are to be believed, people within the power structure and outside it were more outspoken in their conversations with each other than the caution required by 'comradeship' would allow. They did form frank friendships, despite the pressures of politics, and these were very obvious, since the Red Guard critics always assumed that friendship and acquaintance was associated with a political line. People being interrogated or making confessions were always very careful about the extent to which they implicated others. While it would be unrealistic to argue that the Cultural Revolution has

[1] See E. Vogel, 'From Friendship to Comradeship: The Change in Personal Relations in China', *The China Quarterly*, No. 21 (January–March 1965), pp. 46–60.

removed such pressures, in some ways it may have eased them as regards getting to know or retaining relationships with people who have been criticized. On the one hand, nearly all leaders and large numbers of people from all walks of life can be classified as having committed mistakes. Even a long history of participation in revolution did not make a person immune from attack. On the other hand the Cultural Revolution has stressed that class origin and past performance are no guide to a person's present political status. Anyone can develop faults or be reformed. The result is that it becomes almost impossible to draw a line between people who might bring one trouble and people who would not. In addition, the stigma of faults and criticism is now so widespread that it cannot act as a potent deterrent to maintaining associations with people who have been criticized.

Friendship in China today can no longer imply the same kind of obligations and behaviour as it traditionally did. The economic and social structure within which friendship used to operate has undergone fundamental change. Obtaining a job through the intervention of a friend, using personal connections to further one's own project, relying on such relationships for commercial and other economic undertakings are all now much less possible than they were. Nepotism and favouritism are being replaced by more impersonal codes of conduct which, in turn, have been produced by new laws and forms of social organization. Although cases of bias in the traditional manner are still reported, their importance is declining. Moreover, a new ingredient can be found in forming friendships: the commitment to new ideals and a new society. In literature, friendships are now always depicted as centering on shared political outlooks and aims. The reality probably does not match this idealization, but it is not entirely unlikely that friendships are formed in China based on a common vision of the future.

CONCLUSION

The area of change dealt with in this study is both intractable and wide-ranging. There are many other aspects of social activity such as recreation, religion and so forth which might also have been included. Even the topics which have been considered deserve a much fuller study in themselves. However, enough features have been examined to indicate that relations between superiors and inferiors and attitudes towards social involvement are two areas where the Cultural Revolution has had an important impact. Since psychological factors and changes in individual attitudes can have a direct effect on more general social and economic developments, the ultimate effect of these changes may well have much wider implications as time passes. Certainly the Cultural Revolution earned its name in part because of the belief that change at a fundamental level of the kind examined here can deeply affect China's growth.

If we were to examine the outcome of the Cultural Revolution in terms of some concept of an ideal man which it aimed at producing, then we would be forced to conclude that its achievements have been limited. China has not become a country where all have abandoned the habits of tradition and live their lives entirely according to the tenets of Marxism–Leninism–Mao Tsetung thought. It would be unrealistic to assume that one short campaign could achieve that ideal or, indeed, that the 'ideal man' could really exist. On the other hand, the Cultural Revolution did serve to dramatize many of the problems involved in the transition from the old to the new. The limited and uneven changes which can be discerned in family and daily life or in interpersonal relations are all contributing to the emergence of the new society. There has not been a great qualitative change but a reassessment of developments which were already taking place.

Although, during the Cultural Revolution, the Chinese experienced intense influences on their personal, family and daily life, not all of these influences have brought about large-scale and permanent change. At some levels, such as superstitious beliefs and generational relationships, the outcome has been a further shift along lines of social development that were already in process. At other levels such as political attitudes, educational development, and career choice and patterns, the outcome has been twofold. It has emphasized trends which were already present and which dated from the Great Leap Forward, if not Yenan, and it has resulted in a shift away from attitudes and policies for economic and social development prevalent in the early sixties. Eventually, this change of emphasis may produce effects over a wide range of activity. The

Cultural Revolution served to centre attention on the issues involved but did not itself provide the answers. The process of change in the life of the Chinese, as always, consists of an interaction between the constraints of tradition and culture, the conscious effort of revolutionaries, and impersonal, environmental forces. One movement can have an effect but, as in the case of the May Fourth Movement, it needs decades to penetrate society to any great depth. It remains to be seen whether the Cultural Revolution will leave an equally great legacy.

CONTRIBUTORS

MARIANNE BASTID is Chargée de Recherche at the Centre National de la Recherche Scientifique in Paris. She is the author of *Aspects de la reforme de l'enseignement en Chine au début du XX* siècle* and (with J. Chesneaux and M. C. Bergère) *Histoire de la Chine, 1840–1921*, in two volumes. She studied in China from 1964 to 1966.

JOHN GARDNER is Senior Lecturer in Government at the University of Manchester. He has written several articles on Chinese politics and is at present completing a book on mass mobilization in China.

JACK GRAY is Senior Lecturer in Chinese Studies at the University of Glasgow. He is co-author (with Patrick Cavendish) of *Chinese Communism in Crisis* and editor of *Modern China's Search for a Political Form.*

CHRISTOPHER HOWE is Reader in Economics in the Department of Economics and Political Studies at the School of Oriental and African Studies, London University, and, since October 1972, Head of the Contemporary China Institute. He is author of *Employment and Economic Growth in Urban China 1949–1957* (1971) and *Wage Patterns and Wage Policy in Modern China 1919–1972* (1973).

WILT L. IDEMA works in the Documentation Centre for Contemporary China of the Sinological Institute at Leyden State University. He has studied Chinese at Leyden, Sapporo, Kyoto and Hong Kong.

STUART R. SCHRAM is Professor of Politics (with reference to China) at the School of Oriental and African Studies, London University. He was Head of the Contemporary China Institute from its establishment in 1968 until October 1972.

JON SIGURDSON was a Visiting Research Fellow at the Science Policy Research Unit, University of Sussex, in 1971–3. At present he is on the research staff of the Scandinavian Institute of Asian Studies in Copenhagen. He is studying rural industrialization in China and related problems of technological development, and has visited China twice in the course of these studies.

ANDREW WATSON was a Lecturer in Chinese at the University of Glasgow from 1970 until 1974. In January 1975 he took up an appointment at the Centre for Asian Studies, University of Adelaide, South Australia. He lived and worked in China from 1965 to 1967. He is studying the modernization of the traditional water transport system in China, and has edited and translated a number of Japanese studies under the title *Transport in Transition: The Evolution of Traditional Shipping in China.*

331

INDEX

academic criteria and education, 258, 259, 261, 264, 270, 275, 279, 280, 285
accountancy, training in, 276, 277
accounting, 75, 84, 177, 210, 235, 249, 316
acupuncture, 283
administrative methods, 32, 105, 191-3, 196
adult education, 261, 276, 289
advancement, opportunities for, 301-2, 303, 311, 316, 320
Africa, 72, 107; revolutionary movements in, 64
agrarian reform, see land reform
Agrarian Reform Law, 142 n. 1
agricultural and non-agricultural sectors, rotation of workers between, 235
agricultural collectivization, 24, 38, 42, 123, 125, 128-9, 137, 142-3, 163; and education, 120
agricultural experimental stations, 265, 276
agricultural extension networks, 212
agricultural machinery and implements, 56, 63-4, 143, 161, 214, 218, 226; repair and manufacture of, 140-1, 200, 201, 207, 208, 212, 216, 217, 218, 222, 228, 229, 230; research institutes for, 141
agricultural machinery trust, 144, 145, 148
agricultural mechanization, 38, 63-4, 119, 139-43, 148, 201-2, 203, 205, 228, 289, 311; Liuist policy for, 149-50; Soviet, 143
agricultural production, 34, 37-8, 42-3, 55, 59, 132, 135, 144, 148, 161, 178, 209; private, 137
agriculture, 40, 45, 63-4, 106, 111, 112, 113, 114, 119, 132, 133, 134, 137, 170, 171, 191, 215, 231, 288-9, 301, 310; 'blind commands' in, 72; collectivization of, see agricultural collectivization; co-operativization of, 128; and industry, 41-2, 112, 192, 203,

205, 206, 319; see also rural industry
mechanization of, see agricultural mechanization; neglect of, 135; peasant, 110, 113; priority of, 145, 164; production drive in, 124; Soviet, 148; Western, 140
agrochemicals, 209
Alley, Rewi, 125
alloy steels, 214
America and Americans, 125, 265
ammonia, 224
Amoy University, Depatrment of Biology, 282
anaesthetics, 283
anarchism, 93, 95, 326
animal-power farm tools, 141
anthracite, 224
Anti-Party Group, 63
anti-rightist campaign, 51, 131
antibiotics, 283
army, and production efforts, 33
artists, 150
arts, see humanities
Asia, 72, 107, 145; belief in its inferiority to Europe, 25-6; revolutionary movements in, 64
attitudinal change, see change
authoritarianism, 157; and revolution, 94
authority: family, 321, 323; and the individual, 305, 308, 312; reassertion of, 307, 310; and the right to rebel, 86-7; sources of, 94, 99-101; and the young, 309, 312
automation, 221, 227, 228-9
automobile repair shops, 221
autonomy, see local autonomy

backwardness, advantages of, 44-5, 55
bacterial fertilizer, 277
balance ratios, 171
'balanced growth', 110, 112
ball bearings, see bearings

333

INDEX

work teams, 77, 78
worker demands, 236
workers, 31, 81, 126; criticism of leaders, 106; in Europe, 126; factionalism among, 249; freedom or control of movement, 233–4, 237, 239, 244, 245, 247; industrial, 315; Marxist view of, 28; participation in education, 317; participation in enterprise activity, 240–1; in the Party, 24; permanent, 248, 253, 255; and revolutionary struggle, 9, 15, 25; social involvement of, 308; status as proletarian leaders, 25, 37, 92, 317; temporary, 235, 239–40, 241, 245, 248, 253, 255; writings of, 317
workers' colleges, 278
workers' congresses, 236, 316, 325
workers' propaganda teams, 309, 317
workers' provost corps, 326
working hours, 135, 317
world revolution, 13, 26
writers, 150
Wu (Wei Emperor), 65

Wu-ch'i *hsien*, 263
wu-fan see 'five antis'
Wuhan, 13

Yao Wen-yüan, 94, 96, 97, 100
Yenan, 2, 22, 23, 32, 33–4, 43, 51, 56, 98, 107, 124, 155, 260, 292, 329; industrial co-operatives, 125
Yenan Forum on Art and Literature, 24, 33
Young Pioneers, 311
youth: during the Cultural Revolution, 307, 309, 323; education of, 97–8, 270–1; need to learn from veterans, 97–8, 310; and revolutionary enthusiasm, 56–8; role of, 96–7, 303, 312; as teachers, 273, 276; withdrawal of power from, 310; and work in the countryside, 98, 276
Youth League, *see* Communist Youth League
Yu-ch'ang production brigade, 276
Yüan Shih-k'ai, 58
Yugoslavia, 47